The World of Classical Myth: Gods and Goddesses; Heroines and Heroes

The World of Classical Myth: Gods and Goddesses; Heroines and Heroes

Carl A.P. Ruck
Danny Staples

Carolina Academic Press
Durham, NC

ISBN: 0–89089–575–9
LCCCN: 93–74701

Carolina Academic Press
700 Kent Street
Durham, North Carolina 27701
(919) 489–7486
FAX (919) 493–5668

Printed in the United States of America

PATRI

R. E. S.

AMICOQVE

Table of Contents

Mythology is defined as the fundamental structures that a people apply to the interpretation and delineation of what they consider their common or shared reality. It is shown as a kind of evolving pattern, constantly undergoing revision to keep pace with the evolution of the culture, and hence offers an archaeology of a people's changing sense of identity. Contrasts between Myth and Reality offer perspectives upon our individual identities today, or upon our own culture.

Symbolic forms are eternal and indestructible (or archetypal). They are never annihilated, but merely change their appearance to meet the demands of changing times: they undergo transmutation. Hence the iconography and worship of the twelve Olympian deities offers a record of their evolution into their Classical identities. And humankind plays an essential role in stabilizing the evolving world through the institutions of its culture or civilization.

Classical culture is shown as the outcome of a reconciliation between two diametrically different peoples, centering upon the question of whether a Goddess (and her way of life) or a God (and his) would predominate. In the Classical age, the Olympians were ritually reminded of their newer identities, and offered commemorations of their past.

Athena is presented as a formerly predominate Goddess, who has evolved into the Olympian family via her new birth as a daughter of Zeus. The monuments of the Acropolis of Athens demonstrate the transmutation from her (and its) past, where she once reigned as the Queen of a sisterhood, with a consort, who in more recent times has become her Olympian brother Poseidon.

Dionysus similarly experienced a rebirth as a child of Zeus as he evolved into the Olympian age, although he never became anything more than a visiting member of the family; for he maintained an easy (and reversible) pathway of regress to the world of his origins. The ceremonies of the Symposium and the Festivals of the Dionysia contrast with the maenadic revels, and bridge the double aspect of his identity.

Apollo and Artemis were less successful in their transmutations: the absolute perfection of their idealized Olympian natures resulted from a past that went back to their roles in the Labyrinth and had more in it that needed to be hidden. They often require the help of others (who will journey for them back to the origins) in order to stabilize their precarious Olympian identities. The sanctuary of Delphi (which is periodically relinquished to their brothers Dionysus or Hermes) demonstrates a mediation with their former natures.

Like Dionysus, the trickster Hermes became a son of Zeus, with easy pathways of regress. Even as an infant, he took upon himself the job of helping Apollo by stealing away from him his herd of cattle. The final trick, which reconciled the ultimate dilemma of God or Goddess, was his begetting of Hermaphroditos.

The hero is shown as similarly belonging to two worlds. He may be called upon to step forward through the threshold (or limen) where he stands—to found the world anew and help defeat the past; although he could also step back—to fulfill an even higher calling; to become the fundament, rather than the founder of his new city. There are always two ways of telling the hero's story.

Perseus founded the new Mycenae and helped Athena overcome her past as the Gorgon Medusa; but when called upon, he also went back to fulfill his role as the Goddess's man.

The crowning achievement of Herakles' career was the remaking of the entire world, and in particular, the refounding of the sanctuary of Olympia. As the most perfect of the heroes, and a rival son of Zeus, he posed a threat to Apollo, whose place amongst the twelve Olympians he came close to usurping.

Chapter IX: Theseus: Making the New Athens 203

It was Theseus who made Athens over to the ways of the newer times by defeating the Minotaur and transmuting the windings of the Labyrinth into the dancing on the island of Apollo's new birth on Delos; before he, too, took up residence in the fundament of the city he had benefited by burying there so many befriended enemies from the past.

Chapter X: The 'Foreign' Legions 223

What these three heroes did in reconciling the spirits that underlie the present, could also be told as a corporate endeavor, involving legions of supposedly foreign allies. One such tale was the Voyage of Jason's Argonauts. Another was the Wars at Thebes, in which the hero Oedipus had a role.

Chapter XI: The Last 'Foreign' Engagement: Troy 263

The most famous of these corporate endeavors was the War at Troy, which was the final attempt to stabilize Apollo. After the War, the age of heroes came to an end within a few generations.

Part Four: Liminal Heroines 313

The liminality of the male hero involves two versions of his identity. The female has three, corresponding to her additional physiological limen at menopause; maiden, mother, and wet nurse/witch. Through endurance and suffering, she finally ascends to a fearful victory.

Chapter XII: The Two Worlds of Persephone 317

At the village of Eleusis, just across the border of Attica, each year a legion of initiates—living people, and not the heroes of myth—undertook the same age-old journey down into the Deathlands, and returned, having reaffirmed the treaties of family and friendship that join the present with the spirits of the past, and that ratified the triple schism of the Goddess into Demeter, the mother, and her daughter Persephone, with Hekate as the terrible third.

Preface

🛡

The first concern of those deciding to use this book, either to learn more about Classical Myth for themselves, or to teach the subject to others, is apt to be: in whose words will the stories be told?

Ancient tellings? Translated, of course. To use any but our own translations would be unfeasible, in view of copyright restrictions; but although we both as authors have had experience with published translations, it would be presumptuous to assume that single translators could do justice to the vast variety of periods and styles, when others have devoted a lifetime to just a work, an author, or, at most, a genre. And as excerpts, or in their entirety? Both alternatives imply that some ancient telling was, in its time, definitive, which isn't true, although in later ages it may have come to play that role. In its day, it was heard as another telling of the never ending story. And to excerpt, moreover, deprives it of meaning as a work of art, substituting merely a superficial prettification of the plot. But the entirety would make this book an overly lengthy anthology and lose its focus on Myth: for either as excerpts or in the entirety, the story itself tends to get lost in the particular manner of its telling.

We have opted to rephrase the stories in our own words, not trivialized as they might be presented to children, but as a demonstration of their full range of possibilities in different versions, and as a serious study, worthy of an adult or mature student, with the emphasis upon the recurrent elements and patterns that never change fundamentally, despite the tellings. Serious, yes. But not difficult. The patterns are few and constantly reinforced, with **pedagogical aids** (which are a unique feature of this book) to jog your memory. Also unique, the material is presented in a graded progression (as a textbook, whether or not you have a teacher), moving from simpler ideas to more complex; and with a clear indication of what is of primary importance to remember, as opposed to what you may wish to refer back to, as you proceed.

And secondly: **which stories**? For there are so many, some only local, known to the people of a particular village; others, more universal, enshrined in magisterial works of art. The latter is our emphasis, but we have not falsified the subject by ignoring the others, which often help enlighten the meaning intended by the artist. A quick glance at the INDEX will show that our treatment is inclusive, without losing its learnable nucleus: so that the book can also serve for encyclopedic reference.

But finally, the end is just the beginning. The reader is invited to follow our suggestions, selecting to pursue in its entirety (**from the wide array of readily available translations**) whatever seems most enticing, or as directed by the teacher. Myth is not a closed and finished subject, but the more you learn, the more it beckons you onward: to seek its meaning and reflections in religion, anthropology, psychology, literature, art, history, philosophy—and most intriguing, not only as it was in the past, but ultimately still here, hidden within yourself.

This is the World of Classical Myth.

Acknowledgements

Museo Archeologico Nazionale, Taranto
British Museum, London
Vatican Museums, Rome
Antikensammlung, Staatliche Museen zu Berlin
National Archaeological Museum, Athens
Archaeological Museum, Ankara
National Archaeological Museum, Iraklion
Museo Archeologico, Florence
Museo Nazionale, Rome
Metropolitan Museum, New York
Museo Etrusco di Villa Giulia, Rome
Musée du Louvre, Paris
Palazzo dei Conservatori, Rome
Museo Nazionale, Tarquinia
Museum of Fine Arts, Boston
Museum of Corpus Christi College
American School of Classical Studies, Athens
Museum der Universität, Wurzburg
Museo Nazionale, Naples
Museo Jatta, Ruvo
Museo Borghese, Rome
National Archaeological Museum, Delphi
Museo Archeologico Nazionale, Ferrara
Museo Archeologico, Florence
Staatliche Antikensammlungen und Glyptothek, Munich
Museum für Kunst und Gewerbe, Hamburg
Hermitage Museum, St. Petersburg
Municipal Museum, Southampton
Pergamonmuseum, Berlin
Antikenmuseum und Skulpturhalle, Basel
Museo Nazionale, Palermo
National Archaeological Museum, Olympia

Galleria Spada, Rome
Spiridon Collection, Rome
Musée Municipal, Bologne-sur-Mer
Museo Nazionale, Clusone
National Archaeological Museum, Eleusis
Museum für Völkerunde, Berlin

Part I
Orientation

Chapter 1
What is Mythology?

ψ

"That's just a myth! You can't possibly believe that."

We've all heard it said. There's no clearer put down, the absolute debunking. A myth is something that is not true and couldn't possibly be true, despite some other people's belief in it. When labelled a myth, it must be avoided. You are thereby advised to abandon it and join the thinking of all sane people.

Is mythology then the science or 'logos' of lies? And if so, why should you study it?

And yet you also hear of things like the 'myth of the hero,' by which we don't mean that heroism doesn't exist. Or the 'myth of the American West,' by which we don't mean that the West doesn't exist or that events such as those told of it never took place. What we do mean is that the myth defines and informs our perception of heroism, both in the past and in times yet to come, and that the myth of the frontier may have influenced what happened there and the way we have embodied it in history. When subsumed in a different perspective like the role of women or the plight of the aboriginal natives, a different history emerges, more contemporary perhaps, but no less true than the other. We have merely decided to look at something else. We have directed our sight toward a different goal.

Myth is apparently a slippery term. It is used for both what is totally implausible and false and also for what may be the ultimate truth, the underlying pattern for how we interpret what happens and even for what, in fact, does happen.

We inherit the word with its aura of respectability from the Greeks and repeatedly, as they themselves did, we have had to slough off elements that are embarrassingly at variance with our changing view of the world. The early Christians, for example, couldn't any longer possibly accept the doings of the pagan gods, who patently, from the view of the new religion, didn't exist, although it was a dilemma for these people who had been educated in the Classical tradition to find a way not to have to reject the whole preceding culture of literature, art, and law which they cherished as their heritage. But even before them, the great pagan philosophers had also questioned the morality of the amorous Greek gods and the bestiality of their vengeance. And a way had been found to view myths simply as allegories, embellishing a basic truth with the beguiling allure of a fictional narrative. That approach was supposedly devised by the novelist Euhemerus in his imaginary travelogue entitled the 'Sacred Inscription' a couple of centuries before Christ, and even though **'euhemerism'** takes its name from him, the same technique had been proposed by the philosopher Plato. He rejected the validity of myth but saw that its seductive trappings of language and story could be used to deceive a gullible populace into accepting a different truth, one of his own devising, his so-called 'noble lie.' And even today, we are accustomed to believe that the fictions of novelists and poets are in some way true, truer perhaps than the supposedly factual account of the newspaper, although we are not always sure that either we or the author could tell us what that truth is. The best fiction, unlike allegories or Plato's lie, has a life of its own and doesn't seem to be capable of adequate expression in any other terms.

If myth, then, is a fiction, like all fiction perhaps it encapsulates some elusive truth.

The serious modern study of myth received its impetus in the late eighteenth and nineteenth centuries, when Christian missionaries encountered the beliefs of the various peoples they converted to their own faith. Partially from anthropological interest, but also so that they could better counter the native gods they were attempting to displace, these missionaries gathered the mythical traditions of their converts. Information about African, Polynesian, Amerindian, and Asiatic beliefs began to accumulate back in Europe and puzzling similarities with the Judaeo-Christian and Classical traditions, like the common stories of a Great Flood, were increasingly noted. And these peoples seemed to be as devoted to the validity of their implausible histories as the Europeans to their Noah's Ark. Evangelical zeal allowed the mere substitution of the one event for the other, although often the convert failed to totally relinquish the former, but simply added it in some subtly disguised form to the other.

In the latter part of this same period, the demented fantasies of persons who did not seem to be able to fit in with normal views of reality came under more serious study. Their imaginings, both wakeful and in dreams, bore intriguing similarities to Classical myths and even to these more exotic, foreign importations. A doctor could sometimes document the delusion not only with a work of literature or art from the Classical tradition, but also with one of the bizarre idols that were beginning to be recognized by some as works of art. If dreams were a clue to the suffering minds of the insane, the sane often had the same dreams. And artist and writers seemed able to tap the same source with their creative imaginings.

The ground was laid for further study by Sigmund Freud's revolutionary formulation of the situation. Apart from the conscious contents of a person's mind, there was another, forgotten realm of contents — willfully forgotten or suppressed, as he postulated — but not entirely gone. When some forbidding censor of wakefulness was distracted, as through sleep or hypnosis or Freud's new technique of psychoanalysis, or even through an artist's creative inspiration, these subconscious contents could surface and become accessible. Freud argued that these forgotten elements had been dropped off as a person grew into adulthood, often because they were too painful to be remembered. With his patients, he went backwards into memory, guiding them along the way, to teach the troubled adult how to deal with the recalcitrant infant that was still latent with-in each of us. The problems he uncovered displayed a certain commonality and it was almost as if one or the other of the Classical myths was illustrative of the same problem. He even experimented in applying his discoveries to the inter-pretation of literature, art, religion, and entire cultures. Other of his younger associates were particularly intrigued with these possibilities, investigating con-cepts like the hero myth and the 'double' companion or 'Doppelgaenger.' Psy-choanalysis, which had begun as a treatment for the mentally disturbed, seemed to have a lot to say about certain paradigms or patterns underlying the psycho-logical functioning of ordinary and gifted persons.

While Freud, as a scientist, eschewed metaphysical speculation and insisted, at least professionally, that the subconscious contents were suppressed rem-nants of each individual's personal experience, Carl Jung, with a more mystical view, was to diverge from him. He theorized that the recurrent patterns in these subconscious contents, and their similar occurrence in myth, literature, art, re-ligion, and all aspects of culture, had a trans-personal or universal origin in the 'collective unconscious' that was shared by all humans. He called the patterns **'archetypes'** of human experience and saw them as pertaining not solely to the maturation of each person individually, but also to the whole evolution of the species, going back before birth to the infancy of the race and projecting be-yond death toward some as yet unrealized aspiration or goal. The writings of Joseph Campbell made Jung's archetypes known to a wider, nonprofessional public. The archetypes are not really unlike what in different terms might be called instinctual programs: the embryo follows a determined path of develop-ment, or a spider spins a web only of its own characteristic design. However, in a human adult, instinct is overlaid by conscious control and direction and hence is modulated by training and culture. For example, basic drives like sex or hunger can be denied or expressed in sublimated actions.

The theory of the archetypes was anticipated as early as Plato. He, too, the-orized that there were basic building blocks out of which the bewildering array of perceived reality was constructed. These forms or **eide** ('ideas') were the truer, underlying reality that philosophers were to be trained to intuit (or ac-tually 'see' as a visionary illumination) before expressing them for others as the noble lies. In a similar manner, writers and artists after Freud and Jung, and even before them in anticipation of the formulation of their theories, have often consciously encoded the archetypes into their fictions in the belief that that would lend them a fundamental validity. Still more often, however, these ar-chetypes seem to have been rediscovered without the artists' conscious intent, merely as a function of the state of mind or inspiration involved in the creative imagination.

But whether you equate the archetypes with instincts, or the ideas with geom-etry or atomic structure, the search for a definitive enumeration of forms or types eludes scientific certainty. What is clear, however, about the fictions of myth is that they seem to mean something that is somehow true and universal.

Others have attempted to avoid the stigma of speculative psychology and metaphysics by what are assumed to be more scientific methodologies. Max Mueller in the nineteenth century thought all myths were just rationalizations of natural phenomena, a kind of mistaken, primitive science. Rationalization, also, is not new. Plato tried that, too, as when he had Socrates rationalize the familiar story of Death and the Maiden as an accidental fall occasioned by a gust of wind that pushed the girl off a cliff.

Another, more recent approach has sought to see myth as a science of language whose basic words and grammar must be uncovered in order to decode its meaning. This linguistic method, associated with the work of Claude Lévi-Strauss and his disciples, is only speciously more scientific than the archetypes and other attempts to define the basic elements since the investigator is not unbiased in selecting the categories (like 'raw versus cooked' or 'birth from the mother versus birth from the father') under which to classify the narrative items extracted from the myths. Structuralism, as it is called, derives from the work of Vladimir Propp, who analyzed Russian folktales into thirty-one recurrent elements which could be applied universally to the decoding of all such stories. Propp argued that the elements were always repeated in the same linear sequence, whereas Lévi-Strauss grouped his extracted elements diachronically, without regard to their narrative order. Although the choice of categories in structuralism is arbitrary (but influenced by anthropological presuppositions), the method has at least demonstrated that myth seems to be a way of solving problems about binary oppositions which are not reconcilable in more rational terms. Every mother's child, for example, does have a father, and every father's child, a mother, although cultures differ in the emphasis and value placed upon the one or the other ascription. It is a kind of non-rational problem solving for which Lévi-Strauss used the metaphor of **bricolage**, like the work of an inventive repairman who makes do with whatever tools are at hand, for want of something better. The method of structuralism, however, provides just another mode of looking at the kind of reconciliations that are supposedly effected through psychoanalysis or the archetypes, although linguistic and anthropological, instead of through the, to some minds, more suspect techniques of psychology and religion or metaphysical philosophy. Thus, every male is also feminine, both psychologically and physiologically, and every female, masculine.

Semiology or **semiotics** as a method applied to myth refines the linguistic approach and attempts to find the 'words' of its universal language, without regard for what they refer to in individual cultures. For example, mushrooms are mediators, always effecting a reconciliation of whatever binary opposition they are involved in. As hermaphroditic, they mediate male versus female; as cultivatable wild plants, they mediate the wilderness versus civilization; as edible poisons, they mediate life versus death. And so on. Such a function can be noted without speculating upon the cause.

Clearly, the method to some extent determines the findings uncovered in the study of myth. Those who study it often are so addicted to their methodology that they fail to notice that their discoveries are largely analogous.

The following conclusions about myth are probably all true:

1. **Myth is what we call somebody else's reality.** It is not the world we live in, but the one that they do. We should not assume that their world is not real for them. For example, Greek myth commonly narrates adventures of heroism in which the male hero is accompanied and guided by a divine female helper, the goddess Athena. From our point of view, she would be an imaginary presence. But when the Athenians were fighting the Battle of Salamis in a war that had the same meaning for them as the myths of heroism, many people actually saw her ghostly shape leading them into the fray. This on the authority of an historian. A hallucination, we would say, triggered perhaps by their stress. A myth. But that is what they saw. And it was what they, because of their training, would have been expected to see.

2. **Our own myths we call reality.** We, too, have myths, but unless we are making comparisons to other possible ways of ordering our world, we do not call it mythology.

3. **Often, other people's myths surface in aspects of our world that are considered somewhat less than real.** We, too, have that ghostly companion (the **anima** in Jungian terms), but unless we are not sane or are hallucinating, she is confined to our dreams or other non-rational modes of thinking, like fantasy.

4. **However implausible, myth is accepted as historical fact.** It is only when new views of reality evolve (occasioned by newer sciences, methodologies, or modes of thought, or by changes in the structures of society) that the factual validity of myth comes into question. For Greece, this happened toward the end of the fifth century before Christ, in the final decades of what we call their Classical Age. The loss of confidence in their mythical heritage was largely the result of the developing art of reading, which replaced the art of remembering and allowed the reader to compare and assess more rationally what hitherto had been handed down from generation to generation as their oral history. A failure of the Athenian political system and a growing dissatisfaction with the patterns of sexual roles contributed to this crisis of reality.

5. **When the validity of myth within a culture comes into question, ways are sought to salvage some part of it so that the culture does not lose its heritage or roots.** These ways may include rationalization, allegorization, or other attempts to homogenize the doubtful validity of myth with the newer evolving perceptions of reality. To this would also belong the patronizing view that myth is a kind of primitive science, naively mistaken in its conclusions. (For example, it rains because of Zeus.) Etiological explanations (the use of myth to explain the origin of customs, although no one any longer believes it) are similar. For the Greeks of the Hellenistic and Roman periods (third century before Christ and on, until the fall of the Roman Empire), it was particularly important to hold on to their mythological heritage and the litera-

ture, language, customs, and art that expressed it. It was their identity and le-
gitimacy amongst polyglot peoples, often in alien lands, and their unique claim
to glory.

A number of other terms are sometimes substituted for myth, particularly in
the modern era, to downgrade its supposed validity, while maintaining it within the heritage. Such terms categorize by subject matter. Examples are: saga
(historical traditions, eventually in prose and generally implying Nordic origins),
legend (historical story, originally a saint's life), fairy tale (simple cautionary
tales for children, including fairies, ogres, magicians, witches, and the like, similar to those collected from oral traditions by the brothers Grimm), fable (story
generally in which animals act like people), and folklore (beliefs and customs that
persist unreflectively amongst a people as oral traditions). Apart from particu-
larized subject matter and the emphatic distancing of credibility, these terms do
not differ from the more general term of myth. Saga and legend are not really
appropriate for Classical mythology, and particularly the former, which implies
a Nordic heritage. For Greek myth, such historical traditions are called epic, because the earliest extant versions exist in the Homeric epic poems. The stories
ascribed to Aesop are Greek examples of fable and apart from the traditional
personalities characteristic of the various animals (like the craftiness of a fox or
the industriousness of the ant), they were probably never an actual part of the
belief system. The Greeks also had fairy tales and folklore, but since the extant
tradition derives from sophisticated and adult sources, we catch only glimpses
of such, largely lost, oral matter, primarily in the Hesiodic poems and in later
antiquarian scholars.

6. **The salvageability of myth after the loss of confidence in its factual
validity is facilitated by its universal elements (psychological com-
plexes, archetypes, structures, or be it whatever else) that make it always
in some way still true.** As somebody's reality, although not or no longer ours,
it is a human construct and hence a possibility shared by us with all humanity.
It is this that makes the study of myth valuable. It provides an outside vantage
point from which to view ourselves, which is to say, to discover our own myth.

7. **Myth is first and foremost the 'word,' mythos, and primarily the
spoken word.** Myths are stories, and *mythologia* is the 'telling of stories,' and
eventually, of 'tall stories.'

The characteristics of myth are a parallel reflection of the nature of language
itself and in particular, of spoken language, before the stories told are recorded
in writing. When separated from the emotive interaction of the speaker and the
hearer, they begin to lose credibility.

Ancient Greek is more complicated than most modern tongues, and it was
already, in itself, a simplification from the Indo-European language from which
it evolved. In general, the trend in the development of the more modern deriv-
atives of Indo-European has been one of increasing simplification. This is probably true of all languages. They simplify in the course of time and become easier
to manipulate.

Beyond the great demands upon memory required to activate the broad array of forms and linguistic distinctions available in ancient Greek, the speaker also had to depend upon memory to recall the content of traditional and historical material since for a very long time the language had no written form. And even after the invention of writing, the written signs were at first only a partial prompting for memory. The Greeks first wrote their language in a pictographic syllabary adopted from their Minoan predecessors in the Greek lands, a form of writing that is called 'Linear B' to distinguish it from 'Linear A,' which recorded the Minoan tongue. Linear B could not accurately represent the actual sound of the Greek language (since every vowel sound in Greek is not linked with a single consonant, as in a syllabary) and it was used only for the temporary keeping of accounts by a trained bureaucracy of scribes. History and everything else that was important was still a matter of memory, and with the fall of the political system that employed the bureaucrats, the writing of Linear B was abandoned. Some four-hundred years later, in the eighth century before Christ, the Greeks again invented a form of writing, this time adopting a Phoenician consonantal system (with signs only for consonants) and converting it into an alphabet (with signs for both consonants and vowels). The intent was to have an accurate written indication of the sound of the language. With continuing improvements (such as indications of pitch, initial aspiration, and a partial distinction of short and long vowels), this became more and more possible, but only until five hundred years later, and even then, the written record was not completely accurate because the spoken language had continued to develop into dialectal variants that increasingly deviated from what was to become the official orthography, based on what had been the dialect of Athens. Hence modern Greek is still spelled like ancient Athenian Greek, but pronounced quite differently.

Without an orthography, written words cannot communicate as visual signs, but only as directions for sounding out the words, which then communicate orally. This was still the manner of reading for centuries even after the advent of an orthography. One read aloud, not silently. Well on through the Classical period, reading would have been a laborious process of sounding out the letters. None of the improvements that make silent and rapid reading possible had yet been developed. Without word division and punctuation, the deciphered and verbalized sounds would still have to be organized into meaning as they were heard; and reading, such as we think of it today, did not occur.

What was read was usually a text already known, for which the writing was just a mnemonic prompt. Or something like an ordinance or law, whose written promulgation could serve for future reference. Or the text of some new work of literature which was not so much intended for reading as for decipherment and memorization, rehearsing it for performance. Almost all of what we would consider a literature of poetry and history was for the ancient Greeks a performance, something to be encountered aurally by an audience of listeners, and usually accompanied with music and dance. The notable exception is the history of Thucydides, whose exile from Athens denied him of his audience, and the model he followed was that of a medical textbook, analyzing symptoms and recording them for reference so that one could consult it in the future when similar symptoms appeared. Even well after the invention of writing, the stories of Greek mythology were told stories, stories told and heard, in the emotive bonding of performer and audience.

And these stories were the culmination of millennia of tellings, going way back to before the advent of writing as an aid to prompt the memory, going back to even before the Greeks had migrated to Greece, back even to before the language had evolved into Greek. For all that time, the stories survived only through memory, and to facilitate recall, a language of verbal formulae and recurrent situations had developed. When the tellers repeated their stories, telling it as it had been told to them, they were not performing a verbatim version. Without knowing it, they were creating it anew, skillfully manipulating the language of memory and adjusting the story to suit the ever changing interests of newer generations of listeners. An archaeology of the story would reveal fossilized remnants from great antiquity and could trace the path of its evolution, through successive periods of culture and awakening states of human consciousness and aspiration. Only the best mnemonic patterns, the most psychologically emotive and apt metaphors, the most perfect generic situations, the most appealing verbal formulae would survive over the generations, continually undergoing refinement and distillation so that they would best latch onto the listeners' deepest concerns. The 'archetypes' are the inevitable product of such an oral transmission of the verbal heritage, and mythology is inherently a language of archetypes.

The gifted performers and their responsive audience do not know how this amazing feat of apparent recall is accomplished, how this cherished tradition of knowledge is accessed. The performers ascribe it to some outside force, something divine, a Muse that is speaking through them, and the listeners, too, sense that the moment is magic. Neither side has the mental detachment necessary to question its validity, or even to understand what it means in any terms other than its present performance.

To this situation of oral retelling can be ascribed the basic characteristics of myth as a way of thought.

8. **Myths are accepted unreflectively on their own terms as whole blocks of meaning.** To question the meaning during the performance would break the spell of the moment and defeat its purpose, which is the strengthening of cultural solidarity, of belonging to the group. As with a child's singsong recitation of some memorized piece, a gauche interruption would destroy recall. The child hasn't really forgotten. Simply backtracking to get a new start will often carry the performer over the previous hiatus, restoring what had seemed irretrievably lost, since the individual parts of the communication exist not in isolation, but as part of a 'run' linked to the totality. The child cannot improvise and say what the piece means in other words both because the string of memorized words are the key to access the material and because the same material in other words would lose authority.

When Socrates toward the end of the Classical period called the validity of the mythic tradition into question, the method he used was interruption of recall, extracted isolation, and imposed rephrasing. And the reaction he encountered from those he interrogated was anger and frustration at his lack of manners and the suspicion that he was somehow subversive to their culture.

9. **Contradictory myths can coexist with equal acceptance.** Since each myth exists encoded in its own words and each is individually accessed, they cannot be juxtaposed for comparison unless they are interrupted, isolated, and rephrased.

Thus, the oldest, aboriginal olive tree in Greece could be found growing on the Acropolis of Athens (via the myth of Athena's contest with Poseidon for possession of Attica) and also in the sanctuary of Zeus at Olympia (via the myth of Heracles' dedication of the Altis to his divine father), as well as on the island of Delos (via the myth of the death of the embassy of maidens from Apollo's Hyperborean homeland). So too could many cities claim to have been

Athena Reflecting the Gorgon's Head in Perseus's Shield (Apulian Red-figure Pelike, Museo Nazionale Archeologico, Taranto)

the place where the female race of Amazons had been finally annihilated.

10. **Amongst these unnoticed contradictions is a suspension of linear chronology.** Myths are eternal, with all their possibilities simultaneously accessible.

Thus, Athena is often depicted in vase paintings as she aids the hero Perseus to decapitate the fearsome head of the Gorgon Medusa, which she henceforth will wear as a trophy of this victory; but she already is wearing it.

Similarly, Hera gave birth to Hephaestus as retaliation for the birth of Athena from Zeus; but Hephaestus is already present to witness and assist at the birth of Athena.

11. **Logic, which derives from the scientific study of language as a grammar for argumentation, is not dominant in myth, which is unexaminable speech.** Instead, myth is non-logical, like the thinking that occurs in dreams or the free association of ideas. To be examined, speech must be read, with the writing not just a jog for memory; speech must be externalized to be exam-

Hephaestus
Assists at the
Birth of Athena
from the Head of
Zeus (British Mu-
seum, London)

ined, but prior to the art of reading as a means of communication, the performer and the audience are too caught up in the emotional demands of the moment to judge dispassionately. It would be like trying to examine the latent content of the dream or stream of consciousness while still asleep or in a meditative trance. It would be like trying to read yourself. Scientific logic, like the light of day, dispels the truth of myth.

Myth, however, is not primitive thought or a primitive science, since primitivism implies deficiencies that in the course of time will be overcome. Myth is as sophisticated as science as a way of ordering the world, and each is limited by its unique method. When it comes to the ultimate questions, scientists often peer across the boundaries into myth.

12. **The basic categories in the grammar of myth are binary polarities, which are mediated, usually in the definition of personal and cultural identity.** These sets of opposites could be anything and infinite in number, but since culture is human culture and all humans share in human nature, these binary polarities tend to pertain to similar fundamental problems faced by all peoples. For example, is a person male or female, infant or adult, wild or civilized, and for each possibility, what role is expected from society. The problems are insoluble in rational terms, since an individual, both psychologically and physiologically, is one sex only by dominance over the other potential, and the latent infant still resides within the most civilized adult. But myth works out solutions, as many answers as there are questions that can be phrased.

The solutions to these questions that evolved in Classical mythology are of particular power and interest to us today because, by chance of history (which involved the merging of two diametrically different kinds of people, a settled, female dominant, agrarian people with a nomadic, male dominant, hunting people), the polar oppositions that Classical mythology was required to mediate posed a perfect set of problems, almost a laboratory demonstration. They are not only those that are amongst the most fundamental to human nature, but, in addition, the particular formulation of the solutions it worked out laid the foundation for the ensuing millennia of Euro-American culture. It is the Classical model that established the terms for the debate today about such controversies as male and female sex roles and the relationship of developed to undeveloped nations, and even of body to soul.

It is not only, however, the centrality of Classical mythology to our own culture that makes it of particular interest and importance to us today.

13. **Classical mythology is still largely retrievable in the form that it existed before the failure of its belief system.** Many mythologies have been anthologized, and comparisons between different mythologies have established fundamental similarities in their content and method, but most of these anthologies have been compiled by outsiders, usually with the aid of native informants from marginal or moribund cultures. The great tellers were in the past. This is what we used to believe, the informant narrates; or this is what we are trying to make our belief again, as the embattled people strives to revive its lost traditions. This was increasingly the situation also in Classical antiquity, but only after the fifth century, as the art of reading supplanted memory and the use of writing simply as a mnemonic technique. Then, too, myth became the study of encyclopedists, antiquarian scholars, and of literary and artistic imitators. But the great works from the Classical and pre-Classical ages, that survive today, transcribed into writing, belong to a still living mythopoeic tradition.

Much has been lost, of course. But the Homeric epics, the Hesiodic tradition of knowledge poetry, the lyric and epinician poems, the tragic and comic performances for the Attic theater — these masterpieces, that we read today as literature, were vibrant testaments of myth in their own day. Aeschylus, Sophocles, Euripides, Aristophanes are our informants, not some marginal storyteller that the world's history has passed by, not some outsider who doesn't believe the truth of what is gathered. It is a mistake to consider these Classical artists as writers, using myth perforce to say something else. As persons possessed by the mythic heritage, they would have been less able than anyone to step outside the performance. Socrates, in fact, tells us that these poets were totally incapable of explaining their meaning in other words, incapable of rephrasing, although others could make a stab at it. They were amongst the most conservative, for that was their genius, while other of their contemporaries might break with tradition and try out other ways of viewing truth, with more scientific eyes.

14. **Although myth is a story, the stories are told not only through words.** There are also nonverbal ways to access the myth. Since myth is the reality, which is to say, the world in which they live, nothing in that world exists without the myth, whether the story is told or not, or even consciously recalled to memory. Everything that is done in the way that it has always been done

provides access to the myth. Sometimes, in fact, the customary actions outlast the story. Sometimes the story that would explain and justify the action has paled in belief and offers only a trivial etiology, an indoctrination for children, perhaps, but the truth is simply that there is no other proper way to do things.

The way in which food is prepared and eaten, for example, is myth, sometimes with an etiological story explaining why it is done that way, but more often the manners are so ingrained that the procedure itself is accepted unreflectively as the only way. To do it differently is unthinkable. Who can think of a reason to-day for why we don't eat horses? Or dogs and wolves, for that matter? Those sto-ries were forgotten long ago. Only relics remain in our feelings about nightmares and werewolves. Or why don't we call a cow a cow when we eat it? Or why set the table the way we do? Why not eat with our fingers? The whole of what we might call table manners attempts to mediate the problem that the living and all their culture live off the dead and the dangerous recidivist putrefaction that is their realm. The turkey, for example, that we eat traditionally at Thanks-giving is a bird of the New World and commemorates the feast that the Pilgrims shared with the native inhabitants of the land they were settling. The story fas-cinates us, we tell it to children as history, whether completely accurate or not, but we don't consciously access the meaning involved in the millennia of pre-vious eatings that celebrated the harvest, before it was transported with the colonists to the New World.

The Greeks in their myth of Prometheus could cite the reason why they ate the way they ate, but the meaning, like the Thanksgiving turkey, was more elu-sive than they could grasp, and every feasting perpetuated the myth, even with-out the verbal telling.

Myth, moreover, permeates not only what is done (both as sacred ritual and profane custom), but also the whole attitude toward the environment. Should it be overcome, for example, and bent to our will or respected for itself and left to go its own way? We no longer have any stories about Mother Nature, apart from her name, but we cannot build anything upon the earth without betray-ing one of our myths, that we don't even know.

The Greeks, too, unreflectively imposed their imprint upon their surround-ings. Styles of architecture and dress, the design of homes and of the family's life within them, these also are myth, often devoid of words and story to justify the model. No one could say why a pubescent boy should look like an Apollo, or a girl, like his twin sister Artemis. The mere physical appearance of a person could be a nonverbal access to myth. And in a more direct sense, the works of sculp-ture, the decoration of buildings, the depictions on tableware, armor, and the like could immediately access particular myths, and might even be used to occasion a demonstration of memory, a telling of the actual words to prove, not that the myth was true—for that was not the question—but that the teller belonged to the culture.

The sources for our study of Classical Mythology are many and of dif-ferent kinds. But first, we should clarify the subject itself. Classical Mythology is actually ancient Greek Mythology, and not Greek and Latin Mythology, as is often thought.

The Latin-speaking Romans were another branch of the same Indo-European migrations that brought the Greek-speaking peoples into the Greek lands. In the Italian peninsula, the Romans, in contact with different peoples, underwent a similar but different evolution of culture. They had their own mythology. Their own history, customs, stories. Their own particular cultural dilemmas to mediate.

By the time they took serious notice of the Greeks, first as neighbors in the southern part of their own peninsula, and then elsewhere in the Mediterranean lands, the Greeks were already a highly sophisticated culture, much more advanced in art and literature than they. Greece had passed beyond the time of its Classical Age. Science and philosophy had supplanted myth as the primary reality, and myth had entered upon its long period of retention as a cultural heritage, studied, anthologized, and imitated, perpetuated in new works that consciously vied with the grandeur of the masterpieces preserved in writing from the past. In order not to seem provincial and uncouth, Roman writers and artists tried to participate in this dominant Greek tradition. The Romans largely abandoned their own mythology and adopted the Hellenic tradition, equating many of the Latin deities with their related Greek manifestations and homogenizing their earliest history to conform with the epic stories of the Greek heroes. That is to say, they adopted Classical Mythology, which is Greek mythology from all its sources, both Greek and Latin, together with its continuance through the European Renaissance into the modern era. We catch only glimpses of Roman mythology in the later Latin writings of scholars with an antiquarian interest in their own lost culture.

Throughout this long period of transmission lasting several millennia, Classical Mythology has served as a unifying force, lending coherent identity to the educated peoples of diverse cultures, which, like the Romans, lost much of their own traditions and incorporated the Classical view, continually reinterpreting it in new ways and searching for its elusive truth, while accepting it now as a patent fiction.

In this tradition of Classical Mythology, not every story has fared as well as others. Mythology is a constantly evolving view, perpetually reinterpreted and refined by each successive telling. The reality it describes recedes from the dominant truth that prevailed in the time of its sway as the primary mode of thought, into more recondite, unconscious, and occult meanings, forever beckoning to us to reexamine who we really are. Some stories were lost; others barely survive as antiquarian oddities.

Amongst these many stories, primacy of importance belongs to the ones that survive in versions that date from before the failure of the belief system in their authority. These are the *ipsissima verba*, the 'actual words,' for the performances of the works of the great Classical and pre-Classical masters, works which, through the vagaries of transmission of the written text, are still extant, although the performances themselves, and the music and dance that were often a part of them, can only be imagined. Still other works from this period can be partially surmised from surviving fragments and from the mentions in later antiquarians, who had more of the written record at their disposal and could cull these now lost works for summaries of plots that were once dramas and epics. Vase paintings, sculpture, and architectural ornaments, as well as archaeological reconstructions of sacred places provide another source for the mythology during its period of dominance.

Even during that period, however, some stories were losing their interest and relevance, and they were noted only by specialists, historians and compilers of local customs and oddities. Since the imitators who came later were demonstrating their scholarly credentials as perpetuators of the Classical heritage, these oddities often were incorporated in their own works, but usually only as peripheral details to a story that, through their reinterpretation, still had vitality.

Not all of the surviving works from the Classical period had such an enduring vitality. Even though they were all available for anyone who knew the language to read, it was only the most archetypal ones that at first were translated or were the ones that persisted into ever newer imitations and reinterpretations. They are the ones that are still told today.

In presenting this introduction to Classical Mythology, we will not offer a compendium of all the stories, with more names and events than could possibly be learned. That is the subject for a dictionary or encyclopedia.

Our focus will be the manner of thinking that is characteristic of myth, a reconstruction of the Classical world view or reality, and an investigation into the paradigms or archetypes that gave it an afterlife beyond the failure of its literal validity. In all of this, we are establishing a vantage point from which to view our own identity, our own myth.

A Note About Spelling. There is no universal agreement about how to spell the Greek names from Classical mythology, unless they are left in the Greek alphabet. The most ancient way was to convert the names into our alphabet in their Latin equivalents. Hence Greek names ending in -os are changed to -us, and since Greek has a 'k' and Latin a 'c', a name like Kronos can be written as Cronus. But since the Latin equivalence of the mythical figure is often not entirely the same, many people prefer to transliterate directly from the Greek alphabet, where possible. This, however, sometimes makes the name appear unlike what has become its traditional spelling in the modern language. Platon, which is Plato's name in some modern languages, looks strange in English. Similarly, -ai and -oi can be converted to equivalent Latin word endings as -ae and -oe, but in a word like Moerae consistency seems wrong since it isolates the word from Moira, as a given name in English. So, too, with the place name Mycenae, which has become its traditional spelling in English, so that it would appear strange with a 'k' as **Mykenae** or **Mykenai**; and here the 'y' is the traditional transliteration of the Greek 'u', so that the name could even be spelled **Mukenai**, if it did not make it unidentifiable to most people as the city of **Mycenae**.

The procedure we have adopted takes all of these elements into consideration. We have opted to let the words appear Greek where possible, but not where they would seem too strange. Nor have we hesitated to let a name evolve, so that Dionysus becomes Dionysos (but not Dionusos) as the character of the Greek deity develops; and Mycenae shifts into Mykenai as we come to understand its meaning.

A Note About Format. Each chapter presents a discrete, learnable segment, focusing on the major stories and their historical, religious, cultural, and psychological significance. Important concepts and names are highlighted in **bold print**. The chapter is followed by a **REVIEW**, which summarizes the material and lists the most important of the highlighted items. A repertory of **PARADIGMS** or archetypal patterns is recapitulated as they evolve in the successive chapters. **FOR DISCUSSION AND FURTHER STUDY** suggests readings in primary sources and, where appropriate, introduces correlative myths, with questions designed to prompt discussion.

Questions for Discussion

1. What foods do you associate with traditional holidays? What do you think is involved symbolically in the commemoration of Thanksgiving? What foods don't you eat? Why?
2. Why were the mastheads of ships traditionally a woman? Ships are usually referred to as female. If sailors were women, would the ship be male?
3. What difference would it make in your attitude to the environment if you considered it Father Nature?

Suggested Additional Readings

Archetypes:

Carl G. Jung, "Approaching the Unconscious," *Man and his Symbols* (Dell 1968) 1-94.

Joseph Campbell, *The Hero with a Thousand Faces* (Bollingen 1949).

Psychoanalysis and Literature

Sigmund Freud, *Delusion and Dream* (Beacon 1956).

Otto Rank, *The Myth of the Birth of the Hero and other writings* (Random House 1964).

Structuralism:

Claude Lévi-Strauss, "The Story of Asdiwal," *The Structural Study of Myth and Totemism* (Edmund Leach, ed., Barnes & Noble 1967) 1-47.

Semiology:

V. N. Toporov, "On the Semiotics of Mythological Conceptions about Mushrooms," *Semiotica* 53-4 (1985) 295-357.

Part II
Transmutations

☫

The basic building blocks of Myth are symbols. Unlike words, which have a specific reference to objects or concepts in reality, symbols invite us to infer a meaning, which is never specific, but rather like the tangible half of an extremely intriguing missing other half. Literally, the symbol describes a token that has been rent in two: we have only its half, but our half would complete the other missing portion, if we could ever find it. It is the story, for example, of twins, separated at birth and adopted by families in different lands, but entrusted at their parting with the broken tokens, whose enigmatic signs hold the clue to their common origin. Later in life, as chance would have it, the twins, with their quite divergent experiences, may come together again, perhaps even as mortal enemies; but in the knick of time, the mysterious emblem is glimpsed and the two halves that have puzzled each through life mesh perfectly. Or less romantically, the symbol is the proof of some contractual agreement that can be expedited only when the two original partners authenticate their identities by producing, each the other half of the broken token.

Such symbols are typical of the way we imagine our total or complete identity to be, of which we sense that we are only a part, destined one day to rejoin the rest. Our notions about deity are a prime example; and whether they accurately intimate the divine nature or are projections merely of our own human psychology, these images of god have a truth and validity that is eternal and indestructible. All of the tokens, although they may be engraved with different mysterious signs, tell the same story of separation and potential reconciliation; and the different faces on the tokens are simply variations upon the same theme. These variations we call transmutations. It is the way that what is eternal and true defies destruction, changing instead, only to remain the same thing.

In this section we will begin with the problem of whether the god image is more of a male or a female, and what that implies about the peoples who imagine it. Classical Greek culture and its Mythology is the result of the reconciliation of these

Hermes (Amphora, 5th century BC, Vatican Museum, Rome)

two diametrically different views. The outcome was a family of twelve deities who all owe allegiance, in one way or the other, to a supreme Male.

But the old Goddess never ceased to exist: she was transmuted. The story of that transmutation is seen in the myths about the goddess **Athena**.

But even when the Goddess had not yet yielded to masculine dominance, she could not function without her consort; for it is a fact of human nature that we are each differing admixtures of masculine and feminine physiological, psychological, and social identities. No people have ever managed to survive without some kind of accommodation between the sexes. Athena's former consort **Poseidon** survived in transmuted form with a different role in the era of reconciliation.

The old world of the Goddess was transmuted into the new world of the God, but no one can live for the moment only, without a sense of the past. **Dionysus** was a god, both effeminate and very masculine, who easily belonged to both worlds, and continually retraced the pathways of the reconciliation.

That was something he could do, since there was nothing he was ashamed of in his past. The same is not true of the twins **Apollo** and **Artemis**, who once had been consort and Goddess, before they were transmuted into a sibling pair. Their past was too terrible to ever allow them to revisit it. They were doomed to become the most perfect exemplars of what they never were in former times. Such a lack of access to one's past is apt to produce a certain instability, and these two deities were never easy to get along with.

Everybody had to help them, but their baby brother **Hermes** was the best in that role. There was no need to take it all so seriously, he would show. With a little trickery of the sort that Nature can play, it might even be rather funny. Ultimately, Hermes had a son, who turned out also to be his daughter, both at once, a transmutation that was a divine mockery of the whole problem.

Chapter II
God or Goddess

The storytellers had kept the memory alive over the generations, more generations than anyone now could count: their people were not from this place. If the others that they now lived amongst spoke Greek, it was hard to tell who was who any more, so much had the different peoples intermingled and joined their family lines. There were still a few isolated pockets amongst them, cultural backwaters where the people spoke a different language—Pelasgian, true Cretan, as they called it, and the like, and in some places, like Sparta, the aboriginals had been treated like slaves, but for the most part, they all shared the same language now. They were Greeks. It was their language, in its many regional dialects, that gave them their identity, wherever they were living, Greece, the islands, Asia Minor, Italy, even Africa. They shared no unified political structure as a nation. Their allegiance was to cities and tribal groups, but they worshipped the same gods and they met at the same great festivals to renew their common identity, listening to the stories and watching the dances. The others who didn't speak Greek were all barbarians, foreign people who spoke in unintelligible tongues, like just so many senseless repetitions of syllables that sounded to them like 'ba-ba-ba.' But the real Greeks were not from anywhere around these places.

They had come from somewhere far up north, somewhere from beyond the cave out of which the deadly North Wind **Boreas** blew. No one knew exactly where anymore, but it was some kind of paradise, where the people never aged, a place of magical plants and inspired visions, of marvelous animals, too, like the reindeer, a place you might hope to return to when you died. That's where the olive tree came from, so they said, and the laurel, too. It was very far away, too far for ordinary folk in this life, but the poets sometimes still claimed to visit there in some kind of trance, and there were special gateways in the Greek lands, certain caves and sacred places that might afford an easy entrance. This distant paradise was the original homeland of the Greeks. They remembered it as the land of the **Hyperboreans**.

Zeus

What the Greeks remembered as north of them was also toward their east, beyond the mountain pass down which Boreas blew, beyond which lay the central Asiatic highlands. No one knows why they left. To seek a better life, perhaps.

A better climate. Or perhaps it was just the spirit of adventure. To see what lay always beyond the horizon. Why not, after all? They were nomads, then. Hunters. They had no settled way of life.

They left in many groups and over a long period of time. There are no records of them then, except for memory, but toward the beginning of the second millennium before Christ, they began showing up on the doorsteps of the more settled peoples to their south and west. They began making their entrance into history. The migrations had taken many generations, with various routes and stopovers amongst other peoples along the way, from whom they picked up different aspects of foreign cultures. By the time we catch sight of them, they were living in the valley of the Indus and throughout Europe, for which reason they have been named the Indo-Europeans.

Their original language had developed in their different destinations into distinct dialects that were no longer mutually understandable. In India, it became Sanskrit, which is the classical language of Hinduism. Other branches of these migrations that brought them into Europe and Asia Minor evolved various ancient dialects of Germanic, Celtic, Anatolian, and Iranian, most of which are now no longer fully extant from the earliest periods. In the Italian peninsula, their dialect developed into Italic. Amongst these Italic peoples were the Latini, who originally inhabited the plain of Latium on the banks of the River Tiber. They had a knack for government, and through political expansion, they spread their version of the dialect, **Latin**, throughout an ever expanding Roman empire, which eventually overtook the whole peninsula and went on to include most of England, Europe, the near East, and northern Africa. It was a Slavic branch of these migrations that brought the Indo-Europeans into the Greek lands, where amongst their dialects evolved the language of **classical Greek**.

Wherever they went, and despite the different notions they had picked up along their way, they retained a feeling for male superiority and for the freely-roaming life they had followed in their homeland, so many centuries ago. They brought with them also their deities.

Chief amongst these was a male, a Great Father. The Greeks called him **Zeus**. **Zeus pater**, as they often said, 'Father Zeus.' The Romans called this same god **Jove**, or **Jupiter**, which is actually the identical name, a dialectal variant, with the epithet of 'father' no longer separable in Latin, as in Greek. He was so much the supreme god amongst other gods that his name was also responsible for the word for 'god,' itself, in Latin, **deus**.

Like his bands of hunters back home, he reveled in male strength, in physical prowess, and he sought always the open spaces and the high bright air of day. Day and sunlight were his domain, so much so that he even lent his name to the Latin word for 'day' or **dies**. His weapon was the bolt of lightning, which he wielded not primarily as a manifestation of the storm, but as the powerful implement of celestial enlightenment directed against the earth and the powers of darkness.

In Greece, he dwelt upon the highest mountain, **Mount Olympus** in northern Greece, as close as he could get to the Himalayan massif of his original home.

There he was 'father of Gods and Men,' presiding over a family of twelve **Olympian gods**, who included an aunt, several brothers and sisters, one of whom was his wife, as well as several children, including an illegitimate son. In modern terms, however, the Olympians would have to be considered a dysfunctional family. No one could ever control the aunt, who had more power even than he, and although he did father gods, only one of the Olympians, **Ares** (Latin **Mars**), the God of War, was sired upon his wife. Ares's bellicose nature was a clear reminder of the lack of marital harmony that characterized the union of Zeus and his wife. Although she was forced to lend her blessing to the rite of matrimony amongst humans, this was like a final indignity, to make her sanction the double standard, the very ritual that demanded a woman's dutiful subservience to a promiscuous husband; and although no one

Zeus Hurling the Thunderbolt (mid-5th century from Dodona, Staatliche Museen, Berlin)

would ever dare to incur Zeus's wrath by having an affair with his wife, **Hera** was constantly seeking ways to get back at him by playing dirty tricks.

And as for fathering men, it was true that Zeus was responsible for begetting several extraordinary men, including a case of quadruplets of which two were infamous women, but he originally had little sympathy with the race of humankind. His dwelling on Olympus was as far removed as possible from the community of men, whose humanness was basically antithetical to his nature. He and the other Olympians were immortal, ageless, whereas humans are polluted by flesh, are born, sicken, and die. The Olympians couldn't even share the same food as humans at first, but they dined on **ambrosia** and drank **nectar**, special foods that were uncontaminated by death, whereas humans could nourish themselves only with disgusting stuff that once had been alive. In fact, Zeus so much detested humans that he would have destroyed the whole race, had not some spark of the celestial fire been implanted in them, much against his will.

Mother Goddess

As in any dysfunctional family, the problem was caused by the fact that the members had their own private lives and were only gathered together on occa-

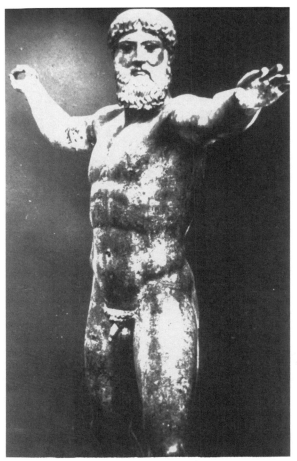

Zeus, Hurling the Thunderbolt (Sometimes identified as Poseidon, from the sea off Cape Artemisium c. 450 BC, National Museum, Athens)

sion as official proof of their supposedly common accord. Each had had a separate existence before being pressed into service with the Olympian family.

When the Indo-European migrators arrived in the Greek lands, the place was already inhabited by a quite different type of peoples. Their common culture, with many local variations and languages, had spread to Greece from Mesopotamia and Asia Minor. Unlike the nomadic Indo-Europeans, the peoples of this other culture had learned to settle in cities and had taken up a way of life that centered upon the tending of crops and herds, a way of life that demanded the solution to the basic problems of pollution and decreasing fertility, that are caused by the continuous living and farming of people in the same place.

For them, the deity was not a freely roaming god, but a goddess, attached, as women are, to the demands of material nurturing. This goddess of earthly nature, this Great Mother had many names in the different languages of her peoples, some of these names were eventually assimilated into Greek. She could be known, for example, as **Persephone**, a fearful name that suggested 'Destruction and Slaughter' by a false etymology, as if the name were Greek. And this Great Mother was, in fact, a goddess of death, but not just of death. Death as birth, and birth as rebirth. Death as the source of life. Another of her names was Deo, the Mother, which was assimilated into Greek as **Demeter**, whom the Romans called **Ceres**. The **cere**al grains that are nourished by the fertile rotting remains of life were her gift. Still another of her names was **Hekate**, the witch, the one who, again by a false etymology, always 'got her will,' the Willful One. The three belonged together inseparable, pacing the three aspects of a woman's experience, as maiden Persephone, mother Demeter, and the postmenopausal crone, Hekate. The Great Mother had always these three aspects, seen also in the phases of the moon, whose lunar periods, waxing, full, and waning, mirrored the fertility of a woman's menstrual cycles. The oestrual madness that drove the beasts to procreate had special sanctity, and the tremendous allure of a cow in heat upon the bull, which was the most powerful of the animals in the herds they kept, lent the goddess bovine attributes, like the lunar crescent worn as horns; and her mate, taurine. The madness was ritualized as hysteria and the women celebrated their solidarity as females, joining together as a tripartite sisterhood uniting the triple aspects of the goddess.

You can imagine the familial problems caused by incorporating this domineering goddess into the group of Olympians. In the case of Demeter, she was separated from her other two selves, allowed to revisit them only on occasion, and was incorporated as a dutiful sister into the family of Zeus, who then completed the insult by fathering her maiden daughter upon her as his own.

There couldn't be a more fundamental problem than this for myth to resolve. Two antithetical ways of life: nomadic males, hunters who needed the spirit of the wilderness to anticipate the migratory patterns of their prey; and domesticated females, farmers and herders, controlling nature with the magic of their own bodies. A male god in the physical power of full paternity, and a female goddess, waxing to the fullness of repeated maternity. The demands of man or woman to dominate.

Mycenaeans

We first caught sight of the migrating Indo-Europeans in the Greek lands through the archaeological excavations of the German Heinrich Schliemann in the latter part of the nineteenth century at the site of Mycenae, a steep hill several miles inland, at the base of the mountains that close the plain that stretches from the port of Argos in the eastern-most peninsula of the Peloponnesos, which is called the Argolid. Schliemann had already astounded the world by demonstrating that his naive faith in the historicity of myth was justified. Fired with an amateur's enthusiasm from his reading of the Homeric epics, he had set out to discover the city of Homer's Trojan War, where the Greek forces of Agamemnon had supposedly confronted the defending troops of Priam and the

Goddess (Cybele), Enthroned, Giving Birth (From Çatal Hüyük, Turkey, c. 6000 BC, Archaeological Museum, Ankara)

Gold Mask ('of Agamemnon,' from Tomb V, Mycenae, 16th century BC, National Museum, Athens)

Trojans, who refused to give back the Spartan queen Helen, who had been abducted from her husband Menelaus by the Trojan prince Paris. And although the precise hillock on the Hellespont that Schliemann identified as Troy may not be the actual city of Priam, his excavation forced a reexamination of the relationship of myth to history. Having found, as he thought, the city of the Trojan War, Schliemann turned his effort toward finding Agamemnon's home back in Greece.

The site was still known as Mycenae, and the ruins had been plundered many times before Schliemann's arrival, but he uncovered tombs that had escaped the robbers, and found hordes of precious ornaments, including sheets of gold that had been pressed upon the faces of the buried corpses to preserve their features for eternity. One of these, he mistakenly identified as the mask of Agamemnon himself, and he rushed off a message to the King of Greece informing him that he had succeeded in finding the tomb of his ancestor, forgetting that the king's lineage was German, like his own, and not Greek.

But this was the city of Agamemnon. This was indeed one of the many places where the battle between Zeus and the Goddess was played out, just one of many, but since it was here that we first encountered them in Greece, we customarily refer to them as **Mycenaean Greeks**.

The visitor today can pass through the fortified citadel's great Lion Gate, which is emblazoned above the lintel with two heraldic lions, flanking a single pillar that tapers toward its base. It is the emblem not of Agamemnon's dynasty, but of the Goddess of the pre-Greek people, whose city this originally was, before it succumbed to the domination of males. It was the city where the Goddess was called Mykene, and Mycenae is named in the plural for the sisterhood of females who tended her there. At Thebes, she was called Thebe, and the city again a plural, Thebae (or Thebes, where the 's' is the plural formation). Similarly, at Athens, she was called Athena, and the city, Athenae (or Athens, again a plural).

Beyond the Gate to the right lies the Grave Circle, a cemetery within the city, where the dead were buried at the bottom of deep shafts, unlike the earlier tombs that line the approach to the city, where the corpses were laid temporarily to rest in state, until they rotted, on a bier in grand subterranean vaulted chambers with the characteristic domed shape of a beehive, the so-called Tholos Tombs. These latter tombs imply a belief in the regenerative transition through death, since they were reused over and over again for successive burials, whereas the former, the shafts of the Grave Circle, suggest an attempt to immortalize the corpse's features for some eternal existence in the other world. Past the Grave Circle, the path makes its way up the hill, through the remains of clustered buildings, of which only the rubble of foundations is extant. At the top of the steep incline is the base of the walls of the royal palace.

It was here that **Clytaemnestra**, named as a 'Maiden Famous for her Bridal Wooing,' murdered her husband Agamemnon. As the tragedian Aeschylus described the event, Clytaemnestra had snatched back the dynastic power in her husband's absence, and upon his return from the Trojan War, she reversed the roles of sexual dominance, becoming a bull that mounted him sexually, as she plunged her murderous sword into him. The deadly controversy between them had begun when he separated her maiden daughter from its mother and slaughtered her in a sacrificial offering, as if the daughter were his child, and not the mother's. It is a story that we will return to later, but the final outcome successfully mediates the problem of matrilineality versus patrilineality, with the solution firmly in the favor of the Mycenaean Greeks. The child is more the father's than the mother's. And Clytaemnestra and her Mykene sisters, or Furies, are coaxed into the subterranean world, where they more appropriately belong.

As the Mycenaean Greeks imposed their own way of life upon the former female rulers of Mycenae, they even gave the city's name a new interpretation. By a false etymology, they could claim that it was named for their own Indo-European religious traditions, rather than the sisterhood of the Goddess. Along with their deities and other aspects of their culture, the migrators brought with them their ancestral attitudes toward sacred plants. The classification of plants and animals would have been their earliest science. In the botany of foods and medicines, a specific mushroom had special sanctity for the Indo-Europeans and they main-

Lion Gate, Mycenae

Amanita muscaria, Fruiting Body

tained remembrance of the tradition wherever they migrated, often substituting other plants as surrogates for the original, either because it was no longer easily available in their new lands, or because it better suited their evolving notions of religion or culture. This plant was a mushroom, the fly-agaric or Amanita muscaria. By this new interpretation, Mycenae (Mykenai, in Greek) was named for the mushroom or 'mykes.' The city got its new name when the hero **Perseus**, a son of Zeus born at that place, refounded it for the Indo-Europeans. That, too, is a story that we will return to later. Other cities that were taken over by the Mycenaean Greeks have similar traditions re-aligning the former peoples and their religion to the culture of the Indo-Europeans.

Amanita figured in Indo-European shamanism. The mushroom contains mind-altering chemicals that allowed the priest or 'shaman' to escape from the body and commune spir-itually with the deities in their celestial domain. Apart from the celestial orien-tation of their traditional, usually male-dominated shamanism, the mushroom's wild, uncultivatable manner of growth fit the Indo-European nomadic style of life as a special found magical plant, mediating as a sacred drug with other of the Amanitas, that include edible mushrooms, as well as deadly poisonous ones. The thunderbolt of Zeus was itself a mediation between the Father God's realm and earth, as the ethnomycologist R. Gordon Wasson has shown in demon-strating the wide-spread belief that mushrooms appear where lightning strikes the earth. Amanita was divine food, not something to be indulged in lightly, not something to be profaned. It was the food of the gods, their ambrosia, and nectar was the pressed sap of its juices.

Minoans

As with the Mycenaean Greeks, our name for the pre-Greek peoples is due by chance to another archaeological discovery. An Englishman, Sir Arthur Evans, was much impressed with Schliemann's excavations of Troy and Mycenae, but he became convinced that the Mycenaeans that Schliemann had uncovered must have had some means of writing. He was intrigued by some mysterious-ly engraved stones that were offered for sale in an Athenian antique shop. He was told that they were 'milk stones' that the women of Crete wore between their breasts as amulets for nursing. Following that lead, he went to Crete and exca-vated the ruins of a site that was traditionally known as the palace of king **Mi-nos**. They say that it was actually a Minos who sold him the plot where he intended to dig, but if true, that was merely a coincidence, just as people can still be named Mary or Jesus.

Just as Schliemann thought he had uncovered his own and the king's Aryan ancestors, Evans discovered what seemed very like the Empire in which he was himself a knight. A few miles upstream on the shallow river that empties into the sea at the modern city of Iraklion, toward the center of the north shore of the island of Crete, he found the ruins of **Knossos**, a maze-like complex of buildings, lacking fortification, which to him suggested that it was the central royal residence of a thalassocracy, an island empire whose powerful navy made local defenses unnecessary.

It was here that Minos ruled, he thought, even though the recent example of his own homeland might have suggested the possibility of a queen. **Pasiphae**, a name which suggests a lunar epithet, 'She who Shines on All,' was wife of Minos. It was she who had the uncontrollable oestrual cravings for a bull in her husband's herd, and disguised as an artificial cow, she managed to conceive a bull-man from the beast, the 'Minos Bull,' or **Minotaur**. Minos himself was also the son of a bull in the famous abduction of **Europa** by a taurine Zeus, unless that was the Minos who was his grandfather, for there were two and they are often confused. The former Minos became a judge of the dead in the nether world. Pasiphae's Minos was a couple of generations earlier than the Agamemnon of the Trojan War. We will return to the fuller story of Europa and Pasiphae later, with the tale of the hero **Theseus**, who did for Athens and Knossos the same sort of refounding or Indo-European reorientation that Perseus accomplished at Mycenae.

Knossos may not have been a palace, as Evans imagined. Amongst the many problems with that interpretation is the fact that although parts of the complex

Knossos
(Reconstruction
drawing)

are extant to the third floor, most are just the remains of the basement, and Evans was forced to fantasize the life of the royal family in those cramped and damp lower levels, rather than in the more desirable, although missing, airy upper stories. The separate building adjacent to the complex, in his view, was the summer palace, although it is unlikely that the king would go only so far as next door for his vacations. And the stone materials out of which the complex is constructed do not seem durable enough for much use, since the ruins suffer today from the abrasive feet of the tourists who have visited it since its discovery.

The confusing maze of corridors, moreover, is an inept design for a residence. But a maze is what one finds at Knossos. A **labyrinth**, to use its real name, a word assimilated into Greek from the pre-Greek language, as is the name of Knossos itself. A labyrinth is the 'place of the labrys.' A 'labrys' is a double axe, an axe with edges that cut in both directions. It was a symbol of the religion practiced at Knossos, like the crucifix in Christianity. Ornamental golden exemplars have been found, as well as much sturdier implements for actual use.

And like the cross, it was the symbol of the sacrificial death. The labrys was used to slaughter the bull, and the bull was the taurine manifestation of the bovine Queen's consort. Originally not a bull, but the consort himself, was the victim. Between the two edges of an axe that cuts in both directions is the sharp divide, the razor's edge, the midmost point—beyond which lies another world. The labrys symbolizes renewal through death, and when kings became less expendable, other humans came to be substituted in the king's role, supposedly as willing sacrificial victims, uniting the living with the dead to revitalize the fertility of the Goddess and of the mortal women who joined as a trinity of sisters in her worship. The labyrinth itself, with its contorted and confusing passageways, was emblematic of the Goddess, like a maze of entrails leading to the womb, which is the gateway for life and death.

At the center of the labyrinth of Knossos was a courtyard, where the offering of human victims was performed as an acrobatic dance with a real bull. Both males and females were afforded this deadly honor, two groups of seven each year, at the time of Theseus, before he put an end to the practice. As the bull lunged, the dancers were expected to grasp the bull's horns and attempt to flip themselves in a somersault through the horns and over the bull's back, to land gracefully upright behind the bull. A difficult task, and more often, no doubt the dancer failed, but even a close brush with death might satisfy the need, or demonstrate the deity's moment of benevolence. The narrow and dangerous passageway through the horns was another way that these people symbolized the point where life and death convened.

The Bull Dance was a rather grisly entertainment to be occurring in the residence of the civilized royal couple that Sir Arthur imagined living there. But it was an intriguing discovery, nonetheless. And Evans did find writing, too, but it didn't at first justify his faith in the literacy of the Homeric Age, for the writing didn't appear to be Greek. Knossos had suffered from extensive destruction twice in its history, apparently from natural disasters, first by an earthquake

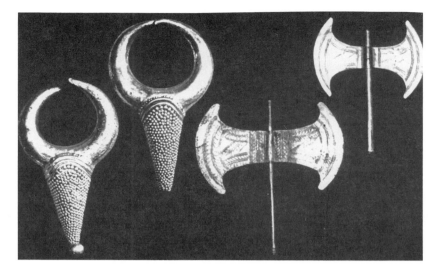

Golden Double
Axes and Bucrania
(or bull heads,
before 1600 BC,
National Museum,
Iraklion)

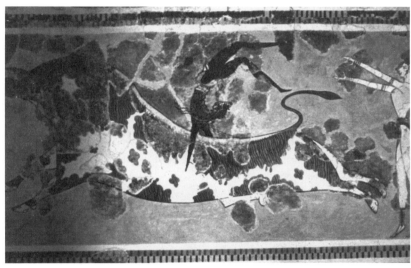

Bull Dance of
Knossos (Men are
brown; women,
white: fresco,
National Museum,
Iraklion)

West Wing,
Staircase Leading
from Bull Dance
Courtyard,
Knossos
(Reconstruction
drawing)

around 1700 BC, and again about a century later, and each time, it had then been repaired and reused. It wasn't abandoned until its final destruction around 1375, after having been severely damaged by the volcanic eruption that blew up the island of Santorini, to the north of Crete. The labyrinth included chambers for storage of agricultural offerings, and by chance, a fire, apparently occasioned by the Santorini disaster, baked the clay tablets on which were recorded the contents of these chambers. The tablets were meant merely as annual accounts, but converted into terra cotta by the fire, they survive until today, long after their intended use. They are inscribed with a linear pictographic script, which Evans dubbed Linear B, since they differ from a similar earlier script, dubbed Linear A. Examples of Linear B have been found, under similar circumstances of accidental firing, at other Mycenaean sites, most notably at the palace of Nestor at Pylos, in the southern Peloponnesos.

It is now agreed that the writing of Linear B is, in fact, Greek, written not in the later alphabet, but employing the pictographic syllabary of the Minoan language. As at Mycenae, the Indo-Europeans had somehow taken over the place, by whatever means is unknown, whether dynastic intermarriage or war, and had assimilated various aspects of the previous culture. The inverted pillar that we saw in Mycenae's Lion Gate is, in fact, the characteristic style in the Minoan architecture of Knossos.

Pillar Lady of the Labyrinth

The excavation of Knossos led to further discoveries on Crete and the islands of the Cyclades and elsewhere, from which a clearer notion of the Mother Goddess in the Greek lands has emerged. Since she is the original deity from whom the women on Olympus evolved, through the assimilation of the Minoan religion by the Mycenaean Greeks, it is essential to grasp certain aspects of her symbolism.

She is the Lady of the Pillar, whom we have already met at the entrance to the citadel of Mycenae. She is the mainstay of the enclosed space, for which the Labyrinth is one manifestation. When flanked by beasts, as in the Lion Gate, she has been dubbed the **Potnia Theron** or 'Mistress of Beasts.' The phrase is a quotation from the Homeric epic tradition, where it describes the Olympian goddess **Artemis** as a huntress. But she was a huntress only after her incorporation into that family as a daughter of Zeus, with her twin brother **Apollo**. In her new role as a huntress, she was forced to abandon certain aspects of her Minoan identity and made to conform to the nomadic traditions of the Indo-European homeland. From that alien northern environment, she even acquired the reindeer, a hind with golden branching antlers, as her special beast, an animal not native to her own Mediterranean and Anatolian origins. It replaced other animals that were originally associated with her as a Mother Goddess. The hind is an animate manifestation of the power residing in the sacred plant of the ancient Indo-Europeans' shamanism, for Amanita is an inebriating mushroom that the reindeer is fond of grazing upon, and the animal's branching horns, supposed-

(left) Artemis as Potnia Theron, Winged, Flanked with Reindeer and Lion Familiars and Wearing Dress with Labyrinth Design (Krater 570 BC, 'François' vase, Museo Archeologico, Florence)

(below) Athena (or Hera or Artemis) with Gorgon Face and Vine as Potnia Theron, Flanked by Pubescent Girl and Boy and Lions, and Wearing Dress with Labyrinth Design (Pithos from Thebes, early 7th century BC, National Museum, Athens)

ly of the same golden color as Amanita, easily suggest botanic affinities with a magical tree. The hind replaced not only the Goddess's other animals, but also the sacred plants that they represented in her former Minoan shamanism.

The Lady of Beasts was never a huntress amongst the Minoans. She and the male deity who would later become her twin brother were originally Lady and Consort, Rulers of the Labyrinth, and their fearful and sinister identities as re-cipients of human victims there required the most strenuous evolution of myth to isolate the two of them from their Minoan pasts and to remodel them both into their Classical identities as the most perfect exemplars of Greek female and male pubescent youthfulness. Artemis, despite her sexual maturity, was even made into a perpetual virgin, denied forever her former role as Mother. But for the moment, we are not interested in tracing the evolution of Artemis into an Olympian, but in the original symbolism of the Goddess she once was.

And it was not only she who could be this Lady of Beasts, but that Goddess lurked in the past of other of the Olympian females, like **Hera**, Zeus's sister and wife, and **Athena**, another of his daughters; although it was only the twins Artemis and Apollo who maintained their ritual and mythical association with human sacrifice even into the Olympian age.

First, what was the realm over which the Lady presided? Unlike Zeus's affiliation with the open daylight sky, the Lady's domain is the enclosed space, the settled city, the house, but also natural enclosures, like caves, or architectural imitations of subterranean chambers, and her time is night, dark places like the tomb or the womb, or architectural imitations of its symbolism, like the labyrinth. She or the Pillar sometimes appears on top of a mountain, or the mountain itself can be substituted for her in the configuration of flanking beasts, but her sacred space is a cave on the mountain, and not the bright Olympian domicile; or the sanctity of the mountain consists in its resemblance to features of the female anatomy, and not, as with the Olympians, in its celestial separation from earth. She sometimes has her eyes closed, as if dreaming or asleep. Narcosis is the experience in her shamanism, unlike the enlightenment of Zeus, and her special plant is not wild, like Amanita, but a cultivar, in particular, the opium poppy, for which it, too, like Amanita, later has purely symbolic surrogates substituted, for example, the rose (for its similar flower and capsule-like hips) and the pomegranate (whose fruit also resembles the poppy capsule).

And what were this Lady's beasts? The beasts that flank or attend the Lady of

Goddess, Eyes Closed, with Crown of Opium Poppies Incised to Extract Opiate (from Isopata, National Museum, Iraklion)

the Pillar are typically of the following kinds: **burrowing animals**, like the prolific rabbit, that makes its home in earth; **serpents**, which similarly burrow into her darkness, and demonstrate their close affinity to her realm by lacking legs, and also because of their obvious phallic appearance and because of their association with venoms or drugs, and also because their shape is essentially just the alimentary canal, a labyrinth of transformation; **birds**, particularly long-necked birds (again for their phallic significance), like the goose, swan, and cock, or the crane (which is also migratory, and hence suggests a trip to another world), or predatory birds (carnivorous, soul-snatching birds), like the owl, hawk, or eagle; **pigs** (which alone of animals respond to the human sex scent); **bulls** (for the power of their arousal by the cow in heat);

and **lions** and **leopards** (probably an Anatolian remembrance, but perhaps, like the bull, also for their mating behavior). **Insects** are also associated with the Goddess, in particular, **bees**, which like serpents have connotations of venoms or drugs gathered supposedly from flowers, a venom that can also be a nutriment in the form of honey; bees are, moreover, queendoms, ruled by the queen bee. The Minoan sisterhoods are sometimes portrayed with insect faces, and the stylized manner of Minoan dress is with an exaggeratedly narrow waist in the manner of an insect. The beehive, as we saw at Mycenae, was the shape of the subterranean grave chamber.

But who was this Lady's Consort? All of these beasts of the Lady of the Pillar have sexual connotations, and like her magical flowers, they can suggest the possessing spirit of her mate or consort. Their attendance upon her derives from her basic nature as primordially both sexes in one, or **hermaphrodite**, male as well as female. This can be blatantly explicit, as in the example of the very early figurine of a goddess with a phallic head.

Goddess, with Head Shaped like a Phallus (from Pharsala, Thessaly 5th millennium BC)

Or more stylized, like the numerous Cycladic idols with exaggeratedly long necks and female bodies that suggest male genitals, the so-called 'fiddle case' goddesses. The same symbolism underlies the portrayal of the goddess as a mother nursing her own male child, or with a child of both sexes, or flanked by human youths, instead of beasts, one of each sex. Sometimes the masculine part of her identity is indicated by the serpents she wields or has twined about her body, the so-called 'snake goddesses,' or by the birds perched atop her head. The bird is often merged as part of her own body, and she is winged, or raises her two arms in the typical prayerful gesture of the Minoan goddess, suggestive, in its painted striated feathers, of her bird-like wings, a pose that also imitates the lunar crescent. Sometimes the pose with the prayerful crescent is only one in a series of idols, where the other versions in the sequence round out the crescent into a full circle representing the phases of the moon, to depict the trinity of her sisterhoods. The bird-like lunar crescent also suggests horns, and she can wear both the crescent or horns also as a crown, amidst the birds on her head.

Similarly, the digits of her fingers on the upraised arms or her toes are often so grossly explicit that you can count them. These pentads of fingers and toes are her **daktyls**, and typically the males who attend her are groupings of five. Her brotherhoods are often comprised of men who are either short or tall, with the shape-shifting magic that characterizes penile erection.

But even without her digital men, even apart from her flowers and the wings or birds, serpents, and beasts teeming about her body, there would be no mistaking the nature of this Lady with the elongated neck and startling face. This is the Lady of the Pillar, the mainstay of the enclosure. She needs no other maleness to complement her own womanhood.

Even as an Olympian assimilation, her primordial hermaphroditism persists. She is Artemis, twinned with a brother Apollo. Or Athena, who dresses in male attire. Or Hera, with the bastard son of Zeus, **Hephaestus**, her son, and her son alone, although some people would deny her that honor, and claimed that Zeus must have been his father. Or **Aphrodite**, the aunt of Zeus, who was transformed into a woman out of her father's castrated genitals.

The Birth of Zeus

It was from a Lady like one of these that Zeus was born into the Greek lands. Since he was originally not from that place, the story can only be that of his rebirth, the story of the coming of the newer Olympian age. And to match the trinity of the Lady, the birthing will require three generations to culminate in the victory of Zeus and his Olympian family.

In the beginning, there was only Earth, called **Gaia**, Mother Nature, male and female together. She brought forth children alone out of her own body, the creatures with which she peopled her universe, females out of her own femaleness, and males out of her own maleness. Most opposite to her own femaleness as Earth, she brought forth a male who was Sky or **Ouranos** (Latin **Uranus**). This was the first generation.

Now with Ouranos, who was once the maleness of her own body, Gaia continued to bring forth children, but in the newer manner, heterosexually. But as she readied each child for birth, Ouranos pushed them all back into her womb, fearful that the next son she bore would be mightier than its father. And as each birth was denied, her pregnancy became more and more unbearable, with the many completed fetuses waiting for birth. One of these was her son **Kronos** (Latin **Cronus**). Him she counseled to play a trick upon his father. When next his father came to her, heavy upon her body, desiring to make love, Kronos was instructed to reach up and sever the genitals off his father's body. This he did. And the waiting siblings in his mother's womb he rescued, freeing them for birth. And this was the second generation.

Characteristic of this generation is the difficulty of escaping from the mother's body. The castration of Ouranos also depicts the female as emasculating, the psychological complex of the 'vagina dentata,' the male's imagined fear of the vagina as having teeth capable of biting off the penis. In this complex, it is the son Kronos, wielding his great sickle, who plays the role of the teeth. His act inaugurated the Kronian age, and he and his sickle persist as our New Year's myth of Father Time, who is Khronos, not the same mythical figure as Kronos (Latin Chronus), but often confused with him.

The castrated genitals of Ouranos fell into the sea, foaming. Buoyed on the foam, they floated to the island of Cyprus, where they came ashore. Rising out of the foam was born the Goddess **Aphrodite**, whose name means 'Foam-given.' She is the goddess the Romans called **Venus**, the goddess of sexual lusting. Although destined to become an Olympian, she is a generation earlier than Zeus.

Characteristic of Aphrodite's birth

Aphrodite, Rising from the Sea at Birth (Ludovisi Throne, Museo Nazionale, Rome)

is the absence of a mother. She is her father's child alone. As the most powerful of the Olympians, more powerful even than Zeus, and born earlier than he, Aphrodite is a remembrance of the original primacy of the Goddess. Her birth from the sea associates her with water as the primordial home of life, and as the metamorphosis of her father's genitals, she is a phallus, despite her seductive femininity. Both the birth from the sea and her phallic femininity are commemorated in her having the conch or other sea shells as her attribute, for molluscs are hermaphroditic, and the spiralling of a conch suggests the womb passageway and the labyrinth. And she is a goddess of madness, the lustful arousal the female can produce in the male. Since her father Ouranos was the phallic nature of Gaia, externalized as a separate male, she is a female's maleness returned into female appearance.

Amongst the children liberated by Kronos from Gaia's womb was **Rhea**, another version of Gaia herself, and often interchangeable with her, but named as 'Flux.' With this sister of his, Kronos now begot children, but like his father Ouranos, he feared that a son would prove mightier than he. His own example had set the precedent, but he was not so foolish as his father to push the children

Rhea gives Kronos the Stone in Swaddling Clothes
(460 BC, Metropolitan Museum, New York)

back into the mother to be used as her ploy against him. As each was born, he took it and ate it, putting it into his stomach, as if the belly could double as his womb. Once again, the mother played a trick. When Kronos came to claim his latest child, she gave him a stone, wrapped in swaddling clothes like a baby, and the son, who was **Zeus**, she hid in the most sacred cave of her Minoan religion on Crete, either on Mount Ida or Dikte. There she tended him, in the old style, like the infant god that repeatedly was born to Mother Nature. Her sisterhood of goddesses cared for him, and to camouflage the baby's wailings, she instructed her brotherhood of ecstatic **Korybantes** to drum upon the tympani, an instrument newly invented for this purpose, and to dance outside the cave. The Korybantes are interchangeable with another brotherhood, the **Kuretes**, who performed the same function at the cave, making noise by the clashing of their spears. Both groups are associated with the orgiastic worship of the Goddess. Zeus was even nursed by the goat **Amalthea**, whose horn became a symbol of the bounteous fertility of the nether world. And it was bees who fed him with their honey. Thus Zeus was given a proper Cretan birth to begin his new life in Greece.

When grown to adulthood, Zeus gave an emetic potion, mixed with honey, to his father Kronos, who vomited up the children he had eaten. These were the siblings of Zeus: **Demeter**, **Hera**, **Poseidon**, and **Hestia**. These four became members of his Olympian family. A fifth, **Hades**, became Lord of the underworld. And this was the third generation.

Characteristic of this generation is the difficulty of being born from the father, whereas the second generation had had that problem with the mother. It also presents Zeus as the rescuer of his own future Olympian brothers and sisters.

In case you doubt the veracity of this story, the stone that Rhea gave to Kronos could still be seen, preserved at the sanctuary of Delphi, where it was tended, anointed each day with oil, like the baby it was. Stone is the substance of Earth. She has the power to change things into stone, and her creatures often use stone as their weapons. Her primordial image is as a faceless stone, without the craftsman's working which would impose a human likeness upon it. This stone that Kronos ate was a true child of Earth, and Rhea deceived her mate into giving it a masculine gestation, while preserving Zeus, the product of her own feminine gestation. The sanctity of the Delphic stone involves the ultimate mediation between Earth and Sky, and mother and fatherhood.

The Coming of the Olympian Age

If anyone could bring these two worlds together, and impress upon them the stamp of Indo-European male bias, it was Zeus. But he had been born as an infant, conforming to the pattern of the divine child in Minoan religion. He would have to grow to his maturity, fixed eternally at the age of fatherhood, avoiding the pitfalls of his Minoan heritage, where he would have remained his Mother's maleness, rather than his own man.

The enemy is always one's other self. Whenever the battle is fought, the opponent is who you hope you are not. In the case of Zeus, it is this Minoan heritage that he must overcome.

There were three versions of the battle. The last was with **Typhon**, like another Zeus, the youngest of the sons of Earth, born after Zeus seemed to have succeeded in establishing his Olympian family. Typhon was a monster, the fearful potential of what Zeus might have been, replete with all sorts of dreadful Minoan attributes, serpents, bull voice, and so on. He managed for a time to imprison Zeus in a cave, and so frightened the Olympians that they, too, reverted to their pre-Olympian animal identities, including Hera as a cow. But even this ultimate foe, Zeus overcame, imposing upon him the same nether world confinement that Typhon had intended for him. Typhon went on to beget many monsters that the heroes, who had not yet been born, would have to confront, in the name of Zeus.

But before Typhon, if we can assign a linear chronology to the events of myth, which is synchronous and eternal, there were two other versions of this battle with the children of Earth. The two are basically identical. The opponents are called either **Giants** or **Titans**. The encyclopediasts could list their names and distinguish between them, although it is generally agreed that the Giants were serpents below the waist and were named as 'Children of Gaia,' while the Titans were 'Stretchers,' probably implying the phallic metaphor of the 'big little man.' Vase painters depicted them sometimes as fighting with stone projectiles, against the much more civilized forces of the Olympians. So evenly matched were the two sides in the battles that Zeus could not have won, except that he managed to prevent the enemy from eating the magical plant that Earth had provided for them, and one opponent from the opposite side came over to the Olympian side and tipped the balance of force in their favor.

This turncoat was the Titan **Prometheus**.

The Creation of Man

There must have been humans in Minoan times, before the coming of the Mycenaean Greeks, but in the mythical traditions, mankind was created at the dawn of the Age of Zeus. It was the role of this new race of humans to mediate between the Olympians and the forces of Earth.

Prometheus made the first man, fashioning him—for it was only the male that he created—out of clay. You could still see the petrified pieces of stone that were left over from this creation at a site in Boeotia near Thebes. And even though it was Athena, the favorite daughter of Zeus, who breathed the spirit of life into the humanoid, Zeus himself was so repelled by the creation that he intended to destroy it. But Prometheus prevented him by stealing some bit of the celestial fire from the Olympians and implanting it in man. Fire is the force of transformation whereby matter is consumed and transmuted into the airy substance of smoke or spirit. It is this heat of transformation that animates the clay. It is the soul, the Olympian nature that the flesh-bound creatures of earth share with this new age of gods. Hence, Prometheus's theft of fire was seen as the origin of man's intellect. Prometheus hid the stolen ember in a stalk of fennel, as if it were the animating spirit of some plant that he was taking from the gods—which actually was the case, for the hollow fennel stalk was what the Minoans used to house the magical herbs they gathered. The theft implies the assimilation of the Indo-European sacred plant into Minoan traditions. And because some part of the celestial nature now resided in earthen man, Zeus was frustrated in his desire to annihilate this creature that constantly by its living mediated between his own realm and that of Earth.

In eating, humans feed that fire. Near Corinth, at Sicyon, formerly called Mekone (which means 'poppy,' probably the opium poppy of the Goddess), Prometheus taught his new creation the proper table manners for the coming age to ritually perpetuate that mediation. Prometheus established the rules for the sacrificial meal.

He played another trick on Zeus, for Prometheus was good at such things: even his name labels him as 'Forethought.' He slaughtered a bull and made two parcels of the butchered meat. One parcel he made of the inedible parts, disguising them with fat and the hide, so that it looked like the better portion. The other parcel he made of the edible parts, camouflaging it with entrails so that it appeared less appealing. Thus he tricked the gods into choosing the worse portion. Otherwise, there would have been nothing left for man to nourish life upon.

This was the precedent for all ensuing holiday feastings, for customarily it was only on special occasions that ordinary Greeks ate meat. Sacrifice was a communal meal. The people ate the edible parts, and the gods' portion was burnt upon the altar, so that its material substance would be transmuted into smoke and spirit that rose to the celestial realm, where the Olympians breathed in its airy fragrance. If the Olympians were to have actually eaten flesh, instead of spirit, they would have been no better than the deadly Minoan Goddess and consort who presided over the Labyrinth, the 'earthly' or **chthonic** deities whom the new Olympians replaced. For those were the two types of deities, the **Olympians** and the **Chthonic** ones (named for a Greek word for Earth, which is 'chthon'). Thus it was that Prometheus not only, by the theft, gave his human creation the fiery power of spiritual transformation, but also, by the trick, he prevented the Olympians from regressing and becoming the same sort of gods as their predecessors.

Every repetition of the sacrificial meal reinforced the progressive cultural evolution both of the human worshippers and of the new age of gods. The animal that was slaughtered represented the primordial chthonic nature of the god to be worshipped, a bull for Zeus, for example, who had replaced the bull consort of the bovine Queen; a pig for Demeter; and so on. The animal was treated like the honored deity it represented, and it had to be tricked into acquiescing in its own death. Water or grain, for example, could be sprinkled on its head, and when the animal nodded to shake it off, the priest could interpret the beast's gesture as a sign of its willingness. Then the butchered beast was cooked on the altar (for an altar was like an outdoor grill) following special culinary procedures that reflected the group's ethnic identity. People today still gather for holiday celebrations in which they reinforce their cultural togetherness by eating the traditional foods of that holiday, prepared in the manner of their own family roots. And we still eat with the refinement of table manners that set our feasting apart from the uncivilized carnivorous gnawing of beasts. But the Greek feast was similar, only more structured: the parts of the sacrificed animal were successively cooked in a sequence that recapitulated both the supposed developmental growth of the animal and the evolution of the culinary arts, with the most primordial organs cooked in the most primitive manner. The feasting was accompanied, moreover, by music, singing and dancing, reiterating the traditional myths and cementing the bonds of family, tribal, and social structures, which were the world these new gods presided over—politics, art, all the good things of civilization. And joining in the feast were the gods themselves, nourished anew upon the demise of their own former selves, transmuted into spiritual essence, as the worst and inedible parts of the sacrificed animal that represented their own primordial, more sinister identity were burnt upon the al-

Sacrificial Feast, Altar with Skewered Meat Roasting (Museo Nazionale di Villa Giulia, Rome)

tar. As the fragrant smoke rose aloft to their celestial realm, the Olympians breathed it in, an inspiration that humans offered to help perpetuate the gods in their newer manifestations.

The chthonic deities could also receive sacrifice, but for them the procedure was different, remembering the tradition that the victims once were human offerings and not fit for consumption. The slaughtered animal was not edible, a food prejudice that often still persists until today, and it was simply tossed in a pit, uncooked, and left to rot. Typical of such chthonic sacrifice was the dog that could be offered to Hekate where three roads met, symbolic of her tripartite nature, an offering that would be made at night, unlike the daylight meal for an Olympian. The dog was considered a tamed version of the wolf, and not entirely incapable of reverting unexpectedly into its werewolf ancestor, with all of its sinister connotations, including the possibility that a human could be possessed by its wild and outlaw spirit. We have inherited this tradition in our attitude toward 'bitches' and metaphors like the 'hounds from Hell.'

Even the art of cooking had a special role to play in the mediation of humankind's dependence upon dead matter for nourishment. It would not be civilized to eat meat raw, like an animal, or like the grave. But cooking softens meat, just like rotting. It is a hastened and scientific putrefaction that renders the food not poisonous, but fit for human consumption. Nor is it simply softened by the cooking, but the food is prepared in the ways of our forebears, expressing our cultural identity. And as the fine cuisine passes through the alimentary canal, as fuel for the fire of life, it undergoes a further transformation somewhere in our middle. What was fine becomes disgusting, to emerge as offal, polluted poison. But even that must not be despised nor neglected. It can be correctly managed so that it will renew the fertility of the chthonic realm, both physically in continuing harvests, and spiritually in the bond with the deceased members of our family. A symbol of this interdependence of life and death is the **uroboros**, the 'tail-eater.' The uroboros is a serpent curved into a circle, sustaining its life by eating its own tail; for amongst its others aspects of symbolism, the serpent represents an animal reduced essentially to just its alimentary canal, whose coiling narrow passageway can also be seen in the labyrinth, especially when it takes its original form as a way from entrance to exit, rather than entrance to the center and back.

This interdependence is what Prometheus foresaw in the theft of fire and the rite of eating, the way to unite his own, and man's, chthonic origins with the furtherance of civilization through intellect and celestial or spiritual aspirations.

He got little thanks for it all from Zeus, at first. It is a story, a myth, that we will come to later. It will require that Zeus learn to avoid the pitfalls of his own past—that Zeus not beget a son, such as he was, who would displace his father, but one instead who will be the most perfect heroic redeemer of humankind. It is a story not unlike the role of Christ. Until that future time, Prometheus was tormented by Zeus in punishment for his thievery. Zeus bound him to a mountain, where a vulture repeatedly eats his liver, the organ of his intellect, which each time grows back, so that he cannot die and end his pain. Eventually, that heroic redeemer who is a son of Zeus—**Heracles** was his name—a man who becomes an Olympian, will set even Prometheus free, but only after another immortal agrees to resign his own rank of immortality and die in place of the liberated Titan. The mountain of Prometheus's torment was sometimes located in the Caucasus, but it was also a nether world place. Prometheus is often interchangeable with **Hephaestus**, Hera's son; and the latter was identified with subterranean fire, the forge of the underworld, and in particular with the volcanic core of various mountains. Chained to his mountain, Prometheus is basically that fiery core itself, striving to unite the dichotomous natures of the man he molded of formless clay and fired like a pot. For the potter's kiln and the metallurgist's forge are attributes of Hephaestus. They are the way he, too, imparts form to the faceless ores and clays of Earth.

Not surprisingly—since he was his mother's child, a son without a father—Hephaestus was called upon to complete the creation of the race of humans, by fashioning the first woman.

The Creation of Woman

Pandora was her name. And she was the first woman, at least so they said—because there must have been women in the days of the Goddess, before the coming of the Mycenaean Zeus-worshipping Greeks.

And Pandora must have been a splendid example of femininity, for all the Olympians endowed her with their own brand of special gift. That was the meaning of her name: the 'Every Endowment.'

Zeus commissioned the work from Hephaestus, who fashioned her, too, like Prometheus's man, out of clay. She was a maiden woman, a female at puberty, and her divine gifts included the arts of wifely duties, but she was also ravishingly beautiful, bedecked in finery and gold, and with a deceptive tongue that would make her a difficult mate for a husband to control.

Prometheus was too smart to accept the woman, knowing that it was some trick of Zeus, but Prometheus had a backward brother, **Epimetheus**, who was the stupid version of himself. Epimetheus was 'Back-thought' to Prometheus's 'Forethought.' It was he who took the bride, despite his brother's warnings to beware of anything that came from Zeus.

Pandora possessed a sealed urn, an enclosed space—which she opened. That was the trick. She scattered its contents throughout the world: toil, disease, and early death. Just one good thing there was in this urn of Pandora's—Hope, and that she trapped inside, replacing the lid before it could fly out of its earthenware prison. Presumably, for we are not explicitly told, that is why the men she has so grievously afflicted with the human condition continually return to her seductive blandishments.

The myth expresses the deeply distrustful misogynistic attitude of the Indo-European males, intensified by their fear of the Goddess's power, but it is also a mediation with the Minoan tradition. Prometheus's man has spirit and intellect, but Pandora is not evil: it is with Olympian attributes that Hephaestus's woman is endowed. Even her deceitfulness is the gift from one of them. Before Pandora came, men lived a longer, trouble-free life, but they could foresee its inevitable end. She shortened the life span and added suffering, but retained Hope, the immortality that humans can aspire to in the successive generation of descendants. And without humans to mediate between the chthonic and Olympian deities, even the Olympian age could not exist.

The Flood and the Coming of a New Age

In some remote pockets left over from the Minoan age, however, people were still practicing the old religion. In the backward regions of Arcadia, which is the central highlands of the Peloponnesos, there were still Pelasgians, and the king of these pre-Greek peoples, a certain **Lykaon** or 'Wolf-man' actually sacrificed a boy to Zeus. Zeus disguised himself as a traveller and visited the house of this Lykaon, and sure enough, that is what they were doing. They had the audacity to serve their Olympian guest a meal of human flesh. He ratified their ungodly primitivism by turning them all into wolves. Now, the wolf was one of the primordial natures of Apollo, and these wolf-men, of which there are quite a few in Classical myth, are always Apollo's darker self, his werewolf persona. Zeus decided to destroy this whole age of humans who still persisted in honoring the ways of the Labyrinth, and he did this by unleashing a huge flood. The story of the devastating Flood that inaugurates a new age is common to people around the globe. It appears to be archetypal, and involves the idea of water as the boundary between worlds, ultimately the boundary between our present humanness and our past aquatic forms, both in the ocean, as a species, and in the womb, as individuals. Each of us, in coming into being, repeats the same sequence of developmental forms that our whole species went through in its evolution from lower, more primordial creatures. Ontogeny recapitulates phylogeny, is the way a scientist would say it: the individual repeats the whole evolutionary history of its species in its gestation. Once again, Prometheus was responsible for saving humankind.

Prometheus and Epimetheus both had children: Prometheus, a son named **Deukalion**; and his brother Epimetheus, a daughter, the 'Fiery' **Pyrrha**, presumably Pandora's daughter, for since Prometheus and Epimetheus and Hephaestus are all interchangeable, there are inevitably various accounts of the genealogy. These, however, were always the people involved in stories about the earliest ancestors of mankind, and some of the versions were kept as secrets in rites of initiation. But we will come to that later. In the myth of the Flood, Deukalion and Pyrrha were a married couple, cousins, male and female from dissimilar fathers, but perhaps both Pandora's children. Prometheus warned Deukalion of the coming disaster and instructed him to build an ark, like Noah's in the Bibilical tradition, but apparently only for himself and his wife.

Now it should be noted that an ark isn't primarily a boat. It is a closed container, a casket, a coffin. Deukalion's ark was a 'larnax,' not a boat, but a box, with definite tomb-like connotations. The same is true of Pandora's urn, which was a 'pithos,' earthenware, but a vase that could have funereal use. The journey over the primordial waters that separate worlds is usually accomplished in such 'vessels,' which have female and womb connotations, as well.

When the waters receded, after nine days of Flood, Deukalion's ark touched down on Mount Parnassos, which was sacred to Apollo, both in his original lupine (or werewolf) nature and in his soon to come Olympian self.

There the final mediation was completed in the making of a new race of humans, more evenly balanced in the representation of males and females. The Goddess and Consort of the ancient Labyrinth-Cavern on Parnassos (for the one at Knossos wasn't the only such place, but only the most elaborate architecturally) advised Deukalion and Pyrrha, in accordance with Zeus's will, to throw the bones of their mother behind them. They interpreted the riddle to mean 'rocks' as the bones of Mother Earth. Thus, throwing stones over their shoulders as they walked forward, they re-peopled the earth. From the rocks of Deukalion, behind his back, men came into being; and from those of Pyrrha, women, uniting not only chthonic and Olympian traditions, but also 'Back' and 'Forethought,' as well. Some even claimed that Prometheus showed up at the last moment to put fire in the new creatures again. In various holy places in Greece you can still see where the last swampy damp spots from the Flood haven't yet quite dried up. There's even one in Athens at the base of the Acropolis.

Deukalion and Pyrrha had a son, **Hellen**, who had in turn three sons, from one of whom (Xuthos) he had two grandsons. The two grandsons (Ion and Achaios) and the other two of the sons (Doros and Aiolos) lent their names to the four great tribal groupings of the Greeks: Dorians, Aeolians, Ionians, and Achaeans; and the whole people, who could claim Hellen as their ancestor, were known as Hellenes, one of the names that the Greeks called themselves.

The Five Ages

Despite the fact that the world has obviously gotten better with the coming of the new age, there was also a certain nostalgia for the olden times, the imagined perfection of the Hyberborean homeland, as well as the higher civilization of Minoan culture that was disturbed by the coming of the Indo-European migrants, especially by a second group of them, who were less acculturated than the earlier ones and were actually responsible for plunging Greece into a Dark Age of about four-hundred years.

In this other view of history, there has been regression, instead of progress. First there was an **Age of Gold**, when Kronos was still king. Humans were like gods, in those days. They lived without having to work, and they didn't grow old, but died, after a long life, without suffering or disease, by simply falling at last to sleep.

Second was an **Age of Silver**, far inferior. It was then that it took children a hundred years to grow up, and when they did, they lived only briefly, engaged in violence. Zeus was king by this time, and he did away with them, placing them, like the former, in Earth, where they comprise a lower class, less honored than the previous, who are holy and protectors of humankind.

Third there was **Bronze**. This time it was of bronze that they were made. And so was everything in their world. They were violent, devoted totally to war, and they died of their own hands, going nameless into the nether world

Fourth there was a reprieve, although not everyone includes this Age in the numbering. This was the **Age of Heroes**, the time when the Great Men lived, whose stories we shall see later, people like Heracles, Perseus, and Theseus, the famous refounders, when the Indo-Europeans were taking over the places of their Minoan predecessors. It was a time of strife, but when they died, they went to paradise, back to the Hyperborean Islands of the Blessed. There in a magical garden, Kronos is their Lord, newly ascended from the nether world, where he had been confined after the passing of the Golden Age. For this was the age, this Age of Heroes, that reconciled Zeus with his predecessors.

Note that the Age of Heroes is the only one in which the humans are not produced by metallurgy, molded in the Hephaestean forge from the ores of Earth.

Last, and worst, came the **Age of Iron**, which is now. It would be better never to have been born, if this is when you must live. This is the time of cold reality, the glaring contrast to myth. There is nothing but work, nowadays. But it, too, won't last forever. It is doomed to end when children are born already gray. And they will not honor their own parents, but argue and fight, and destroy each other through violence. Even the gods will desert us eventually, for Olympus.

* * * *

Review

Classical myth developed through the assimilation of two quite different peoples. We can refer to these two different cultures by using the names of the two places where they were first uncovered through archaeological investigation: **Mycenaean** (Greeks) and **Minoan** (pre-Greeks), but the terms are merely useful and not accurate.

The general trend of the assimilation was to replace female dominance of the Mother Goddess with male dominance of the Father God. This latter was **Zeus**, with his family of twelve **Olympians**, all of whom also have past identities from the **chthonic** religion of the Minoans.

You have met eleven of the twelve Olympians, but you will get to know them all better. So far, this is what you know:

Zeus or **Zeus pater** (Roman **Jupiter**, **Jove**): attribute: lightning bolt, bull

Hera, his wife and sister: patroness of matrimony

Hephaestus, her child, but probably not his; interchangeable with **Prometheus-Epimetheus**, but not as Hera's child; attribute: volcanic forge, torch, a craftsman

Ares (Roman **Mars**), son of Zeus and Hera; patron of war

Aphrodite (Roman **Venus**), 'aunt' of Zeus, born from his grandfather's genitals; patroness of sexuality; attribute: conch or seashell

Zeus's siblings, in addition to Hera:

Demeter (Roman **Ceres**): attribute: pig, ear of grain, pomegranate, roseate poppy flower

Poseidon

Hestia

Zeus's children not by Hera:

Athena

Apollo: attribute: wolf

Artemis, Apollo's twin: attribute: reindeer, golden hind; huntress and mistress of beasts (**potnia theron**)

The twelfth Olympian is another son of Zeus, without Hera, **Hermes**, whose name you have already encountered in the word **hermaphrodite**, which combines his name with Aphrodite

You have also met some of the chthonic deities:

Hades, a brother of Zeus, but not an Olympian

Persephone, his bride, a daughter of Zeus by his sister Demeter

Hekate, the witch; Persephone and Hekate are the chthonic two-thirds completing Demeter; attribute: dog, crossroad where three ways meet

The Goddess was originally hermaphroditic; her maleness or Consort often is represented as part of her own body and takes the following forms:

daktyls or digit-men

Korybantes and **Kuretes** (ecstatic dancers)

serpents

bulls (often worn as her horns)

birds (either as her wings, her digit-men displayed in upraised arms resembling wings and horns, or as attendant bird: goose, swan, vulture, cock)

lunar crescent, resembling horns, but implying as well the lunar phases

plants, such as the opium poppy, functioning in her rites of chthonic shamanism as her spirit mate, for which the pomegranate and rose are common substitutes or surrogates

You have also learned the following stories or myths:

Birth of Aphrodite

Birth of Zeus (**Gaia**, **Ouranos**, **Rhea**, **Kronos**)

Theft of Fire and Rite of Sacrificial Meal

Creation of Humans (**Prometheus**, **Epimetheus**, **Pandora**, **Deukalion**, **Pyrrha**, **Lykaon**)

The Five Ages (**Gold**, **Silver**, **Bronze**, **Heroes**, **Iron**)

You have also seen one of the basic paradigms or archetypes of the creative imagination (of which Myth is one manifestation). You will build up a repertory of such paradigms as we proceed.

1.) The enemy is always the other self. (Example: **Zeus versus Typhon**; also **Zeus and the Olympians versus the Titans and the Giants**)

For Discussion and Further Study

1. Why do you suppose the Age of Heroes is not the product of the metallurgist's art? Can you reconcile the two creation myths (Prometheus and the Five Ages)?

2. Can you suggest another instance in which the apparent enemy is actually very similar (or identical) to its opponent? (Think of novels or plays or movies or comic strips or politics or religion or psychology, etc.)

3. The 'crucifixion' of Prometheus is portrayed in the Greek tragedy *Prometheus Bound,* a drama often ascribed to the authorship of Aeschylus. Read it and consider in particular:
    Why is Hephaestus so unwilling to torment his enemy?
    Whose fire is it that Prometheus has stolen?
    Why is fire called a 'flower'?
    What benefits does Prometheus claim he has given his newly created
        human?
    Why is Zeus portrayed as such a tyrannical master?

4. Mary Shelley's *Frankenstein* is called 'The Modern Prometheus.' Apply the paradigm #1 to an analysis of the relationship of Dr. Frankenstein and the monster he created. Consider that the novel was written by a woman: does that influence her condemnation of Frankenstein's scientific attempt to create life, while neglecting his fiancee and the more obvious means?

5. A fuller account of the Coming of Zeus is given in Hesiod's *Theogony*. In the long series of 'begettings' can you discern a pattern? Trace what ultimately is coming into being.

6. A different version of the origins of humans is given in the comedian Aristophanes' speech in Plato's *Symposium* (189A-193E). Humans were originally of three sexes: male, female, and hermaphrodite, but they were all severed into halves by Zeus in order to keep them inferior to himself; the resulting half-persons are now gay males (from the male total creature), lesbian females (from the female total), and heterosexuals (from the hermaphroditic totality). Bear in mind that Aristophanes is a comedian and that he is telling a joke, but how would you apply this version to the assimilative mediation that we have observed between Mycenaean and Minoan traditions?

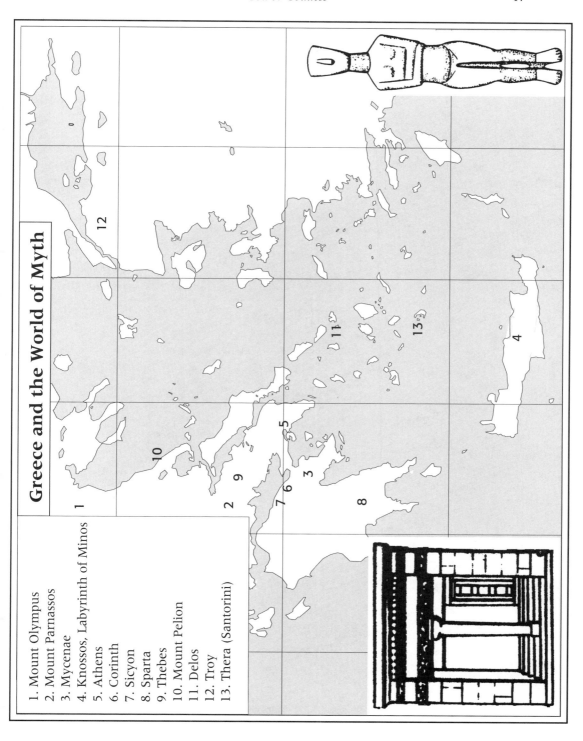

Greece and the World of Myth

1. Mount Olympus
2. Mount Parnassos
3. Mycenae
4. Knossos, Labyrinth of Minos
5. Athens
6. Corinth
7. Sicyon
8. Sparta
9. Thebes
10. Mount Pelion
11. Delos
12. Troy
13. Thera (Santorini)

Chapter III
A Goddess for the Age of Zeus

Athena was already a goddess in the Greek lands before the coming of the Indo-Europeans. Her name belongs to one of the pre-Greek languages and we do not know its meaning. At Athens (which was called that as a plural of her name), she was the Queen of the Athena sisterhood, the Athenai. There, she was associated with various male figures who were later remembered as early kings of Athens, men who were half serpents, like **Kekrops** ('Tail-man,' in appearance), who was a snake below the waist, or sometimes a fish, and who was said to have been born from the Earth; or like **Erechtheus** ('Chthonic-man'), similarly Earth-born, aquatic, and usually serpentine. These so-called kings were originally not the rulers, but the Queen's consorts, for in those days, the Goddess was still supreme, and children were considered the mother's child and not the father's. Patriliny would set in only after the coming of Zeus and the Indo-Europeans. Before that time, it was very hard for a father at Athens to establish a male dynasty through his son: the supposed history of the earliest male dynastic lineage at Athens shows repeated interruptions and disjunction.

The Birth of Athena

To judge by what became of her in the Olympian age, Athena must have originally been a very powerful Goddess, for Zeus made her into his favorite daughter. Not only that, but he used her birth to demonstrate that other females, in general, were henceforth expendable, since by giving birth to his Athena, he replaced the Minoan Goddesses by incorporating femaleness into his own body. It was now Zeus—not Gaia or Earth—who could lay claim to the primordial superiority of being both sexes at once. It was Zeus who was symbolically the hermaphrodite. Or Zeus together with his daughter, for Athena was very masculine, for a female, and never did she do the things that were the basis of a woman's power. She never was an infant, dependent upon the closeness of a mother for nourishment and growth. She never had a consort or husband, although she forever was a female at the ripe age for one, a **parthenos** or 'virgin.' Nor ever was she a mother. And never did she age to the fullness of a woman's suffering endurance that would have given her the terrible knowledge of witchery. And beyond all that, she even dressed in armor as a male warrior, a woman attired as a man.

49

Athena's mother belonged to an aquatic sisterhood, the daughters of Ocean, and when she became pregnant, Zeus feared that the child might replace him on Olympus, as he had replaced his father Kronos; and Kronos, his father Ouranos. So he ate the pregnant mother, forever after keeping her femaleness as part of his own body. It was a better solution than that of Kronos, who had merely eaten the children after they were born and had never acquired a womb of his own. In Zeus, the fetus gestated, and when it came to term, he gave it birth, but not from his lower body, as a woman would, polluted by the proximity of the organs of sex and excretion, and infantile, but pure from his head, like a thought, and already an adult, fully wise. The mystery of this male birthing was not totally a destruction of the Goddess, but a transmutation, a mediation. The 'wisdom' that emerged from Zeus's head was originally a woman's dangerous craftiness, for the pregnant mother that he ate was called **Metis**, which means 'wise and crafty.' But she never had a chance to play a trick, such as Rhea had on Kronos, and Gaia on her mate Ouranos. The goddess that the Romans equated with Athena was named **Minerva** (or Menerva), a word that, unlike Athena, does have an Indo-European etymology. Minerva was named for this characteristic of her transmuted '**men**tality.'

For the birth, Zeus had no vaginal aperture in his head to allow Athena to emerge. So one was provided for him by Prometheus-Hephaestus (or sometimes Hermes). They did this by whacking him on the head with the ancient Minoan double axe or 'labrys', but instead of resulting in the sacrifice of him as the bull or consort whose death would renew the power of the Goddess, Athena emerged from the cleft head, the apotheosis of Zeus's Olympian ascendancy.

Birth of Athena from Head of Zeus with Eileithyia and Poseidon in Attendance with Owl (Musée du Louvre, Paris)

The male deities who were pressed into service for this bizarre midwifery were appropriate agents, whichever version one follows. We will come to Hermes later, but all three are examples of Earth's phallic men, and all three were adept at mediating the dichotomy of male and female. It was Hephaestus, you will remember, who created the first woman, Pandora; and Prometheus-Epimetheus who received her; the deceptive mind of Pandora was a gift from Hermes (whose name you have already encountered in the term 'hermaphrodite'). Remember that in mythopoetic thinking all three versions can be simultaneously accepted as valid since each would be separately accessed and not easily compared to the others; but as is often the case in myth, all the variants basically express the same pattern.

Zeus had already (if one can speak of time in myth) expropriated midwifery by begetting from his own wife, **Hera**, a sisterhood of goddesses who preside over birthing, the three Eileithyiai (although sometimes the three are only one), the 'females who come' at a mother's time of need. And they were often present at the birth of Athena to witness their father's triumph. Zeus's affair with Metis was, of course, an extramarital event, and hence an affront to Hera, who presided over the very same ritual of matrimony that, by the double standard, did not apply to a husband, and particularly to her own. In the Roman tradition, Hera did not even retain a name independent of her husband. She was called **Juno**, which is a feminine form of **Jupiter**'s name, just as wives customarily assume their spouse's surname.

The Birth of Hephaestus

Hera was so incensed at Zeus's usurpation of a female's role, that she gave birth herself to a child without the cooperation of him or of any maleness beyond her own. This was **Hephaestus** (the Roman **Vulcanus** or **Vulcan**, from whose name we have words like '**volc**ano' and '**vulc**anize'). But even that couldn't compensate for her humiliation, for by one of the versions of the myth, this parthenogenic son of hers was used as the agent for facilitating Zeus's demonstration of his own powers of parturition, the Goddess's own son used against her.

Some versions of Hephaestus's birth claimed that Hera was so disgusted with his ugliness that she threw him into the sea, where he was tended by an aquatic sisterhood for nine years. Others were kinder and claimed that Hephaestus's deformity was inflicted upon him by Zeus, who threw him out of Olympus, down upon the volcano on the island of Lemnos, where he was tended by a brotherhood of primordial men. For Hephaestus was the only Olympian who was not perfect. He was lame, supposedly crippled from the wound he received when he fell to Earth. Here, too, both versions were simultaneously accepted; both, in fact, occur in the same Homeric poem. In both instances, whether in the sea or in the volcano, it was this chthonic sojourn that taught Hephaestus his skill as a craftsman: he was devilishly clever at making all sorts of mechanical devices, including robots and automated vehicles. In this amazing skill as a craftsman, He-

Hephaestus
Working at his
Chthonic Smithy
with
Brotherhood of
Cyclopes,
Athena and Hera
in Attendance,
Making the
Armor of Achilles
(Palazzo dei Con-
servatori, Rome)

phaestus was often associated with various primordial peoples who were later suspected of wizardry and black magic, and who sometimes were thought to have constructed the marvelous works of the Minoan age, like the earliest foundations of Mycenae and Athens. There was always something subversive about these automated mechanical devices of Hephaestus, almost as if they represented some threat to the Olympian age, for they could function as matter, inanimately, without a soul. The Greeks maintained this prejudice so that even after inventors had in reality discovered things like the 'steam engine,' they were considered merely as curiosities, just toys, and not anything to put to use, replacing human energy by animated machines.

By the version of Hephaestus's deformity in which Zeus was said to have inflicted his lameness, Hephaestus had angered Zeus by siding with his mother in some marital dispute. Zeus could have quite a temper toward his wife; and apparently on this occasion he had even hung Hera from the skies by golden bracelets fastened around her wrists, further weighting her body down with anvils attached from her ankles. This painful pose is an ironic example of the Minoan Goddess's prayerful display of her digits with upraised arms, together with a sardonic demonstration of the force of Earth's gravity, intensified by the pull of the heavy anvils from the chthonic forge of her son Hephaestus.

The lameness of Hephaestus represents his phallic nature, the metaphor of the 'third leg' and the imagined disabling or crippling spasms of penile erection. There will be other instances in Classical myth of such limping (or maimed) figures, who are dear to Hera or are otherwise chthonic in nature.

Athena's Owl

Athena's miraculous birth represents, as we have seen, the transmutation of the Goddess's trickiness (Metis' and Pandora's deceptive mind) into higher wisdom, through the intermediary of Zeus's head. The transmutation is more complete in the case of the Roman Minerva, who is largely just a goddess of Wisdom, than with Athena, who maintains more of her past. As a Minoan goddess, Athena would have had, as part of her traditional symbolism, an association with a bird, an aspect of her consort attendant. As Zeus's daughter, she still has that bird. It is the owl, and she even retains the honorific epithet of having an owl on her head: **glaukopis**; just as Hera retains the epithet of having cow/bull horns: **bo-opis**. The owl, however, has lost its original meaning as a sinister, carnivorous night predator. It now connotes friendly wisdom, higher arts and inspiration, a meaning that is still traditional today, despite all evidence to the contrary. In antiquity, owls were kept in aviaries in Athena's temples. There were, in fact, so many owls in Athens that 'To carry owls to Athens' was homilitic for an unnecessary task, like 'to carry wood into the forest' in English.

Except when she functions as a stand-in for Athena in Latin versions of Greek myth, Minerva is little more than a goddess of Wisdom. Like Juno, she is a more complete subjugation of the Goddess to male traditions. Although Athena also represents inspiration—more strongly felt as a transmutation from its chthonic origins—another group of goddesses in Greek mythology is closer to the less complex and blander role of the Roman Minerva. These are the **Muses** (or Mousai).

Wisdom in a mythopoeic tradition is a matter of memory, the ability to access and recall the unwritten history that is myth. The goddess who presides over this art of memory is **Mnemosyne**, whose name means '**mem**ory,' formed from the same Indo-European root that appears in the name of Minerva, whose **men**tal powers are really the ability to re**mem**ber. Mnemosyne goes back to the first generation, before the birth of Zeus. She is a goddess born from Gaia and Ouranos. Zeus slept with her to beget a sisterhood of thrice three daughters, the nine Muses (from which we have '**mus**ic' in English, since the mythic tradition was originally a sung, and often danced, recall of the accessed knowledge). The names of the nine are known from earliest Greek times—and the tradition that they could trip you up and give you the wrong truth, if they didn't like you— but only late in Roman times were the nine differentiated into different branches of knowledge: Calliope (epic), Clio (history), Euterpe (flute), Terpsichore (dance), Erato (lyric), Melpomene (tragedy), Thalia (comedy), Polyhymnia (mime), and Urania (astronomy). With these nine daughters, Zeus could lay claim to all aspects of higher civilization, presiding over a world that had once been the Goddess's, but was now encoded into the Greek linguistic formulae of his own people.

The Contest with Pallas

The first task, as always, is to confront the enemy, who is one's other self. **Paradigm #1**. Athena does this three times, destroying her own Minoan past and, as in the case of her owl, reconciling it to the new Olympian age of Zeus. The three are **Pallas**, the **Gorgon Medusa**, and the spinstress **Arachne**.

Pallas was a beloved friend of Athena. You can get some idea of the nature of this friend from the fact that in primordial times there was a group of children at Athens who were called the 'children of Pallas,' the Pallantidae, and they were said to have led revolts whenever a king tried to pass the dynasty on to a son. Pallas was a name for the primordial Athena of matrilineal times. Nor is it clear what sex Pallas was. Although a female in the contest with Athena, there was also a Pallas who was a male Giant that Athena destroyed in the great battle of the Olympians against the children of Earth. And the name of Pallas merely indicates a pubescent youth, of either sex, for the Goddess in those days was still hermaphroditic; nor did she refrain from sex, like the later Athena, for it was also a term for non-matrimonial sexuality, for polyandrous concubinage. Nor can we be sure that Pallas was even human in shape, for there was a Pallas who was a wolf—and even a goat. The most ancient talismanic effigies of Athena were called palladia. These were magical found objects, faceless pillars of Earth, in the old manner, before the Goddess was anthropomorphized and given form through the intervention of human intellectual meddling.

Pallas was Athena. And Athena, as the daughter of Zeus, had to destroy her.

Pallas was an aquatic female with whom Athena played warlike games, and by accident she killed her. Zeus had momentarily distracted Athena's attention by displaying a goatskin, such as Athena herself had once worn, fringed with serpents; and without thinking of what she was doing, Athena struck Pallas with her spear, forgetting that it was in jest. The 'brandished' spear that resulted in Pallas's death became the false etymology of her name. And Athena so grieved for her mistake that she forever afterwards wears that fringed goatskin, the **aegis**, as a commemorative expiation for her lost friend. She even added her name to her own, so that she can be called **Pallas Athena**.

Since the enemy is the other self, it can never be completely destroyed: it must be confronted and reconciled. Paradigm #2. Anything else would be suicide. No on can live as only half a person.

The Contest with the Gorgon Medusa

If ultimately we do not know what Pallas looked like, the same is not true of the **Gorgon Medusa**, the conniving 'Queen' (which is what Medusa means) of the Gorgon sisterhood, of which there were usually three members. These sisters were the third group, completing a triad of aquatic sisters, the three nubile **Hesperides**, and the three crones with a single eye, the **Graeae** (or 'Gray Ladies'). We have many pictures of the Medusa. And like the goatskin aegis that commemorates the former Pallas, Athena will also wear the decapitated head of the Medusa, again as a memorial of who she, now as a daughter of Zeus, no longer is. For in the Athens of earlier times, Athena was the Medusa. The Athenai sisterhood were the Gorgons, the 'Terrible Women'.

The Medusa had bulging eyes, puffed cheeks, a lolling tongue, and fangs for teeth. The hairs of her head were hissing serpents. For a body, she could be a goat, and some people claimed that was where the **aegis** skin came from that Zeus used to distract Athena's attention from Pallas. (One of the last 'kings' of Athens was a 'goat-man,' **Aegeus**, and his son **Theseus** was responsible for putting down the dynastic claims of the Pallantidae, but that is a story that we will come to later.) More often, the Medusa had a horse's body. She was a nightmare, a sinister female horse.

And her eyes had the primordial power of Earth to turn you to stone if you looked at her. And she was winged, a bird woman.

And worst of all, she was bearded—a woman who was a man.

She was ugly, terrifying, petrifying. Although, perhaps she was beautiful—too beautiful. There were people who claimed that she only got to look like such a monster after she had angered Athena by impersonating her and having sex in her temple.

Athena, in Armor, with Aegis and Gorgon Head (Painted for the potter Andokides, c. 525 BC, Staatliche Museen, Berlin)

Freud interpreted the Medusa as the projection of a man's fear, what the emasculating power of such beauty might do to a man. The tongue and fangs to him, suggested that emasculation, the metaphor of the *vagina dentata* (the vagina with teeth), and her appearance is simply, as Freud thought, her sex displaced to her face.

To destroy the Gorgon Medusa, Athena needed a man of the new age, one of the human heroes, who was a son of Zeus, the hero **Perseus**. We will come to his story later, but typical of the male hero is his role in defeating the old order or in some other way acting to establish the Olympian age. Perseus helped Athena destroy the Gorgon Medusa at Mycenae; **Theseus** did the same thing at Athens and Knossos. Even for the greatest of the heroes, the hero **Heracles**, Athena was a constant companion; his task was not to change just a single city, but to refound the entire world in its new order for the age of his father Zeus; and not to help just Pallas-Medusa-Athena displace her past identity, but to perform this same function for the Olympian wife of Zeus, Hera. These stories, too, we will come to later. Athena is often the 'best girlfriend' of the hero, the unsexually involved female companion who helps him along in his task. She is particularly good at this because she is such a perfect transmutation of the enemy—the

Gorgon metamorphosed into Athena. He needs her, and she needs him, for, as we shall see, he, too, is a creature of the new world, a person who was formerly a different sort of man.

When it was all over, Athena wore the decapitated head of the Medusa, resting on top of her aegis shawl, and she took the honorific title of knighted woman, 'horse-woman,' Hippia. **Paradigm #2**. And the Gorgon head on her breast could still, if she so wished, turn you to stone.

The Contest with Arachne

Arachne (the 'Spider,' from which we have words like **arachn**id in English) was a spinstress in Anatolia, which was often considered the homeland of the Goddess, and the daughter of someone who was known for his 'Knowledge.' Although we learn of her myth only from Roman sources, the involvement of Athena in spinning and weaving goes back to earliest times. Athena had been Arachne's teacher in needlecraft but the student's skill rivaled that of her master. Disguised as a gray-haired crone, Athena advised the girl to acknowledge the goddess's superiority, but when Arachne refused, she revealed herself and entered into a competition with her. Each produced a beautiful tapestry, but Arachne's work, which depicted the Olympians engaged in indecent sexual escapades, so infuriated Athena that she tore it up and beat the girl with the shuttle from her loom. In grief, Arachne hanged herself. But then came the reconciliation. **Paradigm #2**. Athena brought her back to life with a magical herb, but changed her into a spider, the spinning insect that is forever abhorrent to the goddess; and Arachne climbed down to safety on the ropes of her web.

There is much involved beneath the surface in this simple story. We tend to forget in English that a spinstress (or spinster) is a female spinner. We think of her instead as old, no doubt ugly, and unmarried, assuming that there was probably something about such a woman that made her undesirable for matrimony, perhaps not pretty enough, or just too bossy. This sinister connotation we inherit from the ancient tradition of the spinning Goddess.

First, it is unfair to impute that a spinstress couldn't be married, rather than she simply chose not to marry—not to make herself subservient to a husband. Such independent women arouse fear in a man. And even if we do think of this unpleasant hag as a spinner, whiling away her mean old age with some kind of incessant knitting, or the like, we tend to suspect that there is something dangerous or ominous in her handicraft, the product of her long, bony fingers.

In Classical myth, the **spinning Goddess**, usually multiplied into a sisterhood of three, presides over Fate (Roman **Fata**, the 'decrees of destiny'). In Greek, the fates are thought of as the allotment of human life, and the sisters are named collectively as the **Moirai** (or Moerae) (the 'Apportionments'), and they were individualized as **Clotho** (the 'Spinstress'): she spins the wool from her distaff into the thread of life on her spindle; and **Lachesis** (the 'Alloter'): she measures the length of thread allotted with her ruler; and **Atropos** (the 'Irreversible'):

she cuts the thread with her scissors, allowing no turning back. Zeus obviously had to assimilate this spinning Goddess, and he made them into his daughters, too, although not by all accounts, for even he was bound ultimately by Fate.

As with the role of bees and their matriarchal societies, careful observation of the spinning insect that Arachne became appears to lie at the origin of this metaphor for Fate. It is the female spider that spins its web. The male is dispensable, and it is not only the black widow (a New World spider) that commonly does just that, usually right after benefiting from insemination by her mate. The articulated joints of the spider's limbs, like the fingers and lengthened nose of an old witch, suggest, moreover, the phallic digits of this terrible female of Death.

Athena was once Arachne (**paradigm #1**), and not in a trivial sense, as in the playful myth of the contest of sewing. That displaced identity required repeated appeasement. **Paradigm #2**. Every fourth year in Athens, Athena was honored, in an especially elaborate celebration of her annual birthday party—the birth as an Olympian daughter of Zeus—as the patroness of spinning, at her Panathenaea ('All Athens') Festival. An embroidered robe was hoisted on the mast of a ship, like its wind-driven sail, and the ship, as if coming from the goddess's former aquatic homeland, was drawn on wheels through the city, to her temple on the Acropolis, where the robe was presented as her new piece of clothing for the effigy of Athena. This cloth was a breath of wind, a newly repeated 'inspiration' for the remade Goddess. The needlework of this robe, and its embroidered mythological themes, represented higher art, displacing the sinister webster's craft. And it had been specially woven in a manner that would ritually isolate it from any weird involvement with female sexuality; it was made by an honorific sisterhood, composed only of pre-pubescent girls, and under the direction of a post-menopausal priestess. And with music and dance, with a sacrificial meal, and with the performance of athletic games, the people of Athens thus perpetuated anew their Goddess in her Olympian identity.

Athena and Erichthonius

As the virgin goddess, Zeus's daughter could never again have a Consort, never have a child. But once that would have been her role, and her former identity as a mother also could not be obliterated, but merely transmuted. She even in some localities would retain her epithet of 'Mother.' And in Athens, she was closely associated with a serpentine male, who was almost her son, but in the nick of time, he turned out to be only her foster child.

Hephaestus attempted to beget that son on Athena. It was inevitable that those two, united in their births, should come together: Hephaestus, the male with only a mother for parent; and Athena, the female with only a father. She repulsed his advances, stepping aside at the last moment, so that his ejaculation fell on her robe. She wiped if off with a wad of wool ('erion') and threw it to Earth, who was fertilized instead of her. Earth bore the son intended for

Athena's child. **Erichthonius** was his name. And he was a serpent. His name combines 'Chthonic' with the wad of 'erion' from her robe, but he is often merely a double for one of the early serpentine 'kings' of Athens, **Erechtheus**, whose name combines 'Chthonic' with the ground 'rending' moment of his emergence from Earth's womb.

Athena became the foster-mother of this son, that she wasn't allowed any longer to have herself. But since he originally should have been the Medusa's child at Athens, she entrusted him with two precious drops of blood from the defeated Gorgon Queen: one drop was a deadly poison; the other, a miraculous panacea.

And then, by mistake (**paradigm #2**), she got rid of the Athenian sisterhood of Gorgons, as well. She gave the infant Erichthonius into the keeping of three sisters, who were daughters of 'king' **Kekrops**. Athena hid him in a chest, with the instructions that they were not ever to open it. Just like Pandora, they disobeyed. By some accounts, the serpent bit them. They went mad and fell to their deaths from the Acropolis. (The leader of the three sisters, Aglauros, some claimed was turned into a stone, like an ancient Mother Goddess, and was still worshipped on the Acropolis: the group of three was named Aglauridai after her.) Erichthonius often appears beside Athena in her iconography, a serpent, such as she would once have had as a Minoan snake goddess.

Erechtheus, like Kekrops, had a sisterhood of three daughters, each of whom he sacrificed on behalf of the city as they reached puberty—although they may have volunteered for this honor, themselves. A fourth (named 'Queen') survived, outliving her father. From her was born **Ion**, the founder of the Ionic tribal group of Greeks. He was really his mother's son, but everybody thought that he was his father's son, instead of hers.

Athena and Erechtheus-Poseidon-Triton

In addition to a son, Athena would once have had a Consort, as well. This, too, she had to be deprived of—and then be reconciled with in a new role.

One version of this Consort at Athens was **Poseidon** (equated with the Roman **Neptune**). Eventually he became one of the Olympian family, a brother of Zeus, sharing with him and another, non-Olympian, brother, **Hades**, a third of the world: Zeus received the sky as his realm; Poseidon, the sea; and Hades, the underworld—three brothers who henceforth would manage the world that formerly had belonged to the triform Goddess. But like all the others, Poseidon represents an assimilation of the Minoan tradition by the Indo-Europeans. His name, if it is truly Greek, describes his previous role as 'Consort of Earth' ('Posis' or husband of 'Deo,' which appears to be one of the names of the Goddess), a male obviously subservient to his Queen, since he is named after her, rather than imposing his own name upon her. It would have been what the Indo-Europeans called him, in terms of what they saw to be his role amongst the Goddess worshippers when they got to Greece, but the etymology is doubtful and not ancient, and the name may not be Greek. What is certain is that in the Mediterranean regions he did function originally as such a Consort and that he was associated with springs, subterranean waters, and the sea. At Athens, he was sometimes equated with Erechtheus, with whom he shared the phenomenon of earth-rending, the earthquake, accompanied by chthonic thundering, which announced the birth of an Erichthonius emerging from Earth.

In those earlier days, Poseidon was a horseman, and slept with the horse-woman Medusa, in what would eventually become a temple of Athena. He, too retained the epithet of Hippios, as Athena did Hippia.

Since the sea was a topographical phenomenon of the natural world unknown in the Indo-European homeland (and even the Greek word for 'sea' was assimilated into Greek from a Mediterranean language), Poseidon's attribute as a sea god cannot derive from the Indo-European tradition, but the same is not true of the horse. His equine attribute must be Indo-European, since the horse evolved in the Asiatic steppes and came with the Indo-Europeans on their migrations. The equine manifestation of the Medusa, Athena, and others of the Minoan goddesses was perhaps imposed upon them later through their continued association with Poseidon as their Consort after the arrival of the Greeks with their own gods.

Amongst the Indo-Europeans, the horse was a **totemic animal guide** and friend of the warrior-hunter. It was his link with the wild spirit of the animals he hunted and the steed that carried him into battle with his human enemies; it was his companion in acts of heroism. The horse is a large tamed animal, but only marginally tamed, easily startled and rendered again dangerously wild. 'Alogon,' they still call it in Greek, as in antiquity: the 'crazy, irrational thing.'

In Classical mythology, there are two chthonic brotherhoods of horsemen; both function as mediators of this dichotomy of wild versus civilized: one is the group of **centaurs**, wild, often drunken men who are four-legged horses below the waist, of whom only one is wise, with the wisdom of the wilderness—the centaur **Cheiron**; the other is the brotherhood of **satyrs**, two-legged, uncontrollably lascivious goat-men, usually also with equine attributes, such as their tails and ears—of whom again only one is wise—their father, **Silenus** (sometimes multiplied into a whole group of older satyrs or **silens**). These brotherhoods, like the equine manifestations of the Goddess, represent attributes that the Minoan tradition acquired from the Indo-Europeans: Cheiron, for example, is named for the 'Hand,' and hence the centaurs are similar to the digit men or daktyls, whose phallic nature is evident also in the ithyphallic satyrs.

As this animal guide, the horse was set aside in the classification of animals; although edible, it was not something to be eaten, just as one would not eat a friend. We have seen a similar taboo with the wolf-dog. The goat is even more special, since it is a wild friend, who allows itself to be eaten as sacrifice. And when the warrior died, it was the custom back in the Indo-European homeland to kill his horse at the funeral, so that it could continue to aid him by carrying the spirit of the corpse on into the afterlife. This funereal role of the horse would have facilitated the insertion of the Indo-European horse-god into the complex of symbols identifying the Consort of the Goddess, especially since the horse-god, while still in the Indo-European homeland, seems to have been associated also with springs and water. (The name of Neptune is Indo-European and involves the idea of 'wetness,' but not of the sea; as with Juno and Minerva, Neptune, except when he is a stand-in for his Greek equivalent, is a less colorful and complex figure, and a more complete instance of assimilation.) Further facilitating the assimilation of Poseidon as the equine spirit of water, was the similar association of the Minoan Consort with the sea, as the primordial aquatic home of life. And in the sea, the Indo-Europeans even found a miniature fishy version of the sacred equine, the sea horse. Poseidon sometimes has the sea horse as an attribute, and the sisterhoods of the deep can use it as their steeds. Water, moreover, is an obvious attribute for the Consort figure, since fertility of both Earth and animals depends upon a flow of fluids.

Poseidon invented the horse, it was said; and Athena, its bridle. Through Athena, the horse was controlled. Using the help of the hero **Perseus**, Athena even managed to mold the horse for higher things, giving it a purified birth, like her own, from the head. When Perseus decapitates the Medusa, Poseidon's child that she was pregnant with was born. This was the horse **Pegasus** (the horse of the 'Spring'), who flies as the mount for the victorious hero. Wherever it touches down to earth, a miraculous spring of inspiring waters bursts forth from the ground. There were several of these Horse-springs to be found in the Greek landscape, tended by the triple triads of Muses, who were daughters of Zeus. But that is a story that we will come to later.

As an Olympian, Poseidon is anthropomorphized as another Father god, a male at mature age, bearded, and indistinguishable from his brother Zeus, unless he wields the trident, whereas the latter has the thunderbolt. The trident presents Poseidon as a fisher god, the lord of aquatic life forms, including ours. Although a fishing implement, the trident is also a triple fork, with three horn-like prongs; for Poseidon, like his brother, also had bull manifestations. Other aspects of the trident may go back to the Indo-European homeland, where

Poseidon and Athena (Black-figure vase by Amasis painter 540 BC, Musée du Louvre, Paris)

it seems to have been a stylized sacred tree and the emblem of the shaman priest who communicates with the spirits of the afterlife.

Earlier, less anthropomorphized versions of Poseidon, the Consort, were probably fish-like, as well as equine—a fish or dolphin below the waist, a merman or male mermaid. Of such shape was the son **Triton** he begot from his mate, the water maid **Amphitrite**: both have names that suggest the 'Trinity,' although as Minoan deities, their names may not be Greek. Athena could have a similar name, too. She was **Tritogeneia**, the one 'Born of Triton,' which in this instance was thought of as a lake in Libya, but the epithet probably remembers her special former association with Triton-Poseidon. The myth

Birth of Erichthonius: Athena Receives the Infant, with Kekrops Attending (5th Century, Staatliche Museen, Berlin)

that she surfaced from the waters of the lake in Africa represents her 'black' identity: there was a tradition that represented the primordial and chthonic version of the self as dwarfish black Africans.

Triton, like the other brotherhoods, could be multiplied into a whole group, and the sea that was Poseidon's realm was peopled with such creatures as these dolphin-men, riding the foaming waves as they trumpeted the conch shell of Aphrodite. The dolphin, itself, as an attribute of Poseidon, is another example of an animal guide; for dolphins, like their human friends, are intelligent mammals—named, in fact, for their supposed similarity to the shape of the 'womb.' And with them in the waters, were the sisterhoods, such as the **Nereids**, daughters of **Nereus**, the Old Man of the Sea; and the **Oceanids**, daughters of Ocean, who was the great stream of water encircling the whole inhabited world. The entire subterranean aquifer was linked and interconnected; hence you could find such creatures also lurking beneath the surface in springs, rivers, and lakes: sisterhoods such as the **Naiads**. And out of rivers or sea could often emerge these chthonic abductors, seducing both men and women to enter their subterranean realms. The female seducers, in general, could be called **nymphs**, or marriageable brides. Nor were they confined to their watery places; other sisterhoods lurked in groves of trees: **dryads**, originally only in the oaks (a tree sacred in the Celtic-Druid tradition of the Indo-Europeans: Zeus imposed his rule over these sisters, for the oak was his tree; in the olden times, people could live on acorns); and **caryatids**, in the nut trees, of various kinds; and the **Meliai**, a sisterhood of the ash tree, supposedly born from the blood of Ouranos when Kronos castrated him (another tree sacred to the Indo-Europeans: Zeus took them over, too; the Meliai tended the infant Zeus in Rhea's cave). And there were others: nymphs of mountains, meadows, glens.

It was no easy task to withstand their allure, and the hero who was fighting on the side of Zeus would often have to face one or the other of them in combat. Understandably, Poseidon was seldom of any help; water was the ultimate enemy.

Such was the aquatic world that once belonged to Athena, before Zeus rescued her to be his virgin daughter. In Attica, which was the land of Athens, Athena contested Poseidon, this former Consort of hers, for control of her country. The contest took place in the time of Kekrops and its outcome was cited as the precedent both for the disenfranchisement of women and for the naming of children no longer after their mothers.

Triton, Wrestling with Heracles, Surrounded by Line Dance of Water Sisters (Museo Nazionale, Tarquinia)

It was a close judicial decision, hinging upon a single vote that tipped the scales in favor of Athena's age of patriliny. Each of the deities produced a miracle—and hers was judged the greater. Poseidon struck the ground on the Acropolis with his trident and caused a spring to flow in a cave beneath it, the source of water for the citadel. Athena retaliated by causing the first olive tree to appear beside the trident marks in the stone.

The olive became the new botanic attribute of Athena, displacing the plants, like poppy, that served in her former Minoan shamanism. The olive represents the evolution toward the culture of the Olympian age. The olive is a weedy growth, sending out many worthless shoots from its spreading roots; these must be repeatedly pruned away, forcing the wild olive to grow into the valuable fruit-bearing tree. Even its fruit, however, is usable only after further human intervention, either pressing the oil from its olives, or soaking the fruits in brine to wash away their bitterness. This olive tree on the Acropolis was claimed to be one of the first ever to grow in Greece; the olive originally was said to have come from the Indo-European homeland of the Hyperboreans—where, actually, it isn't native. The sanctity of the olive derives from its symbolism as a substitute for the sacred plant of the homeland which it commemorates, Amanita, which similarly in Indo-European tradition is 'pressed,' and called, in fact, in the Hindu tradition 'Soma,' the 'Pressed One,' for that act of pressing. The olive, perhaps was even better than the original Amanita, since it is cultivated and has no psychotropic properties for shamanism: the Indo-European tradition was never at ease with the need to depend upon the body to see the deities.

In this way, Athena not only dispensed with her Consort, who was nevertheless still honored at Athens, but also implanted a symbol of the newer Olympian order of celestial religion.

The Acropolis of Athens

Acropolis. The 'High City.' The sacred citadel, rising sharply out of the plain of Attica. Here was the original home of the Queen and her Consort, remembered later as the place where the kings once lived. Towering much higher above it, is the mountain of Lykabettos, a huge rock that Athena intended to add to the fortifications of the Acropolis, but she dropped it where it now is when she saw that the three daughters of Kekrops had taken a look at the infant Erichthonius in the chest. It would have made a higher citadel, but it lacks the supply of water that Poseidon provided for the Acropolis. By the Classical age, no humans lived any longer on the Acropolis; only the goddess had her dwellings there, Athena, and most important, her **Parthenon** temple. You can still see the marks in the stone where Poseidon struck his trident to call forth the spring deep beneath it. And beside those three holes from the trident, Athena's olive tree, still growing today, although not the same one; it was replanted nearly a century ago—on Washington's birthday, to link the new world symbolically with the old. And on the Acropolis there are still the ruins—magnificent ruins of the former glory, the monuments of the ancient city, but lacking the color that once enlivened them, and suffering more today than through the earlier succession of millennia because of the pollution of the modern age. But still sacred, still assimilating newer religions, just as the Olympian had its predecessor. The Parthenon became a church of the Virgin for many centuries, and then a mosque, before it finally lost its roof in 1687, exploded by the Venetians when they attacked the Turks, who were using it for a gunpowder magazine. But below, in the cave, a woman still replaces the flowers today in a Christian shrine, where once the ancient sisterhoods performed their chthonic rituals, commemorating the old Athena, while the new one basked in the Olympian sunshine above.

Athens is an eternal city, a cultural heritage claimed anew by each generation that elects to follow in her footsteps, whiter and purer than she ever was, more beautiful recreated from her ruins. The historian Thucydides predicted the outcome, in writing of the war that Athens and her empire states were fighting with Sparta and its allies during the last third of the fifth century BC, the culmination of the Classical age, and a war that Athens finally lost, lost because of her uncontrollable pride and the bankruptcy of her myth of reality. Anyone in future ages, he said, coming upon the ruins of this city would think her much greater than she actually was—so lavishly had Athens decked herself out with splendid monuments. Under Pericles and his successors, Athens misappropriated the money extracted from its unwilling alliance of city states to finance a massive program of public construction. Athens had the money for art, and craftsmen and artists flocked to the city to sell their skills. The beautification of the city justified Athens' claim to be the cultural leader of the Greeks, the manifest destiny of Athens, the inevitable role that by chance had been thrust upon this hitherto rather ordinary city by its victory over the forces of barbarism that had come against Greece, and in particular against Athens, in the wars with the Persian Empire at the beginning of the century.

And not only the monuments, but the literature, the drama and dance. Greek culture, and Classical mythology in general, bears the Athenian stamp. The stories that we have are largely the way they were told at Athens. Even the epic tradition derives from an Athenian recension, a written version of the oral history prepared at Athens. Elsewhere, there were different versions of the myths, different aspects to the process of assimilation. Hera was more important at Argos; Apollo and Aphrodite at Corinth. Apart from worshipping together at the great Panhellenic sanctuaries like Delos and Delphi and Olympia, the Greeks never achieved a national identity, never molded a unified political structure. They were people of their cities (the **polis** or 'city-state'), and secondly of their tribal divisions.

Athenians were indoctrinated into this city's particular world of myth not only by the performances of the stories, but by everything around them that might trigger access to this heritage of traditions: things like the toys of children; or the decorations on tableware, and the social rituals for which they were used; and the noticeable features of the surrounding landscape, steeped in remembrances; and the monuments, through which the artists lent the land speech.

Acropolis of
Athens
(Reconstructed
model)

The Gateway or Propylaea

The Acropolis is approached from the west, up a steep incline to the **Propylaea** or 'Gateway,' which affords access through the fortifications to the monuments beyond it. It was constructed to the design of Mnesikles, originally intended to be a building at right angles to the newly completed Parthenon Temple, rising above it, and of the same floor area, but it was never completed, and the size was modified, and asymmetrical, probably so as not to encroach upon the property of the little Temple of **Athena Nike**, the Goddess of 'Victory,' adjacent to it, to the right, above on the Acropolis. (In the Nike Temple, Athena's ancient sisterhood of attendants was represented by a sculptural group of 'Victories,' Athens triumphant over the forces that would threaten its culture and way of life.) In one of the rooms flanking the passage through the Propylaea was housed a collection of paintings, a Picture Gallery, so that one's way up to the Goddess was through a Museum, a repository for the higher artistic inspirations offered by the daughter of Zeus.

Athena Promachos, 'Who Leads in Battle'

Through the high colonnade of the Gateway, the first glimpse was, at foot level, of the Goddess, a colossal effigy looming so high above that the sun glancing from her spear was visible miles away at sea, as her sailors returned home from battle, having rounded Cape Sunion, past the Temple of Poseidon, into the Saronic Gulf. It was the work of Pheidias, cast in bronze, around the middle of the fifth century, out of the spoils taken from the Persians. And ranged around her, were other trophies of victory, shields and weapons, prows of ships, booty taken from the enemies that had come against the city. Just as she did with the heroes in myth, Athena led her soldiers and sailors in battle. She was the **Promachos**.

Many had even seen her in person at the Battle of Salamis, where the navies of the Greeks, following a stratagem of the Athenian Themistokles, had defeated the vastly larger Persian fleet. The victories in the Persian Wars led to Athens' ascendancy as a naval power, a role that was only natural for a city that could claim Poseidon, as well as the Goddess, amongst its sponsors. The gods were on their side. Even the wind, for they could count Boreas as an ancestor, through his son Xuthos, the one who had recognized the 'Queen's' son **Ion** as his own, in the transition to patriliny. Many said that it was Boreas who had sent the sudden windstorm that had greatly weakened the Persian armada as it made its way toward them down the coast of Greece.

Myth had prepared them to experience this view of reality, with the divine Promachos fighting beside them. The best friend of the hero 'inspires' the battle, like a wind of change, an animating force. With the help of the friend, the terror is on their side, terrifying the enemy. That is exactly what another of the deities had promised earlier in the Wars, before the battle of Marathon. The goat god **Pan** had materialized and predicted that he would strike 'panic' fear in the

Persians. And he did. The 'friend' is the turncoat, like Prometheus siding with Zeus to tip the scales in nearly equal combat. You need something of the enemy on your side.

Paradigm #3: the enemy transmuted into a helper. The Jungian term for this helper is **anima** (for a female helper) and **animus** (for a male helper), two words in Latin meaning 'wind' or 'inspiring **spirit**,' differing only in grammatical gender. The archetype of these 'animating' helpers usually involves the metaphoric association of them with wind. A modern popular example would be the figure of the Lone Ranger, fighting Indians with the help of Tonto, an Indian on his side in the encounters with the wild men of the Frontier. He is the 'lone' good horseman (presumably you cannot trust any of the other guys); his enemies are outlaws—but then so is he, masked just like one of them. The Greek term for **anima/animus** would be **Promachos** (for both male and female).

The Promachos effigy was literally cast from the weapons captured from the enemy. But beyond that, Athena, as we have seen, is the Aegis-Pallas-Medusa-Tritogeneia and the other way of life, transmuted into the Olympian, who fights on the side of Zeus. She is Arachne, 'blowing' with the transmuted webwork of the tapestry as she sails anew, each Panathenaic Festival, from her former aquatic home. The same is true of Poseidon, not the old god, but the new, appeased friend of Athens. This metaphoric association with the 'wind-spirit' is an essential part of the archetype. Even the Aegean, the sea of the Ionian peoples, stormy with its sudden aegis-like 'goat squalls' (called aegis) and named for the Athenian 'goat man' Aegeus was on their side, the basis for their naval superiority and their island Empire. Athena even transmuted, as we shall see later, the hissing of the Medusa's serpents into music by inventing the flute, a wind instrument, to imitate their hideous sound in art.

The glory of Athens was the result perhaps of the perfection of its **anima**ting Promachos.

Erechtheion

Beyond the Athena Promachos, to the left of the Parthenon Temple, is the **Erechtheion** (or Erechtheum), replacing an earlier temple of Athena that was destroyed when the Persians sacked and burned the Acropolis. This House of Erechtheus-Poseidon, built toward the end of the century, is of unique design in order to enshrine some of the city's most sacrosanct antiquities. Here you can still see the trident marks; the well below gave forth the sound of waves when the wind blew. And in an enclosed courtyard, Athena's olive tree: it sprouted again miraculously after the Persians attempted to destroy it. Kekrops was buried nearby. Here too was the **palladium**, the most ancient of the Athenas, made of wood; it was to her that the Panathenaic robe was presented at the festival. Other curious antiquities included a folding throne from the Minoan age. And most unusual, is the Porch of the Maidens, where the colonnade of supports for the roof is composed of **Caryatids**, a petrified sacred grove of Athena's sisterhood of maidens. In the basement was the serpent, a still living version of Erichthonius, Athena's child.

Parthenon

This was the fourth temple to Athena, replacing the earlier ones. It was her House. Inside, was another Athena that Pheidias made, constructed of sheets of ivory (for the fleshy parts) and gold (for the rest), hung upon an interior armature of wood. A giant serpentine Erichthonius coiled about her feet, and she wore her aegis shawl, with the Medusa head. From her helmeted head rose monstrous beasts, transcendent. And she held out her arm, holding as her offered gift, the ancient figure of the bird goddess, now a winged 'Victory.' Her shield portrayed the battle of the Olympians against the Giants, on one side; on the other, the annihilation of female dominance, in the battle against the Amazons. The pedestal beneath her feet showed the birth of Pandora.

To enter the Temple, you had to walk all the way from the Propylaea on the west to the **Parthenon's** eastern facade. That was the custom with an Olympian temple: the doorway faced the rising sun, with its back toward the more sinister direction of the night.

Pheidias oversaw the construction of the entire Parthenon, which was completed in 432, with the final dedication of the statue. The temple was a marvel of science—and an optical illusion, improving on Mother Nature and the laws of perspective. The floor was curved upward, to compensate for the natural order, which would have made it appear concave instead of flat. And the columns tilted inward, so that they would not appear to be falling out under the weight of the roof; and they bulged in the middle of each column, so that they would appear straight and tapered, and not concave. This was not something in the old style, a faceless found object, imbued with the sanctity of Mother Earth.

In the gable or **pediment** at each end, in the low triangle formed beneath where the roof peaks, there is a ledge which generally is ornamented in a Greek temple by a grouping of sculptures, with the tallest figures filling the space below the apex. The western pediment depicted the contest of Athena and Poseidon for control of Attica, with their respective offerings of miracles. Even more optimistic was the eastern pedimental group: the birth of Athena, witnessed by the other assembled Olympians.

The columns, again as is typical for a Greek temple, completely surround a central building, with a doubled rank of them at the front and back to form **porches**. The entire design architecturally imitates a sacred grove, and like the pitched roof of the temple, is probably an Indo-European tradition from more northern environments. (Minoan buildings were of the Mediterranean type, with flat roofs, since there is no need to shed the weight of snow in the warmer climate.) In a continuous band toward the top of the exterior walls of the building enclosed within the colonnade, Pheidias designed and directed the carving of a

frieze depicting the Panathenaic procession, beginning at the western back and proceeding simultaneously along both sides toward the front, where, just above the entrance, the newly woven robe is presented to the goddess, attended by the members of her Olympian family. The frieze, too, is a masterpiece of optical deception, depicting, in bas relief, what appears to be a parade of people and animals several ranks deep.

A Greek temple typically affords still one more space for decoration. This is where the bottom edge of the pitched roof meets the supporting colonnade (just below where the gutter would be on a modern house). Filling the spaces between the exterior projecting ends of the timbers that would support the interior ceiling of the building are a series of plaques or panels facing out, called **metopes**, interspaced by narrower plaques covering the ends of the beams themselves: these latter are decorated by a triple geometrical design, for which reason they are called **trigylphs**. The metope sequence of the Parthenon Temple depicts episodes from a fight that occurred when centaurs got out of control at a wedding party; they tried to abduct the bride, who was rescued by the other male guests: the battle of the Centaurs and Lapiths. Such a contest represents the transition from primitivism to male dominant control of women, through the ritual of marriage.

The entire temple is a symbolic evocation of the deity whose House it is, perpetuating the transmuted identity.

* * * *

Review

Athena, as a daughter of Zeus, is a transmutation from her former identity in Minoan times. She continues to bear commemorations of her past. These are her bird-goddess aspect: **owl**, winged-victory or **Nike**; hermaphroditism: **Pallas**, male armor; snake-goddess: **Erichthonius-Erechtheus**, serpent fringe of her **aegis**, serpent locks of her **Medusa** head; consort: **Hephaestus, Poseidon**, also the 'kings,' like **Kekrops, Erechtheus**; spinning goddess: **Arachne**, the Panathenaic robe; water-goddess: **Tritogeneia, Poseidon**; (shamanic) plant goddess: **olive tree**; goat goddess: **aegis**, the 'king' **Aegeus**; sisterhoods: daughters of **Kekrops**, the **Caryatids**, the **Nike** sisterhood. From the Indo-European tradition, like the other versions of the Minoan Goddess, she acquired equine attributes: **Pegasus, Hippia**. As a possessing goddess, her shamanism was reoriented from chthonic to celestial, and she becomes an inspirer of higher arts and wisdom: this aspect is even more apparent in her Latin name, **Minerva**.

Review of the twelve Olympians (thus far—more later—with Latin names):
Zeus (**Jupiter**): thunderbolt, oak tree, bull
Hera (**Juno**): cow, matrimony
Ares (**Mars**): war
Hephaestus (**Vulcan**): volcano, chthonic smithy, torch; lame
Aphrodite (**Venus**): conch

Demeter (**Ceres**): pig, ear of grain, pomegranate, poppy

Poseidon (**Neptune**): ocean, springs, horse, sea horse, trident, dolphin, fish; mate: **Amphitrite**, a **Nereid**

Hestia (**Vesta**)

Athena (**Minerva**): olive, goat, horse, spinning-weaving, male warrior; flute

Apollo (same name in Latin): wolf

Artemis (**Diana**): reindeer, golden hind, huntress and mistress of beasts (**potnia theron**)

Hermes (**Mercury**)

Sisterhoods: **Muses** (daughters of **Mnemosyne** and **Zeus**); **Moirai** (**Fata**, sometimes made into females as **Fatae**): **Clotho, Lachesis, Atropos; Aglauridai** (daughters of Kekrops); **Gorgons; Hesperides; Graeae; Eileithyiai**(daughters of **Zeus** and **Hera**; preside over birthing); **Oceanids, Nereids, Naiads, nymphs, dryads, caryatids, Meliai**

Brotherhoods: **centaurs** (**Cheiron**); **satyrs** (**Silenus**); **silens**

Myths: **Birth of Athena**
Birth of Hephaestus
Contest with Pallas
Contest with Gorgon Medusa
Contest with Arachne
Birth of Erichthonius
Birth of Pegasus
Contest with Poseidon
Battle of Centaurs and Lapiths

Monuments of the **Acropolis**:
Propylaea
Athena Promachos
Erechtheion
Temple of Athena Nike
Parthenon Temple
chryselephantine ('gold and ivory') **Athena Parthenos** (also called **Athena Polias**, 'City')

Paradigms

#1. The enemy is always the other self. (Examples: Pallas, Medusa, Arachne)

#2. Since the enemy is the other self, it can never be completely destroyed: it must be confronted and reconciled.

(Examples: aegis shawl, Gorgon head, Pallas Athena, rescue and metamorphosis of Arachne into a spider, Panathenaic robe, mistake that led to the death of the Aglauridai daughters of Kekrops)

#3. The enemy transmuted into a helper (anima/animus). The friendship with this helper is already an instance of partial reconciliation with the other, but the helper is needed to complete the confrontation and transmutation-reconciliation. (Examples: Athena Promachos, Athena as helper for Perseus in decapitating the Gorgon Medusa, and her similar help to the other heroes; often involves the metaphor of **wind-spirit**: invention of the flute, tapestry sail; Boreas, aegis 'goat-squall,' **inspiration** of higher arts)

The helper (as in hunting) is the **totemic animal guide**. Hence, the **anima/animus** or **promachos** often has an animal manifestation (example: Athena's owl) or is part animal. Typical in this role, as we shall see later, is the good animal-human, amongst the bad animal-humans (example: Cheiron, amongst the other centaurs; or Silenus, amongst the lascivious satyrs). Note also that Athena, wearing the aegis shawl, is a goat-serpent woman, and hence is similarly an animal-human combination, even if she is no longer portrayed as **glaukopis**, an owl-woman.

For Discussion and Further Study

1. The transfer of Ion from being actually the biological son of his mother 'Queen' Kreousa to being accepted as the supposed son of his mother's consort Xouthos (or Xuthus) is the plot of Euripides' comic *Ion* tragedy. Read it and consider in particular:

What are the details of Ion's conception in the cave of the Aglauridai sisterhood at Athens?

Why does Xouthos assume that he might have begotten a son at Apollo's sanctuary, Delphi?

What were the symbolic tokens that Kreousa left with the infant Ion when she exposed him to die on the mountain?

What Gorgon-like qualities does Kreousa display?

What does Ion's new name mean (compare **ion** in chemistry) and what is comic about the scene in which Xouthos gives him this name?

What was Ion's name before he is named by his new father? (**Ion** is also the name of the sacred violet flower.)

2. Another Athenian story about the olden times is the **Myth of Philomela and Procne**:

Pandion was another of the early kings at Athens. He had two daughters, **Procne** (or Progne) and **Philomela** (or Philomena), who are interchangeable in the telling of their story. One of them was married off to **Tereus**, like Xouthos another king from the north, and again as a reward for fighting as an ally of Athens. She bore him a son, **Itys** (or Itylos). Tereus, however, fell in love with his wife's sister. He pretended that his wife had died and claimed the sister-in-law as replacement. When she came to him, her sister managed to communicate the truth to her. Tereus had taken the precaution of cutting out the former wife's tongue so that she could not speak, but the woman wove the story into a tapestry. Or some said that Tereus merely raped his sister-in-law when she came for a visit with her sister and then cut out her tongue (hers, and not his wife's), again so that the truth could not be told, but again the woman (this time the sister-in-law) wove the tapestry that told the truth. The two sisters conspired to get revenge: they slaughtered Itys and served him to his father as food. Then they revealed what they had done. They were all turned into birds: Philomela became a nightingale; Procne, a swallow; and Tereus, a hoopoe. The son, too, became a bird: a sandpiper. (But here, too, there were other birds sometimes mentioned, and there were still other ways of telling the story, in which the mother killed her son by mistake.) Tereus, as a hoopoe, eternally pursues the sisters with an axe, crying 'pou, pou' (which in Greek means, 'Where' are they?); and the nighingale repeatedly mourns her murdered son, crying out his name, 'Itu, Itu.'

Because of its many variants, this myth invites intriguing speculation. Which of the following ideas do you think are worth pursuing, and why?

Ancient historians tried to make patrilineal sense out of the early history of Athens by citing a list of five 'kings': **Kekrops**, **Erichthonius**, **Erechtheus**, **Pandion**, and **Aegeus**. Why five? (There was a similar handful of early kings at Thebes.) Pandion's name became an Athenian Festival, the Pandia, a festival of Zeus.

The feasting on human flesh occurs in other myths: you have already encountered it in the story of **Lykaon**, the wolf-man who tested Zeus's Olympian status. There is a wolf-man in the Athenian traditions also: **Lykos**, who is a brother of Pallas and a son of a Pandion, although supposedly not the same Pandion who was father of Philomela and Procne.

Like Xouthos (from Thessaly), Tereus comes from the north (Thrace). Both are also associated with the region of Apollo's Delphi.

Should we compare the telltale tapestry to Arachne's weaving? Or Kreousa's in the *Ion*?

Should we think that this myth disposes of Minoan-type bird-people, and hence that it clears the Acropolis again of a sisterhood?

Should we consider whether the butchering of Itys involves a controversy over which of the parents has a better right to lay claim of ownership to the child, the mother or the father?

3. There is still another tradition about early Athens. This is the **Myth of Oreithyia and Boreas**.

Oreithyia was a daughter of either Erechtheus or Pandion. She was abducted from the banks of a river or 'blown' (as some claimed) from a mountaintop (the meaning of her name implies the latter) by the north wind, **Boreas**, the king of Thrace, and bore him twin sons, **Kalais** and **Zetes**, who grew wings when they reached manhood (perhaps not that unusual—since Boreas is winged); and also two daughters: **Chione** (the 'snowmaiden'), who was taken by Poseidon; and **Kleopatra** ('famous for her father'), who was taken by a similarly chthonic mate. The Athenians worshipped Boreas as a son-in-law and built him a temple on the banks of the river after he aided them in the battle against the Persians. Oreithyia, like Kreousa, was a member of an Apolline sisterhood at the time of the abduction; her group was called the Pharmacids, named for the sacrificial human victim and for the sacred pharmacological plant.

Which of the following ideas seem worth pursuing, and why?

Kreousa, like Oreithyia, was also picking flowers and in a place where her sisters had, one by one, previously been offered as human victims, when she conceived Ion by Apollo. There are many versions of such abduction episodes in Classical mythology. It is the theme of 'Death and the Maiden.'

Should we think of these various bird-people when we read the scene in the *Ion* where Ion is chasing birds away from Apollo's temple at Delphi?

Can you compile a list of common elements in all these traditions about early Athens?

4. Can you list other occurences of heroes with helpers (or sidekicks)? (Think of movies, comics, novels, plays.) To get you started, how about: Robinson Crusoe and Friday? Be prepared to explain why the relationships you propose fit the situation of **paradigm #3.**

Chapter IV
The Two Worlds of Dionysus

𝕻

Bacchus was his name in Anatolia, where he was called that as the 'mourned' consort of the Goddess, her divine infant, destined to die each time he grew to fulfill again his duty as her lover. As with Athena, Zeus had to make him, too, into one of his children, even conferring upon him his own name of Zeus, as **Dionysus**, the 'Zeus of Nysa'—**Nysa**, which was the sacred place of his former Anatolian homeland. The Romans knew him primarily by his more ancient name of Bacchus, but apart from some mystic cults, he was just a jolly god of drunkenness and wine for them. His other aspects were considered too disruptive to the stability of the Roman state. One of the earliest documents in Latin is a decree of the Senate forbidding the enactment of his orgiastic rites, which were seen as a dangerous contamination spreading northward from the Greeks who had colonized the tip of the Italian peninsula.

Dionysus was not the only former Consort who was assimilated into Indo-European traditions. We have already seen how **Poseidon** ended up being a brother of Zeus; and **Apollo** and **Hermes** (and sometimes **Hephaestus**) were also turned into sons. But like Zeus's other brother, the chthonic **Hades**, Dionysus was not admitted to the Olympian family, except on special occasions, displacing one of Zeus's sisters, **Hestia** (Latin **Vesta**). He is one of the group of deities in the pedimental sculptures of the Parthenon called upon, as a visitor, to witness the miraculous birth of Athena from Zeus's head.

On such public occasions, Hestia usually could be expected to stay away, keeping the home fires burning. For that was her primary function, the Goddess of the Hearth, the king's communal fire at the center of government. In both Greek and Latin, she is named with the Indo-European word for that 'burning' hearth. Its perpetual burning was essential, like a magical life-spirit, to assure the continued power of the state, and nothing was ever allowed to distract her from her duty. Although she could be offered the kind of sacrificial victims in Greece appropriate to the Goddess—a pig or a cow —, she stayed a virgin, never had any interest in a love affair, and remained a rather dull and faceless deity. She was somewhat more important at Rome, where her fire was tended by a priesthood of **Vestal virgins**; although Greek cities also maintained a public hearth at the centers of their governments. Athena at Athens had a lamp of her own, perpetually burning, in front of her palladium in the Erechtheion. The lamp was another marvel of science, requiring refueling just once a year.

Dionysus's inclusion in the official Parthenon grouping was only to be expected, for a god who had meant so much to the city. Originally rural and more popular with the lower classes, his welcoming into Athens proper occurred as part of the social reconciliation that led to the founding of the Athenian democracy. From the beginning, his religion was most important at Thebes and Athens, and it was the Athenian view that no other city (and certainly not Thebes) could ever honor him so well as they. The glory of Athens, both in its day and for future times, was as much the result of him, as of their goddess. Like Athena, Dionysus was a perfect transmutation, to guide them to their destiny.

The Birth of Dionysus

There were always people so backward as to disbelieve in the miracle of the birth that made Bacchus into a son of Zeus. For those people, Dionysus had only a mother. They could not accept that he was born twice, that he was a child in the newer, patrilineal style—and that he now had a father. Although Athens could not claim that the birth took place in their city, but, as everyone knew, in Thebes, a neighboring city that they were often not on the best of terms with, they liked to think that the Thebans, in this, as in so many other ways, belonged to the backward group of gainsayers, who were the god's traditional enemies in the battle to establish the age of Zeus. Besides, the birth of Dionysus was much like that of their own Athena. Both were physically born from a male, instead of a female, and both births were essential to the demonstration of Zeus's ascendancy over the Mother Goddess.

Semele was a Theban female, back in those early days when there were just five autochthonous 'kings' at Thebes. Her name is not Indo-European, but is another of the pre-Greek names for the Goddess. It was she who was chosen to be Dionysus's mother, and when the whole ordeal was over, she, too, achieved another name as **Thyone**, a Greek—and 'spiritual' name, meaning 'Incensed,' like the rising smoke of sacrifice. And she was even bodily resurrected from Earth to ascend amongst the Olympian family, although not as one of the canonical twelve—so effective was Dionysus as a mediator between the two worlds.

At first, Semele had assumed that it was an ordinary male of the chthonic sort with whom she was making love, but it was Zeus, disguised as a man. Hera was jealous of her husband's infidelity and played a trick on Semele. Approaching her in the likeness of a crone, she tattled on her husband, making Semele want to experience her lover in his full Olympian manifestation, as when he made love to his own wife. That's what Semele requested when Zeus next came to her. The true manifestation was as a thunderbolt. Semele was destroyed, leaving behind, in her dying, three incredulous sisters. But Zeus took the fetus that she was pregnant with from her incinerated womb and sewed it into his own body, in the thigh between his legs, as if it were just a phallus taken from the Goddess—

which, of course, it was. When it grew to term, he removed it, now from his own body, as his son Dionysus. Unlike the birth of Athena from his head, this was a lower birth, in the manner of women, not cleansed of chthonic pollution. And just as Athena could dress as a man, Dionysus, although as male as a bull, could often disguise himself in female garb.

The Wilderness Sojourn in Nysa

But Dionysus was born as an infant, not full grown like Athena. Every Greek infant, male or female, was born into a woman's world. Only later did a son enter the masculine world of his father. And every child is born as a primitive, knowing none of the things required of an adult in civilized society. As a mediator between two worlds (male and female, primitive and civilized), Dionysus will repeatedly move back and forth across the boundary.

Upon his birth, Dionysus was entrusted to his brother **Hermes** (Latin **Mercury**), who carried him back to

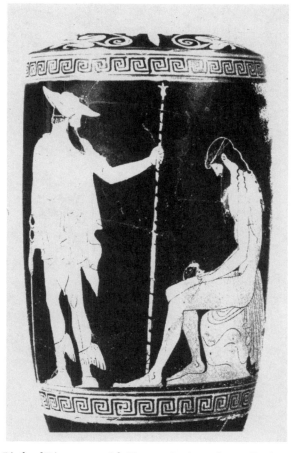

Birth of Dionysus, with Hermes in Attendance (Red-Figure Vase 460 BC, Museum of Fine Arts, Boston)

the former world of his Goddess, the homeland of his infancy in Nysa. Although geographically located in Anatolia, Nysa could be many other places as well; it could be anywhere that you might expect to encounter the primordial world. In Nysa, the baby Bacchus-Dionysus was turned over to the care of Papa Silenus, the good father of the wild satyrs and leader of the troupe of silens. It was his task to educate the child in the good lore of the wilderness, so that he would not forever be limited by the wildness of the other goat-men. There, in Nysa, the infant was nourished by a sisterhood of Nysian nymphs. It was an infancy that mirrored the experience of his father Zeus, when he was tended by the Cretan sisterhood and the brotherhoods of Korybantes and Kuretes.

Nysa was a place where things grew wild, a place of poisonous plants, a place lacking the culinary arts and the refinement of table manners. A mountainous place, usually. A place even of cannibalism. Food was eaten raw there, pulled to pieces with your bare hands. And Dionysus, like any infant, was still wild.

Hermes Entrusts the Infant Dionysus to Silenus
(Kalyx krater 440-30 BC, Vatican Museum, Rome)

But in Nysa, he discovered a marvelous plant that allowed him to bridge the passage foreward to the Olympian age. This was the vine, from whose fruit could be manufactured a transmutation of the natural poisonous growths of Nysa into a civilized drink, a sophisticated inebrient—which is wine.

Symposium

Dionysus sailed back from Nysa, bringing with him this marvel of science. In some places—and even in Thebes, where he had had his first birth —, his arrival was met with disbelief. These were the backward people, like the Theban **Pentheus**, a son of the serpent-man, who was one of the handful of early 'kings' from the olden times, and a cousin, in fact, of Dionysus, himself: Pentheus (named as the 'Sufferer') had all of the 'suffering' that his name implies, but he refused the alleviation that this new drink would provide, preferring instead to nourish his deranged mind upon the poisonous plants of the pre-viticultural Nysian world. Or like the Thracian 'werewolf' **Lykourgos**, who attacked his Nysian sisterhood with a cattle prong and chased the god back into his aquatic realm: Lykourgos went blind and even killed his own son with an axe, mistaking him for a tree, before finally chopping himself down, as well. Serpent-men, digit-people, wolf-men, cowboys, plant-men, demented people, lacking inspired vision—these are the god's enemy: they are the god from the single, maternal birthing; they are the former identity of Dionysus. The enemy is always the other self. **Paradigm #1**.

But those who accept the gift of wine know that it is not an emasculating drink that might make you subservient to women. It is a drink that inspires masculine courage, one that doesn't derange the mind, but inspires instead wisdom and the higher arts.

The proper way to drink wine was at a **symposium**, a 'communal drinking,' something like a cocktail party. For both of these, we have inherited favorable connotations of intelligent conversation, learning, and social and political bonding—setting it decidedly apart from something like a brawl, which was the sort of thing you could expect from centaurs when they got near wine, as in the myth of the **Centaurs and the Lapiths**.

The symposium was exclusively for men, since wine was emblematic of the second birth that had transmuted Dionysus into the Olympian age. The men at the party were often homoerotic couples, as at Plato's *Symposium* dialogue. Homoeroticism (or homosexuality) for the Classical Greeks was considered a situation that intensified masculinity, not only because it excluded women, but because it functioned physically and spiritually as a furtherance of all aspects of male-dominant culture. It was here that the friendships were expressed that would be the basis for political and business endeavors. It was here, too, that the mythical heritage would be accessed, through the recitation of poems or the citing of myths in intellectual argumentation. The expensive tableware, with its mythical ornamentation, might serve as a stimulus for exegesis, as well as to offer an opportunity for the host to make a display of his own wealth, sophistication, and culture. Or a father might summon his son to introduce him to influential friends, requesting him to demonstrate the progress of his education by performing a recitation.

If women were present, they were females of the professional class of entertainers, the so-called **hetaerae** or 'female companions.' Unlike the wives and daughters of the citizenry, these hetaerae had received an education in music, dance, myth, and all the other subjects that would make them interesting intellectual company for men. And also unlike the wives and daughters, these women were sexually sophisticated. With them, a man might experience the kind of physical gratification that he might expect with another man, but which would have been unseemly with a wife. For the hetaerae were also prostitutes, and since they were not of the citizen class, sex with them posed no threat to the males' dominance of society.

It was considered incorrect behavior at a symposium to become drunk, and this was true even though the whole ceremony of the drinking was planned as a step by step advance toward the limits of sobriety. The drinks were drunk in a sequence of rounds or toasts. The pace was determined by the host or leader, who was in charge of the whole procedure. He proposed the topic of conversation and

Men at a Symposium, with Hetaera, Performing on the Double Flute (Kylix 5th century BC, Corpus Christi College)

also determined the potency of the drink: for Greek wine was too intoxicating to drink undiluted with at least three or four parts water. The 'mixture' (which is still the common word for wine in modern Greek: **krasi**) was prepared in the **krater** or 'mixing bowl' and then ladled out to the guests to drink from their individual cup or **kylix**. As proof of sobriety, the end of the symposium often involved the playing of a game of skill, called *kottabos*. The guest attempted to fling the last drop of wine from his kylix into a distant metal basin.

More often than not, however, drunkenness was the actual result. Even in Plato's *Symposium*, where the guests have decided not to drink too heavily since they are still hung-over from the party on the preceding day, the drinking lasts all night long, with most of the participants having fallen asleep by its end in a drunken stupor.

Wives and daughters, too, of course, might drink wine, but not at a symposium. They lived in their own separate quarters, protected in the back rooms of the house, or in its upper storey—either location customary to deprive them of easy exit from the house, for ordinarily they did not go outside, even for shopping, which was considered a man's job. And when seen in public, women were veiled, being properly seen only by their husbands. Men suspected, however, that when women drank, it did not further the cause of respectable society. They got drunk, it was imagined, and plotted against their husbands, planning to overthrow the government, or having illicit sexual affairs and bastard children that they might try to pawn off as their husbands' legitimate heirs.

Maenadism and the Return to Nysa

For certain ritual and religious occasions, however, women left the house. Unlike Athena, who merely bore the name of Pallas, tacked on to her own as a commemoration of her former identity, the reconciliation (**paradigm #2**) between the Dionysus-Bacchus of the Olympian age and his precedents allowed the god to go back and forth between his two worlds. Since he never became an Olympian, and since he was born not as an adult, but as an infant—nor was he immortal, but repeatedly died, was reborn, and grew again to maturity —, his primordial self was constantly a part of his identity. He and his enemy were the same person.

To honor the former Dionysus was the appropriate task of women, the wives and daughters of the city. They, who ordinarily could not leave the house, met together in the wilderness of his Nysian past, in the sacred places on the barren mountaintops, joining into the sisterhood of the olden times, into groupings of three: prepubescent, maternal, and postmenopausal. There with him, they regained their lost power from the days of the Goddess.

We have only the metaphors for what they did there. But emblematic of their ritual is the **thyrsus** (or thyrsos), a word from the pre-Greek language. The thyrsus is the implement of women who pick and gather—not cultivated, but— wild plants or herbs. It traditionally was the hollow stalk of some reed-like plant, such as the giant fennel, into which was stuffed the gathered specimens, in this case, a bouquet of the leaves of ivy. Ivy symbolized the pre-viticultural antecedents of the grape vine. Ivy was seen as the sinister other self of Dionysus, the plant of his infancy in Nysa. Through the scientific arts of agriculture, the ivy had been hybridized into the vine. Ivy with its tiny dry berries was considered a poison, capable all by itself, in its natural state, of deranging the mind; whereas the vine, with its luscious fruits was nourishing, and through the science of the oenologist, its juice could be used to grow the civilized intoxicant that is wine. Even in its manner of growth, the ivy mocks the vine. Through the heat of summer (a season that was supposed to decrease the sexual desire of males, while that of women, unfortunately out of sync with their mates, increased to its peak), the ivy trails limply along the ground, while the vine grows upright. But with the coming of winter (when men's potency returns), the vine perversely dies, and the ivy enters its second birth, sending upright shoots, in the manner of its civilized descendant. The vine had been tended through the summer—pruned, since like the olive, it requires the intervention of the farmer to produce its fruit; and then after the harvest, the women, in the winter, sometimes even in the midst of snow, performed their mountain ceremony, consorting with the primordial god, with a sexual abandon that would have been totally improper with their own husbands.

They became 'mad'—for which reason, they were called **maenads**. (They were also called **Bacchants**, after the more ancient name of Dionysus.) The ivy was merely the emblem of the god's identity, in terms of his evolution into the vine; ivy has no chemical properties to induce such madness, although other non-viticultural predecessors, such as the opium poppy, sometimes figure in

Dancing Maenad— Hermaphroditic, Wearing Goatskin and Phallus, with Seated Dionysus, Holding Thyrsus (Early 4th century BC, American School of Classical Studies, Athens)

the symbolism. If they drank anything—since we often see them portrayed with cups —, whatever it was, it was supposed to symbolize the natural, pre-scientific world, magical springs pouring from the earth itself. No men were actually present at these revels—no humans, at least; and the maenads cavorted sexually with the brotherhood of goat-men or **satyrs**, who invariably attack them in states of high arousal. One other male was present. This was the god, himself, passing through their midst, sometimes bearded, sometimes not, but an adult, their friend, posing no threat, as a real man might: he even dressed in female robes. And never in person does he assault them sexually. And also he is there in his infancy, still their baby.

For the revels, the maenads dressed like primitives in skins of animals that symbolize the animate nature of the god from olden times, in particular the dappled skins of fawns or leopards, like the pelt that Hermes had used as swaddlings for the baby when he first delivered him to Nysa. And like the Minoan snake goddess, the maenads wove serpents into their hair, or held them in their hands, or used them to belt their robes. And they were said to hunt for their god, again like primitives, with only their bare hands; and he, for his part, hunted for them. The maenads, without nets or weapons, plucked rabbits from the mountainside, presenting the bunnies, with their sexual connotations, to their fellow hunter. And the eating, too, was in the most primitive manner—raw, pulled to pieces with their hands, even cannibalistic—feasting upon their own divine infant in his primordial identity.

And all of this was a return to the utopian past, a marvel of the natural world. It had to be, otherwise the enemy of the god's Olympian identity would be left without honor. Otherwise, women would be deprived of all the rights they once had. Otherwise, Nature would be disowned by Science.

Nor, however, could the world forever be just the past. The maenadic revel was a temporary regression. The women returned to the city, to their looms, to their mundane household tasks. This god of the mountain revels had to volunteer to give place to his future self. (**Paradigm #2.**) The god's enemy must be befriended and agree to die, to make way for the other. The sacrificial victim, as always, is the new god's former self.

For Dionysus, the victim typically is the goat, like one from his brotherhood of satyrs, who represent his infancy in Nysa and the irrepressible libido of the Nysian revels. Even in its grazing habits, the goat was thought to pose a threat to the cultivating of the vine—and to all cultivated plants: the proper pasturage for goats is the wild mountainous scrub of land too poor for agriculture. This was the animal chosen to be the god's scapegoat. And after the sacrifice and the ceremonial feasting upon the correctly cooked flesh, the goat's skin became the container for the wine, which was his better nature.

In Euripides' *Bacchae*, the enemy of Dionysus is portrayed as the king of Thebes, **Pentheus**. As his name implies, he is the 'suffering' complement of the god, essential in his demise for the god's evolution into the Olympian age. In his kingdom, the necessary return to Nysa is denied: the maenadic revels are forbidden, and the dishonored natural world revolts, returning his land to primitivism, unredeemed by the easy back and forth from world to world that the god's troupe of revelers extols. He agrees to dress in the female robes that are the god's disguise amidst his revels and willingly is led to the sacrifice that will make him the victim of the pent up rage that is not allowed to express itself, as in the harmonious reciprocity of the rituals in a city like Athens, where the myth of the double birth of Dionysus is properly accepted.

Entheogen: (W)oinos or 'Wine'

The drink that symbolizes the two worlds of Dionysus is wine ('woinos,' in ancient Greek). It contained the possessing **spirit** of '**the god within**' it: for this reason, it is appropriately called an **entheogen**. No other term (like 'drug,' 'hallucinogen,' etc.) is correct or has the right cultural, psychological, or religious connotations: the spirit, for example, need not be chemical, as is the case with the ivy and the olive: and yet the god was felt to be within them; nor need its possession be considered something detrimental, like drugged, hallucinatory, or delusionary: but possibly instead an invitation to knowledge or whatever good the god's spirit had to offer.

The discovery of this drink called woinos was the **vehicle** that occasioned the god's return from Nysa to claim his Olympian birthright. It was this drink, too, that provided the vehicle for the men of the symposium to access their traditions of myth, the priceless, age-old knowledge that could surface miraculously into consciousness through the dangerous, but controlled irrationality of communal inebriation. It was the drink also that was the vehicle for the recidivist compensatory return to the ancient realm of Nysa through the female hysteria of the maenadic revel. Wine was the mediating vehicle, reconciling past and future, Minoan and Mycenaean traditions, men and women, validating the balanced roles assigned for each in Classical society.

As an entheogen, this woinos of Dionysus should not be confused too easily with what we now call wine, although many of its present connotations derive unreflectively from the ancient tradition. Woinos was a complex drink combining and transmuting, into one spiritual potion, the two worlds of the god. And it was the vehicle for the ritualized journeys into one realm or the other.

Although we retain the term 'spirit' for the intoxicant in wine, alcohol was not isolated or known as a substance in antiquity. Isolation requires the art of distillation—a procedure that was discovered much later, and first applied to the sublimation of metals, and only later by the alchemists to the extraction of alcohol, which was termed 'aqua vitae' ('water of life') or, using the Arabic term from the metallic distillate, 'al kohl,' which is pulverized antimony, employed as a darkening cosmetic for the eyelids. Distillation and the isolation of alcohol are also required to elevate the alcoholic content of wine above what can be produced through natural fermentation. Hence, woinos was not a 'fortified wine,' like sherry or brandy, with an artificially elevated alcoholic content. Nor, of course, was it anything as strong as brandy. And yet, it had more 'spirit' than any of those. As little as four cups, diluted with water, could exceed the boundary of propriety.

It was, however, recognized in Classical antiquity that fermentation was a fungal growth. It produced heat, and like cooking what would otherwise be raw, it hastened the softening that is characteristic of putrefaction, but controlled it, so that the end result was not like the poisonous moldering of the tomb, but—if not entirely edible—at least, a beneficial inebriant, a transmuted mediation with the chthonic realm of poison and death. As part of this mediation, woinos contained in its mixture not only the ferment from the juice from the grape, but also other entheogens, spirits from other botanical identities of the god, that accrued to him in the course of his evolution from the earlier times of Nysa—the 'bouquet,' as we still call it, of the wine, some purely symbolic, some chemically potent as inebriants. These were added both during the manufacture of the woinos and at the time of mixing the drink in the krater, to choose the particular effect planned by the host. Amongst these additives was the resin of pine, a tree sacred to Dionysus, imparting to the woinos the distinctive taste of pitch, which is still traditional in the **retsina** of modern Greece.

The Indo-Europeans did not originate viticulture, which is not native to their homeland. When they encountered it in their migration, they named the inebriating ferment with the word for their own sacred drink, woinos (etymologically, a common pictograph for a mushroom cap as a spoked wheel). They recognized it as the entheogen of Zeus and of their own traditions of shamanism, the Amanita mushroom and the 'pressed' juice of Soma—but better, since no longer unpredictable and wild, the way it was found amongst the Hyperboreans: as befit their own assimilation of agrarian modes of life, the fungal entheogen was now cultivable. Dionysus became the 'Nysian Zeus,' inseminated upon the Earth-mother Semele by the thunderbolt—which was thought to be the origin for the sudden, unexpected growth of Amanita, thrusting its phalloid fruiting mushroom bodies upwards with a ground-shattering roar of quaking earth, proclaiming its chthonic birth amidst the fallen needles at the base of pines and other such trees, and bellowing like a bull to its awakened sisterhood of cows. Such are the metaphors that resulted from the amalgamation of the Indo-European and Minoan traditions.

The Making of (W)oinos

In the fall, at the time of harvest, Dionysus, who had grown from infancy, tended with the vine through the summer months, died, in the picking of the ripe grape clusters. Alone of the gods of the new age, he acquiesces in his own demise, the way he did in the olden times of the Goddess, in order to fulfill his role of savior for humankind. But the harvest is murder; and the pressed juice, the slain god's blood. Hence the harvest was conducted like a funeral, to the accompaniment of wailing music; and to deflect the blame upon his own proper enemy, the harvesters were masked, disguised as satyrs.

Satyrs (or Silens) Treading the Grapes to the Music of Flutes with Juice Channelled into Subterranean Pithos (Archaic Vase by the Amasis Painter, Museum der Universität, Würzburg)

The juice was channeled into subterranean vats, entombed in the 'cellarage' for its fermentation. The crushing of the grapes places the sugars of the juice in contact with the yeasts that occur naturally on the skins of fruits, and the yeasts produce a foaming boil, as they give off gas or spirit, which is engendered as they grow upon the sugars, converting them in the process into alcohol. The whole process continues until either the sugars are depleted or the concentration of alcohol halts the fungal growth by pickling the yeasts and killing them. The heat and effervescence indicate that the god, although now in the chthonic realm of his mother's womb, is not really dead, but gestating for a future birth and return.

But while he is absent from this upper realm, the world reverts to primitivism. All that is left is his empty mask and his clothes, displayed on a pillar, awaiting his return. This is the time of year that is given over to the ivy, to the satyrs, to the maenads, to popular carnivals, and to the ancient pillar god and his phallus, which represents the obscene anti-social libidinous drives that resist control through civilization and its institutions. The latter emblem, this phallus, in giant form, was paraded through the rural areas of the city state or polis, for this was the old Dionysus, the god of the country folk who had been displaced by the coming of the new age of aristocracy. Various rituals paced the god's gestation through these months of winter: the ferment was sampled; the January sisterhood of maenads, called **Lenai**, after the 'wine press,' convened at the god's tomb to encourage his approaching thunderous emergence from earth, with the playing of tambourines and tympani.

February, called Anthesteria (for 'the flowering bouquet'), was at last the month for the resurrection. The newly reborn spirit was welcomed back in a three day festival. First was the 'Opening of the Pithos,' when the earthenware burial urn or **pithos**, where the fermentation had taken place, was finally exhumed and its seal broached. And with the opening of this wine cask, the graves of Athens similarly were thought to come unsealed, to release their spirits to return for a visit and join in the communal celebrations with the living.

For this shared feasting between the living and the dead, special table manners were in order, to guard against any contamination from the revenant ghosts that were wandering abroad. One preliminary precaution was to cleanse the digestive systems of the living from all of their own residual putrefaction: hence, to prepare themselves for the banquet, the living chewed upon the root of a plant that was associated, in connotations, with the chthonic deities and which had chemical properties as a purgative laxative. Separate but welcome, was the rule for this holiday. So, the second precaution: which was to eat at separate tables, and, instead of mixing a common potion in the krater, the wine was drunk from individual, triple-lipped 'pitchers' or **choes**. The first occurrence of this special separate drinking procedure was said to have been back in the time of myth, when the citizens devised these pitchers as a way of offering hospitality to a mad man (**Orestes**, from Mycenae) who had come to Athens, seeking a cure for his dilemma, hounded, as he was, by his dead mother **Clytaemnestra's** sisterhood of infernal ghosts—was he more his mother's child or his father's? Athena decided in favor of the latter, a decision determined not only by her own motherless birth, but also one in keeping with this festival that celebrated the second birth of Dionysus, in which he, too, acquired a father. Once again, as was the Athenian view, it was in their own city that problems at other places, like Mycenae or Thebes, were finally settled.

It was these **choes** that gave their name to the second day of the festival, which was called 'Pitchers.' The whole three days were a celebration for the entire family, males and females together. It was the time when children, at the age of three or four, were introduced to the new vinous spirit, which, like themselves, had just recently been born. Children, with their own miniature versions of the choes pitchers, were initiated into the meaning and experience of inebriation, drinking wine for the first time. The choes vases depict these children cavorting with ghosts and chthonic beasts at the grave sites, and also impersonating their parents in performing various of the adult rituals for Dionysus. At such an early age, were they thus indoctrinated into the myths that would determine the way they saw the world, their society's reality.

As part of these three days of festivities, there was also celebrated a 'Rite of Swinging.' Maiden girls played in swings hung from trees, swinging over the pithos urns, sunk beneath them in the ground, those containers that served both for graves and for the wine's fermentation, imagining that they were being pushed, unseen from behind, by satyrs. It was a celebration of spiritual liberation. In this way, they, too, like another Semele transmuted into Thyone, escaped from the grave into the levitating lightness of air, redeemed from maenadism into the Olympian age. Their playful swinging, assisted by the well-behaved satyrs, was supposed to commemorate a swinging of a different type, again an event that had occurred back in the time of myth. When Dionysus first came to Attica, back in the days of 'king' Pandion, he was welcomed by **Ikar-ios**, whose hospitality he rewarded by entrusting to him the gift of wine. When Ikarios shared the wine with his fellow men—unfortunately straight or neat, forgetting to dilute it with water (in fact, he seems to have made his wine without the use of the vine, as well), they thought it was a poison and began to see double; they turned on Ikarios and killed him, making him the Athenian equivalent of the Theban Pentheus. Ikarios's daughter **Erigone** went looking for her father, with her dog **Maira** ('Sparky'), who had witnessed the murder, and when she found him dead, she hanged herself from a pine tree, in grief. Now, here was a daughter who knew how to honor a father—we never hear of Erigone's mother. The swinging ritual redeemed the city from an ensuing plague: all the maidens of Athens had taken to hanging themselves, just like Erigone. Ikarios, of course, like Pentheus, was the primitive Dionysus, and his inadvertent death is another example of **paradigms #1&2**. Maira was a chthonic bitch, a vengeful woman metamorphosed into a dog, like the maenadic hounds of Clytaemnestra—or the deluded pack led by Pentheus's mother. At Athens, Maira was transmuted to the heavens as Canis Minor, the constellation of the Lesser Dog. With Sirius, the Canis Major, she ushers in the dog days of summer with her morning risings, the days whose unbearable heat makes women's uncontrollable sexuality still dangerous, as in the old days: for men, the month for a safe marriage was January; but transported to the skies, these dog days produce the heat necessary for the ripening of the grapes, as well as the dryness that drives off the damaging blight or black rot that would destroy the crop with the kind of fungal mold that is the antithesis of the beneficial yeasts—and which is the curse these chthonic hounds would place on cities who do not know how to appease them, as they are at Athens.

Another of the events in these three days of Anthesteria, was a contest in drinking, in which the contestants competed at drinking to excess. The winner demonstrated his endurance at withstanding the adverse effects of drunkenness by triumphing over the goat, the primitive god's identity, by balancing himself on a greased wineskin. The meaning of the contest is the same as that of the game of kottabos at the symposium.

The last day of the festival was more solemn. It was called 'Pots,' after the **chytros** pots, in which the people boiled up a porridge of seeds, which they offered as a final meal to the ghosts, who were escorted back to their graves and bade farewell until the next year. Their gateway back to the nether world was the Swamp in Athens, an area of moist ground that marks the place where the last of the waters had receded from the Great Flood that had destroyed the people of the pre-Olympian age. Here there was a temple of Dionysus in the Swamps that was opened only this once each year.

It was in this Temple in the Swamps that a ritual that dated back to the earliest times was still performed. Even though the city had become a democracy—and there hadn't been any 'kings' since the days of Aegeus—there was still a woman who bore the title of 'Queen.' She now received that role by virtue of her marriage to her husband, the man who was called King Archon (or 'magistrate') and was in charge of the sacral affairs of the city. In this temple, a group of women prepared the 'Queen' for a secret ritual, her sexual union with Dionysus. Again, we have only the metaphors for what actually took place: she did something that in myth was described as 'Queen' Kreousa's encounter with the primitive god in a cave, attended by the Aglaurid sisterhood, as she picked a sacred flower and conceived Ion, at the beginning of partilineal traditions at Athens.

The Theater of Dionysus

Dionysus is the only deity who is ever represented by a mask, an empty mask and a suit of clothing, waiting for the animating spirit to return from the tomb to give it life, as at the January ceremony of the Lenai sisterhood. The mask is a symbol that goes back to the burial customs of the Greeks at Mycenae.

On the south slope of the Acropolis of Athens, was the Theater of Dionysus, where masked dramas were performed. It was a particularly Athenian ritual, dating back to the dramatist **Thespis** in the last third of the sixth century BC., apparently as part of a populist political program under the tyrant **Peisistratus**. Precedents for it include the dramatic recitations of Homeric epics at tribal gatherings by singers called **rhapsodes**, rural dances, itinerant minstrel shows, and the masked enactments of the life story of famous people at their burial sites. There was also a ceremonial plaza at Knossos, in addition to the 'bull dance' courtyard, but there is no indication of what it was used for. But drama like that performed in the Theater of Dionysus was an Athenian ritual, a reflection of the special importance that they accorded to that god at Athens. The success of the Theater, even in the Classical age, was largely responsible for Athens' dominance as a cultural leader, and the phenomenon was soon imitated elsewhere.

There was a sanctity to the mask. After it had been used, it could not be simply thrown away. The masks from previous dramas were hung in the Theater grounds, swaying in the wind, leering and smiling, waiting for the passage of time to desanctify them. In the dramas, they had been alive, they had been given spirit through the actors, who had felt themselves possessed, through the sponsorship of Dionysus, by the characters they impersonated, calling them back into life from out of the mythical heritage, so that through them their story, the myth, could be told—and the possessing spirit could spread abroad still further, catching upon the minds of the spectators as well, as they sat there on the sloping hillside, laughing, crying, giving themselves over entirely to the story. They were learning the myths, uncritically—in the visceral way that would make them forever a basic part of their cultural indoctrination. They might recall the myths later to examine them, to wonder at their meaning, to rephrase them in other words, if so forced, and dispel their possessing grip upon their minds—but in the Theater there was no time for that. One story came at them fast upon the previous, throughout the day, and day after day, as they sat there, at ease, drinking wine, and reaffirming their solidarity as a people.

As at the Anthesteria festival, Dionysus could bring back the ghosts in a way that was a benefit to the world, a ratification of its reality (rather than a delusionary disruption), through the perfect mediation he afforded. Those who did not accept his guidance could expect their cities to become undone— not his beneficial inspiration, but the madness which is its antithesis. The maenadic revels commemorated—and appeased—the latter; the Theater, like the Symposium, was the former. Hence, it too was a matter for men. By the fourth century, Athenian life had changed and women were admitted to the Theater, but in the Classical age, the audience was composed only of the men. And only men

Actors Contemplating the Masks of the Characters Each will Impersonate (Polychrome vase, Museo Nazionale, Naples)

were the actors, impersonating, behind their masks, all the roles, both male and female—and often of females doing things totally uncharacteristic of what their wives or daughters would, or could, ever do. For these were the women of myth, doing the sort of things that men in a male-dominant society forever fear or suspect their women might do.

The Theater, as we see its remains today, is largely a structure from the mid-fourth century, replacing the Theater of the Classical age, which had wooden bleachers arrayed on the hillside, in place of the present tiers of stone seats, and a 'scene' building (**skene**, literally 'tent') constructed of wood and canvas, as a backdrop for the action. The layout, however, is basically the same. The dramas were sung and danced enactments, with the accompaniment of musical instruments. The dancing, by the troupe of dancers, called the **chorus**, occurred in a circular dancing area, called the **orchestra**, at the base of the semicircular auditorium of seats on the hillside. In the center of the orchestra, was an altar of Dionysus, which could be called upon to represent a tomb, a monument, etc. The acting area was a rectangular dais, tangent to the circumference of the orchestra on its far side and elevated no more than a few steps from it, unlike a modern stage. At the back of this acting area, was the skene, sometimes painted as a scene indication, and of substantial enough construction to allow further acting upon its flat roof, to depict a rooftop, a city wall, or the like. Inside the skene were stored whatever props were needed for the enactments; it also provided cover for the actors to change costumes and masks—for the actors usually had to impersonate a series of different characters for each drama. The skene could be called upon to represent a house, a city's walls, a cave, and so forth. A broad door on the skene afforded entrance into it from the acting area; generally, all action was supposed to take place outdoors, but indoor scenes could also be displayed: a 'roll out' device or **ekkyklema** could be extended through the central door, and whatever took place upon this platform was considered an indoor event. Entrances and exits for the actors and chorus were to either side of the skene or through its central door. It was also possible to stage a flying entrance by the use of a crane device, called the 'machine' or **mechane**.

Various types of enactments typically were produced at a festival: **dithyrambs**, **tragedies**, **satyr plays**, and **comedies**. Apart from country celebrations, there were two festivals of drama held in the city of Athens: one in January, called the **Lenaia**, like the **Lenai** sisterhood; the other in March, called the **Great Dionysia**. The season for neither is appropriate for outdoor drama. January is a decidedly cold and stormy time, and although the seas have calmed down sufficiently by March to allow foreigners to visit the city—as they did— for the dramas, the climate is still windy and chilly; even if one wanted to avoid the dry heat of the summer, May and June, or September and October would offer more dependable and pleasant times: the scheduling of the festivals was clearly determined by ritual symbolism, instead of comfort for the spectators.

Originally, **comedy** was produced at the Lenaia; and **tragedy** at the Dionysia—a distinction that reflects the difference in religious meaning of the two genres: but the popularity of the productions soon led to the inclusion of both at both of the festivals.

Comedy belongs to the gestation period of the woinos, when the cultivated god is absent and the world has been given over to his primitive precedents. It is the 'song of the **komos**,' the disorderly drunken carousal that is the antithesis of a **symposium**. Rather than the reaffirmation of society, the komos is its radical destruction—and the imagined remaking of the world to one's own liking. This is the time of the phallus, when its libidinous whims defy civilized standards of control. The actors and choral dancers in comedy were costumed with large leather phalluses, and much of the action is determined by fantastic metaphors for this apparatus. And although mythical figures often appear in comedies, the plots are new inventions, not reiterations of the traditional heritage—in fact, tradition is held up to ridicule: the most prominent political and cultural leaders in Athens are usually the brunt of the joking. A typical comedy is the *Birds* of Aristophanes, first produced at the Dionysia of the year 414 BC. The metaphor for the phallus is the archetypal one (going back to the Minoan traditions) associating it with the erect heads and the flight of birds, and the choral dancers impersonate an outlandish troupe of birds. Two commoners from

Athens have decided that they can't make it any longer in Athens: so they follow where their own 'birds' direct them, out to the countryside, where they form a conspiracy with the bird-men (led by the hoopoe Tereus and his nightingale wife) to construct a natural city of their own devising. The new city places an embargo on sacrificial smoke rising up to the Olympians—the ultimate treasonous act, since it would necessitate the reverting of all the Olympians into their primitive identities. The Olympians are forced to come to terms with the conspirators, who demand Zeus's daughter as payment. And the two Athenians, who couldn't make it in Athens, get to make it with Athena herself—probably impersonated by a nude hetaera (who as a professional entertainer, would not be restricted by the conventions that applied to female citizens).

Tragedy, on the other hand, belongs to the time after the return of Dionysus, as he begins his growth as the vine through the cultivated season. It is the 'goat song,' the song for the sacrificial demise of the goat or **tragos**. The primitive identity must give way to its civilized replacement: Pallas must cede to Athena; Bacchus-Pentheus, to Dionysus, and so on. Since tragedy is one of the major sources for what we know of the hero's story in Classical myth, we will return to this pattern later, in the next section of this book.

The goat, however, had the last say in tragedy, for there must always be the reconciliation (**paradigm #2**). A performance of tragedies was concluded by a **satyr play**, in which the chorus impersonated satyrs and the plot was a humorous mythical event and even the language of the poetry mocked the serious metaphors of tragedy. Apart from fragments, only one satyr play has survived from antiquity: the *Cyclops* of Euripides.

Dithyramb, a word that appears to be a pre-Hellenic name, like Bacchus, for Dionysus, was a sung dance—circular in choreography, unlike the rectilinear movements in tragedy. The only complete examples extant are by **Bacchylides**. At Athens, the dithyramb was danced by amateur male dancers, unlike the professional dancers of the comic and tragic plays.

A typical schedule of events for the Dionysia began with the welcoming of the rural, primitive god into the City, by escorting his ancient effigy in parade from its customary home in the frontier town of Eleutherai into the Theater. Political announcements and awards were followed by twenty dithyrambs (two groups of ten, danced by boys and by men, from each of the ten regions of Attica); for the next three days, on each day a single playwright produced a sequence of three tragedies, followed by a satyr play; on the fifth day, five comedians each produced a single play. Prizes were awarded for best plays and actors, by a committee of ten judges—although the actual decision was partly a matter of chance (to allow the god to decide) by selecting at random only half of the votes cast by the judges.

Over more than a century, hundreds of dramas were produced. Of this huge output, only a few have survived, and of those few, still fewer are commonly read today. Apart from fragments and the names of other poets, we have works only from the end of this period: three tragedians (each from successive generations) and one comedian—seven tragedies of **Aeschylus** (of which one may be by a different author), seven tragedies of **Sophocles**, twenty tragedies and one satyr play of **Euripides**, and eleven comedies of **Aristophanes**. The selection was determined by what plays were being studied in schools over a century later, except for the additional number of Euripidean tragedies, which was the result of chance.

Dionysus and Ariadne

What the sisterhood prepared the Queen of Athens for in the Temple in the Swamps was the consummation of her **sacred marriage** to Dionysus. A sacred marriage is a union between someone living and a spirit, a bond between dissimilar creatures, at a magical place, such as the Swamp was, where two worlds come together at a common frontier, a place that is thought of as the 'axis of the universe' or the **axis mundi,** or the 'threshold' or **limen** to another world. It is a union between matter and soul, a union between what is living and whatever there is other than this present form of living. It inevitably involves the idea of death and whatever lies beyond the grave. It is the theme of Death and the Maiden; or conversely, it is the theme of the Bride who Wore Black. Rituals of human marriage—marriages between dissimilars, although both human—are reflections of this metaphysical marriage: preparing the bride—or bridegroom (depending on the orientation of the society) —for death: the loss of identity, the loss of home and family, as prelude for the acquisition of a new role and world. The sacred marriage often involves an **entheogen** (either chemical or purely symbolic) as the means for summoning the possessing spirit, and the axis mundi is sometimes thought of as a magical garden, a grove of trees, or a single special tree (the **world tree** or the **cosmic tree**), whose fruit is the entheogen.

Although all the maenads are brides or 'nymphs' of Dionysus, the queen of them all is **Ariadne**, the 'Holy One.' We will come to her story later. She was one of a triad of females from the Labyrinth of Knossos, and she was almost brought to Athens by **Theseus** to be his 'Queen' there, but Athena intervened in the nick of time, so that he abandoned her on the island of Naxos. She is another of the primal identities of the Goddess, and Athena, as daughter of Zeus, got rid of her, too. Left to her fate on Naxos, Ariadne was caught up in a maenadic revel and became the 'Queen' of Dionysus. The two of them, Dionysus and Ariadne, are lurking just beyond the grave, waiting to consummate with one of us the sacred marriage that bridges the journey of the living from this world into the other world. Dionysus is Death for the maiden; Ariadne, the Bride who wore black.

The maenadic revel is a common theme in the decoration of sarcophaguses. And on vases, Dionysus is often portrayed in this role of final bridegroom. The woman prepares herself for her divine lover, fixing her hair or anointing her body with perfumed unguents—assisted by satyrs, for this is a marriage that offers all of the voluptuousness that would have been improper in life. And the drink (or entheogen) is poured into a portable metal pail (an implement of the funeral ceremony), or sometimes a goatskin instead, to be taken along on the journey, often with the satyrs leading the way, and lighting it with a torch. And Dionysus, as a beardless young man, more handsome probably than her mortal husband ever was, and more gentle, often is shown summoning her, offering a bridal wreath, or ringing a bell, or contemplating an egg in his hand, with the implied suggestion of re-birth or resurrection.

For Dionysus knows the pathways back and forth between his two worlds. Repeatedly he dies and re-turns. And he alone of the gods offers himself in sacrifice, not only the primitive victim that is the goat, but also his finer self, in the drink that is his wine.

* * * *

Review

Dionysus with a Bell, Summoning a Woman (Apulian krater, Museo Jatta, Ruvo)

Dionysus-Bacchus-Dithyrambos was a Consort in the Goddess re-ligion, assimilated into classical traditions as the 'Nysian Zeus,' son of Zeus and the Earth Mother **Semele**, whom he redeemed eventually from death—in cor-poreal assumption onto Olympus—as **Thyone**, just as he holds out to all his worshippers a similar resurrection. Unlike Athena, he has both a mother and a father (by the mystery of his double birth)—and he alone of the gods had a physical gestation and birth passage—witnessed—from a father. He belongs both to the women's world and to the world of men, both to the Minoan past and the Indo-European Classical age. From his wilderness sojourn in Nysa, where he was tended by **maenadic nymphs** and **satyrs** (and **silens),** and educated by Father **Silenus,** he acquired the secret of the **(w)oinos** drink, which he brought back to civilization. It is a perfect mediation of his identities and of the rival tra-ditions underlying the evolution of Classical culture: it mixes together the Soma tradition and the fungus of viticulture, with symbolic and chemical commem-orations of antecedent entheogens, and in addition is something grown and manufactured, rather than natural or primitive.

The civilized nature of Dionysus is celebrated by men in the **symposium** and the Theater; its wilder antecedents are commemorated by the **maenadic** (or **bacchant**) **revel** and the **komos**, and in wintertime phallic carnivals. And the Theater itself combines both the primitive aspects (**comedy, satyr plays**) and the sacrificial demise of primitivism, as the necessary prelude for the liberation of more civilized culture (**tragedy**).

Ivy and the **thyrsus**, the **phallus**, the bull, leopard, fawn, serpent, bunny, and the goat (**tragos**), and the poppy are symbolic of the Nysian revel; the (w)oinos drink, of the cultivated god. The mask (or prosopon) is a mediating symbol.

Myths: **Birth of Dionysus**
Contest with Pentheus
Contest with Lykourgos
Contest with Ikarios, Erigone, and Maira
Marriage to Ariadne

Athenian Festivals: **Lenai sisterhood** (January)
Lenaian drama (January, originally only comedy)
Anthesteria: Pithos-Opening (Pithoignia), Choes, Chytroi (February)
Great (or City) Dionysia drama (March, originally only tragedy)

Vases: **krater, kylix, pithos, chous** (plural **choes**), **chytros**

Theater: **skene, orchestra, chorus, ekkyklema, mechane**

Paradigms

Paradigm #1 (other self as enemy) and **#2** (reconciliation). The other self is found at a gateway to another world, a **limen** or an **axis mundi**. The journey to that place requires a **vehicle** that is in some way magical, often involving the metaphor of 'inspiring wind.' An **entheogen** is such a vehicle, often found growing as a magical plant at the axis mundi. **Paradigm #3** (helper: **animus/anima**). Just as the helper often involves the metaphor of a beneficial wind and is a transmutation of the enemy into a friend, the helper often offers the **entheogen**, not as a poison, but as a beneficial and magical food. Dionysus is a prime example in his role as mediator between his two worlds.

For Discussion and Further Study

1. The contest between Dionysus and Pentheus is the subject of Euripides' *Bacchae*. Read it and consider, in particular, the following:

What use is made of the stage altar in the play?

Dionysus is disguised as the prophet of his new religion. What does his disguise consist of? He changes costume later: what is his second costume? Pentheus changes costume, too. What is it?

There are two groups of maenads in the play. How do they differ?

How is the earthquake (supposedly, the destruction of the **skene**) staged? And what does it mean?

How does the relationship of Dionysus and Pentheus illustrate the situation of **paradigms #1&2**?

There are two descriptions of the mountain revels of the Theban women. What happens in these episodes? And why are they not like what the Asiatic (or Nysian) maenads describe?

2. Another version of the Sacred Marriage occurs in the myth of **Eros** (**Amor**) and **Psyche**. Unlike the myth of Dionysus and Ariadne, which has to do with death and the final dissolution of the body, Eros and Psyche is a metaphor for the incarnation or beginning of material life. Also, 'matter' is usually considered feminine, but in this telling of the story, Psyche (whose name means 'Soul' or 'Spirit') is a maiden. Psyche is also the word for 'butterfly,' the beautiful flying insect that is metamorphosed from the wormlike grub: the grub eats, whereas the butterfly procreates, but no longer eats. Her love affair with the handsome Eros is ethereal—until she is tempted to look upon his body. She had been tricked into suspecting that the man she slept with each night, unseen, might be a beast, but her true torment—and slavery—begins when she sees what he really looks like. The myth of Eros and Psyche is told in the Latin novel of Apuleius, *The Golden Ass* (or *Metamorphoses*). Read it and consider, in particular:

What transmutations of the Goddess's symbolism are involved in making her into spirit as Psyche?

3. The myth of Eros and Psyche is told from the point of view of Psyche's ugly jealous sister in C. S. Lewis's *Till we have Faces*. Read it and consider:

What has Lewis changed in reinterpreting the story as a Christian myth?

Chapter V
Dancing the Labyrinth

𝕄

Apollo and his twin sister **Artemis** were also children of Zeus, in their Olympian identities. The Romans equated their own goddess **Diana** with Artemis, although only a few of their manifestations are the same: as Diana, she even has an Indo-European name, etymologically (Di-) associated with the same root that occurs in the name of Zeus and Dionysos (Dionysus), and she was a wood nymph of the sacred oak grove, as in the Druidic traditions of the migrating Indo-Europeans. But like the other Olympians, they are an assimilation and transmutation from their former identities in the religion of the Goddess. Diana means the 'Shining One,' although the shining is lunar, rather than solar, like Zeus. And Apollo in Greek also had the name **Phoebus**, which similarly means 'Shining,' and although he later becomes associated with the shining of the sun, the name is actually matrilineal: he is named after the lunar goddess, **Phoebe**, who ends up becoming his grandmother. He could also be called **Letoides** or 'Leto's Child' (Latin **Latoides**) and **Letogenes** or 'Leto-born', again matrilineal, after his mother **Leto** (Latin **Latona**), whose name is not Indo-European. (It may be Anatolian for 'Lady.') Nor are the names of Apollo and Artemis Greek—although they may be given false etymologies which betray an awareness of their pre-Greek identities: Apollo is the 'Destroyer;' and Artemis, the 'Slaughterer.'

(As with Athena-Minerva, the Latin versions of the twins are more Indo-Europeanized than the Greek: **Dione** in Greek, which is the equivalent of the name of Diana, is a mate of Zeus at his sacred oak grove at Dodona, and by some very ancient accounts, the mother of Aphrodite, who can therefore be called Dione; and Apollo in Latin is more associated with the sun than he is in Greek.)

Apollo and Artemis were once Goddess and Consort, before they became twin siblings, and in former times, they presided over the Cretan bull dance in the Labyrinth of Knossos. Even after their transmutations, they could still be offered human victims, although supposedly only a token death now would satisfy them—a mere scratch on the neck, for example, or a whipping, or at most, a fall from a cliff, in the vain expectation that some beneficial gust of wind would intervene at the last moment to soften the landing.

The story of their birth as children of Zeus, therefore, is really the story of their rebirth into their Classical identities: Apollo, the favorite son of Zeus; and the twins, boy and maiden, each the most perfect exemplar of Hellenic youth.

The Birth of Apollo and Artemis

Other places laid claim to being the site where the twins were born, but it was the island of **Delos** that won out. Zeus had begotten the children upon **Leto**, but no part of Earth was willing to allow the pregnant mother to rest long enough to bring them to birth—so adamantly opposed was Hera to this infidelity of her husband. A trick had to be devised to deceive her: there were those who claimed that Leto disguised herself as a she-wolf from the Hyperborean homeland; or Poseidon may have flooded over the island, so that the twins were actually delivered in the aquatic realm; the Delian version of the tale is that the island was actually floating at the time and not yet an anchored part of Earth: in reward for allowing the delivery, the island received its present stable fundament; still others claimed that the birth was forestalled until the birth goddess **Eileithyia** was bribed to attend, against the express commands of her mother.

In any case, the birthing was long and painful, but finally the twins came into being. Their mother held onto a palm tree on the island in her labor: the tree is sacred to the Mother Goddess. And perhaps Artemis, who was born first (as is only appropriate, in view of her former primacy in the religion), immediately assisted her mother in the birthing of her twin. The tree could still be seen, venerated in the sanctuary of Apollo on the island of his birth. And in the old fashion, they were even mountain children, **Cynthius** and **Cynthia**, named for Mount Kynthos on the island. The island even changed its name because of the birth: Delos, named as the 'Shining Island,' used to be called 'Quail Island' or **Ortygia**, after that bird's migratory habits, which made it appropriate to the Minoan Goddess's bird manifestations and the soul-journey of her Consort; Artemis could still be called Ortygia.

The Contest with Niobe

There was a pair of Zeus begotten twins also at Thebes, **Amphion**, a musician, who played the lyre, and his bellicose brother **Zethos**, an archer and hunter who despised the other's effeminate talent. (Zeus was often the begetter of twins, and if they were not actually so different as male and female, they were always in some way antithetical versions of each other.) Thebes was founded, and came undone, several times in the course of its evolution, as we have already seen happen in the case of Pentheus. In one of these acts of colonization, Amphion and Zethos were said to have built the walls of the encircling outer fortifications, famous for its seven magical gates. Despite their differences, the two brothers cooperated: Zethos laboriously dragged the stones—which are pieces of Earth—into place, and Amphion charmed them into harmony with the music of his lyre. (In a previous colonization at Thebes, which had resulted in the fortification of the inner Acropolis citadel (called the **Kadmeia**), harmony out of dissonance had also been the thematic pattern: **Harmonia** or 'Harmony,' who was the daughter of **Ares** and **Aphrodite**, had been given as wife to the founder **Kadmos**; and the Olympians, themselves, had attended the sacred marriage.)

Amphion and Zethos were the outcome of another of the marital infidelities by which Zeus merged his lineage with the chthonic aboriginal inhabitants at the various settlements he took over in the Greek lands. At Thebes, one of the surviving handful of digital men was **Chthonios**; **Nykteus**, a 'Man of the Night,' was his son, a figure of the same generation and background as Pentheus. (Pentheus was the son of another of the five digital men, the 'Serpent-man' **Echion**.) It was the daughter of this Nykteus, **Antiope**, who was chosen to bear the twins of Zeus at Thebes, both male this time: Amphion and Zethos. The name of Antiope, which means something like 'Opposite Face,' suggests that she is a transmutation of a more sinister identity, like the reverse reflected image of a Gorgon Medusa. (There was an Antiope also at Athens, as we shall see later, and there, too, she was a transmutation of a Gorgonesque female.) It was through this Antiope who was mother of the twins that the religion of the Goddess would be turned around for an attempt at establishing Olympianism at Thebes.

Before the twins could build the fortifications of this newer city, they had been required to rescue their mother Antiope from her former Gorgonesque identity. For she had a mortal and chthonic Consort, as well as the Olympian Zeus for her mate. This other mate was the werewolf 'king' at Thebes, a man called **Lykos** (**Lycus**) or 'Wolf,' another son of Chthonios and a brother of Nykteus. When Antiope became pregnant by her Olympian lover, she ran away; and in her absence, there was only her former self left in residence: instead of the 'turn-face' Antiope, Lykos had her darker identity as Goddess, in the person of **Dirke**. (Her name, which is probably not Greek, associates her with 'Destruction' and a chthonic entheogen, the hallucinatory Datura.) Dirke and Lykos are the arch-enemies of Antiope.

The runaway (or turncoat) Antiope sought protection from the ruler of Sicyon (there were other instances of turncoats at Thebes, and they always seek foreign alliances); but Lykos killed her protector and brought her back as a slave to Thebes. And Dirke tried to keep her pregnant rival (and other self) in an appropriate chthonic environment—a subterranean prison (this, too, is common: to bury the turncoat); but Antiope escaped to the upper light just in time to bear her twins on the mountain of Kithairon. But there were other ways of telling the story: the twins may actually have been born in the chthonic prison, and Lykos sent them off to the mountain as infants, like the wilderness sojourn of the baby Dionysus on Nysa, for Kithairon is the maenadic mountain of Thebes. Hence, just as it is not certain that Antiope was successful in her transmutation, it is not clear what sort of identity her 'hillbilly' twins are to have. They, no less than she, will have to prove that. The twins were rescued by herdsmen, who raised them like animals; and when they were grown up, we find them living in a cave, still underground. It was then that they had to confront the challenge as to their Zeus-born identity.

Antiope escapes from Dirke and her sisterhood who have gone to the mountain for a maenadic ritual—they had intended to tie Antiope to a bull, and then let him tear her to pieces, an appropriate, although sadistic, mating of the chthonic Antiope with her Consort, which would have settled the problem of her identity, once and for all. And her twins, too, almost killed her, but just in the nick of time they recognized their mother—and then did to Dirke what Dirke had intended to be Antiope's fate (which is obviously a much better outcome than what happened between Pentheus and his mother **Agave**'s maenadic sisterhood on this same mountain). In this way, the mother and her twins were all redeemed from their more sinister potentials—and Amphion and Zethos showed who their father really was: Zeus, instead of perhaps Lykos. From the mangled body of Dirke, the spring which is named after her came into being. (By some accounts, this was the same spring that Kadmos had confronted in his 'earlier' (remember that linear time doesn't matter) founding of the city: she had a serpent Consort in those days, and Kadmos had to destroy it in order to fetch the water and earn his bride Harmonia. He then planted the fangs of the serpent in the ground; from them grew a crop of men, who fought amongst themselves, until only five remained, the digital men of Thebes, who were called a brotherhood of 'Sown-men' or **Spartoi**.)

So, from such lineage they came; and Zethos and Amphion ruled jointly at Thebes (again a situation that is common at Thebes, where dissimilar brothers rule in uneasy alliance.) Zethos took the aquatic nymph **Thebe** (of the Thebai sisterhood, after whom the city was named) as his bride; and Amphion took as his wife, **Niobe**.

Which of the brothers made a better marriage would be hard to decide. In view of the city's problems with fountain nymphs like Dirke, it is not optimistic that both Thebe and Niobe became springs. And Thebe was the daughter of a river, as had been her mother; at least Niobe, whom the musician Amphion chose, was a foreigner: she was a sister of the **Pelops** who would eventually give his name to the Peloponnesos, which is a story we will come to later. But she came from Anatolia, a place that often figures as the 'motherland': the Goddess's palm tree, in fact, was called in Greek after the name of her eastern homeland. And also the foreigners were often not foreign at all, but just in a different realm; so that when the founder reached out for a foreign alliance, he had merely to reach down for a chthonic helper.

Zethos's marriage was apparently without issue: Zeus or Apollo may have abducted Thebe; but Niobe and Amphion had many children. The number varies, but often it is fourteen, seven boys and seven girls, a pair for each of the Seven Gates of Thebes, and twice the seven which was the day of the month on which Leto bore her Zeus-begotten twins.

Niobe boasted, in fact, that her own feat of motherhood was far superior to the puny birthing of just two, as Leto had done. Clearly, Niobe was similar to Leto, and a rival (**paradigm #1**). Apollo and Artemis vindicated their mother Leto's primacy and put Niobe back in her proper primordial role. They shot Niobe's children with their arrows, all fourteen of them, and killed them. Then they turned the people of Thebes back into stone—and did the same thing to Niobe, herself: as she grieved for her lost children, she was metamorphosed into a mountainside on the Anatolian coast, with a spring from her eternal weeping streaming down the cliff, which bore a resemblance to the features of her face.

Some claimed that two of Niobe's children were spared (**paradigm #2**): these were **Amyklas**, who was the supposed 'king' of the Amyklai sisterhood, whose god was a still primordial Apollo; and **Meliboia**, the 'Honey-cow,' who similarly was destined to remain in her chthonic role: she changed her name to 'Pale-green' (**Chloris**), like a plant (**entheogen**) and married one of a pair of dissimilar twins, who became lord of a place that was mythically a Gateway (**limen**) to the netherworld.

Archery and Intoxication

Apollo and Artemis both are archers: none of the other deities, except for **Eros** (Roman **Cupid** or **Amor**), has the bow and quiver of

Apollo and Artemis Shooting Arrows at Niobe and her Fourteen Children (Red-figure vase, Musée du Louvre, Paris)

arrows as an attribute, although several of the heroes were also famous archers. In Classical myth, arrows are poisoned arrows, dipped in the toxins from the botanical world of the Goddess (**entheogen**).

In the case of Eros, he comes by his poisons through his close association with his mother. Eros is the winged bird-boy—who had a mother, but no discernible father. It was debated in antiquity amongst scholars as to who might have been the male who sired him. But a mother, he definitely had. He is Aphrodite's son, and he could even be multiplied into a whole brotherhood of **Erotes** (or **Cupidines** or **Amores**). Anyone whom Eros struck with his poisoned arrow lost all rational control and fell under the erotic spell of the Goddess, indissolubly bound as a slave to the beloved object. The symbolism persists today in our notion of the heart smitten by love's arrow, as in valentines.

The arrows of Eros induced the madness of love, but Apollo's archery shot the toxins of death—disease and plague; as did the arrows of Artemis, too, although in particular she managed the pains of menstruation, childbirth, and the other female troubles. Conversely, both Apollo and Artemis could also be

Aphrodite Teaching Eros Archery (Gilt bronze mirror cover 4th century BC, Musée du Louvre, Paris)

called upon to alleviate these same maladies, which in their nastier identities they had caused.

The poisons of these arrows involve the metaphor of intoxication: the same word in Greek means both 'arrow' and 'venom' (**ios**); the word for 'bow' is **toxon**—we get our English word 'toxin' via the Latin (**toxicum**) for the poison in which arrows were dipped. 'Intoxication' derives from a verb meaning 'to poison the arrows.'

The archer controls the toxin, and by shooting the arrows, the enemy or prey becomes intoxicated with the victor's poison. In shooting the poisoned arrow, the archer alienates his or her own toxicity to the enemy—who, is, as always, the other self (**paradigm #1**). By intoxicating, the intoxicator becomes purified or sober. The two identities hence are often mediated by the exchange of the toxin or **entheogen**. We have already seen how such an interchange mediated between the two worlds of Dionysos (ivy versus the vine, wild mushroom versus the cultivated ferment, sacred plants of the Indo-European tradition versus the plants of the Minoan Goddess, masculine sobriety and intellect versus female maenadic hysteria).

In intoxicating Niobe's fourteen children and turning their mother and the aboriginal inhabitants of Thebes into stone, Apollo and Artemis have alienated their former 'toxic' identity in the Goddess's religion and validated their newer role in Olympianism as children fathered by Zeus.

There were several entheogens associated with Apollo and Artemis's archery. The Dirke drug, Datura, was one of them. Another was wolfsbane (or aconite), which was named for the same metaphor in Greek: the 'bane caused by the wolf,' **lykoktonon**. This is the toxin that involves the twins in the traditions of the werewolf. (By some accounts, as we have seen, it was as a wolf that Leto bore her twins. Their birth on Delos as Zeus's new children allowed her to become a woman.)

The metaphoric effect of wolfsbane in Classical myth is that it supposedly induces a maenadic regression to the pre-Olympian world (when primordial 'wolfmen' like **Lykaon** or **Lykourgos** (**Lycurgus**), or the Theban **Lykos** opposed the advent of the newer gods): in particular, wolfsbane causes the madness of rabies (called **lyssa** or 'she-wolf'). Lyssa makes the hunter's tamed dog revert to its primitive ancestor as a wolf, turning upon its own master. That is to say, wolfsbane is a recidivist agent, causing the world to regress to the primordial age.

Apollo and Artemis were always precarious in their newly transmuted identities as Olympians. The wolf was their ultimate enemy (**paradigm #1**), and as always, it was dangerous to allow anything to remind them of their former selves. Hence, not even dogs were allowed on Delos; nor was anyone supposed to be buried there, lest they recall the past when they had demanded human victims. On several occasions, it was discovered that the prohibition on burial had been violated, and the corpses were exhumed and reburied elsewhere to avert disaster. It was chancy even to let either of the twins look upon someone dying.

This wolf manifestation of the twins connects them back to their homeland. Just as Bacchus-Dionysos could call Nysa his home, and Tritogeneia-Athena came from a lake in Africa, Phoebus-Apollo and Artemis-Ortygia had Lycia (Lykia) as their motherland. It was a country in Anatolia, named as the 'wolf-land,' and a place that still actually existed in historical times: the people there persisted in the custom of naming their children after their mothers, instead of their fathers. And just as Bacchus (or Bakchos) would return to Nysa whenever his Olympian identity went into eclipse, the twins could similarly return to Lycia, upon the temporary demise of their newer selves.

Lycia, however, was not their only homeland. There were Indo-European traditions (including northern versions of the werewolf), as well as Minoan precedents, lurking in the past of the two Olympians. Hence, their homeland could also be found amongst the Hyperboreans. And Delos, the island of their birth into the Minoan Mediterranean world, coincided with another 'Shining Island' that the Indo-Europeans remembered as their own other-worldly paradise, where the souls of the departed found their eternal rest, just as the migratory quails once repaired to the Isle of Ortygia.

In addition to being able to alleviate the plagues that Apollo shot with his arrows, this archery had another Olympian transmutation. The baneful twanging of the archer's bowstring could be imitated in the harmony of music, the plucked chords of the seven-stringed lyre, which, along with the bow and quiver of arrows, is a common attribute of Apollo. Its sound could stun the entire universe with its 'bolts' of melody, so that the primordial world fell into a peaceful trance that allowed the accession of the Olympian age. Music is the better aspect of the baneful entheogens of former times. In this way, Apollo, like Dionysos and Athena, was the source of higher inspiration.

The lyre was actually invented by Apollo's brother Hermes, who then gave it to him. Even in its construction, it represented a symbolic mediation between chthonic and Olympian worlds. The sounding board was formed from the shell of a reptilian mountain tortoise, covered with cowhide; and the seven strings were strung on a brace made from a pair of horns from cattle. (The other musical instruments, as we shall see, had similar mythical inventions, transmuting Minoan symbols into Olympian harmony.)

Dionysos had his troupe of maenads, but Apollo, when he played his lyre, was the leader of the sisterhood of nine Muses: then, his epithet was **Mousagetes**, the leader of his own band of transmuted sisters.

This symbolic opposition between archery and music should remind you of the uneasy alliance of Amphion and Zethos in constructing the walls of Thebes.

The Contest with Hyakinthos

Not only could Apollo and Artemis never be allowed proximity to dogs and death, but even sexuality might disturb the delicate and precarious balance of their

Olympian transmutations. Both of them are fixed eternally at the age of puberty—but their love affairs were always disastrous. Apollo is never seen bearded (unlike Dionysos, who has no problems with sex and can be bearded or not), for the growing of facial hair implies the onset of puberty. When boys reached that stage of maturation, they offered their first shavings of hair to Apollo, as a token death of their youthful self. And girls dedicated to Artemis the cloths soiled with the blood of their first menstruation. Boys and girls at this age, the so-called **kouroi** and **kourai**, were the traditional representation in art of the Zeus-begotten twins.

Amongst the loves of Apollo was the beautiful boy **Hyakinthos**, of Amyklai, near Sparta in Laconia, a stronghold of the Goddess and named, like other pre-Greek cities, in the plural for her Amyklai sisterhood of devotees (although later patriarchal historians invented the male **Amyklas**, the one surviving son of Niobe). The beard of Hyakinthos had just begun to grow, and he may have even once been a child of Artemis, or tended as an infant by the Amyklai sisters. Like Athena with Pallas, Apollo inadvertently killed him (**paradigm #1**): for Hyakinthos was Apollo, back in the days when Apollo was the divine darling of the Amyklai sisters, and consort of Artemis, instead of her twin. Again, it was a contest gone wrong. Apollo and Hyakinthos were playing at throwing the discus, and Apollo fatally struck the boy.

Some claimed that it was a 'wind' (**animus**) from the sinister west (the wind called **Zephyrus**) that misdirected the missile to its target: Zephyrus was also in love with Hyakinthos and didn't want to share the boy with Apollo. A vase painting, in fact, shows Zephyrus, instead of Apollo, killing the boy, abducting him in an explicit sexual assault. Zephyrus, like the **aegis** of Pallas, instead of the newer Apollo, could thus be blamed for the murder of the former self. Both the aegis goat persona (**totem**) and Zephyrus, the 'wind that blows from Darkness,' are examples of **paradigm #3**: the helper syndrome, where the helper is the enemy aiding the victor's combat with the other self.

From the boy's blood grew the flower (**entheogen**) that is named after him: on its petals you could discern the cry of the god's grief for what he had done (**paradigm #2**). Hyakinthos, like another Bakchos (the 'cry of Sorrow'), is the lamented child-consort. The hyac**inth** flower, whatever it was—for it was not the one that we now call by that name —, was a word assimilated from the same pre-Greek language as the Cretan labyr**inth** (for -inthos is not a sound that occurs in Indo-European). At Sparta, the death of Hyakinthos was commemorated in a festival, which included a performance by a choir of boys, singing to the music of lyres.

Some people knew a version of the story in which it was not Zephyrus who was Apollo's rival for the favor of Hyakinthos, but a poet, **Thamyris**, a famous musician on the lyre. He challenged Apollo to a competition, with the Muses as judges, and lost. He was blinded; and his voice and instrument, destroyed. This version apparently took place, not in Laconian Amyklai, but in northern Greece, in Thessaly; but Apollo is frequently associated with both places: myth, beneath what may appear as divergent versions, is basically the same story. Similarly, the 'wind' is sometimes cited as the North Wind **Boreas** (the 'Devourer'), instead of the dark Zephyrus.

The Contest with Daphne

Apollo was no more successful in his love affair with **Daphne**. She was either a maenadic member of an aquatic sisterhood (a river nymph of Laconia or Thessaly) or actually one of the Amyklai sisters; and Apollo had an 'equine' and Dionysian rival in the person of a certain 'White-horse,' called **Leukippos**. Apollo often ran the risk of becoming confused with the darker aspects of his brother Dionysos, who (unlike him) never had trouble reverting back and forth in his sacred loving between the two worlds of his identity: hence, he could be counted on to substitute for his brother whenever the situation became too compromising for Apollo. Like another Pentheus-Dionysos, Leukippos even disguised himself as a woman in order to participate in Daphne's mountain revel. As the maidens prepared themselves for the sacred marriage by the ritual of their pre-nuptial bath, Apollo contrived that Leukippos be revealed as a man when they saw him nude—and Artemis, the virgin, shot him dead.

But Apollo was allowed to be no more successful than Leukippos in his courting of Daphne, for the nymph fled from the god; and as he began to overtake her, she prayed to her parent (either Earth or an aquatic male) to rescue her. Just as Apollo caught up with her, she was metamorphosed into the laurel or bay tree, which is called **daphne** after her. Apollo adopted it as his special plant (**entheogen**). Chewing upon its leaves was supposed to induce a fit of clairvoyant possession, as was repeatedly done ritually by the many priestesses Apollo used as his spiritual brides in the shamanism of his prophetic oracle: for Apollo, as we shall see, was a god of prophecy. Like the werewolf tradition, Apollo's prophetic shamanism appears to derive from his role in both his Lycian and Hyberborean homelands, and it is the fundamental basis for his assimilation into his Hellenic manifestations.

The laurel (Laurus nobilis) contains, in fact, nothing that chemically would be active in inducing such prophetic seizures: it is purely a symbolic commemoration of the entheogens that once figured back in his homelands. Like Athena's olive, the daphne has Hyperborean associations, supposedly first transplanted by Apollo into the Mediterranean world via Thessaly; and like the olive, it is a surrogate for Amanita, the Indo-European sacred mushroom. But like the woinos of Dionysos, it also had Minoan antecedents: for Apollo, these included, as we have already seen, the Dirke Datura and the Lykos wolfsbane. In the assimilation of the two traditions of shamanism, the hysterical shrieks of Apollo's tormented brides became interpreted, not as a message from the chthonic underworld of the Goddess, but a clue to comprehending the mind of Zeus, himself. The fact that the possession was purely spiritual now, without any chemical inducement, made it even more appropriate to the aspirations of Olympian shamanism.

We should have no difficulty in surmising that Leukippos and Daphne are former versions of Apollo and Artemis (**paradigm #1**); and the twins effectively disposed of them, too, by converting Daphne into a commemoration of the enemy (**paradigm #2**) and then using her as the helper (**paradigm #3**) for the god's future consorting with his Goddess of earlier times. As usual, the helper has metaphoric connotations of inspiration or 'wind' (**anima**) and a sacred plant (**entheogen**).

The Contest with Actaeon

Actaeon (or Aktaion, apparently an aquatic 'Man of the Seashore') had a fate similar to Leukippos. He was a Theban, and what happened to him took place in exactly the same sacred spot on Mount Kithairon where Pentheus was torn to pieces by his mother's pack of maenadic hounds. Actaeon was a son of **Aristaeus** and **Autonoe**, one of the Theban sisterhood, which included Dionysos's mother Semele and Agave, Pentheus's mother.

Apollo and Daphne (Bernini, 17th century Italian, Museo Borghese, Rome)

Aristaeus was himself a son of Apollo, and so it was not until the next generation that Apollo and Artemis disposed of their former identities, in this case, in the person of Apollo's grandson (**paradigm #1**). Aristaeus's mother was a huntress, like Artemis: **Kyrene** was her name, and she represents Apollo's African phase, like Athena's Tritogeneia. Apollo saw Kyrene wrestling with a lion on the mountain in Thessaly and abducted her to the region in Africa that bears her name, Cyrene. There she bore their son. Aristaeus, himself, is otherwise known for his own attempt to abduct a chthonic Goddess: this was **Eurydike** (**Eurydice**), the wife of **Orpheus**, who was another 'Man of Night' and an earlier 'priest' of Apollo. Like Kadmos, Aristaeus came as an 'outsider' to Thebes, where his royal role depended upon his relationship to the sisterhood and his wife Autonoe. He was also known for his tending of 'bees.' All of these elements, of course, betray his chthonic and Minoan heritage.

Actaeon was the son of this Aristaeus. He had the misfortune while hunting to see Artemis nude, as she, like another Daphne, bathed with the sisterhood on the mountain for the pre-nuptial rite. And Artemis obviously had to get rid of this so-called grandson of Apollo, lest he awaken some threat to her new Olympian virginity. She shot him with her rabid arrows, poisoned with wolfsbane, just as he metamorphosed into an antlered stag, the animal (**totem**), with tree-like horns (**entheogen**), that is her special attribute. As he changed into an animal, his hunting hounds turned upon their master, as they, too, metamorphosed, reverting from dogs to wolves, possessed by the werewolf goddess of rabid madness, **Lyssa**.

There were also people who claimed that Actaeon's offense was that he courted Semele. The variant, as usual, presents the same theme: for without the second birth as son of Zeus, Dionysos would be only the chthonic mother's child that his enemies, like Pentheus and the Theban sisterhood, claimed he was, denying his Olympian identity.

Like Tritogeneia-Athena, Apollo could tack his African identity onto his name. He was called **Aristaeus** (or Aristaios, the 'Best'), **paradigm #2**: commonly in Greek, things that are too sinister to name can be called by their opposite: like **aristera** for the 'left hand,' which Latin more honestly calls **sinister**.

The Contest with Koronis

Like Athena's owl, Apollo, too, maintains bird-man or ornithological attributes from his Minoan past. One of these birds was his bride **Koronis**, the 'crow' or raven, black and predatory.

Koronis was an aquatic nymph of a lake in Thessaly and a sister of **Ixion**, whose hallucinatory attempt to abduct Hera was the origin of the whole race of Centaurs. (He thought he was raping Hera, but it was only a 'Cloud' (**Nephele**) that happened to deceive him by looking like Hera. He was bound to a spoked wheel as punishment and now whirls, dizzily, for all eternity. The son of Ixion by Nephele mated with mares to produce centaurs. Ixion's misguided sacred marriage with the Goddess in her new role as queen of Olympus involves the hallucinogen Datura (**entheogen**), which in Greek is called 'horse-mad,' as well as dirkaion: it is a plant that makes horses behave like centaurs when they graze upon it.)

Apollo slept with this Ixion's sister Koronis, but while he was away, leaving her with a white crow as guard, she slept with

Actaeon, Shot with the Arrows of Artemis, and Set upon by his Hounds with Lyssa, Wearing a Wolf Headdress (Red-figure vase, Museum of Fine Arts, Boston)

a mortal—chthonic and Bacchic (**Elatos**, the 'Pine-man,' son of the 'Mad Woinos-man,' **Oinomaos**). When Apollo learned (as some claimed, from the crow) of his nymph's infidelity, he changed the bird's color from white to black. Artemis then contributed her help: she killed Koronis with an arrow, although Apollo may have shot her himself. As Koronis's corpse was burning on its pyre, Apollo took the fetus he had begotten from her body (like Zeus with Semele's Dionysos) and gave it to the good centaur (**totem**), who was called **Cheiron** (a digital 'Hand-man') to educate with all the beneficial lore of the wilderness and its drug plants, and their use in archery (**paradigm #2**).

This son of Apollo was **Asklepios** (Latin **Aesculapius**: a corruption of the same name, when he was imported into Rome in 293 BC to cure a plague). Through Asklepios, the toxins of the wilderness and the uncivilized nature of centaurs were transmuted into the beneficial science of medicine. Asklepios was the patron of the brotherhood of doctors, who in Greek are called 'druggists' (**iatroi**, literally **ios**-doers).

Apollo typically resolves the dilemma of his dichotomous identities with the help of a son (**paradigm #3**). The mortal son can solve what the immortal father cannot, for the father's immortality allows no mediation with the mortal human condition. We have seen the same theme in the begetting of Kreousa's **Ion** at Athens, where the mother's chthonic child is passed off as the result of the father's infidelity with a woman from an Apolline maenadic sisterhood. (Ion's name is given the false etymology of 'Moving,' but its true meaning is the name of another Apolline flower (**entheogen**), the '(v)iolet,' which is itself involved in the symbolism of the **ios**).

But even Asklepios, as a mortal version of Apollo's druggery, had to be gotten rid of (**paradigm #1**). Artemis had a particular favorite, a 'Horse-man' called **Hippolytus**, a man born out of wedlock (in the older fashion of the days when women and the Goddess controlled the world); and he was a matrilineal child, named after his mother **Hippolyta**, Queen of a race of dominant horsewomen (the **Amazons**) of Anatolia. There was just a possibility that this Hippolytus would turn out all right: his father was **Theseus**, the founder of Athens, and Hippolyta was another attempted 'turncoat,' with the name **Antiope**. It is a story that we will return to later, but it didn't turn out all right. Hippolytus unfortunately was in love with Artemis; and she, with him. The two of them consorted in a special garden, where he even picked a wreath of flowers (**entheogen**) as a love offering to her. So, he had to die, too.

When Hippolytus died, Artemis, of course, dared not watch it happen; but she bribed Asklepios to use his drugs to bring him back to life for her. He complied, and Zeus had to destroy him with a thunderbolt. Apollo, himself, was not personally responsible for the death of Asklepios (a variant of the accidental murder): he could do nothing to retaliate, beyond killing the **Kyklops** (**Cyclops**, one of the brotherhood of craftsmen in the chthonic forge of Hephaestus) who had made the thunderbolt for Zeus.

Apollo in the Bonds of Death

Murdering the Kyklops in retaliation for the death of Asklepios was not Apollo's only reconciliation (**paradigm #2**) with the other self that his son represented (**paradigm #1**). In getting rid of Asklepios—albeit indirectly—, he had killed himself; and as commonly happens in Classical myth, this implies that the victor, like anyone dead, must descend into the underworld. Unlike Dionysos, Apollo has no easy converse back and forth; but when he leaves, as he repeatedly does so as not to have to see his other self, this world reverts to maenadism—and Apollo betakes himself to either of his two primordial homelands.

Apollo spent a year in bondage in order to atone for his murder. During this period of expiation, he tended the cattle herds of **Admetos** of Pherai (another place named in the plural for its sisterhood, although again there was supposed to be a male named Pheres). Pherai was in Thessaly, and Pheres' son Admetos was the husband of the queen **Alkestis**. There were other men named Pheres, and all of them are as sinister as he: the name means 'Undertaker.' Admetos is the 'Indomitable;' and Alkestis, the 'Strong.' They all have names that are appropriate characteristics for the rulers of the Underworld.

But they were unexpectedly kind to Apollo, who found himself thus bound into Death. And Alkestis was so unlike the Goddess that she offered to do what no other wife had ever done: namely, to consider herself more closely related by kinship to her husband than any member of his family who was related by blood, as of course she was not—closer even than his own mother or father. For Apollo had discovered from the Moirai sisterhood of Fates that Admetos had to die, like any proper Consort of the chthonic Queen. In return for the royal couple's leniency toward him, Apollo got the sisterhood drunk and wrangled a favor from them: Admetos could live if someone else would take his place. Everyone refused—but Alkestis volunteered.

She was saved from death at the last moment by the hero **Herakles**, who was also visiting Admetos at the time—drunk and himself in one of his own chthonic phases—but that, too, is a story that we will return to later.

The Contest with Phaethon

The 'shining' **Phaethon** was another identity of Apollo, involving him in his supposed 'solar' symbolism, like **Phoebus-Apollo**. Phaethon was the son of **Helios**, the Sun—but since his mother **Klymene** (the 'Famous') was one of the Ocean sisterhood, the Sun must have begotten him during one of his diurnal eclipses: each night, Helios got drunk in the West and sailed back through the primordial waters in his drinking cup (**entheogen**) to the dawn in the East. There were other nymphs called Klymene, however, and the mother of Phaethon may have been one of the maenadic sisterhood associated with the primordial inhabitants of Thebes, their **Minyan** neighbors—but, as usual, the variant would be the same theme, and the locality of Thebes would even suggest the complicity of Apollo in the begetting. (There were actually ten women called Klymene, but they all, in different versions, present the same metaphor of the chthonic Queen.)

Phaethon appeared to have no father when he grew up—only a mother, as a matrilineal child. Taunted as a bastard, he inveigled from his mother the disclosure that Helios was his father. So he journeyed to the dawn in search of Helios, and begged him to be allowed to drive the sun's chariot through the sky for a single day. The task proved to be too much for him. The horses went wild and the earth was in danger of burning up. Zeus killed him with a thunderbolt.

He fell into the Po River (called Eridanos), in northern Italy, another stopover of the Indo-Europeans on their migrations from the Hyperborean homeland. On the banks of the river, Phaethon's sisterhood of **Heliades** eternally mourned his death. They were metamorphosed into poplar trees, weeping the sap that becomes, as they thought, the magical stone called amber (**entheogen**).

Phaethon had a male lover also, a certain **Kyknos** (Latin **Cygnus**), the 'Swan' (**paradigm #1**). He was a notorious 'enemy' of Apollo, and even wanted to build a temple of skulls at the god's sanctuary of Delphi as an affront to his new Olympian identity. (Kyknos was given various genealogies: as a brigand, he was a son of Ares, like Dirke's serpent, stealing the offerings made to Apollo; as an aquatic creature, he was son of Poseidon, or else he drowned himself in the same lake as his mother; or he was a kinsman of Phaethon and king of the people of the Po valley; or he was actually a son of Apollo. The variants are, as usual, all the same theme.) In grief for the loss of Phaethon, Kyknos was metamorphosed into a swan, which is the other bird sacred to Apollo.

The swan is a large ferocious bird, with a long phallic neck and no song to speak of, except for its rasping, serpentlike hissing; but just before it dies, the swan sings one beautiful song, its swan song. This is because it is Apollo's bird, and at the threshold of death, it has the gift of prophecy from him: it looks across the boundary between this world and the next, and its swan song is its final (altered) vision—a description of the coming paradise on the Shining Island.

The clairvoyance of Kyknos and of the prophetic brides of Apollo was considered a phenomenon similar to the medical arts of Asklepios and his Asklepiad brotherhood of doctors; for medicine in Greek antiquity was not so much a matter of effecting a cure, but rather of knowing the normal course of a disease so that the doctor could note its critical threshold moment and then predict its outcome—whether the patient would live or die.

The Contest with Kassandra

One of the most famous of Apollo's prophetic brides was the Trojan maiden **Kassandra**. She was courted by the god, who promised her whatever she wanted in return. She asked for the gift of prophecy, but then refused to accept his sexual advances. Since the gift had been already granted, it could not be rescinded; but Apollo cursed her so that no one would ever understand her predictions until it was too late. She never had anything good to report, and finally died, trying to make people understand that she was about to be murdered by the Queen of Mycenae.

Troia, which is the city of Troy, is another place named for the trinity of its sisterhood, although, as with Amyklai and Pherai, here, too, it was supposedly named for its 'king' **Tros** ('Triform'). Apollo had a hand in founding this city, too, which like Thebes, was the theme of a Great War that would eventually be fought there to settle, once and for all, the proper roles of males and females.

One tradition was that the people of Troy came originally from Minoan Crete, and even named a mountain there by the Bosphorus **Mount Ida**, after the Cretan mountain where Zeus had been reborn into the Mediterranean lands. They had been told to settle wherever earth-born creatures attacked them. These turned out to be a plague of mice—from which Apollo saved them: acquiring thereby the name of 'Mouse-god,' **Smintheus Apollo (paradigms #1&2)**.

In the Trojan War, Troy figured as the ultimate enemy of the whole Indo-European way of Hellenic life. It is a story that we will come to more fully later. Apollo Smintheus had predicted that the Trojans would be invincible so long as they preserved the most ancient (which is to say, not transmuted) effigy of Pallas: this was the **palladium** of Athena, in the days when she was still a Spinstress Goddess.

Another of the primordial 'kings' at Troy was **Ilos**, after whom the city could also be called Ilium, just as it was also known as Dardania after 'king' **Dardanos**. There were five 'kings,' in all, the digit men of Troy (unless you add an **Erichthonios**, as in some accounts: since Athena could not do without him), the last being **Priam**, who was 'king' with his Queen **Hekabe** (Latin **Hecuba**) at the time of the Trojan War: they were the parents of Kassandra.

In the generation before Priam, under 'king' **Laomedon**, the walls of the city (which was sited on the 'Hill of **Ate**' or 'Demented Destruction') had been built by Poseidon and Apollo—both in the bonds of Death, as slaves of Laomedon, in order to expiate for their attempt to overthrow Zeus in the revolt that had been led by Hephaestus on behalf of his mother Hera. Poseidon , like Zethos at Thebes, did the manual work, while Apollo, like Amphion, played the lyre; Apollo also tended cattle, as he did for Admetos of Pherai: cattle-tending was the typical occupation in the bonds of Death. After the work was done, Laomedon refused to pay the indentured gods their wages. Poseidon retaliated by sending a sea monster as a deadly consort for one of the daughters in the sisterhood of Laomedon. Her name was **Hesione**. Herakles, the hero, rescued her, too, like Alkestis.

Again, however, Laomedon reneged on his agreement. He was supposed to pay Herakles with a magical team of horses that Zeus had given to Tros, as recompense for the loss of his son **Ganymedes** ('Bright-lord'), whom Zeus had loved and taken away to Olympus to serve as cup-bearer at the gods' feastings. Herakles destroyed the city, saving only Priam, who up to that time had been called **Podarkes** ('Swift-foot' or perhaps 'Bearfoot': both are possible, and the latter associates him with the ursine characteristics of Artemis, as we shall see;

for this Apolline consort of the Goddess was given a second chance with the name of Priam, the 'Bought-man.').

Priam suspected that the Hill of Ate might be a bad place to found a city. So he consulted the oracle of Apollo at Delphi, but his ambassador fell in love with one of the priests of Apollo and abducted him, like another Ganymedes, to Troy. (Unfortunately, Delphi in those days was still an Earth oracle, and Apollo was not yet his Olympian self.) Thus Priam never learned the Olympian god's opinion, but instead, he made the abducted 'holy man' into Troy's Apollo—and he rebuilt the city on its old foundations. During the Trojan War, Troy's primordial version of Apollo was the enemy of the Greeks and sent a plague upon them, shooting them with his poisoned arrows.

Kassandra, like Apollo and Artemis, was a twin (**paradigm #1**). She and her brother **Helenos** were amongst the many children that Priam and Hekabe had (fifty sons and twelve daughters, in all), and both Kassandra and Helenos were prophets. By one account, they received the gift of prophecy in the sanctuary of Troy's **Thymbraios Apollo** (named for the 'Savory-mint' and also called 'Black-flower' **entheogen**): their parents got drunk in the temple and staggered back home without them; when they returned they found serpents licking the children's ears; the serpents escaped into boughs of laurel. This tending of an infant by the **ios** ('arrow-poison') of serpents was a traditional sign of the child's future clairvoyance.

Just before the city was finally taken at the end of the Trojan War, another of Priam and Hekabe's children, **Laocoon**, who was a priest of their Apollo, tried to prevent his fellow Trojans from accepting a Greek horse, a dedication to Athena, but a serpent came from the sea and strangled him and his two sons, **Thymbraios** and Black-flower, **Melanthos**.

Troy could only be taken by usurping and matching its chthonic defenses by their transmuted equivalences. A similar pattern occurs in the taking of the seven-gated city of Thebes. Thus, the palladium had to be stolen away and its power converted into the ruse of the **Trojan Horse**: this was an artificial wooden horse that concealed Greek warriors inside, a centaur symbol of Athena now on their side. The poisoned arrows of Herakles also had to be brought against the city. The hero **Achilleus** (Latin **Achilles**), who bore the epithet **Podarkes**, would kill one of Priam's sons, **Hektor**; Hektor's sinister brother **Paris** would shoot Achilleus in his vulnerable foot; and finally Achilleus's son **Neoptolemos** ('New-war') would fatally shoot Paris in the foot with the poisoned arrow. (Paris had another name: **Alexandros** ('Warrior'); and he and his sister Kassandra are dual versions of the same identity, for she could also be called **Alexandra**: the two are another version of the Trojan Apollo-Artemis duo.) The only son of Priam who would eventually survive was Helenos, a male version of the **Helen**, whose abduction by Paris had been the whole cause of the war.

When Kassandra was finally killed at Mycenae, it was over a debate by a husband and wife as to which of them had a better right to claim ownership of a child.

The father **Agamemnon** had sacrificed a daughter, **Iphigeneia** (which was a name of Artemis as 'Strong in her birth'), in order to rouse the wind for his journey to Troy. The wife **Clytaemnestra** did not approve, and she murdered him and Kassandra when he returned with her from the Trojan War. Then Apollo ordered Agamemnon's son **Orestes** to avenge the father's death by killing the mother. He did, went mad, and sought a cure to free him from the sisterhood of spirits that hounded him—first from Apollo and Artemis, and finally at Athens. He arrived, as we have seen, at the Feast of Choes. And the problem was finally decided in favor of patriliny. Not only was Apollo vindicated, but there were some who claimed that Iphigeneia hadn't really died, but, in typical fashion (**paradigm #2**), the redeemed Artemis had been lenient and at the last moment had spirited the maiden away to another world, leaving a reindeer (stag, hind) in her place as victim.

It took several generations and a whole army of agents and actually three wars to finally put down Apollo and Artemis at Troy. And in the Athenian view, it finally was resolved only at Athens.

The Contest with Kallisto

The story is variously told, but there was a maiden named **Kallisto**, the 'Best, Most Beautiful,' similar in meaning to what we have said about Aristaios. She disguised herself as Artemis (**paradigm #1**). And Zeus made love to her, although he may have disguised himself, too: either as the werewolf **Lykaios** or even as Apollo himself. Obviously, this could not be allowed to happen.

While bathing with Artemis, Kallisto was found to be pregnant. Either Hera or Artemis changed her into a she-bear; and Zeus-Lykaios killed her, or Artemis shot her. But the son she had conceived was saved, **Arkas**, the 'Bear;' like another Dionysos, he was given to Hermes and raised in the wilderness. In some versions, Kallisto did not die immediately, but wandered about for years—and met her son while he was bear hunting; he would have shot his mother, but Zeus prevented it by changing them both into the two Bear constellations, Ursa Maior and Arctophylax (**paradigm #2**). And Artemis tacked the name **Kalliste** onto her own. Arkas was the ancestor of the Arcadian branch of the Greek peoples, who settled the central highlands of the Peloponnesos.

At Brauron on the east coast of Attica, Artemis was known as **Iphigeneia**, whose tomb was there. Here, the new Artemis required only a scratch on the neck from her human male victims; and she was a goddess of childbirth, honored by a sisterhood of girls called **arktoi** or 'bear cubs,' who danced a bear dance, as initiation to cleanse them of the pollution of their imminent pubescence.

The Contest with Orion

Orion, like Actaeon, was a hunter. Although his story, too, was variously told, his background was definitely chthonic and Dionysian, from the primordial world. He was a gigantic child of Earth, or else aquatic, a son of Poseidon who walked on the waters. His first affair was with a nymph of the pomegranate tree (**Side**, an **entheogen** of the Goddess, and one of the Sidai sisters after whom her city was named), before he tried a second sacred marriage with a Minoan bee-lady (**Merope**), who was daughter of a 'woinos-man,' (**Oinopion**). (Merope's name is not Greek, but someone remembered that it meant 'bee-eater'—an epithet of the honey-loving bear: 'honey-intoxication' remained the basic word for 'drunk' in Classical Greek.) Orion had lost his first bride Side because she was tossed into Hades for daring to rival Hera's beauty (like Nephele, the 'Cloud' who was Ixion's hallucinatory bride). The second marriage wasn't very successful, either: Oinopion made him drunk, deprived him of vision, and threw him away by the seashore. In his blindness, like another drunken Helios, he wandered through the sea (or on it) to the East, where a ray of the sun restored his sight. Some people claimed that Orion even found time somehow to fit in a marriage to one of the crow-girls, the **Koronides**.

Artemis destroyed him. The Dawn (**Eos**) fell in love with him; Artemis was jealous (apparently he should have been her lover—at least in the olden times), and shot him with her arrows—on the island of her Olympian rebirth, Delos. Or he may have been playing at throwing the discus with her, like another Hyakinthos. Or he may have tried to violate one of a sisterhood of Hyperborean maidens (or else, Artemis, herself) who were delivering a secret plant (**entheogen**) to Delos from the homeland. The variants all tell the same story of transmutation from the older to the newer versions of Apollo and Artemis— Orion was Apollo, or a regional version of him, and Artemis was his Goddess (**paradigm #1**).

One further version suggests the identity of the secret Hyperborean plant whose arrival marked the death of the older traditions. Orion's birth involves an entheogen. He comes from the Boeotian town of Hyriai, another plural, named for the sisterhood, and again, someone remembered that these would be the ladies who were the 'Swarm of the Beehive.' The 'king' was having trouble begetting a son, and was advised by a trio of male gods to urinate on a cow's hide and then bury it in the ground. The child who was thus born from the chthonic realm was destined to surpass his Minoan begetting and to become a celestial sign, like another Apollo. He was supposedly named Orion because of his begetting via this act of **uri**nation (although the etymology is false, an Indo-European meaning that has been forced on a name that is not Greek). When he grew up, he attempted still another sacred marriage with the Pleiades sisters: they were all turned into constellations (**paradigm #2**)—the Pleiades as a flock of seven doves, fleeing from the Hunter. The one that Orion raped was the 'Bee-eater,' Merope: like another Niobe, continually grieving she is the star that is not always visible, since she hides her face in shame for her former chthonic marriage.

The tale of Orion's conception via urine (this son of a 'king' in a land where men could not beget sons) marks the transition to the newer traditions of Indo-

European shamanism. One of the characteristics of Amanita is that its metabolite in urine maintains its chemical efficacy—so that the urine of the shamans or animals, like the reindeer, that eat it is a second source of the entheogen. This was the plant offering that was supposedly being delivered by the sisterhood from the Hyperboreans. Orion's death and redemption on Delos is an essential element in the mediation of the Indo-European and Minoan traditions of shamanism.

Apollo tacked the names **Loxias** ('Oblique') and **Hekaergos** ('Working from afar') onto his own in commemoration of two of the Hyperborean maidens (Hekaerge and Loxo) who died there at Delos (**paradigm #2**). But even with these names, as with Letogenes and Phoebus, he is still being called after his Goddesses.

The Contest with Diktynna

Artemis also had the names of **Diktynna**, **Britomartis**, and **Aphaia**—three names for a single goddess, commemorating her former identity on the island of Crete, where she was the Goddess of a consort who was the lord of the Minoan labyrinth.

'King' **Minos**, who was the son of a cow-woman, **Europa**, and the husband of the woman who bore the 'Minoan bull-man' (the **Minotaur**), courted the nymph **Britomartis**, one of the sisterhood that hunted with the hounds of Artemis. Her name is supposed to mean the 'Good Maiden'—which like Aristaios and Kalliste, is probably a euphemism for its opposite, the Maiden of Death. She fled from him and tossed herself off a cliff to escape. But as usual, the Apolline sacrificial victim was spared via the twins' leniency in their newer transmuted manifestations. As Britomartis fell, with the abducting wind (**animus**) rushing past her, Artemis contrived that fishermen, netting their aquatic prey, would catch her in their net, whence her name was changed to **Diktynna**, the 'Net-woman.' Artemis-Diktynna was credited with inventing the net, which in less auspicious times would have been a piece of more sinister weaving by the huntress-spintress. Diktynna fled to the island of Aegina, in the Saronic Gulf, off the coast of Attica, and another holy place of the Goddess, originally colonized by 'wolf-people' from the Lycian homeland. (One of the island's former 'kings,' **Aeacus**, became a judge in the underworld because of his 'goodness,' joining Minos and his brother **Rhadamanthys** in that reward—making three judges, in all, **paradigm #2**.) There Diktynna hid in a grove of Artemis and was worshipped as **Aphaia**, which was a name interpreted as meaning that she disappeared, although formerly she would have made you disappear.

Her late archaic temple (6th-5th century BC) still stands on the island, one of the best preserved from antiquity, on the hill overlooking the shore, above the fishing village of Agia Marina, which is named for the Blessed Virgin, the 'Holy Lady of the Sea.' Thus the mantle of sanctity passed on to an even newer religion. On the other side of the island are the remains of the temple of Apollo.

The Contest with Python

Each of the contests represents Apollo's victory over himself at the various sites where the Goddess once ruled, but his greatest triumph was at Delphi in the contest with **Python**, for Delphi was destined to become his most important shrine—one of the Panhellenic sanctuaries, a place where all Greeks, regardless of local and tribal affiliations, came together to worship the god. It was here, on the high slope of **Mount Parnassos**, that Apollo took over the oracle of Earth and realigned it to the traditions of the Olympian religion of his new father Zeus.

When Apollo was born on Delos as Leto's son, he had as yet no piece of Earth to call his own. How could he? Earth would not have even let him come to birth, were it not for the mediating role of turncoat that the island of Delos was made to play. That island became his other Panhellenic sanctuary, although it was primarily honored more by just the Ionian tribal group of Greek peoples.

The infant god, just a few days old, went in search of a piece of property to claim for himself. And he found it, after many stops at other chthonic shrines along the way, at Delphi. And apart from its sheer beauty, a better piece of sacred real estate would be hard to imagine: Delphi was the 'navel' (omphalos) of Earth herself; two eagles (or swans or crows), released from the opposite extremities of the earth, met at this point and dropped the navel stone that marked the place. But unfortunately, like any colonist, Apollo found Delphi already inhabited by its aboriginal owner. This was Python, a serpent, sometimes male (coiled around the omphalos), but also sometimes a female monster, a dragon-lady. It was also said that Python was the consort of a Goddess called **Delphyne**, the 'Womb-lady,' after whom the place was named Delphi, as it was also called Pytho. By other accounts, the lady was a she-dragon who had nursed the monster **Typhaon**, whom Hera had born, all by herself, like another Hephaestus, in outrage for Zeus's solitary begetting of his daughter Athena. Or Python, as some claimed, had actually been sent by Hera to persecute Leto during her pregnancy with the twins. Or it may have been something left over from the stagnant waters receding after the Great Flood that had destroyed the olden age. The truth is simple: Python-Delphyne was the Minoan Goddess, both sexes in one, Mother and child consort. And Apollo shot it with his poisoned arrow, either on Delos itself, or at Delphi (**paradigm #1**). At Delphi, the monster was an oracle of Earth in a cave high up on Parnassos, tended by a sisterhood of 'Gray-ladies,' called **Graiai**, at a gateway (**limen**) that tunneled down to the other world.

The victorious Apollo took possession of the oracle, and gloated over his victim, telling the writhing serpent 'to rot' (**pytho**) as fertilizing nutriment for the earth upon which it had been a bane. Thus did he pun upon its name and transmute its poisonous nature into something beneficial (**entheogen**). By further punning, **pytho** was given another false etymology, interpreting it as the Greek word that means 'to learn by inquiry,' as in the future everybody would when they came to consult the newer oracle, which would henceforth reveal, not Earth's wisdom, but the mind of Zeus (**paradigm #2**).

And even the name of the place as Delphi was given a new meaning, too. In Greek, it is a masculine plural (Delphoi), anomalous amongst so many places named in the plural of the sisterhood, and no longer was it interpreted as the 'womb;' instead, it was derived from the 'dolphin,' the aquatic mammal that is Apollo's special sea-creature. As with Poseidon, the dolphin represents an animal friend (**totem**) in the primordial waters of Earth's womb. Apollo chose as his first brotherhood of priests for Delphi a group of Minoans from the Cretan labyrinth of Knossos. Apollo pirated their ship as it journeyed on the sea, appearing to them as a dolphin; and he stole them away to Delphi to become his ministers in the new version of his religion. This priesthood of 'Dolphin-men,' the Delphoi, replaced the 'Gray-ladies,' but the oracle itself remained in the hands of a woman, the **Pythia**, whose title was the Queen Bee in this hive of men (**paradigm #2**).

As with the murder of the Kyklops, the death of Python required expiation by a sojourn in the bonds of Death. Apollo went into a period of exile in the **Valley of Tempe**, a utopian other-worldly paradise in Thessaly, the nearer version of the Hyperborean homeland. It was there that he had his contest with Daphne. And every eighth year at Delphi, the murder and expiation was reenacted in the ritual of the Presentation of the Holy Branch. A noble boy (a kouros) destroyed a temporary building that was supposed to be the house of Python; then he journeyed north with attendants along the Sacred Way through the plain of Thessaly to the Valley of Tempe; there, he was purified, and returned bearing the branch of laurel (daphne) which symbolized the new sacred plant imported into Greece from the Hyperboreans to replace the plants of the Goddess's religion (**entheogen**).

In addition, athletic contests (eventually, every fourth year) were held at Delphi, the **Pythian Games**, as was the custom upon the graves of dead heroes, to honor and commemorate them. And Apollo tacked two more names onto his own: **Pythios** and **Delphinios**.

The Sanctuary of Delphi

The site of the Classical sanctuary is supposed to be on the spot of the original cave of Python, although the cave is not there, but actually much higher up the mountain, a subterranean labyrinthine cavern of forty interconnecting chambers, with stalactites and stalagmites, the **Korykian Cave**, named for a cave in Anatolia, in the god's Lycian homeland: the people in the nearby mountain village were said to have been Werewolves, and it was wolves who had led their Wolf leader to this spot on Parnassos. (Apollo had to kill the 'Wolf' **Lykos**, as well as Python, at Delphi, in order to wrest control of the oracle, **paradigm #1**.) In the eighth century, the oracle was moved to its present more accessible location, below the south slopes of Parnassos, at the base of the twin cliffs, called

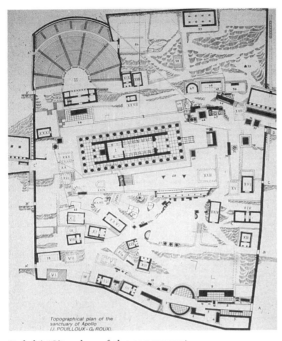

Topographical plan of the
sanctuary of Apollo
(J. POUILLOUX - G. ROUX)

Delphi (Site plan of the sanctuary)

the 'Shining Rocks.' From their summit, human victims were still thrown to their Apolline death, but only on occasion, and only those who were demonstrably deserving, as criminals convicted of sacrilege in the sanctuary. Below the site and funneling up towards it, spreads the fertile plain of Krisa, which is the town at its far end on the Gulf of Corinth. Most pilgrims would approach Delphi by sea, through the port of Krisa, or else overland, along the pass on the south slope from Thebes and the plain of Boeotia.

The approach to the Temple of Apollo, where the Pythia sat when she was in residence for oracular consultations, was up the steep Sacred Way, past the **treasuries** that line it on both sides, amidst the many sculptural works of art set up as dedications by athletes who had been victorious in the Games, or by cities commemorating victories in war, private and public donors—all testifying to the importance and validity of the oracle and to their own favored role as proponents of the Hellenic way of life. The treasuries themselves were like bank vaults, storing the dedications from different cities, and votive offerings from their citizens in gratitude for past responses from the oracle. Everyone vied for a lot on this sacred road, demonstrating by the graceful design and ornamentation of their own city's treasury that they had a right to claim preeminence as representatives of the Hellenic culture that the Olympian Apollo had come to represent. And since he was good in such matters (as witnessed by his own conquest of Earth's former sacred site), Apollo's oracle was often consulted about where it would be auspicious for a particular city to found a new colony of its own brand of culture elsewhere on the inhospitable earth, in the midst of alien peoples, often in southern Italy or on the coast of Africa. (The oracle was also consulted frequently by married individuals who were having trouble begetting a son for the father, since Apollo as Zeus's son, was obviously good at that, too.) But the Greeks were a very competitive people, and a city tried, in particular, to occupy a better piece of property on this Sacred Way than its neighbors or enemies. The higher up, the better: no position on this road was without significance. Just where the road turns, highest and closest to the retaining wall that is the foundation for the Temple of the god himself, is the **Treasury of the Athenians**. It is the only one that stands restored today, its walls inscribed with over 150 separate records of Athenian commendations and honors.

The Way zigzags back at this point, which is below the back side of the Temple, toward the sharp incline up to the Temple's entrance, on the terrace above and facing typically eastward. Along the retaining wall for the Temple's terrace platform (which is formed of closely fitting polygonal blocks of stone, a form of construction that is supposed to go back to Minoan times and to have been built by Kyklopes), and extending right up to the end of it, where the incline up to the Temple's level begins, is the **Stoa of the Athenians**. At the beginning of the fifth century, Athens had played an important role in leading the Greek cities in the wars against the Persians, whose invasion of Greece was seen as the ultimate threat to Hellenism. The building of the Treasury was financed out of the spoils from one of these Athenian victories; and in the Stoa, which was a roofed colonnade, with the retaining wall itself as its back side, was displayed the mastheads of the destroyed Persian ships, as well as the cables from the pontoon bridge that had been constructed across the Hellespont for the invasion by the land forces of the Persians.

There was no better location than these two pieces of Athenian dedications—and they served, as well, as embarrassing reminders to the god himself that he had let his cowardly oracle side with the Persians in the wars. This was the area that commemorated the very foundations upon which the Olympian Temple stood, the god's own triumph over the chthonian Python. And now that the Athenians had moved in, Apollo—and every pilgrim who made this programmed ascent to the Temple—could be reminded of how much he owed them in gratitude for perpetuating his better nature. Here beneath the back side of the Temple, was enshrined the cleft in the rock that commemorated the original Cave of Python up on the mountain. Here, too, was the symbolic Threshing Floor where the combat with Python was reenacted for the Festival of the Presentation of the Branch at the beginning of the Pythian Games: a threshing floor is a place where the grain (or good food) is separated from the chaff by tossing it in the wind (**animus**). Here, too, between the Treasury and the Stoa, was the Meeting Hall for the priesthood that governed Delphi. And the former Goddess was commemorated by the monument of Leto, the mother of the god's Olympian identity. Only the island of Naxos, which administered the sanctuary of the god's birthplace on Delos, had previously been honored in this critical area: they had erected a pillar, thirty feet high, surmounted by a Sphinx, a winged lion with the head of a woman, as a commemoration of the former Goddess who once presided at the Cave high up the mountain. The island of Naxos had been granted in perpetuity the right to be first on any occasion to consult the Pythoness.

On the upper level, in the plaza in front of the Temple's entrance, was a similar commemoration of the rituals at the Cave: a column surmounted by three dancing **Thyiads**, a maenadic sisterhood: in another version of the transition from female to male control of Delphi, one of these sisters is supposed to have given birth to **Delphos**, a son of Apollo, after whom, in appropriate patrilineal fashion, the place could now be named.

Here in the plaza were also numerous dedications of **tripods** of bronze or gold. As with Poseidon's trident, these three-legged cauldrons were Apollo's way of commemorating the former trinity of the Goddess. He or his priestess often used the tripod as a throne: its symbolism as a cooking vessel implies transmutation through the mediation of fire.

The **Temple of Apollo** that now stands in ruins dates from the fourth century, replacing the sixth century temple that was destroyed by an earthquake. The latter had been completed with the aid of large donations from an Athenian family, then in exile, as a way of furthering their political ambitions back home. It had not been the first temple at the site. Tradition recalled that earlier temples had been constructed of laurel or of beeswax—like a beehive (**entheogen**).

For a consultation, the Pythia prepared herself by bathing in the **Castalian Spring**, which flows from the ravine where the two cliffs of the Shining Rocks meet: **Kastalia** was once like Daphne an unwilling bride of Apollo; she turned into the spring to escape from him: its waters were sacred to the sisterhood of Muses (who could be called **Kastalides**) and were supposed to inspire poetry. Apollo was said to have transplanted the daphne-laurel from Thessaly beside this spring (**entheogen**). (Everyone who came to consult the oracle similarly purified himself in these waters.)

Then the god's willingness to be consulted was ascertained: a priest sprinkled cold water on a goat who signified its acquiescence in its sacrificial offering by shaking the water off its head. Only if the goat agreed to die, could one proceed further; otherwise, it would be too dangerous for the oracle. Then, the Pythoness, a simple peasant woman who had been awarded this role by the priesthood because of her special clairvoyant talents, entered the subterranean chamber at the back of the temple. She drank from the water of another spring, the Delphousa, which was channeled into a reservoir in this chamber, chewed on the

Apollo, Seated on a Tripod in his Temple with Omphalos and Laurel (440-430 BC, Museo Archaeologico Nazionale, Ferrara)

leaves of laurel, and sat on a tripod, above what was supposed to be an opening into the cave below. She felt herself become possessed by the god, sometimes in bestial forms, as a horse or a goat. On one occasion when the sacrificial goat had refused to cooperate, they had held the consultation anyway, and the experience nearly killed the woman.

She probably could not recall what she said for a consultation but the priests outside the chamber, interpreted her babbling shrieks as the response, and they rephrased it into an elegant enigmatic verse, which often would leave the client who had consulted her as baffled as before. It is significant that the oracle remained a female at Delphi, but she was handled now by men (**paradigm #2**).

A similar transmutation of irrational possession into harmony was celebrated in the **Theater**, which was built into the hillside above the Temple. Here were performed contests of music. Still higher up the slope, was the **Stadium**, where the athletic Games were performed. (In the plain of Krisa below, there was a hippodrome for the races with chariots, since the Stadium was not large enough to accommodate such events.)

In keeping with the topographical symbolism of transmutation as ascent, just below the area of the Sacred Way and the Temple, there was yet a further commemoration of the former Goddess, an area that was now assigned to Apollo's sister Athena. Here there was a **Tholos** temple, round, in imitation of the beehive. There were also temples to Athena and a **Gymnasium**, where the visiting athletes would exercise for their final preparations for the Games. (Artemis is noticeably absent from Delphi: her relationship with the athletes would perhaps have been too liminal, recalling her unfortunate affairs with figures like Actaeon or Hippolytus.)

As further commemoration of the past, Apollo each year deserted Delphi for the winter months, retiring into the bonds of Death in his homeland. Then, the old Korykian Cave again became the focus of ritual. Since Apollo was not in residence, he turned the cave over to his brothers, sometimes Hermes, but more often to Dionysos. And the chthonic sisterhoods returned again to prominence with the enactment of maenadic rituals above the original cave of Python.

Dancing the Labyrinth at Delos

Apollo killed Python by himself at Delphi, but he needed the help of the Athenian hero **Theseus** to destroy the **Minotaur** at the labyrinth of Knossos and to purify the island of Delos of his former self. We have mentioned a similar pattern in the aid that the hero **Perseus** gave to Athena in killing the Gorgon Medusa.

These are myths that we will treat more fully later when we come to the stories about the heroes. In the case of the Minotaur, Athens had been under an

Theseus Disembarking with the Dance Troupe of Liberated Victims (Krater 570 BC, 'François Vase,' Museo Archeologico, Florence)

obligation to provide human victims for the bull dance in Minos's labyrinth, twice seven victims, like Niobe's children, seven boys and seven girls. Theseus went as one of them to dance the dance. He killed the Minotaur and rescued the victims. On the way back to Athens, his troupe stopped off on Delos and transmuted the windings of the labyrinth into art by imitating its steps in a line dance on the island of the twins' new Olympian manifestations.

The ship that Theseus had used to sail to Crete was still in existence a thousand years later, carefully preserved and constantly repaired. It was used to send a troupe of dancers each year to dance the dance again. The twins no longer demanded that these victims die, but the dancers were flagellated in their dancing, as a reminder of former rituals (**paradigm #2**). And while the dancers were away, no public executions could be held in Athens, lest the gods be reminded of their more sinister role in earlier times.

* * * *

Review

Apollo and **Artemis** (**Diana**) were reborn on Delos as twin offspring of Zeus and the Earth Goddess **Leto** (**Latona**), but in their earlier identities they were Goddess and Consort, closely involved in the symbolism of the Minoan labyrinth and rituals of human sacrifice. In their transmutation into Olympians, they are strenuously isolated from anything that might trigger a regression to their former selves. Both are represented as perfect exemplars of Hellenic youths, the so-called **kouroi** and **kourai**. Although they are twins, they do not always share the same attributes. They claim two homelands, the Indo-European **Hyperboreans** and the Anatolian **Lycians**, and they derive aspects of their identities from an assimilation from both sources: in both, Apollo was a god of prophecy and of shamanism with entheogens.

> **Apollo Phoebus Letoides (Latoides) Letogenes**: epithets **Mousagetes**, (**Hyakinthos**), **Lykios (Lykus)**, (**Aristaios**), (**Phaethon**), (**Kyknos**), **Smintheus, Thymbraios, Loxias, Hekaergos, Pythios, Delphinios, Cynthius**
> Attributes: bow and quiver of arrows; lyre; laurel (daphne); wolfsbane; savory; tripod; omphalos (navel stone); never bearded; crow; swan; dolphin; wolf (dog)

> **Artemis Letoides (Latoides) Letogenes Kalliste Iphigeneia Diktynna Britomartis Aphaia Cynthia**
> Attributes: huntress, with bow and quiver of arrows; reindeer (hind, stag); lion; wolf (dog); bear; virgin (bathing); fishing (hunting) net

Myths: **Birth of Apollo and Artemis**
    Contest with Niobe
    Contest with Hyakinthos
    Contest with Daphne

Contest with Actaeon
Contest with Koronis (Birth of Asklepios)
Servitude to Admetos
Contest with Phaethon
Contest with Kassandra
Servitude to Laomedon
Contest with Kallisto
Contest with Orion
Contest with Diktynna
Contest with Python
Contest with Lykos (Lycus)

Sisterhoods: **Heliades, Kastalides, Thyiads (Thyiades), Pleiades; Graiai, Koronides**

Winds: **Zephyrus, Boreas**. Also **Notos**, the 'Damp' South Wind; and **Euros**, the 'Drying' East Wind. They form a brotherhood of **Aiolides**, with their father **Aiolos**, the 'Changeable' Lord of the Winds, as the fifth. They all blow from subterranean caverns and are soul-abductors.

For Discussion and Further Study

1. *The Sibyl* by Pär Lagerkvist tells the story of a Pythoness at Delphi who does the same thing to Apollo as Koronis: she cheats on her vows to Apollo and has an affair with a mortal, for which she is expelled from her role as priestess. She has had a weird son and is living up in the Cave on Parnassos, and is visited by another person who has been cursed by god, to whom she tells her story. Read the novel and consider:

What similarities of metaphor describe Apollo and the mortal lover?

What is similar about the experiences of the Sibyl and her visitor?

What happens to the Sibyl's son at the end of the novel?

2. Another myth about the 'enemy' of Apollo is the **Contest with the Aloidai**.

There were two of them, **Otos** (a 'stupid' owl?) and **Ephialtes** (a Nightmare-demon, and also the name of a magical herb to prevent nightmares); they were sons of the 'Thresher-man' **Aloeus**, who was one of the children of Earth; some people, however, claimed that they were only his bastard sons and that they were really sons of Poseidon. Their mother was a 'Strong Queen' **Iphimedeia**, who was the daughter of a 'Triple-man' **Triops**: she poured ocean water upon herself by the seashore to beget the twins. Aloeus, himself, was a son of **Helios**.

Supposedly named after their father, the Aloidai grew quickly (nine digits a month) into Giants, as big, some said, as Orion. After capturing Ares and confining him in a brazen vessel, they intended to make war upon the Olympians, piling mountain upon mountain, but they were destroyed just before they could grow a beard. The reason for their enmity with the gods was that they wanted to have affairs with Hera and Artemis.

They also had a better nature: they founded cities, and originated the cult of the Muses. They were localized in Thessaly and Boeotia, and rescued their mother and sister from the Goddess and from Dionysos.

Apollo and Artemis (or perhaps Artemis by herself) killed them. A hind (or Artemis disguised as a hind) ran between them, and they shot at it, killing each other. In the underworld, they were bound back to back to a pillar, on top of which perched an owl.

Otos was buried in Crete, and the two were honored as dead benefactors of mankind.

Would you consider the Aloidai as candidates for **paradigms #1&2** with regard to Apollo and Artemis? Why?

Chapter VI
Playing the Tricks of Nature

⚸

Hermes, too, underwent a new birth to become one of the Olympian family. He is a young god, eternally young, whether bearded or not—for he has none of the troubles that haunted Apollo about his sexuality, and although young as an Olympian, his youthfulness has great antiquity, for his origins in the Mediterranean world are probably of the most primitive.

Before becoming anthropomorphized as a young man, he was represented, in those earlier times, simply as a sacred pile of stones, a **herma**, as a magical guide along the roadside. In modern Greece, Christianity has assimilated this ancient symbolism in the many shrine posts that still line the highways: they commemorate someone who died there, at each location, lost in some fatal accident. For as a guide along the way, Hermes also knew the pathways from this world to the next, and he was a frequent traveler, escorting souls back and forth: it is a job that earned him the title of **Psychopompos** or 'soul escort' (**animus**: **psyche** or soul is the animating spirit wind). In the Classical age, you would be apt to find him at a grave stele or pillar, visiting with the ghost of the body buried there. Traveling is so much a part of his identity, that he commonly is seen wearing the broad-brimmed hat of a traveler, a style that was much in vogue with the human adolescents who were of the same age as he (roughly 17-18 years old).

And even though he was commonly portrayed with a human body, there were still aniconic or only partially anthropomorphized versions of him simply as a pillar. These could take the form of a square stone post, surmounted by a carved head of a bearded male, but with no other indication of his human features, ex-

Hermes (350 BC column base from Temple of Artemis at Ephesus, British Museum, London)

(right) Hermes and a Dead Woman, Crowned for her Sacred Marriage, at her Grave Stele (Lekythos, Staatliche Antikensammlungen und Glyptothek, Munich)

(below) Herm of the Entrance to the Athenian Acropolis

cept for his genitals, in the appropriate place on the pillar. These so-called **herms** were numerous in cities, stationed as magical guardians at the gateways of private and public buildings, permitting access only to the friendly spirits.

Hermes was so closely associated with the symbolism of the herm pillar, that frequently even in anthropomorphic sculptural representations of him, he leans on his pillar. The pillar is not there simply to help support the free-standing figure; for even in vase paintings, Hermes often leans on his pillar. Like the masked pillar of Dionysos, the herm clearly indicates the phallic nature of the god. He, too, was originally a Consort of his Goddess, from whom he derives his fundamental role of trickery, the 'little-big man' magic that we have already noted in the manifestations of the Giants, the Titans, and the digital kings. Through Hermes, the old tricks of the Goddess were realigned to serve the furtherance of the Olympian world. Hermes, the trickster, is a thief—but always in a good cause. Never does he play a nasty trick. He becomes the patron of the controlled thievery that is the basis for commerce and trade. When he was imported to

Rome, where he always maintained a Greek identity, he was renamed in Latin for this patronage of 'merchandizing' (or **merx**) as **Mercurius** or (in English) **Mercury**. This same thievery underlies his patronage of oratory, as the quibbling verbal cleverness that steals the verdict in courts of law and politics.

Because of his frequent traveling and ease in commerce, he was employed as a messenger from the gods, shuttling from Olympus to earth or the chthonic underworld. The emblem of this role is the herald's staff, a rod tied with a ribbon to signify the joining of sender and recipient; but when emblematic of Hermes, this staff takes on a somewhat different configuration. It becomes a rod, with the ribbons replaced by two intertwined serpents, facing each other at the top. This was supposed to be the pose assumed by serpents when they copulated; and seeing it was said to produce a gender change in the viewer. This rod is called the **caduceus** (which is a Latin version of the Greek **kerykeion** or 'herald's wand'). It occurs today as an emblem for the medical arts, and was associated also with the Asklepiads and prophecy in Classical antiquity. Its connotations include magical drugs (**entheogen**) and the threshold between worlds (**limen**), as well as the mediation between masculine Olympianism and the female chthonic world. Sometimes it is winged, as well; more often Hermes has wings on his boots or on his hat, allowing him to fly as swiftly as the wind; for Hermes is another transmutation of the Consort bird, as well as of the Goddess's phallic nature.

The botanical aspect of his identity is the magical plant called **moly**. Its properties are an antidote to the grievous drugs of the Goddess and the underworld. This is probably the most important part of its symbolism, for Hermes frequently functions as a mediator with his former self in Minoan times: like his sister Athena (**anima**), he is a perfect transmutation, making him a fitting helper and companion for the hero's confrontation with the 'enemy' self (**paradigm #3**). Although his moly was identified in later traditions with various known drug plants, the original moly remains a mystery. What we can know is that it is named with an Indo-European word that means a **moll**ifying 'drug root.' It is supposedly hard to dig up; and it is black, with a flower like milk.

In keeping with his chthonic origins, Hermes displays some of the same kind of mechanical wizardry that characterizes Hephaestus. Amongst his inventions were counted the art of cookery (by which the deadly process of putrefaction is transmuted into the beneficial hastening of edibility); and the invention of fire itself (probably via the use of the phallic fire drill); the lyre, which he gave to Apollo, was another of his inventions: from what we know of Apollo, he could never have invented it himself—but we will come to that, in a moment. First we should get Hermes born.

The Birth of Hermes

There really isn't much to tell. The event occurred on Mount Kyllene in Arcadia; and his mother was **Maia**, which merely means 'Mother,' or 'Wet Nurse,' or 'Midwife'—all of which were commonly called Maia as a term of respect and affection. She was one of the Pleiades sisters; and Zeus slept with her, in the black of night, when Hera, his wife, was fast asleep. Kyllene herself nursed the new-born infant in her cave; and Maia, too, lived in a deep cave, for we are back again at the transition to the Olympian world: the good Maia is just the newer version of Kyllene. Hence, Hermes could bear her name, as **Kyllenios**: Kyllene is otherwise known as the mother of the Arcadian werewolf **Lykaon** by the pre-Olympian 'king' Pelasgos, who lent his name to the pre-Indo-European peoples of Arcadia. Hermes could also be called 'Maia's boy.' Maia wrapped the infant Hermes in swaddling clothes and laid him on a winnowing fan (**animus**). No sooner born, than he was off to help his brother Apollo—for the baby Hermes was a wonder child. It wasn't noon before he'd invented the lyre; and he managed to take care of Apollo before nightfall of the day that he was born. But before we let him get on with that adventure, we should make him first put his own house in order.

The Contest with Argos

When the contest was over, he added the name of **Argeiphontes** or 'Argos-killer' to his own, and he had helped his father Zeus, as well, get over the embarrassment of his former identity, just as he had his own. Hermes is the only Olympian who makes it thus explicit what his relationship to his former identity is: he has triumphed over his past as Argos, and it was a victory that aided Zeus also to escape from his own involvement in Minoan traditions; Hermes is

Hermes Killing Argos Panoptes (Red-figure amphora 490 BC, Museum für Kunst und Gewerbe, Hamburg)

not simply Hermes-Argos, like Pallas-Athena, but actually the 'killer' of Argos (**paradigms #1&2).**

Argos was a herdsman, and the cow he had to guard was something special. Zeus had made love to an aquatic nymph, the '**ios**-Lady' **Io**: he was not in his right mind at the time, but under a spell cast upon him by a 'love-bird' charm. Io was a priestess of Hera, or more precisely, she was what the 'Cow-Goddess' Hera was back in those earlier times. Hera accused Zeus of marital infidelity; and to hide what he had done, he disguised Io as a cow. But Hera was not to be deceived. She changed the 'love bird' (**Iunx**, a granddaughter of Hermes) into the wryneck bird; and then demanded custody of the cow who was Io. Hera gave this cow to Argos to watch.

Now Argos would be good at watching, for he had a hundred eyes that never slept: for which reason he was called 'All-Seeing' or **Panoptes**. Even his name Argos means 'Quick-eyes,' like a watchdog. Hermes, however, charmed Argos to sleep with the music of a flute, an instrument whose reedy sound was supposed to represent the transmuted hissing of serpents. Then he murdered Argos.

Hera took the eyes of Argos and placed them in the tail feathers of the peacock—which is her bird familiar: (Zeus had assumed the disguise of woodpecker to show Hermes the way to Argos). And the ghost of Argos became one of those insects of the Minoan Goddess, the stinging gadfly, which pursued the Cow Io, pecking and goading her with the poisons of her oestrual madness. Io, in heat, roamed the world, tormented by the ghost of Argos.

Finally, Io was responsible for establishing the African manifestation of Zeus. At the source of the Nile, amongst the black digital people of Ethiopia, who are called pygmies or a 'fistful,' Zeus laid his finger on Io; and she at last was delivered of a child. This was **Epaphos**, the 'Man of the Touch.' Epaphos became the father of Libya or northern Africa; and Io was worshipped in Egypt as the goddess Isis.

And Zeus owed it all to Hermes, who managed to sort out the proper roles, not only for himself as Argeiphontes, but also for Zeus and Hera. There were still African versions of a black Hermes, who was known as a little Kadmos or **Kadmilos**, one of the primordial men.

Rustling Cows from the Bonds of Death

In the evening of the day that he was born, which was the fourth of the month, just as the sun was setting, the infant Hermes set off to Olympus to steal the cattle of his brother Apollo. For they were still tending cows back in those days in the coastal plain of **Pieria** along the base of the mountain: Apollo was in one of his periods of servitude, keeping the flocks, in that place where the Muses would eventually be born; but in those days, the **Pierides** sisterhood could not yet really be termed the Muses, for Apollo didn't even get his lyre until the whole affair with Hermes had been settled, the next day.

Apollo once again was stuck in bondage. Argos (presumably not the same person that Argeiphontes disposed of) had a son called **Magnes**, who lent his name both to the fatal chthonic attraction of the 'magnet' and to that whole region, which was called Magnesia: it was here that the wild race of centaurs first was born. This Magnes was consort of a daughter of the 'Indomitable' **Admetos**, lord of that same Pherai sisterhood of 'Undertakers,' where Apollo often tends the flocks. The daughter was called something like 'Herds-woman,' **Perimele**; and she and Magnes had a son, **Hymenaios** or 'Wedded Bondage,' for whom poor Apollo was desperately in love, like another Hyakinthos. Apollo just could never break himself away from the House of Magnes.

While his brother was thus distracted, Hermes drugged the herd dogs and stole fifty cows. The manner was extremely clever. He made the cows walk backwards, and he himself wore oversized wicker shoes worn backwards—so that the footprints from the theft seemed to lead, not to where he'd taken the cows, but to where they'd been to begin with. And he drove them through a place called 'Gateway.' This was all a kind of magic to undo the binding that had brought the beasts into the chthonic fold.

Just one witness there was to his theft, as he went through 'Gateway.' This was an old man named **Battos**, a 'Stammering-Chatterbox.' Hermes warned him to keep the secret of what he had seen. At first he did, but Hermes checked to make sure, and the babbler divulged everything. Hermes turned him into a stone, a herm. ('Gateway' was on the way to Delphi, and eventually Apollo sent Battos to Libya: Battos founded Africa, receiving a clod of Earth from Triton himself, and was finally cured of his 'barbaric' stuttering voice. Thus Apollo and Hermes cooperated in transporting their own primordial selves back to their darker land.)

At the Gateway, the baby Hermes sacrificed two of the cows, making twelve portions—one for each of the Olympians, for he, this newest and last son of Zeus, was now one of them. As hungry as he was to taste the flesh, he didn't (for as an Olympian now, he shouldn't); but he burnt all twelve of the portions in proper ritual observance of an Olympian offering. Then he returned to his cave on Kyllene, and cuddled up in his crib like the baby that he still was.

Apollo discovered the ruse and tracked down the culprit, who denied everything—he was too young, as he claimed, even to know what a cow was. He even further disconcerted his elder brother by passing wind—or worse —, like any baby, while cradled in the other's arms.

Apollo hauled the infant off to Olympus to confront their father Zeus with this totally outrageous behavior. There, before the assembled Olympians, Hermes brazenly gave a demonstration of his shameless thievery and litigious effrontery, adding insult to injury by stealing Apollo's bow and arrows, right from under his nose. But the quarrel ended amicably, and the whole family was charmed by the baby's precocity.

Apollo fell in love with the lyre that Hermes had invented the day before; and he traded it for the cows he had lost. Henceforth, Hermes would tend the herds, instead of him. And Apollo also got rid of another embarrassing tie to his former identity: he handed over to Hermes the **Thriai** sisterhood: the 'Ecstatic' Gray-haired Minoan Bee-maidens who devined in the Korykian Cave on Parnassos—since now Apollo's sanctuary would be the newer Olympian site of the Delphoi brotherhood. The divination of the Thriai was reorganized under Hermes into a no longer ecstatic ritual, one simply based upon the interpretation of pebble tossing—for remember: the aniconic Hermes was, after all, just a pile of stones.

Apollo's Contest with Autolykos-Sisyphos

In future generations, Apollo and Hermes continued to face off; for Apollo needed a lot of help to overcome his past, and Hermes, who was the last of the Olympians and the latest in the grand tradition of thieving Promethean creatures, was ideally suited for the role of helper. Apollo's own sons, Ion and Asklepios, had effected some manner of mediation between Apollo's Olympian and chthonic identities: Ion bridged over the problem of matriliny, and Asklepios helped settle the fatal involvement with human sacrifice and his father's deadly drug problem. Hermes contributed three sons of his own as negotiators for a settlement of these same problems; all three represent darker aspects of Apollo, himself: the 'Truly Werewolf' **Autolykos**; the 'Pastor-Herdsman' **Pan**; and the 'Laurel-boy' **Daphnis**. And not only did Hermes father these three Apolline sons, but he offered them as surrogate substitutes—to play the role of 'enemy' in Apollo's continual battle with his own darker self.

For this role of surrogate 'enemy' to work, the son had to be not only the son of Hermes, but in some way a quasi-son of Apollo: hence Apollo and Hermes cooperate in the begetting of the surrogate. This is clearest in the case of **Autolykos**. Although he is a son of Hermes, he is actually the twin brother of a son of Apollo. And his 'enemy' **Sisyphos** is a cousin who was begotten just like another Hermes, but in a way that implicates Apollo and Artemis as the actual parents.

Let us look first at the 'Werewolf' **Autolykos**, who bears the 'Wolf' (**Lykos**) epithet of Apollo. Autolykos is Hermes' son, by a 'Snow-maiden' named **Chione**, a granddaughter of Prometheus-Epimetheus, in the first generation of new people who were created out of stone after the Great Flood; and yet, Autolykos might have been Apollo's son, instead: for both Apollo and Hermes slept with Chione on the same night. When Chione gave birth, it was to twins. The offspring at first had only a verifiable mother, but as it turned out, however, Autolykos must have been Hermes's son, for he became a notorious thief, like his father, when he grew up; while his twin brother **Philammon** became a musician, and hence took after Apollo, although it was the darker Apollo, the African one: for Philammon is the 'Beloved of Ammon,' and Ammon is the prophetic Libyan Zeus. (These dissimilar twins are similar to the Theban story of the musician Amphion and the warrior Zethos, who were sons of Zeus, although Lykos was their mother Antiope's mate.)

And, of course, if Apollo is involved in a sexual encounter, we might expect to find Artemis implicated as well. This is indeed the case in the making of Autolykos and Philammon: for Chione, their mother, fancied herself more beautiful than Artemis—and so, obviously, Artemis had to get rid of her. Artemis assigned the proper Minoan role to this other self who was a mountain snow nymph, a daughter of Earth, and mother of a wolf—and a prophetic African musician. The Olympian Artemis could never be allowed again to be Apollo's Mother and Goddess. Chione was changed into a hawk.

Now although this Philammon was the actual twin of Autolykos, it is with **Sisyphos** that the story continues. Sisyphos, although the son of neither Hermes nor Apollo, was born in a situation that suggests the spiritual sponsorship of them both, and again implicates Artemis, too. Sisyphos was a chthonic 'wind,' one of the Aeolid brothers, and hence a brother of Magnes: it was Magnes who was the father of Hymenaios, the boy (like Hyakinthos) for whom Apollo felt the fatal 'wedded' attraction while tending cows in bondage; and it was Magnes who discovered the magnet when his shoes were attracted to the ground; it was also Magnes who was turned into the magnet stone by the Goddess, in one of her identities; and it was Magnes, the son of Argos, who had one of the 'Undertaker' (Pherai) sisters, the 'Herds-woman,' as wife—but the Magnes who was brother of Sisyphos is supposedly not the same Magnes; just as the Argos of the Pherai sisters is supposedly not the same Argos whom Hermes Argeiphontes killed. (The confusion of identities results from the assimilation of various local versions of the same story: in particular, the Arcadian and Thessalian regions. It is only when a myth received a major telling through an important artist, that it tended to displace the local variants—making some myths seem more simple than they originally were.)

All these traditions seem to suggest that the darker identities of both Apollo and Hermes lurk in the background of Sisyphos. And this is true also in his mating: for Sisyphos took a Pleiad sister for wife—not Kyllene, who was the wet-nurse for Hermes (and chthonic substitute for his mother Maia); but the 'Bee-eater Maiden' **Merope**—otherwise known as a wife of Orion, Artemis's 'enemy' lover: Merope mourns equally as a Pleiad for what happened both to Orion and to Sisyphos.

In the case of the Autolykos-Philammon twins, both Hermes and Apollo are explicitly cited as mates for Chione-Artemis. The same pattern, less explicitly, underlies the begetting of Sisyphos, although as a single entity, he cannot easily be divided into the separate aspects of the twin sons of Apollo and Hermes: making him thus the perfect surrogate for the two Olympian brothers. Although Sisyphos, as husband of Merope and brother of Magnes, implicates the Apollo-Artemis dilemma, his nature, like that of Autolykos, must have been derived from Hermes: for Sisyphos is also a thief and notorious trickster. His name is synonymous with 'Cleverness,' although it is not Greek (and only falsely connected etymologically to **sophos** or 'wise').

Autolykos, the 'Wolf' (or Apolline Hermes' son) and Sisyphos, the 'Clever' (or Hermes-like Apolline son) were neighbors in Arcadia, and, true to form, they didn't get along very well: they were 'enemies' and like the twins Autolykos-Phil-ammon, they were dissimilar. Autolykos, like his father Hermes, rustled cows re-peatedly from Sisyphos, who, like Apollo, tended a famous herd of them. And Sisyphos, also like Hermes, played a trick with the cows' feet. What exactly the trick was is variously told, but it involved something like placing heavy ('mag-netic' or Earth-rooted) lead shoes on the cows, engraved with a brand that ac-cused Autolykos of being the thief. Although Autolykos had the gift from his father of being able to cause hallucinations (**entheogen**), namely to disguise the cows as whatever other animal he wished, Sisyphos (like another Apollo, tend-ing cows, in bondage) tracked down the cows' footprints and confronted Au-tolykos with the theft.

While Autolykos, like Apollo confronting the baby Hermes, was distracted by all the commotion of the ensuing litigation, Sisyphos seduced his daughter **Antikleia**. (She has a turncoat name, like Antiope: she is 'Reverse-fame,' for from her will come the pivotal change to the newer order.) The son she bore was the great heroic trickster **Odysseus**, who was only nominally the son of Antikleia's husband **Laertes**, but who derived his thieving nature from both his grandfa-ther Autolykos (the son of Hermes, not Apollo) and his father Sisyphos (the cousin of Hermes, and again, definitely not Apollo's son), as well as ultimately from his great-grandfather Hermes; and still further back, from Prometheus, himself, for Antikleia (through Chione) was a second generation descendant of that greatest of all tricksters, the creator of mankind. Odysseus was responsible for the ruse of the Trojan Horse, which would finally free Apollo from his fatal involvement with the city of Troy.

And through all of this, one can detect the hand of Hermes. Ultimately, he con-tributed not only his thieving nature to the creation of Odysseus, who would res-cue Apollo, but also the darker self of himself, which he shared with his brother Apollo: Sisyphos eventually tattled on Zeus, for one of his illicit love affairs with an aquatic nymph, the island of **Aigina**, who was a sister of **Thebe**; and Zeus condemned him to the underworld. Fixation to stone is the Hermes-like death, and Sisyphos eternally rolls a stone up a mountain, only to have it roll back down. The actual stone that Sisyphos must labor with was said to have been the stone that Zeus had disguised himself as in order to escape detection in this particular episode of marital infidelity; it was also said that Sisyphos had played one last trick to escape from the netherworld, and that Hermes had been called upon to haul him back down to Hades' chthonic realm. Hence, as with the af-fair with Io, Hermes once again successfully sorted out the proper role for his new Olympian father.

Although Sisyphos ended up confined to the underworld, his grave was hon-ored on the Isthmus of Corinth, and he had a shrine on the Acropolis of that orig-inally pre-Greek city. He was responsible for helping to change the world to the new order: in particular, at Corinth he created the new race of inhabitants out of mushrooms, substituting the Indo-European entheogen for the former tra-ditions of the Goddess and her shamanism.

Apollo's Contest with Pan

The 'Pastor' **Pan** was another son of Hermes, although many different women were named as his mother. (Hence, he is more patrilineal than matrilineal, which is a good sign. Another phallic son of Hermes displays the opposite potential: this is **Priapos**, who is portrayed as a grotesque, often dwarfish man, endowed with a gigantic erection; his mother was Aphrodite, but Hermes shares the honor of having fathered him, along with several other contenders.) Pan, too, like Autolykos-Sisyphos, represents the chthonic aspect of Apollo; and he is another contribution of Hermes to aid the transmutation of his troubled Olympian brother and that brother's twin sister. Pan looked like a satyr, with the ears, horns, tail and hind legs of a goat; and like a satyr, he was also ithyphallic, incredibly lecherous, and even boasted to have slept with every maenad that ever was—to facilitate that extraordinary feat, he could be multiplied into a whole brotherhood of **Panes**. It was Pan's role to negotiate a purification of Apollo's Dionysian contamination—similar to the surrogate role that Hermes and Dionysos play in taking over the responsibility for Apollo's Korykian Cave at Delphi. (Pan's maenadism was something you might see while tending herds, for the mad wildness of a stampeding herd was known as 'panic' fear.) Like Apollo with Daphne, Pan pursued a nymph called **Pithys**, who escaped by turning into the Dionysian 'Pine tree,' which is named after her. Another nymph, **Syrinx**, turned into a swamp of 'Reeds' to escape. Pan gathered a bunch of these reeds and fashioned the wind instrument called panpipes or syrinx, just as his father Hermes once had invented the lyre. It is in this latter episode with Syrinx that we see Pan more clearly in his role of Apollo's 'enemy.'

He challenged Apollo to a contest of music: he, on the panpipes; and Apollo, on the lyre. The mountain who acted as judge found the music of the lyre superior to that of the pipes. Only 'King' **Midas** (a son of the Goddess and a satyr, back in the Trojan homeland) dissented. Apollo made his ears grow like an ass's—an animal henceforth known for its lack of musical judgement, as well as its general stupidity. Midas tried to hide his deformity by wearing a turban—but his barber knew the truth, for Midas had to remove his turban to have his hair cut. The barber dared not reveal what he knew, but the urge to gossip got the better of him: so he dug a hole in the Earth and divulged his tattletale secret into it; then he buried it. A bed of reeds grew on the spot, and whenever the wind blows through them (as it regularly does, of course, also through the panpipes), the sound reveals the secret—that the mistaken judge has the ears of an ass.

Thus the 'wind' of Pan's nymph Syrinx forever testifies to the superiority of Apollo's Olympian lyre. Hermes not only invented the lyre for him, but he provided the son Pan, whose chthonic music was judged inferior.

Apollo's Contest with Daphnis

And finally, **Daphnis**, the 'Laurel-boy' who is the male equivalent of Apollo's Daphne. He, too, was a son of Hermes, this time in Sicily, rather than in Arcadia, like the other two. He helped Apollo purge himself of his Daphne involvement: as an infant, Daphnis was left in a grove of laurel, and he was raised by shepherds, pasturing their flocks. Pan was his teacher in music, and Apollo was in love with him, as was Artemis, too, with whom he used to hunt. Daphnis, obviously, is another Hyakinthos-Hymenaios boy-love of Apollo, and another of Artemis's beloved hunting companions—and in dying, as he must, this son of Hermes would save Apollo and Artemis from their fatal attraction to their darker selves, and each other.

His story is variously told, but he seems to have fallen in love with a nymph. For some reason, she was unattainable—either he or she was frigid, or he may have been unfaithful to her. He was blinded (and hence given inspired second sight), and spent his life singing pastoral poetry, which was his invention. Thus through him, the herding occupation of Apollo's periods of chthonic bondage was transmuted into higher music. When he finally died, he, too, like Sisyphos, achieved the Hermes type of primordial condition: Hermes made him into a stone (**paradigm #2**).

Apollo's Contest with Narkissos-Echo

This theme of (Artemis's) unattainable love occurs also with a third love of Pan. In addition to Pithys and Syrinx, Pan fell in love with **Echo**. Like the stammering Battos and the babbling barber and the tattling telltale Sisyphos, she, too, was a chatterbox, always distracting Hera, when Hera was trying to keep track of Zeus's many infidelities; for which reason, Hera reduced her voice to an echo, so that she could only repeat or stutter something back when it was said to her. Echo refused Pan's love; and Pan maddened the shepherds so that they tore her to pieces, leaving only her voice. She, too, was changed into a stone, a cliff echoing back her voice.

There was another way of telling the story in which Pan was not involved, nor are Artemis and Apollo directly mentioned, although the result is the same: to separate the twins from their role as lovers. This version also removes Apollo from his Minoan drug involvement, like the myths of Daphne and Hyakinthos.

Echo fell desperately in love with a frigid youth (like Daphnis) called **Narkissos** (Latin **Narcissus**) or 'Narcotic Flower' (**entheogen**: although not Greek, its etymology, which is assimilated into the Greek language from the Minoan tongue, is 'narcosis'). And some people claimed that it was because Narkissos would pay no attention to her that she wasted away to a mere echo. Or it could be that she was unattainable since she was only a voice (which was the only safe way for Artemis to appear to her boyfriends). As an Echo, all she could do was repeat back to him his own voice, as it bounced off her cliff face. (Remember that Apollo and Artemis were represented by the twin cliffs of the Shining Rocks at Delphi, and that a fall into the 'wind' from a cliff was the manner of an Apolline sacrifice.)

While Narkissos paid no heed to his own reflected voice, beckoning him to make love with the chattering stone maiden, he fell in love with his own reflection in a pool of water; bound irrevocably to this aquatic attraction (which some people claimed was his sister), he pined away, turning into the flower that bears his name, a flower that is not the same as the one that we now call by that name.

At his birth, it had been predicted that Narkissos would live to a ripe old age, provided he never came to know himself. 'Know thyself'—the challenge that Apollo at Delphi offered to all who consulted him.

In all these ways, Hermes, through his sons, negotiated the separation of Apollo and Artemis.

Hermaphroditos

With one more son, Hermes, the great negotiator, managed to mediate the whole problem of male versus female traditions. This was the son called **Hermaphroditos**, whom he had from a love affair with Aphrodite. The child was neither matrilineal nor patrilineal, but shared a name with both his parents.

An aquatic nymph called **Salmakis** fell in love with him in Anatolia; the waters from her fountain were said to render men effeminate. Hermaphroditos refused her advances, but she prayed to merge her body with his while he was bathing in her fountain. This came to pass. Salmakis and Hermaphroditos became the first hermaphrodite, a trick of nature: a single human bearing the signs of both the sexes. In Classical art of the fourth century, he/she was portrayed either as a young adolescent with developed female breasts, or as an Aphrodite with male genitals.

There were two other versions of this mediation. One was **Aphroditos**, a male-female, who took his name from his mother. The other was **Hermione**, which was one of the names for the Goddess as Demeter; she took her name from the herm stone.

* * * *

Review

Hermes (**Mercurius**) is the last of the Olympians: **Zeus** (**Jupiter**); **Hera** (**Juno**); **Ares** (**Mars**); **Hephaestus** (**Vulcan**); **Aphrodite** (**Venus**); **Poseidon** (**Neptunus**); **Hestia** (**Vesta**); **Athena** (**Minerva**); **Apollo**; **Artemis** (**Diana**); **Demeter** (**Ceres**)—who will be studied more fully later. Hermes bears the traditional title of his 'enemy' **Argos**, as **Argeiphontes**. It is Hermes' role to put the finishing touches on the mediating transmutations that produced the rest of his Olympian family: hence, he functions as an **animus** (or **psychopompos**), making him often the male counterpart to Athena, the **anima** (or **promachos**). He seems to be intimately involved, in particular, in rescuing his brother Apollo from his 'enemy' identities, since the Apollo-Artemis duo are always marginal or unstable in their newer Olympian manifestations—the most perfect exemplars, since they have the most sinister pasts to live down.

Hermes has the following attributes: **caduceus** (which was originally the emblem of his role as herald or messenger); wings (either on his hat or shoes, or on his caduceus); pillar (**herm**, since he was originally just a pile of stones: although this represents his Earth-phallus role, he never is himself shown as ithyphallic—although this is the way his sons **Pan** and **Priapos** are always portrayed; even on the herm, although the genitals are prominently displayed, the penis is not erect); brimmed hat of a traveler, characteristic, as well, of his male human age-mates; either bearded or not; sometimes his Dionysian nature is represented by a leopard skin: he took the infant Bakchus-Dionysos to Nysa. The caduceus represents his serpent nature, as well as his botanic and entheogenic manifestations, but no particular plant is associated with him, except for the **moly**, which occurs only in one episode of the *Odyssey* epic as an antidote to chthonic poisons. Hermes is a **trickster**, and as an Olympian, he has transmuted thieving into beneficial social functions: merchandising, legal oratory.

His sons function to further his helpful role in bringing about the stability of the Olympian order: **Autolykos**; **Pan**; **Daphnis**; **Hermaphroditos**.

Myths: **Birth of Hermes Kyllenios** (mother **Maia**; wet-nurse **Kyllene**)
    Invention of the Lyre
    Theft of Apollo's Cows
    Contest with Argos Panoptes
    Theft of the Cows of Sisyphos and Seduction of
        Autolykos's Daughter Antikleia: Mother of Odysseus
    Contest of Pan and Apollo
    Death of Daphnis
    Seductions of Pan: Pithys; Syrinx; Echo
    Death of Narkissos

For Discussion and Further Study

The story of Hermes' theft of Apollo's cows is told in the Fourth Homeric Hymn (to Hermes). Read it and consider, in particular, the following:

What aspects of the portrayal of the infant Hermes do you think are not so much traditional or symbolic, but taken from actual observation of infant behavior? What would you identify as the former, the mythopoetic?

How does the account given in the Hymn differ from the composite and summarized account presented in this chapter?

The crow who guarded Koronis was also a telltale chatterbox, like Battos, the barber, Sisyphos, and Echo. What do you think the theme of the tattler means?

Part III
The Liminal Hero

With the cast of twelve Olympians now in place, we will turn our attention to the role of the human participants in the drama of Classical mythology. Or more precisely, we will look at the males, the heroes, before examining more closely the goddess **Demeter** and her relationship to her chthonic manifestations, **Persephone** and **Hekate**—which will introduce us eventually to the fuller significance of the heroines, the human participants who are female.

We have already seen several of the heroes lurking in the sidelines, as the Olympian and chthonic worlds sorted out the terms of the truce that allowed them both to coexist. These are men like **Perseus**, who laid the foundations for the newer civilization of the city of Mycenae; and **Theseus**, who did the same sort of thing for Athens and helped Apollo to overcome his sinister involvement with the Minoan labyrinth; and **Herakles**, who helped Zeus subdue the Goddess, wherever she was found; and **Odysseus**, who played the final trick that rescued Apollo from his fatal Trojan involvement. All of these heroes were winners. But there have been others as well: men like **Hippolytus** and **Orion** and **Lykos** and **Pentheus** and **Asklepios**, and so on—men who were losers, but still heroic: for these heroes, losing was a more important role for them to fulfill, since their winning would have derailed the process of the great reconciliation that allowed for the emergence of figures who are more essential than they—their betters, for whose good they are sacrificed.

We will study first three heroes: **Perseus**, **Herakles**, and **Theseus**. For each, we will see that the same basic story is told: the hero is **liminal**; he stands at a threshold (or **limen**) between two worlds, at a moment of crisis for his identity—whether he belongs to the older order of Minoan traditions, or to the newer evolving order of the Olympian age. The story is of a journey across that threshold—in either direction, into either world. In each, he would be a different person: it all depends on which is more essential—every hero can be both a winner and a loser. There are really, therefore, two versions of every hero, himself and his 'enemy' self (**paradigm #1**). The journey, into whichever world, tells the story of the confrontation of these two heroic identities, leading to the defeat of one and the victory of the other and their reconciliation, since they both are the same single hero who stood in the doorway before the journey began (**paradigm #2**). For this journey of confrontation, the liminal hero will require helpers (if he is to be the winner) or deceptive disablers, false helpers (if he is to be the loser). These helper-disablers are the figures we have identified as **animus** and **anima**. They represent the 'enemy' (male and female) transmuted into his companions for the journey (**paradigm #3**). Typical in this role are **Athena** as **promachos** ('leader for the battle') and **Hermes** as **psychopompos** ('spiritual guide'), although others, both divine and human, can also play this role. Ultimately, the hero's winning or losing is not a private affair, but has an effect on the stability of the Great Reconciliation.

For each hero, we will see that the liminality of his identity involves an ambiguity about his parents: was his father someone from the new world or the old; and the same for his mother. And as for him, when it is all over, could we say he is more a matrilineal or patrilineal child?

Sometimes the story is told not about a single hero, but about a whole corporate endeavor of heroes, but the pattern will be the same. We will look at the heroes **Achilleus** (**Achilles**) and **Odysseus**, and the story of the **Trojan War**. Two earlier occurrences of such corporate endeavors were also told: the **War of the Seven Against Thebes**, which will involve the hero **Oidipous** (**Oedipus**); and the **Voyage of the Ship Argo** or the **Journey of the Argonauts**, which involves the hero **Iason** (**Jason**).

Chapter VII
Perseus: Making the New Mycenae

🔱

It was from Africa that Perseus's family came—although, since he was conceived under the earth, perhaps it was just a matter of reaching down to the chthonic realm to find his mother. And she was one of a sisterhood of **Danaids** (or **Danaides**). And as to what their name meant: it may not be Greek, but the ancient grammarians thought it had something to do with 'Corpses,' 'Death,' or Daphne. But there were good signs, too. Only one of those fifty Danaid sisters was willing to accept the dominance of a husband in marriage (all forty-nine of the others murdered their mates on their marriage night); and Perseus's mother was descended from that single turncoat: and, moreover, she was called **Danae**, after her male ancestor, **Danaos**, who lent his name to the new people of Greece, for **Danaans** was one of the ways the Greeks called themselves in those early days, when they were just beginning to take over control of the Goddess's lands. They could even imagine that the word had something to do with Zeus, who sometimes was called 'Dan.'

As for **Perseus** himself, there were darker versions of his identity, too: his name means the 'Destroyer,' a good name for a warrior, but also for a Lord of Death; but he was—probably—the son of Zeus, which is a more optimistic sign for his identity. And the culmination of his heroic career was to be the rescue of **Athena** from her sinister past as the **Medusa** of the **Gorgon** sisterhood; not only that, but Perseus was to prove of service to **Hermes**, too: **Argos** became his kingdom, and Hermes **Argeiphontes**, like Pallas Athena, became his companion and friend. Perseus even rescued an African Medusa, **Andromeda**, from her chthonic and aquatic consort; they named one of their own daughters after Athena as the 'Gorgon-killer' **Gorgophone**. He also was responsible for reorganizing the traditions of the **Mykenai** sisterhood of Mycenae, reinterpreting its name so that henceforth it would conform to the new shamanic customs of the Indo-Europeans and their entheogen, the sacred mushroom or **mykes**.

The career of Perseus is shadowed by a mysterious double of his own identity: **Bellerophontes** (or **Bellerophon**), the 'Killer of Belleros,' a name like Argeiphontes, the 'Killer of Argos.' Bellerophontes was a grandson of **Sisyphos**—who, as we have already seen, did the same sort of reorganization for the city of Corinth, where the new race of people was metamorphosed out of mushrooms. Bellerophontes and Perseus are two versions of the same hero. They both shared a common other name as **Chrysaor**, the 'Golden Sword.' And both of them have the same magical horse, **Pegasos**, who was born from the slain Medusa. And both Perseus and Bellerophontes, after an initial successful career, will have unfortunate deaths at Argos.

As to who this Belleros was whom Bellerophontes killed, we can only guess, for the name is not Greek and has no known etymology—unless it is related to the Phoenician **Ba'al**, which means 'Lord.' Obviously, Belleros should be someone like Argos, whom Hermes Argeiphontes killed; or someone like the consort of the Gorgon, whom Perseus and Gorgophone killed; someone like the 'African' monster from whom Perseus rescued his bride Andromeda.

Belleros, that is to say, must be the 'enemy' of Bellerophontes and Perseus; an Argos, for Hermes to slay; a primordial Triton-Poseidon, for Athena to be rescued from; even, perhaps an Artemis's Apollo, for Hermes to lend his aid to (**paradigm #1**).

The Contest of Danaos and Aigyptos-Argos

The family of Perseus goes back to twin sons who were born to the African **Belos** (a name like Belleros and which, in this case, seems definitely to be Lord Ba'al). This Belos was the offspring of Poseidon and Libya (granddaughter of Io and daughter of Epaphos, who was Io's son via the digital pygmies of Ethiopia); and Belos was himself the twin brother of **Agenor** (the 'Valiant'), from whom would come the 'foreign' and 'African' founder of the new Thebes (**Kadmos**, whose story we will tell later). These twin sons of Belos, who was twin of Agenor, were **Aigyptos** (after whom Egypt was named) and **Danaos** (after whom Greece was to be named); between them, they divided up the lands of Africa and the Near East, the traditional lands of the other world and the primordial past.

Their mother was aquatic, one of the Nile sisters, although further back, she was descended from a sisterhood of ash trees, the **Meliai**, and a river not in Egypt, but in Greece: **Inachos**, who flows through the plain of Argos, and was its first 'king.' (The Meliai or 'Honey-trees' secrete a sweet gum or manna, which was reputed to be intoxicating, or hence an entheogen; the grove of sisters first sprouted from the drops of blood that fell to Earth from the castrated genitals of Ouranos; they are sisters of the dread chthonic 'Furies' or **Erinyes**; and all these sisterhoods are sisters of Aphrodite, although it was only she who was admitted into the new Olympian family.) The combining of Nile and Inachos in the genealogy of Danaos and Aigyptos is not surprising, for all rivers flow from beneath the ground out of a common, interconnected subterranean reservoir, which is ultimately **Ocean** himself, the great river that cradles and encircles the inhabited continent: beyond the frontier of Ocean and the sisterhood of **Oceanides** lies the other world.

The twin sons of Belos typically did not get along well with each other. Aigyptos had fifty sons; and Danaos, fifty daughters, the **Danaids**, named after their father, although their mother was one of the Meliai sisters, and they could have borne that name, instead. In an attempt to patch up their differences, Aigyptos proposed that his fifty sons marry the fifty daughters of his brother. Danaos refused, suspecting that the males would prove to be chthonic consorts of his daughters, escorting them into Death. He took the 'African' Athena with them and fled to Greece, landing at the city of Argos (which lies on the shore, at the broad end of the triangular plain that stretches inland back to Mycenae at its vertex), with the fifty sons of Aigyptos in hot pursuit.

The 'king' of Argos at this time was, as we might expect, apparently a Hermes-like figure, a trickster named the 'Joker' (**Gelanor**). He at first laughed at the preposterous idea that Danaos take over the 'kingship' of Argos. But in the night, a wolf attacked the cows in the Argive herd, killing their bull; and Danaos recognized that the wolf was really Apollo: and he dedicated the famous shrine of Apollo Lykeios at Argos, interpreting the omen as a sign that at this spot the new Apollo had killed the bull/wolf of his former identities—no longer tending the herds in the bondage of Death. As it turned out, both Argos and Danaos contributed their names to the naming of the new race of Pelasgian peoples (or pre-Greeks of the mainland, like Minoan for Crete), for the Greeks called themselves **Argives**, as well as **Danaans**.

As to how Danaos and the Danaids got to Argos from Africa, the story could be told of his journey across the Mediterranean. But there were other more direct routes, for Argos at that time was, of course, a stronghold of the Goddess, and there were several sacred entrances in the environs there that led straight down into the subterranean aquatic world.

In a story similar to Athena's contest with Poseidon for control of Attica, it was told that the plain of Argos was suffering from a drought because of a contest between Poseidon and the primordial Hera, who was the Goddess in that land, with him as her consort, before the coming of Zeus. (Hera was always to remain the powerful deity at Argos, like Athena at Athens.) In the Argive version of Poseidon's contest, the plain has been awarded to Hera, instead of him; and he has retaliated by causing all the water to dry up from the land. One of the Danaid sisters was named **Amymone** (the 'Flawless,' but perhaps she was called that to fend off the more obvious truth of her chthonic identity, like the names of Artemis as Kalliste, Britomartis, and the other 'good ladies'). Amymone, while hunting a deer—just like an Artemis, roused a sleeping satyr (or primitive Apollo?), who tried to sexually abduct her; but Poseidon rescued Amymone, hurling his trident into the rock—and then, he, instead of the satyr, slept with her. As Poseidon's mate, it is as if Amymone had simply popped up through one of the subterranean channels to get from 'Africa' to Argos: for when it all was over, Poseidon instructed Amymone to pull the trident from the rock; and as she did, the famous spring of Amymone flowed from the three holes left by the prongs of the trident, ending the drought—as sign of the reconciliation of the new Poseidon and Hera, a Poseidon who had redeemed the Meliad daughter of Danaos from a chthonic and maenadic Artemis-like involvement. Amymone bore a son to Poseidon. This was the hero **Nauplios**, the 'Navigator,' who settled his African

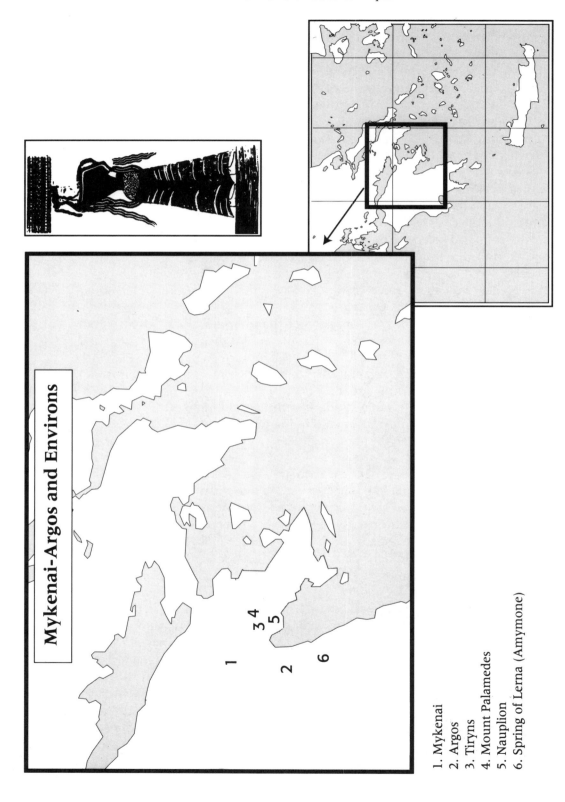

Mykenai-Argos and Environs

1. Mykenai
2. Argos
3. Tiryns
4. Mount Palamedes
5. Nauplion
6. Spring of Lerna (Amymone)

kin at Nauplion, on the other side of the bay of Argos. Through him, the sinister aspects of Ocean were transmuted into the art of navigation—although there was another Nauplios who lured ships to disaster (**paradigms #1&2**). Nauplios was to have a heroic career of his own that would pit him against another version of the Gorgon Medusa, in the form of the witch **Medea**; for he sailed on the **Argo** ship, with the crew of **Iason** (**Jason**) and the **Argonauts**.

Even though Apollo Lykeios, Artemis, Hera, and Poseidon had all changed upon the coming of Danaos to Argos-Gelanor, remnants of the old order remained for future generations to cope with. It was here at Amymone's triple spring at **Lerna** that Hera's terrible water monster called the **Hydra** still lurked, waiting for the day when the hero **Herakles** (whose family dynasty traced descent from neighboring **Tiryns**) eventually would come to complete the conquest of the lands for the newer order of Olympians, destroying the ancient power of the Goddess Hera.

The Birth of Perseus

But Amymone was not the only turncoat amongst the Danaids. There was another way of telling the story, and this one leads to the birth of the hero **Perseus**.

At Argos, Danaos agreed to the marriage of his daughters to the sons of Aigyptos—in order to avoid the drought, but he instructed them all to murder their husbands on the bridal night. All but one did as their father had commanded. This time it was **Hypermnestra** (the 'Great Bride') who brought about a reconciliation. She spared her husband **Lynkeus** (the good-sighted 'Lynx'). Her father brought her to trial at Argos, but she was acquitted: in commemoration of the judgement, Hypermnestra made dedications to Artemis and the Wolf Apollo. Her acquittal ratified that she was a woman of the new order, who, like another Alkestis, considered herself closer to her wedded husband than to the family of her own blood kin. The other Danaids were condemned to the underworld, where they eternally attempt to draw water with sieves for their nuptial bath. The corpses of the dead African husbands were tossed into the waters of Lerna. The water leaking from the Danaids' sieves oozes upwards into this world to feed the 'hundred' springs that are the heads of the Lernean (or Lernaean)Hydra, three of which form the fountain of the Flawless Amymone.

From Hypermnestra and Lynkeus, in the third generation, was born **Danae**, who was to be the mother of Perseus.

Before proceeding with the story of Perseus's birth, we should learn what sort of thing to notice in a mythical genealogy. The traditions would at first have been an oral history, of importance mainly to the family involved; but to publicize and preserve it, the family would have commissioned musical-poetic-danced performances for private and public (often religious) celebrations. Both the oral transmission from generation to generation and the poetized codifications would inevitably open up the probability of fanciful distortion, but the factual validity of the account would not be questioned, especially since many aspects of the

Genealogical Chart: Perseus

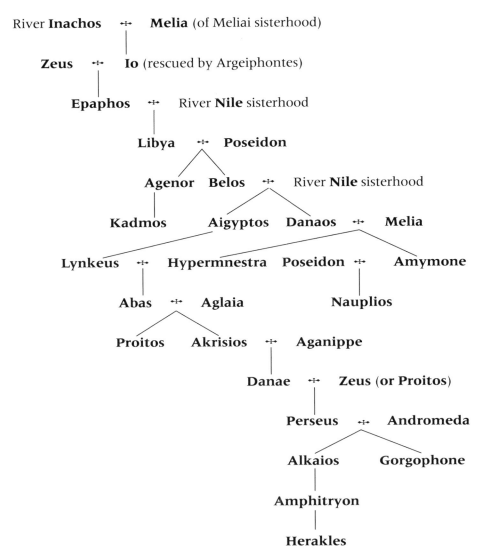

River **Inachos** ⚭ **Melia** (of Meliai sisterhood)

Zeus ⚭ **Io** (rescued by Argeiphontes)

Epaphos ⚭ River **Nile** sisterhood

Libya ⚭ **Poseidon**

Agenor Belos ⚭ River **Nile** sisterhood

Kadmos Aigyptos Danaos ⚭ **Melia**

Lynkeus ⚭ **Hypermnestra Poseidon** ⚭ **Amymone**

Abas ⚭ **Aglaia Nauplios**

Proitos Akrisios ⚭ **Aganippe**

Danae ⚭ **Zeus (or Proitos)**

Perseus ⚭ **Andromeda**

Alkaios Gorgophone

Amphitryon

Herakles

genealogy were verified by the physical and sacred topography of the environs. The account would eventually become the source material for antiquarian historians, who would attempt to interpret and regularize the genealogy to conform with their preconceptions about the nature of their culture. Although the genealogy was their view of reality, we need not accept it as entirely consistent with our own views of reality. For one thing, the historians would have assumed that there was a continuous descent through the male line and they often try to bridge over instances of disjunction or interruption; but even more distorting is the assumption that the genealogy is patrilineal, instead of the actual situation, which was one of transition from female lineage to male, and of the realignment of the entire divine contingent of participants in the events.

The following items can be noted in the genealogy of Perseus's family, whether Perseus, himself, ever actually lived or not.

1. Hermes plays a dominant role. Argos (one of his former identities) and Gelanor (the trickster) are early 'kings' of Argos. The ship Argo has the same name: it was built by an Argos. Even though we are not told that 'king' Argos is the same one that Argeiphontes killed, the name is supposed to imply 'quick-sightedness:' hence the epithet of Panoptes or 'All Seeing.' The same characteristic occurs in Lynkeus, the 'Lynx-man,' an animal notorious for its eyesight—and even as a cure for bad sight. Even Athena at Argos has this epithet of 'Sharp-sight' (Oxyderkes): a son of Nauplios dedicated a temple to her as Oxyderkes for the gift of sight. The sight implies the rescue from darkness, the vision of a newer kind of sight, a newer order involving different ways of seeing: hence, in all probability, the involvement of entheogens in the transition from one world order to another.

2. The genealogy involves repeated instances of sisterhoods of water nymphs: the Meliai with River Inachos and again with Belos, the Danaids with the sons of Aigyptos; and of sacred marriages with Poseidon: Libya, Amymone, and probably Hera, too (in the story of their contest for Argos).

3. Prominent is the connection of the family to Africa (as Libya, Egypt, Ethiopia, and the Near East), but this does not necessarily imply that it actually came from Africa. Io, after all, came from Argos; and one of Perseus's sons, **Perses**, was considered the ancestor of the Persian kings (of modern Iran). The African world is a metaphor for the primordial world, which is synonymous with the chthonic realm; and Africa and Greece are interchangeable, until the genealogy eventually manages to sort out the proper roles for each.

4. Perseus and his daughter Gorgophone (and son Perses) probably indicate that Perse was one of the names for the (Athena-Hera-Artemis) Goddess; and Perseus, originally her matrilineal consort. Indeed, **Persephone** (or 'Killer of Perse') is what the Death Goddess was called when she was made, like Athena and Artemis, into a daughter of Zeus. And there was a Perse in the Oceanides sisterhood, who was mate of Apollo and mother by him of a Perses.

5. The genealogy has two instances of the **warring twins** pattern (like Amphion and Zethos at Thebes): Aigyptos and Danaos; and, as we will see, Proitos and Akrisios. This warring is an expression of the hero and 'enemy' paradigm (**#1**). In a hero like Perseus, the battle is fought between the two aspects of the single hero's liminal identity: Destroyer of Perse or Perse's man.

6. The primordial past in this geneaology has maenadic aspects, synonymous with the African and chthonic worlds. Hence, Nauplios was Poseidon's son, but almost begotten by a satyr, instead. Lynkeus as a Lynx is not only quick-sighted, but also an animal that draws the cart of Dionysos-Bakchos. And Proitos, as we will see, is father of a maenadic sisterhood and a Pentheus figure (**Megapenthes**).

7. Other aspects of the genealogy recall situations familiar in Minoan-Pelasgian traditions: the bovine Io; Proitos is going to have a bovine wife; Apollo, the 'Wolf-killer,' attacks the bull in the cow herd of Argos.

Let us continue now with the story of how Perseus was born. To Lynkeus and Hypermnestra was born a son, **Abas**, a name without clear etymology (unless it means 'Not-Walk,' stationary like a herm), otherwise known only as a chthonic male in Persephone's house. His bride was 'Joy' (**Aglaia**, perhaps too optimistic not to imply her opposite). In any case, the twins she conceived were so antithetical in nature that they began fighting with each other while still in her womb.

She bore **Proitos** ('Primordial') and his brother **Akrisios** ('Injudicious'). They were supposed to alternately share the rule of the 'kingdom' they inherited. But Akrisios refused. Proitos fled to the Apolline 'Wolf-land' of Anatolian Lycia, and took the 'king' **Iobates**' daughter as a wife. She was called **Sthenoboia** (or 'Bovine Strength'); her father Iobates' name, if Greek, means that like another Argos he 'Walks Io,' and hence is the herder of the cow that is his wife (perhaps that he does what Proitos's father Abas didn't do). From Sthenoboia, Proitos begot three daughters, the **Proitides** sisterhood, and the Bacchic son **Megapenthes** ('Great Suffering'). He may have also slept with his brother Akrisios's daughter, **Danae**.

Proitos returned with a 'foreign' army. A great war was fought between the rival forces of the twin brothers—without a decisive victory. The brothers had to divide the lands. Akrisios took Argos; and Proitos, Tiryns (which had been founded by the son of Argos, Tirynx, and named after him, in the pre-Greek language): its famous fortification walls were reputed to be the work of primordial craftsmen, seven Kyklopes, who were called the **Gasterocheires** or digital men with the attribute of being the 'Hands for the Belly-Womb.'

Akrisios in neighboring Argos had a 'Gentle-horse' named **Aganippe** for wife: the (night)mare attribute of Aganippe does not bode well, and even her 'gentleness' is perhaps too optimistic to be true, since it is associated with the 'easy death' that Apollo and Artemis might afford. She was, however, a suitable daughter-in-law for the Danaid Hypermnestra, for Aganippe became a famous fountain, flowing out from Mount Helicon into the River Parnassos of Apollo's Delphic sanctuary on Mount Parnassos. The fountain of Aganippe was sacred to the nine Muses and was said to inspire the higher arts of music and dance. It was not always such, however; it changed its nature only after the good horse **Pegasos** was liberated from its mother, the Medusa, by Perseus—where it touched the Earth on Helicon, there flowed the 'Horse Spring' **Hippokrene**. Other tellers of the story knew of Perseus's mother more simply as a **Eurydike**, the chthonic 'Maiden of Justice,' a Persephone figure who made a suitable mate for her 'Injudicious' consort.

The neighboring households of Argos and Tiryns were, therefore, equally chthonic. But from Akrisios was born the daughter who would become the turncoat, to turn the worlds around: **Danae**, the last of the Danaids and named for her great-great-grandfather, and from a lineage surviving only via the earlier turncoats Hypermnestra and Amymone. This is a typical feature of the hero's mother: since he is **liminal** (or has a dual identity), in each of his two potential identities, he takes after his turncoat mother, looking either backward to her primordial world, or forward to the Olympian age.

Akrisios had this Danae as his daughter, but he managed to beget no sons. There was no patrilineal male to inherit the 'kingdom.' When he inquired of Apollo's oracle at Delphi, he was told that he would never have a son—and that Danae would conceive a son who would kill him. This eventually did happen, in the familiar manner of the accidental murder (like Apollo's murder of Hyakinthos, and Athena's murder of Pallas): in a game of discus throwing in Apollo's Thessalian homeland to celebrate the reconciliation of Perseus and his grandfather, the missile accidentally killed Akrisios, striking him on the foot. This was the way that Perseus was to prove of service not only to himself, but to Apollo (the consort of Perse) in ridding them both of their own chthonic pollution.

Their 'enemy' Akrisios had done his best to keep this from happening. To prevent the birth of his grandson, Akrisios buried Danae in a subterranean bronze chamber, like a tomb—or the House of Persephone, complete with a guardian bitch at its gateway. But despite his efforts, Danae conceived a son. Either her uncle Proitos was his father, or Zeus. This, too, is typical of the hero myth: just as the hero's liminality is expressed by the dual potential identities of his turncoat mother, the father, too, is in doubt—even more so than the mother, for the child does come physically from her womb, however ambiguous her nature may be, but no one can prove who the father was: it depends on what kind of world the child is born into. The hero thus has **two fathers**, one for each of his dual liminal identities.

Proitos visited his niece in her subterranean prison, just barely escaping with his own life: if Perseus was begotten by him, he was clearly chthonic, both from the place of conception and the background of the inseminator. But Zeus visited Danae also, in the form of a golden fall of rain, celestial water for the former Danaid: if Perseus was begotten by him, he is the opposite of the other possibility. But he will have to prove it by what he does: he will have to contest his 'enemy' or 'enemies,' who are his other self (**paradigm #1**). It is harder for him than for a god or goddess, for he must bear the 'enemy' always within himself. And even with Zeus as one of his two fathers, there is always the possibility that it was the Zeus of the olden times, rather than the Olympian Zeus. After all, the celestial rainfall had to seep beneath the Earth to reach Danae; and some tellers of the story knew a version that made it not rain, but a golden fall of snow, in which case, the conception occurred in the maenadic season, and he would then be not like another Dionysos, born of Zeus, but his Bacchic avatar—another **Megapenthes**, the son of Proitos, who fathered the **Proitides** sisterhood, as well.

There are always two ways of telling the hero's story, one for each of his two identities. In one, he is the winner in the contest with his 'enemy.' In the oth-

(above) Danae, Receiving the Golden Rainfall (by the Triptolemos painter 490-480 BC, Hermitage Museum, St Petersburg)
(below) Perseus Receives the Challenge to Heroism, with Both Versions of his Liminal Identity Present ('The Call of Perseus' by Sir Edward Burne-Jones 1877, Municipal Museum, Southampton)

er, the **tragic** version, he is the loser, losing because there can be only one winner, and it is more essential for the evolution of the world that his 'enemy' prove to be the winner.

In addition to sorting out the two possibilities of the hero's liminal identities, his heroic career, whether successful or tragic, will have a stabilizing effect upon the evolving world order: whether he wins or loses, the deities are the ultimate beneficiaries, they and the culture they preside over.

The Contest with the Gorgon Medusa

In the contest with the Gorgon Medusa, Perseus won, vindicating his Olympian heritage and saving Athena and Hermes from their former roles at Argos; and also rescuing Apollo, for whom the obliging Hermes once again acts as a convenient stand-in for his troubled brother.

Danae gave birth to Perseus in the subterranean chamber. She had a wet nurse with her, for the child was to belong to two worlds: and a wet nurse nourishes another woman's baby with the milk that she cannot offer to her own child, who died at birth. There were toys buried also in the chamber, as was the custom—so that a dead child might still play in the other world.

Akrisios heard the laughter coming from beneath the earth, and exhumed Danae and her entourage. When he discovered his former lack of good judgement, he did it all over again. He had a chest constructed, imprisoned Danae and her baby in it, and set them adrift on the Ocean—to send them to their death.

That makes it two times that the baby Perseus had trouble separating himself from his mother.

They came ashore on the rocky little island of Seriphos, in the group of Aegean islands called the Cyclades, a circle of islands around Delos, the birthplace of Apollo. Why Seriphos? Perhaps it was prominent in the cult of the Goddess— we can only assume; but if you wanted to send someone to Hell on earth, Seriphos is the island for you: the Romans used the barren place later for a penal colony.

Seriphos, at that time, was ruled by two **warring brothers**, **Polydektes** (the host who 'Receives All') and his primordial brother **Diktys** (the 'Net-man Fisherman')—both appropriate characteristics for chthonic lords. Diktys was the better of the two: it was he and his brotherhood of satyrs who netted the chest and brought it ashore. He is, of course, the male complement of Diktynna, the 'Good Maiden' Britomartis-Artemis who was rescued from her deadly fall by the fishermen at the base of the cliff: for both Diktys and Diktynna, the netting is a transmutation from more sinister aspects of spinning, such as we saw in the contest of Athena with the spider-spinstress Arachne.

There, on this island of Seriphos, Perseus grew to puberty, under Athena's care—although she had yet to prove which Athena she was, for she was the Goddess of this other-worldly place. And Diktys and his satyric brotherhood of the Dionysian wilderness performed the tradition-al role of tutelage for the young hero, instructing him in the knowledge of the primitive world. And Danae, as a slave in bondage, was detained in the hospitality of Polydektes' 'kingdom.'

When it was time for Perseus to chose a mate, Polydektes, also, de-cided at last to consummate a union—ultimately with Danae, the daughter of 'Gentle Horse' Aganippe; although another horsewoman is cit-ed (**Hippodameia**) by those fami-lies who wanted to work their genealogies into this illustrious lin-eage: but amongst the women with this name, there was a Hippodameia (or 'Wedded Horse') who was Queen

Gorgon Medusa, Head with Lizards and Vine (Attic amphora handle decoration, by the Amasis painter c. 540 BC, Musée du Louvre, Paris)

Decapitation of the Gorgon Medusa, with Perseus Dressed as Hermes, and Gorgon Head in the Kibisios (Red-figure vase from Capua, British Museum, London)

of Argos, although the more famous Hippodameia was responsible for the **warring brothers** who would eventually contest the nearby 'kingdom' of Mycenae. But a (night)mare, in any case, was Polydektes' choice for mate.

And it was his choice also for Perseus. All the guests for the wedding had to bring a (night)mare to the wedding party. Perseus's assignment was to fetch the **Medusa** (**Medousa** or 'Queen') of the **Gorgon** sisterhood of 'Bogey Women'— for the revel that would confirm his chthonic potential.

Hermes as **animus** (or **psychopompos**) and Athena as **anima** (or **promachos**, to use the Greek terms) went with Perseus on the quest. Each is a transmutation of the 'enemy' into a helper (**paradigm #3**). Athena, until the completion of this heroic task, was still the Gorgon Medusa; and the power of the Medusa's 'sight' was to turn Perseus into stone, like the herm of Hermes' former role as consort of the Goddess.

Each contributed an essential element toward Perseus's victory. Athena advised him not to look at the Medusa, but to look instead at her.

And Hermes provided him with a special purse, the **kibisios**, into which he should put the head of the Medusa, after he had cut it off—so that he could keep it hidden from sight until he needed it as a weapon to turn his opponents to stone, as he might have been, himself. This was the first use of the kibisios purse: it continued to be employed in Classical times to store the secret dangerous antique relics of the old Mother Goddess religion; they were handled and viewed only on special religious occasions, commemorating the mediation between the old and new world orders. In the pre-Olympian age, Perseus would have been the herm-like consort of the Athena Medusa; hence, it was only fitting that Hermes' aid also included allowing Perseus to dress up in the attributes of his own transmuted identity: Perseus wore Hermes' winged sandals (or perhaps only one of them) and his traveler's hat for the contest with the Medusa.

And there was a trick also involved, like Hermes' trick of the backward foot-prints of the rustled cows. Perseus would find his enemy, not by looking at her—which would prove fatal, but by looking at her reflection in his shield, her reverse image, her turncoat transmutation, her opposite—which was Athena. Anyone who has tried to use a mirror to guide an action knows how confusing this can be.

So, off they went: Perseus, with Hermes and Athena. But where could you expect to find this Medusa? At the **limen**, the threshold frontier between realms; at the **axis mundi** or world axis, the sacred tree in its magical garden. This special place could be found in the far East, where the sun rises; or the far West, where it sets. Or South, to Africa and Ethiopia and Libya. Or north, to Thessaly, and beyond, to the Hyperboreans. Or, more simply, straight down, right beneath where you are: beneath Argos and Tiryns and Mycenae; right down under Seriphos, to the chthonic foundations of the Earth. The four cardinal points converge eventually back there.

And these places are in the keeping of the sisterhoods. Perseus had to confront a trinity of triple sisterhoods, thrice three. First there were the fountain nymphs, **Naiads**, the 'Sisters of the Flow,' who are another version of the **Danaids**: straight on down through the holes welling with subterranean waters was the pathway—it was they, in some tellings, who lent Perseus the accoutrements for his disguise as Hermes, that let him seep on down.

Then the 'Gray Witches' or **Graiai**. Much worse than the maidens of the fountain. These three were the guardians at the entrance to the subterranean cavern, perhaps beneath Seriphos, itself (also known as the magical garden: of **Kisthene** or the 'Rockrose') where the Medusa lurked—unless it was underwater, for there are many ways of telling the story, although they are all essentially the same. The Graiai had just a single eye (**entheogen**) amongst them, sharing it back and forth; they are like the single-eyed Kyklopes (the Gasterocheires or 'Hands for the Belly-Womb') who built the walls of Tiryns; and like the multiple-eyed Argos Panoptes, whom Argeiphontes killed. Perseus either slipped by unseen while the eye was in transit; or he stole it: some claimed that he tossed it away into the lake where the African Athena as Tritogeneia had been born. In any case, the capsular fruit of the rockrose would be commemorated in later days (**paradigm #2**), imitated in the hampers called **kistos** (Latin **cista**), named after it: these **kistos** hampers were used, like the **kibisios** purse, to hide the sacred antiques from common view. It was never safe to look upon the Gorgon head with profane eyes.

And finally, the **Gorgons**, themselves, (sometimes only two, with the Medusa their third)— although some tellers knew them also as the **Hesperides**, 'Sisters of Evening,' in the Gateway Garden (at Gibraltar, opposite the Atlas mountains in Africa) where the magical tree grew, commemorating the spot where Zeus and Hera first consummated their sacred marriage: it was a place where the fountain flowed with ambrosial waters (**entheogen**). And perhaps, the Medusa was a sow, for some people remembered that Perseus, as her appropriate mate, had to im-

(above) Athena Playing the Newly Invented
Flute, with Perseus Holding a Mirror Reflecting
back Athena's Face like a Gorgon (Red-figure
vase, Fine Arts Museum, Boston)
(right) Decapitation of the Gorgon Medusa with
Perseus Harvesting a Mushroom from the Tree
(Amphora c. 325 BC, Pergamonmuseum, Berlin)

itate a boar (**totem**) to approach her: the
fangs of her yawning grin were taken to
be the tusks of a pig. (The 'Boar Hunt,' as
we shall see, is a common theme in the
stories of heroes.) Still others remembered
that the event had actually taken place
nowhere other than at Mycenae—and the
Gorgon Hesperides were just the **Mykenai**
sisters: Perseus plucked a mushroom at
Mycenae, and from the spot flowed the
spring, deep beneath the citadel, that was the well for the fortress (like Poseidon's
spring on the Athenian Acropolis). In any case, killing the Medusa was like harvesting a plant, for everyone remembered that it was a pruning hook or sickle
that Perseus used to decapitate his 'enemy' (the same implement that had once
been used by the Goddess to harvest the genitals of Ouranos).

When it was all over, Hermes and Athena joined Perseus in contemplating
what they had done together, by inspecting the mirrored image of the decapitated head in the reflective surface of the shield.

Athena even transmuted the dreadful hissing of the serpents of the Gorgon
head into music, by inventing the flute, which in Classical times was a double-
reeded instrument, like the oboe. It requires that the player hold the reeds firmly between the lips and blow—hard, causing the eyes to bulge and the cheeks
to puff out. Athena tried it herself, but threw it away in disgust, for it made her
look too much like the Gorgon Medusa.

Others could play the flute, but not she. But she forever after would commemorate her former identity by wearing the Gorgon head as her breastplate.

The Birth of Pegasos and Chrysaor

The Medusa was a (night)mare, and pregnant at the time of her decapitation. Poseidon, as a stallion, had mounted her—just as, in former times, he had been Athena's mate. When Perseus severed her neck, he provided a higher aperture for her birthing, similar to Athena's own birth from the head of Zeus. From the headless neck emerged the hero **Chrysaor** ('Golden Sword') and the magical flying horse **Pegasos**, named the 'Fountain Horse,' since wherev-

Birth of Pegasos and Chrysaor (Sir Edward Burne-Jones, Municipal Museum, Southampton)

er he touched Earth, springs of inspiring water (**entheogen**) flowed forth, like that of Danae's mother Aganippe ('Gentle Horse') and Hippokrene ('Horse Spring') on Mount Helicon.

Pegasos became Perseus's steed. Mounted on it, he is the triumphant hero, the perfect asexual mate for the former horsewoman that was Athena. A third time, he had managed to separate himself from his 'Mother' Goddess. He had almost this time been turned into a pillar of stone, a herm, in the Medusa's cavern-womb; but instead, he had escaped, with Athena and Hermes' aid—and managed to give birth to himself as Chrysaor, the transcendent hero, pure, like the goddess herself, and now also like her, ratified in his role as a child of the new Zeus.

The Rescue of Andromeda

Through the labyrinthine interconnections beneath the earth, flying with the 'wind,' the hero **Perseus-Chrysaor** (**Bellerophontes**) **Pegasos** wended his way back home. Where he might pop up was anyone's guess.

He was said to have enjoyed a feast amongst the Hyperboreans. And, of course, as we have seen, he surfaced also in Thessaly, and accidentally got rid of the anti-Apolline Akrisios—and by so doing, he vindicated the infallibility of the new Delphic oracle.

In Ethiopia (or sometimes Israel, at what is called the seaport of Jaffa—someone remembered that it was supposd to mean 'Crossroads'), he redeemed the 'African' Medusa Athena, in the form of his own future bride **Andromeda**, the 'Man-Queen.' He sighted her at first in chains, a prisoner being offered up to a Sacred Marriage with a monstrous (sea) boar (**paradigm #1**), that was approaching her, like a primitive Poseidon, from out of the Ocean: in any case, it was Poseidon who sent the beast.

(Why Jaffa, we may ask. Joppa, Jaffa, was a major port, a Gateway or Crossroads to the Near East, and hence an 'African' entrance to the 'foreign' Danites of Ethiopia—but its Greek name of **Io**-pe made it a likely place for an 'Io-sighting.' You could still see the marks there in the rock where Andromeda had been imprisoned—like a 'she-herm' or Hermione—awaiting her lover from the sea.)

Andromeda's father was the Ethiopian (or 'Black-face') 'king' **Kepheus**, who, to judge by his name, was the 'Gardener.' His Queen was apparently the garden he kept: her name was **Kassiopeia**, a woman who had the look of the 'Cassia' or cinnamon tree—although it may not have been the 'look,' but the 'voice,' for she was also known as **Kassiepeia**: both sight and voice suggest that her tree was an **entheogen** for their shamanism. Kassiopeia had angered the sea nymphs by contesting them in 'beauty;' and the offering of the black Andromeda to the aquatic boar had been demanded to appease them.

Perseus defeated the beast—this was probably the **Belleros** that earned him the epithet of Bellerophontes. Perseus harvested his head, too, with his sickle as Chrysaor, while the boar was distracted by the shadow Perseus cast of himself (**paradigm #1**). Or he may have displayed the Gorgon head as his weapon. Then he laid the fearful thing face down on a bed of seaweed—which instantly became petrified: this was the origin of coral, the branching, plant-like aquatic growth (**entheogen**).

Perseus thus won Andromeda as his bride. But Kepheus had a brother **Phineus**, to whom Andromeda had previously been betrothed; and he claimed the bride for himself (much as Proitos claimed Akrisios's Danae). Perseus displayed the Gorgon head and turned him, too, into a pillar of stone (**paradigm #1**).

Or it may have been **Agenor**, the twin brother of **Belos** (and father of the twins **Danaos** and **Aigyptos**) who showed up to claim the bride—although he should have lived fully six generations earlier. But the outcome was the same. Perseus turned him to stone, along with twice one-hundred of his men.

Or maybe it didn't all take place in Ethiopia, at all. In any case, there was another wedding going on at this same time; and Perseus popped up on Seriphos, displayed the Gorgon head, and turned all the guests being entertained there for the marriage of Polydektes into stone, too—after first justifying himself, in proper Hermes-like fashion, with a disquisition at law. If you visit the island today, you will see these former wedding guests everywhere in the rocks that litter the land. Perseus awarded the rulership of the island to the 'Netman' Diktys, and escaped with Andromeda, and now Danae, as well.

The Contest with Sthenoboia

After such a spectacularly successful career, Perseus-Chrysaor-Bellerophontes was needed for something else. From his blood would come eventually the new hero **Herakles**, but the death of Chrysaor is shrouded in mystery—although we can surmise what his problem was. Perhaps he could have gotten on safely with Athena, despite his closeness to her, or with Argeiphontes, despite their similarities; but Apollo and Artemis, however distant, are a different matter—and he may have even begun to encroach upon the stability of his father Zeus. We tend, as humans, to focus upon our successes, but inevitably, we all have to die—and we might as well make a hero's death serve some purpose.

As a loser, Perseus is Proitos's son (instead of Zeus's), the other half of his liminal duality. No one remembered exactly how it happened (or, more probably, there were many ways of telling the story). But after the accidental murder of his grandfather Akrisios, Akrisios's twin brother also died, leaving the 'kingdom' of Tiryns in control of his son **Megapenthes** and his sisters, the **Proitides**. Perseus assumed the control of neighboring Argos, but as the murderer of its previous 'king,' it was inappropriate for him to continue in that role. Instead, he and Megapenthes exchanged cities—and Perseus ended up thus inheriting the chthonic citadel of his non-Zeus parent and the 'foreign' Queen. It was Perseus's fate to play Megapenthes' role of 'Great Suffering' amidst the three maenadic 'Daughters of Proitos.' By taking on that role of 'Suffering,' Perseus became the sacrificial offering, the 'enemy' that he previously had been defeating. This was his ultimate benefit to humankind—to become the Argos for Argeiphontes, and all the others, including Dionysos. It was thus that he not only had a hand in making the new world of Mycenae, but, in dying, he joined the underpinnings needed to support and perpetuate the Olympian age. As the founder, mourned and honored in the chthonic realm, the people of his lands could count upon a friend in the other world (**paradigm #2**). There can be no greater mediation than to become the 'other.' This was the use to which all the heroes, as we shall see, were eventually put.

To return to the story of his death, these Proitides sisters had apparently offended Hera, and she turned them all into the same thing as **Io**: they went mad with oestrual cravings, roaming the mountains like cows, stung by the gadfly **Argos**. And instead of managing to rescue them, as Argeiphontes had, Perseus was torn to pieces as he tended them, being obliged to fill in for Argos-Bakchos as a Pentheus in the losing half of the equation. He had attempted to use the Gorgon head to destroy the maenads, and even may have killed Dionysos's bride Ariadne by turning her into another 'she-herm.'

The Proitides were cured of their madness eventually by an 'African' **Melampous** ('Black-foot'), who came from the 'Gateway' and brought the art of tempering wine with water to Greece, and who also discovered the magical properties of 'rust' (another fungal **entheogen**)—but those stories take us too far afield. What we do know, is that Perseus's corpse joined the bodies of the slain husbands of the Danaids in the Springs of Lerna. It was said that you could summon back Dionysos there out of the waters by playing a trumpet. Thus, it would seem that ultimately Perseus was needed more back in 'Africa,' to free Dionysos and Hermes for their higher roles in the age of Zeus.

Others knew of a simpler death for Perseus. He merely went into exile after

Genealogical Chart: Bellerophontes

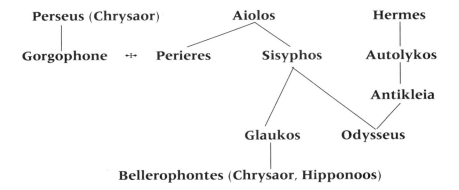

the murder of Akrisios in Thessaly—passing over into 'Africa' via the Hyperborean passageway: it was thus that his son Perses founded the race of Persians. (It was a myth that the Persian kings later would use to justify their invasion of Greece as kindred peoples.)

But there was still another way of telling the story of what happened at Tiryns, and this one involves Perseus in the form of his double **Bellerophontes**. (Probably Perseus and Bellerophontes were two different ways of telling about the defeat of the 'African' Ba'al-Argos and the founding of Mycenae-Corinth, but the two overlapped and were regularized into a genealogy: Bellerophontes ended up being the son of a **Glaukos** or 'Owl-man,' and hence an appropriate mate for **Glaukopis Athena**, a relationship that is similar to Perseus's involvement with Athena as her quasi-son(s): Chrysaor and Pegasos, who were rescued from their mother, the Medusa—henceforth transmuted into the **Gorgophone Athena**. In the genealogy, Bellerophontes occurs three generations later than Perseus; their lineage links via Perseus's daughter Gorgophone: she is a sister-in-law of Sisyphos (the sinister double for Hermes' son Autolykos); Sisyphos is the father of Glaukos, who is the father of Bellerophontes. This Glaukos, incidently, was equine: and he kept a herd of mares at a place called **Potniai** or the 'Ladies,' in the 'Cow-land' of Boeotia around Thebes: he was in the habit of feeding these (night)mares with human flesh—until they eventually ate him. Bellerophontes apparently took after his father before he killed Belleros and earned the name of Chrysaor, for Bellerophontes was formerly known as **Hipponoos** or 'Horse-perception.'

In telling the story with Bellerophontes, instead of Perseus, Proitos hasn't died yet (despite the three generation gap), but was still 'king' at Tiryns with his Queen of 'Bovine Strength,' the Lady **Sthenoboia**. Bellerophontes came to Tiryns to serve out a term in the Bondage of Death—either to expiate for the killing of his 'enemy' Belleros or for the murder of his own brother, a certain **Deliades**, who can be no one other than the matrilineal consort of **Delia** or Artemis. When the Queen saw this magnificent horseman, Hipponoos-Chrysaor, the 'Killer of Belleros(-Deliades),' flying down to her chthonic realm on the winged Pegasos, she fell desperately in love with him, but he refused her advances—as well he might. For if this horseman were to take up again with the Lady, it would merely redo the whole erotic episode of Poseidon and the (night)mare Gorgon Medusa. (There would be no point in his having killed Belleros: Athena's chthonic consort, or Hermes' primordial predecessor, Argos, or the primitive Apollo.)

Sthenoboia, however, was determined to have her way. She told her 'king' to get rid of Bellerophontes, accusing him of having raped her. Proitos sent Bellerophontes on a mission down to his Queen's 'foreign' homeland of Lycia, with a baleful note instructing **Iobates**, Sthenoboia's father, to entertain him in Death.

Like Polydektes with Perseus, Iobates, too, sent the hero on an errand. This time, it was the **Chimaira** (Latin **Chimaera**) that the hero had to fetch. The Chimaira was a 'Yearling,' a she-goat that had lived a winter and hence was ready for breeding: in English, she lends her name to an illusionary beast, for in addition to her goat body, she breathed fire like a Hephaestian volcano, and had the triple head of a lioness, with the tail of a serpent.

Although—contrary to expectation—Bellerophontes succeeded, Iobates was not satisfied, but sent him against two other 'enemies,' before finally having to admit defeat. These were the **Solymoi** (later identified as the people of Jerusalem or Hierosolyma, although they were originally just another of the primordial people of Apollo's Troy, and not males, either, but another 'foreign' city of the sisterhood, the **Solymai**); and the **Amazons** (a race of horsewomen in Asia Minor who raised only their daughters, while disposing of their sons—all the heroes eventually came up against these matrilineal Queens in their careers). Bellerophontes even defeated a contingent of Lycians or 'Wolf-people,' and refused the blatant sexual advances of a whole tribe of their female allies, the **Xanthians** or 'Tawny-yellow' women—Apollo's favorite color: they attacked Bellerophontes, with their skirts raised to expose themselves, but he had no more interest in them than he had previously in Sthenoboia.

By enduring all these tests, Bellerophontes earned the right to Iobates' 'foreign' daughter, not Sthenoboia, but her turncoat sister, **Antaia** or 'Reverse-woman' (often confused with her sister): on whom he begot several children, in that other land: the most famous was his son **Sarpedon**, who would fight alongside the Trojans against the Greek heroes in the Trojan War, together with his companion, another **Glaukos**, who may be Bellerophontes' grandson.

Having sown his seed in 'Africa,' Bellerophontes returned triumphant to Tiryns, just as Perseus did to Seriphos. Sthenoboia was still in love with him, perhaps even more so now that she thought he was dead. She was mourning at his tomb when he popped up. And this time he agreed to satisfy her passion. He swept her up onto Pegasos with him, and they flew away. Bellerophontes dropped her to her death as they passed over Milos, another island of the Cyclades and a stronghold of the earlier civilization of the Goddess.

But he, too, had his final 'fall' from grace. As he ascended to Olympus, encroaching upon the divine family's new celestial status, Zeus sent a gadfly to sting Pegasos so that the good horse would be maddened by the scent of (night)mares in oestrual heat: Bellerophontes was thrown from Pegasos, down into his 'foreign' land. He was maimed by the thorny rockrose bush that broke his fall, and he limped his way, like another Hephaestus, throughout Asia Minor, a bitter creature, wandering—in the 'Plain of Wandering'—and forever shunning the company of men, as he contemplated the human condition, until he finally died.

But Pegasos was admitted to the stables on Olympus (**paradigm #2**).

You will probably want to ask yourself what thanks Perseus and Bellerophontes got for all the good they did. Well, go ahead. Ask yourself.

It is a hard fate to live a life so close to the gods. As the Greeks said, the ones that the gods love die young.

* * * *

Review

The **Gorgon head** represents the fearful power of the Goddess: it was clearly involved in her traditions of chthonic shamanism. In the Olympian age, it was hidden away within the rockrose capsule and supplanted by the **mykes** mushroom of the Indo-European tradition. (The original plant of the Goddess has even been deposed from its role as an active chemical agent: the rockrose hip imitates the capsule of the opium poppy, just as its flower imitates the flower of the poppy, but it has lost all its power; the rose became an emblem of the goddess transmuted into the Olympian age.)

The Gorgon head is most associated with Athena, but it was also worn by Hera and Artemis in earlier times. The heroic career of **Perseus** centers on the region of **Argos**, **Tiryns**, **Mycenae**, and **Nauplion**, where Hera continued in Classical times to be the prime deity; in the pre-Olympian age, her 'king' was an **Argos Panoptes**, a **Hermes** herm, a 'limping' **Hephaestus**. And Artemis and Apollo also had their common problem in the region. As did Athena with her Poseidon. It was no easy task to settle this region and make the new Mycenae. Even with all that Perseus did, it was not completed until three generations later, with his great-grandson **Herakles**: his dynastic seat was at Tiryns, which seems to function as a prime stronghold of the Goddess, and like the **Danaid** Springs of **Lerna**, an interconnection with the chthonic 'foreign' realm.

Although Perseus and **Bellerophontes** represent two ways of telling the story, there are differences in emphasis. Perseus is more involved with Hermes and Athena, while Bellerophontes is more involved with Hera and Hephaestus: he is also the more solitary—except for receiving **Pegasos** from Athena, his heroic career is lacking the **psychopompos** and **promachos** (**animus/anima**) aid, which is so much a feature of Perseus's confrontation with the **Medusa**. There is also a difference in the threats posed by their 'monsters:' the Medusa is very much involved in the theme of petrification (or herm-conversion); whereas, the **Chimaira-Sthenoboia** threatens sexual dominance, which finally does overtake Bellerophontes when Pegasos is maddened into arousal by the gadfly (Argos) and the scent of (night)mares in heat. A similar end awaited Perseus, who was torn to pieces by the maddened heifer daughters of the Cow Goddess, Sthenoboia.

The myths about **Perseus Chrysaor** and **Bellerophontes Hipponoos Chrysaor** (with their shared horse **Pegasos**) involve the theme of 'Africa' as a metaphor for the chthonic other world: this continent includes the whole arc of trans-Mediterranean lands that stretches from Troy (or actually from Georgia, at the far end of the Black Sea—as we shall see) through Anatolia, Lycia, Phoenicia (with the port of Joppa—the name of Phoenicia is Greek and means 'Death'), Ethiopia (again a Greek word, meaning 'Black-face'), Egypt, and Libya, to the southern shore at the straits of Gibraltar and the Atlas mountains. (The crossing at the Hellespont near Troy is one of the major 'entrances' to this 'foreign' realm.) As the two heroes shuttle back and forth (across a **limen**), and up and down (along an **axis mundi**), they are repeating the career of Hermes as **Argeiphontes**, in managing to settle the cow maiden **Io** in her appropriate 'African' transmutation. (The Phoenician Ba'al, whom Bellerophontes killed, or Zeus Ammon Argos, whom Argeiphontes killed, is her 'African' consort.)

The Greeks used the term Africa only in the most restrictive reference and not for the entire region. Africa is what the Carthaginians called their own country, and the Greeks used the word only for Carthage.

Review of Paradigms: #1 the 'enemy' as other self; **#2** mediation; **#3** the 'helpers' as transmuted 'enemy.'

As part of **#1**, we often find the theme of **warring twins or brothers: Aigyptos** and **Danaos**; **Akrisios** and **Proitos**; **Bellerophontes** and **Deliades**; **Kepheus** and **Phineus**; so, too, **Belos** and **Agenor**; and **Sisyphos** is a quasi-brother of **Autolykos**.

Just as the twins are dissimilar, we often find the theme of the **two fathers**, one for each of the two aspects of the hero's liminal identity: **Proitos** and **Akrisios** as fathers of **Perseus**; **Poseidon** and (the **satyr**) as fathers of **Nauplios**; so also, **Sisyphos** and **Laertes** as fathers of **Odysseus**.

The hero, despite his liminality, cannot have two mothers, for there are witnesses to a child's physical birth from a woman—such as there are not for the father's act of begetting. But the nature of the mother is always in question, looking back to the primal matrilineal world, or forward to patriliny and the matrimonial bond to a single, verifiable husband. Hence, the theme of the **turncoat mother**: she is pivotal in the conversion to the newer order: **Danae**; **Hypermnestra**; so also, **Athena-Gorgon Medusa** as mother of the twins, **Chrysaor-Perseus** and **Pegasos**.

Since the liminal hero is only half of his total identity, we also find the theme of the **maimed hero**. Often this takes the form of some injury with the leg or foot, or some problem with walking—although any missing body part involves

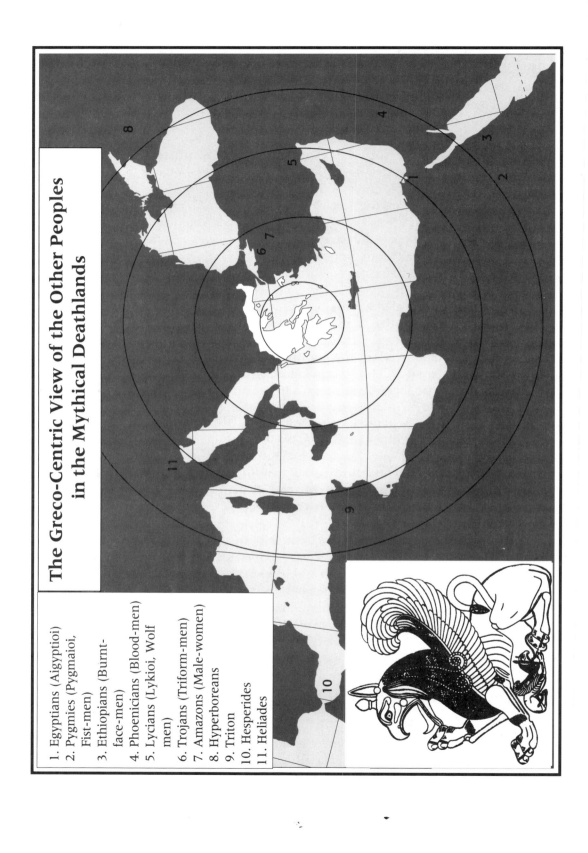

The Greco-Centric View of the Other Peoples in the Mythical Deathlands

1. Egyptians (Aigyptioi)
2. Pygmies (Pygmaioi, Fist-men)
3. Ethiopians (Burnt-face-men)
4. Phoenicians (Blood-men)
5. Lycians (Lykioi, Wolf men)
6. Trojans (Triform-men)
7. Amazons (Male-women)
8. Hyperboreans
9. Triton
10. Hesperides
11. Heliades

the suggestion that the missing part must be someplace else, like the otherworld. Thus, Perseus, in some accounts, receives only a single sandal—Hermes must be wearing the other one ('helper' paradigm). So, too, the maiming of Bellerophontes. The limping often implies the metaphor of a single leg (or a third leg), which has phallic implications. It often becomes the role of the 'helper' to help by becoming the recipient of the successful hero's maimed identity; whereas, the unsuccessful or **tragic** hero becomes the maimed one: hence, **Perseus** versus **Megapenthes**; so, also, **Bellerophontes** versus **Pegasos**. In both cases, the duos are **warring brothers**.

Finally, the hero's liminality usually is expressed by the opposition of the (infantile, natural, maternal) wilderness versus the (adult, masculine) civilization. Hence, we often find the theme of the **wilderness sojourn**: the infant, as mother-dependent and pre-socialized, is sent off to its appropriate place in the wilderness—where 'helpers' educate him with the lore of the otherworld, in order to prepare him to confront the 'enemy' and return across the **limen** or **axis mundi** to found the new order of civilization. Thus, the hero often has a problem in separating himself from the 'womb' world of the 'wilderness.' Examples are: Perseus's subterranean birth, and the floating ark that takes him to Seriphos; also the subterranean cavern of the Medusa, as well as the Medusa's pregnant body; on Seriphos, he is raised by the 'good' **Diktys** and the brotherhood of satyrs.

These, therefore, we can add to our repertory of themes: **warring brothers, two fathers, turncoat mother, maimed hero, wilderness sojourn**.

Myths: **The Marriage of the Danaids and the Sons of Aigyptos**
The Marriage of Amymone and Poseidon
The Marriage of Hypermnestra and Lynkeus
The Birth of Perseus
The Contest with the Gorgon Medusa
The Marriage of Andromeda and Perseus
The Birth of Chrysaor-Pegasos (Bellerophontes)
The Contest with Sthenoboia
The Contest with Megapenthes

For Discussion and Further Study

The arrival of Danaos with the Danaids at Argos is the plot of Aeschylus's *Suppliants* tragedy. How does it differ from the version of the myth that you have learned?

Chapter VIII
Herakles: Making the New Olympia

There was still much left to be accomplished after the death of Perseus. Athena had been put down and transmuted into a hero's friend and ally—at least in some parts of Greece—, and Hermes had shown that the tricks of Nature could work in mankind's favor; but Hera was still a Goddess to contend with. It was left to **Herakles** to complete the task begun by his great-grandfather. In the course of his career, he would visit the Danaid Springs of **Lerna** and all the other sites of the Goddess throughout the world, to conquer almost every conceivable 'monster' of Nature and rededicate the primordial world to its new master, his Olympian father. The crowning achievement of his career would be the transfer of the sanctuary of **Olympia** from its former Goddess to the Father of the new Indo-European peoples. He even put his hand to Troy and Thebes, as well as to the Labyrinth of Knossos—but Apollo was to prove his ultimate 'enemy;' and those sites and a few other odds and ends were left for other heroes to complete.

When he began, back in the earlier days, he was called **Herakles** (or **Heracles**, Latin **Hercules**), because like any proper 'digital' man, he took his name or 'Calling' (-**kles**) from his Goddess: he was 'Hera's Man.' That was always the 'enemy' self against whom he had to contend (**paradigm #1**); but when he was finished, he was known, still as **Herakles**, with the same name, but with a new meaning: he had his 'Calling' because he had defeated Hera. (It was a name like Gorgophone or Bellerophontes or Argeiphontes or Persephone, but more ambiguous—for he never did manage to kill Hera, since in the meantime, she had ascended to the rank of Queen on Olympus, as wife of her brother Zeus.)

The two different interpretations of Herakles' name represent the polarity of his liminal identity: it is the theme of the **two names**. (We have already seen this theme in Perseus, as 'Perse's Man,' or the 'Man with the Destructive Power of Perse.') Sometimes the hero actually has two different names: Perseus-Chrysaor; similarly, Bellerophontes-Chrysaor, or Bellerophontes-Hipponoos.

In the end, the liminality of Herakles' identity would result in his actually dividing into two heroes. As the successful opponent of the olden Goddess, he—and he, alone, of all the heroes—was accepted into the Olympian family, as a thirteenth member, adopted by Hera as her son (as he had actually been in former times), and married off to her daughter **Hebe** ('Youth'), who used to pour the cups of sacred drink (**entheogen**) for the gods, before she was replaced by the Trojan **Ganymedes** or 'Happy Lord': for which reason, Hebe was also known as his female equivalent, **Ganymede**. (She was replaced as cup-bearer to the Olympians because she had indecently exposed herself—and from the pairing of the names Ganymedes-Ganymede, you can surmise what her problem was.) Under her influence, Herakles became immortal, continually replenishing his youthfulness and felicity with her drink. But the other Herakles was not so fortunate: he made less 'happy' marriages and was poisoned by other of the toxins that came from Hera. That **tragic** version of Herakles was needed to help alleviate some of the lingering problems with Apollo. And ultimately, this Herakles took up residence in the chthonic realm from which he had emerged—a role of sacrifice that obviated the need to expel some other of the Olympians from the even dozen that was their full number. Like all the heroes (or 'Hera-men'), he, too, would have to lose, so that someone more important could be the winner.

The Birth of Herakles

Herakles' dynastic home was the sinister 'foreign' citadel of Tiryns, but he was born away from home, at Thebes, from a (**turncoat**) mother in exile from her native land, **Alkmene**, the 'Strong,' like another Sthenoboia. His father **Amphitryon** ('Harrassed on Both Sides') was also a 'pivotal' turncoat, and in exile as well at the time—which helped free him, too, from some of the chthonic burden of his heritage. For Amphitryon had been 'king' of his Goddess at an entrance to her underworld at the city of **Troezen** (or Troizen, named for the 'Triple Enthronement' of the triform goddess): it was a place across the mountainous spine of the Argolid, on the northern shore of the peninsula, but its sacred fountain, flowing profusely from the Entrance gorge was really not that far from Lerna via the interconnecting subterranean aquifer, for all the waters were thought to flow from a common reservoir beneath the earth. (Troizen was later to be used by Herakles as one of his paths of exit from the netherworld.)

Before telling the story of Herakles' birth at Thebes, however, let us see why Amphitryon and Alkmene were in exile at the time.

Perseus had had the full complement of five 'digital' sons from Andromeda, plus the 'foreign' Perses and the daughter Gorgophone. These five 'kings' spread out to service the Queens of his Mycenaean lands. Perseus's son **Alkaios** got Troizen, while **Elektryon** took over the chthonic responsibilities of Tiryns, and a third son, **Sthenelos**, got Mycenae as his portion; the two others were dispatched to more distant regions and took up 'foreign' affairs in the West, to balance Perses' eastern entanglement.

Meanwhile, there had been another outcropping of 'foreign' blood, coming this time from Phrygia, which was the Trojan land in Asia Minor: this 'foreigner' was **Pelops** (or 'Mud-face'), after whom the whole of the southern Greek mainland would be named the Peloponnesos or 'Island of Pelops.' Pelops, as we mentioned earlier, was the brother of **Niobe**: their father was **Tantalos**. We will tell the story of Pelops more fully later, but, like another Perseus, he managed to rescue still another (night)mare, **Hippodameia**, this one in the West at the future sanctuary of Olympia: and from her, he begot several offspring, including the **warring brothers, Atreus** and **Thyestes** (who would eventually fight it out over possession of Mycenae), as well as daughters who married, amongst others, both Sthenelos and Alkaios. These Pelopid brides were genealogically responsible for uniting the lineage of several of the heroes with the Phrygian or Trojan influx of chthonic and dominant females.

From his own Pelopid bride (**Lysidike** or 'Judgement Dispenser'), Alkaios begot Amphitryon and a daughter, **Anaxo**, the 'Queen.' Her uncle Elektryon took this daughter of his brother to wife and begot Alkmene: thus Amphitryon and Alkmene were cousins; and Amphitryon's claim to Tiryns was via his wife's father, who was his father's brother.

Now, the reason for the exile of Amphitryon and Alkmene at Thebes was that Amphitryon had 'accidently' murdered Elektryon, his **wife's** father, who was also his **sister's** husband and his father's brother—the sibling pair who had a **mother** in common, the 'foreign' Andromeda. That is to say, the murder was a symbolic way to slough off some of the burden of female relationships and to purify his own wife Alkmene from the grievous heritage of the 'foreign' citadel. Elektryon, whose wife was the 'Queen' **Anaxo**, had a chthonic name of his own, as well; for although it mimics the name of Amphitryon, it suggests a dynastic attribute of the netherworld as the realm of metallic wealth and magical 'magnetic' stones: he is the man of 'Silver-Gold-Amber.'

This is how the 'murder' took place. In the heroic career of Herakles, the gap between the far-flung 'foreign' realms of East and West would be narrowed: both he and his great-grandfather Pelops would focus upon Olympia; and just as his great-grandfather Perseus had taken control of the eastern islands of the Aegean, the 'western' islands of the Ionian Sea were next to fall under the realm of Zeus. Off the western shore of Olympia lay the imaginary islands of the **Taphians** (or 'Entombments') and the **Teleboans** (or 'Distant Voices'). Their king was a 'Birdman,' **Pterelaos**. He was a western descendant of the 'foreign' involvement of one of Perseus's sons. And he had magical hair, of a marvelous tawny-golden hue—which was the talisman of his power: so long as he had it, he remained invincible. (A similar pelt of golden fleece would be the center of controversy for the rulership at Mycenae.) And still worse, Pterelaos was a herdsman and a cattle thief: both are attributes that implicate him in the religion of the Goddess. He popped up with his brigands right outside Mycenae and demanded as his dynastic heritage, the 'kingdom' from his 'brother' Elektryon. A battle ensued, and the Taphians drove off the Mycenaean cows to Olympia. Amphitryon rescued the 'cows,' and won Alkmene as his bride; but then the 'accident' occurred: Amphitryon threw a club at one of the cows; it bounced off the cow's horns and struck and killed Elektryon, the 'bull,' by mistake. His uncle **Sthenelos** banished him, and took control of Mycenae and Tiryns, himself,

Genealogical Chart: Herakles

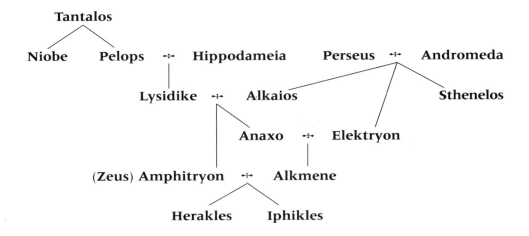

leaving the lesser portions of the lands to the two sons of Pelops, **Atreus** and **Thyestes**—who would fight it out eventually, over the possession of the golden Mycenaean fleece.

Thus, Amphitryon and Alkmene fled to Thebes. There, she refused to consummate their marriage until her husband took vengeance on the Taphians, for the 'accidental' murder of her father. Amphitryon left her, still a virgin, at Thebes, and took off for the 'western' lands. The military expedition turned out to be a success. The daughter of Pterelaos, who was called **Komaitho** or 'Bright-hair,' fell in love with one of the invaders and betrayed her father by turning over the miraculous golden hair that would have kept her father invincible. (This may have been to Amphitryon, himself, or to an Athenian ally named 'head' or **Kephalos**. It was he after whom the island was renamed Kephalonia: its remarkable topographical feature is a labyrinthine cavernous aquatic passage, through which the seawaters wash from one end to the other.)

While this 'foreign' affair was going on, Zeus appeared to Alkmene at Thebes, disguised as her own husband, Amphitryon. Zeus had a golden drinking cup (**entheogen**) that he showed to Alkmene, telling her that it was proof of his victory over the Taphians (like the pelt of golden hair that had been betrayed into the keeping of their enemy). And so Alkmene slept with him, thinking he was her victorious husband, returned from the 'west.' On that same night, Amphitryon did in fact come home, and he, too, slept with Alkmene, so that on the same night, she actually slept with both a god and a man (**two fathers**)—who both looked identical. To accommodate so much love-making, the one night was lengthened into three, with the moon rising three times: and the child she conceived was called 'three-moon,' which would be an appropriate lunar attribute for him in his involvement with the triform Goddess.

But actually, when Alkmene was delivered of her child, she gave birth to twins (**warring brothers**): one was the son of Zeus; the other, the son of the mortal Amphitryon. Only the outcome of their ensuing careers would be able to prove which was which. One of them was **Herakles**. The other, **Iphikles**, had a name that mimics his brother's: Iphikles has his 'Calling' (or **kleos**) because of his 'Strength'—but it wasn't the same kind of strength that Herakles would have; Iphikles derived his strength from the Goddess.

Iphikles, however, was not the only **warring brother** whose strength Herakles would have to contend with in his career.

The Birth of Eurystheus

There was another strong man who was to be Herakles' ultimate 'enemy' (**paradigm #1**). This was the Mycenaean overlord, his cousin **Eurystheus** or 'Broad-strength,' a man with the strength of the Goddess and her chthonic realm to back him up.

As the day for Alkmene's delivery approached, Zeus boasted that he was about to have an heir to his Olympian realm. Hera tricked him to ratify the boast with an oath. Then, she rushed to Mycenae, where the Pelopid bride of **Sthenelos**, by name **Nikippe** or 'Victorious (night)mare,' was pregnant with his child. She speeded up her gestation, so that Eurystheus was born, two months premature; and Hera slowed Alkmene's labor, causing Nikippe's son to be born first, ahead of sequence—so that he, instead of Herakles, was born at the appointed time: her own choice, instead of Zeus's, as Olympian inheritor.

Thus, the stage was set to see which way the new Olympian world would go.

The Contest with Hera

Hera was always the force behind all the 'enemies' that Herakles would confront in the course of his heroic career, but she didn't wait for him to grow up to demonstrate her hostility. She sent two serpents against the twin sons of Alkmene while they were still infants, asleep in their crib, nestled beneath the pelt of tawny hair that Amphitryon had won from the Taphians. Herakles strangled the 'monsters' and rescued himself and his cowardly twin, proving, while still just an infant, exactly who was who, of the two of them.

Apart from being rescued as an infant by Herakles, Iphikles had no career, to speak of. He is a double for the role of chthonic usurper that Eurystheus would play. He apparently went mad and volunteered to be a henchman of the Mycenaean overlord. Somewhere along the way, Iphikles begot a son, **Iolaos** or 'Io-man:' his mother was **Automedusa**, the 'Very Medusa.' Iolaos, like Perseus's Hermes, became the helper and companion of Herakles on several of the exploits of his heroic career (**paradigm #3: animus**).

The Wilderness Sojourn

As an infant, Herakles was subjected to the obligatory wilderness sojourn.

Alkmene left him in a stony field outside the walls of Thebes, later remembered as the 'Plain of Herakles.' Athena (**anima**) plucked the child up, like some wild flower, and gave it to Hera, persuading her to give it suckle, as if it were still her own child (as once it would have been). The baby, however, bit her breast, like the serpent he once would have been; and Hera's milk flowed into the sky to become the Milky Way, which was supposed to be the pathway to the celestial realm.

There was, however, another way of telling this story of the wilderness sojourn. It may have been Hermes (**animus**) who tricked Hera into nursing Herakles—but the outcome was the same. Again, Herakles transmuted the Goddess's milk into the Olympian bridgeway.

During this period of his youth, Herakles wandered the mountainsides outside Thebes, living as a herdsman, tending cattle. As he grew to manhood, he became the darling of the Thespiai sisterhood, a town on the lower slopes of Mount Helicon, and named for these 'Prophetic' or inspired women. There, in the region of Apollo's Delphi, he was required to service all fifty of them, some claimed on a single night, while he dawdled in the bondage of their 'hospitable' father. Or rather, all fifty, but one, like the Danaids: the one who remained virgin became the first of the line of priestesses who tended his temple at Thespiai, where he was honored as a 'digital' man.

It was during this period also that, like Dionysos in Nysa and Perseus in Kisthene, he discovered a miraculous plant (**entheogen**) that would free him from the wilderness: he would bear it with him forever after throughout his heroic career. It was Hermes (**animus**) who showed it to him, the herm-like Hermes, as they said: for Hermes bore the epithet of **Polygyios**, phallic, with 'Mul-

Infant Herakles
Rescuing Iphikles
(Stamnos 500-
475 BC, Musée
du Louvre, Paris)

tiple Limbs.' (Other tellers claimed that actually Herakles was to discover this plant three times—to match the demands of the triform Goddess.) The plant was Athena's wild olive. Herakles picked it, roots and all, on Mount Helicon; and made a club out of it, which became one of his characteristic weapons: we should not overlook that this club is both a magical plant and his phallic Hermes wand; it is also liminal, since it hardly could be considered, in any other hands, as a civilized instrument—if indeed Herakles is civilized. At the end of his career, he leaned it against a herm at Troizen, and it took root, growing back into an olive tree (**axis mundi**).

It was here, too, during this period of sojourn, that Herakles defeated the first of the many beasts that were his 'enemies.' This was a lion that attacked the herds; and he wrestled with it, taking its tawny pelt for his own clothing, and wearing its gaping jaws like a helmet over his own head. In this manner, he laid claim to the talismanic pelt (**totem**) that had conveyed the right of sovereignty amongst the Taphians and the Mycenaeans. (The tawny color is probably emblematic of the shaman's 'animate' plant or entheogen.) Like the club, the lionskin was a typical aspect of his attire—although some claimed that his pelt was not from this lion, but from the more famous one that he would encounter later at Nemea. And like the club, the lionskin is liminal: for if Herakles dresses like a beast, could he be a beast—or just the 'killer' of the beast (**paradigm #2**)?

And from here, too, Herakles derived the third aspect of his typical iconography; his bow and poisoned arrows—although he would repeatedly replenish his supply of toxins by dipping his arrows in the noxious blood of the many beasts (and their 'animate' plants) that he would encounter in his career. The arrows, too, are liminal: are they his weapon, like Perseus's Gorgon head; or if he bears the poison upon himself, is he actually poisoned or 'intoxicated'? In the **tragic** versions of his career, he will become mad, like Iphikles, and be poisoned by his own toxins that he once had won from the beasts. Nor did Herakles always display the social graces that would distinguish him from a beast. He was never a man to hold his wine well—nor mind his table manners or control his gluttonous appetite. He was even wont to beat his teachers.

The Contests with Hera's Eurystheus

Amongst the many successes in the heroic career of Herakles, there was a canonical list of twelve contests (or **Labors**) that pitted him directly against his Tirynian 'enemy' Eurystheus—twelve, to match the number of Olympians. Six of these occurred in the Peloponnesos, culminating in the conquest and rededication of the sanctuary of Olympia; six others were part of this same sequence, but took him farther afield. In all of these, the same pattern is repeated. Herakles was sent to fetch various magical animals and/or plants, or to perform certain tasks of pacification and resettlement. The sites selected were all previously strongholds of Hera or the 'Goddess' and were Entrances to the netherworld—similar to Apollo's contest with Python at Delphi. By successfully performing

Herakles, with Liminal Attributes: Lionskin, Bow and Arrows, Olive Club, and Wine Cup (Red-figure amphora by the Berlin Painter 500-475 BC, Antikenmuseum und Skulpturhalle, Basel)

the tasks, Herakles defeats Hera and displaces Eurystheus from the role he had usurped as Olympian heir—forcing him back into the chthonic realm and thrusting upon him the grievous 'intoxication' of the entheogens from the old order of shamanism; for ultimately, the battle was fought on the botanic level. Eurystheus, in fact, was so disconcerted by the 'animate' creatures that Herakles fetched back to him at Tiryns that he had a subterranean wine vat constructed; and when Herakles displayed his catch to him, he was in the habit of cowering from its sight and seeking refuge in that aquatic realm of chthonic intoxication and entombment.

There was no definite order to the sequence, for the story could be told in different ways, or only in part. Nor is there any one way of explaining why he performed the labors—although ultimately the reason is simply that the 'enemy' is there to be confronted.

Near at home to Tiryns, Herakles completed the conquest of the Danaid Springs of Hera's **Hydra of Lerna**. This 'Water Serpent' or Hydra was also described as a 'bitch,' and her breath alone (**entheogen**) was enough to induce a fatal swoon in any man. And although a serpent, it was also a tree (**axis mundi**), both in its lair, which was in the roots of the Danaid Amymone's gigantic plane tree, and in its own branching form: for it had multiple heads, perhaps as many as one-hundred, as some tellers claimed—as many as the fifty Danaids and their Egyptian mates. Botanic, too, were its heads, for just like Perseus with the Medusa's head, Herakles sometimes was depicted with a sickle for his harvesting weapon, although this wasn't the only way of telling the story. The difficulty was that each head grew back double as it was severed; and besides, there was a giant Crab at it base: it bit Herakles on his foot (**maimed hero**) as he struggled with the Hydra. Only one of the heads was mortal, and the task of seeing the contest through to its end became increasingly more impossible, as the monster's immortality increased by each unsuccessful plucking.

A trick of Nature was required. Iolaos cauterized each neck as Herakles sev-

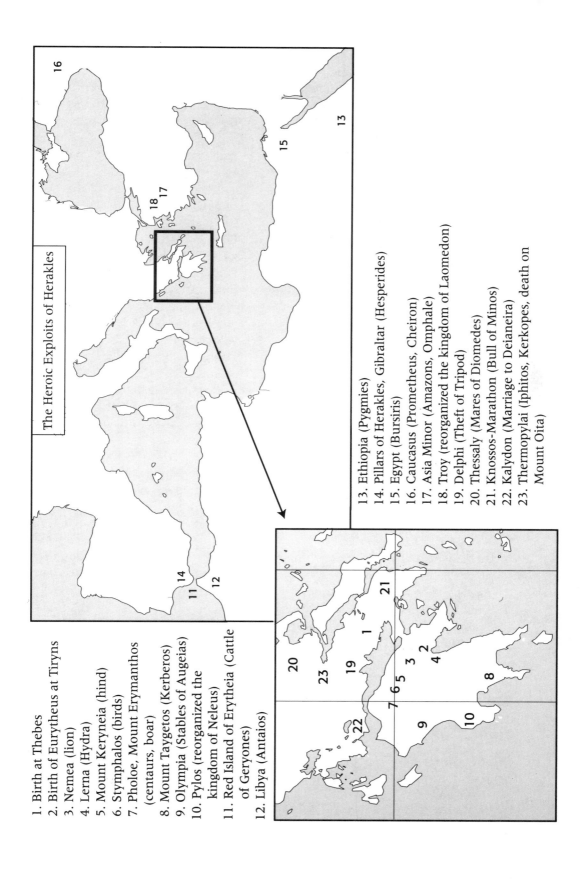

The Heroic Exploits of Herakles

1. Birth at Thebes
2. Birth of Eurytheus at Tiryns
3. Nemea (lion)
4. Lerna (Hydra)
5. Mount Keryneia (hind)
6. Stymphalos (birds)
7. Pholoe, Mount Erymanthos (centaurs, boar)
8. Mount Taygetos (Kerberos)
9. Olympia (Stables of Augeias)
10. Pylos (reorganized the kingdom of Neleus)
11. Red Island of Erytheia (Cattle of Geryones)
12. Libya (Antaios)
13. Ethiopia (Pygmies)
14. Pillars of Herakles, Gibraltar (Hesperides)
15. Egypt (Bursiris)
16. Caucasus (Prometheus, Cheiron)
17. Asia Minor (Amazons, Omphale)
18. Troy (reorganized the kingdom of Laomedon)
19. Delphi (Theft of Tripod)
20. Thessaly (Mares of Diomedes)
21. Knossos-Marathon (Bull of Minos)
22. Kalydon (Marriage to Deianeira)
23. Thermopylai (Iphitos, Kerkopes, death on Mount Oita)

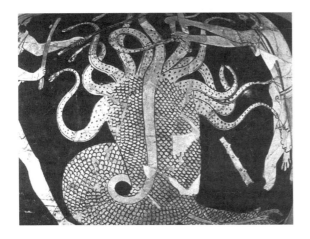

Herakles and Iolaos, with the Lernean Hydra (Red-figure vase 5th century BC, Museo Nazionale, Palermo)

ered its head, thus preventing them from regenerating. Herakles used the Hydra's venom for his arrows; and the dead Crab was transformed into the Cancer of the Zodiac (**paradigm #2**).

Nearby, in a valley of the mountains that close the northern edge of the plain of Argos-Tiryns-Mycenae, lay the sacred site of Hera's **Nemean Lion**: the region, like Lerna, is characterized by a subterranean maze or labyrinth of interconnecting caverns. It was inhabited by a lion, which, like the Hydra, was also serpentine and a bitch, at least in her lineage—which could also be traced back to 'African'

single-eyed, (night)mare manifestations. The Nemean Lion, too, was noxious (**entheogen**), capable of inducing the slumbering swoon of death. Its tawny pelt was impervious to any weapon; and Herakles had to wrestle, barehandedly, with it, falling asleep in the process—and, according to some versions, losing a finger, as well (**maimed hero**). When he awoke, the plant had been transmuted into the wild celery, henceforth associated with Poseidon (whose plant, in former times, may have been the deadly hemlock herb, which it resembles): it was thereafter used to garland graves and to weave the wreath that was presented to the victors in the athletic contests that were later held at Nemea to commemorate Herakles' conquest of the Lion; and hemlock was reserved for official executions. The forest that now covers the mountainside was supposedly planted (**axis mundi**) also as a commemoration by the 'king' of neighboring Kleonai, who had offered Herakles 'hospitality' when he arrived. The town was named for its sisterhood of olden times, the Kleone maidens, who traced their descent from an aquatic father, a local river. The Lion, too, was transmuted to the celestial realm, joining the Crab as Leo amongst the signs of the Zodiac (**paradigm #2**).

Sometimes the monsters were not directly the beasts of Hera, but belonged to the pre-Olympian form of Artemis, who we have seen was also dominant in those parts. The **Boar of Mount Erymanthos** in the highlands of Arcadia was hers. (The mountain takes its name from one of the 'lovers' of Artemis who was blinded for having seen the goddess bathing.) The region (called **Pholoe** for its 'caverns') was inhabited by centaurs, and one of them, **Pholos** or 'Caveman,' entertained Herakles 'hospitably' in his cave, by offering his guest raw meat (although Herakles opted for his own portion cooked), and by opening a new subterranean vat of special wine (**entheogen**). The centaurs became dangerously drunk, and a riot ensued. The battle raged all the way from the caverns of Pholoe to the rugged tip of Mount Taygetos, at the southernmost shore of the Peloponnesos, where there was a famous Entrance to the netherworld. There another 'good' centaur had his cave: this was **Cheiron**, a 'digital' creature, named, as we have seen, for the 'Hand.' These 'good' centaurs, Pholos and Cheiron, amongst the wild rioters who were their brothers, sided with Herakles (**paradigm #3, animus**). They both became the **maimed** versions of the hero they helped. Pholos pulled a poisoned arrow from one of the centaurs that Herakles had shot, and 'accidentally' dropped it on his own foot—and died. Herakles buried his 'friend' (**paradigm #2**). A similar thing happened to Cheiron. One of the arrows that Herakles shot 'accidentally' struck Cheiron in the knee. Since Cheiron was immortal he could not die, but neither could the terrible suffering from the poison be alleviated. He was reserved, as loser, for a role opposite another eventual winner, in an even more essential mediation. Herakles arranged to substitute Cheiron for Prometheus, allowing the centaur to die at last, when Herakles liberated the trickster Titan who had created mankind. The Centaur joined the Zodiac signs as Sagittarius, although opinions differ as to whether it was Pholos or Cheiron. Amongst the centaurs who escaped was **Nessos**, who eventually will be responsible for giving the poison back to Herakles and causing the hero's death, when it comes to be his turn to play the tragic loser.

As for the Boar, itself, Herakles tracked it down in its cave, netted it and dragged it back to Eurystheus at Mycenae, forcing his 'enemy' to cower down in fright in his subterranean wine vat.

The boar's tusks eventually found their way to Apollo's temple at Cumae, an Italian Entrance, with one-hundred openings, into the netherworld; there they were venerated as relics from the antique world (**paradigm #2**).

The **Hind of Mount Keryneia** (or **Cerynea**) in the Arcadian highlands neighboring the Argive plain also belonged to the old Artemis: in those regions, she was known as the Woinos maiden. It had golden antlers, arboreal branches (**entheogen**), like the Hydra; and since it, too, was female, it was a hind of the the reindeer family, for only those deer have horned females. Before it became a hind, however, the creature had been the goddess after whom Mount Taygetos was named; but she had offended Artemis by losing her virginity; and so, Artemis had turned her into her animal familiar.

The special danger of the Hind was not her ferocity, but the mental effect she had upon her pursuer; for she became an obsession, forever enticing further pursuit, and yet eluding capture. Eventually, she too, could lure you to the otherworld. This she did with Herakles. He finally chased her all the way through the lands of the Hyperboreans (where reindeer, which are not found in the Mediterranean, are native and are associated there with the sacred fungal entheogen of the Indo-European traditions); and he caught up with her, either amongst the Hesperides sisters at the Rock of Gibraltar—henceforth known as the Pillars of Herakles (where Perseus had also harvested the mushroom fruit of its magical Tree, **axis mundi**); or perhaps Herakles caught her in Apollo's nearer Italian 'foreign' lands amongst the Po valley peoples, where she lived in the company of wolves. In either case, when he brought the hind (or perhaps only

Herakles Presenting the Erymanthian Boar to Eurystheus, who Cowers in his Wine Vat (Black-figure vase 6th century BC, Musée du Louvre, Paris)

her antlers) back to this world, her fruit had been transmuted into the olive tree. Herakles planted the 'first' specimen of this new plant in the sanctuary of Olympia, which prior to this time had been treeless.

Some people claimed that Herakles actually met Apollo and Artemis, his Olympian siblings, when he popped up in the Peloponnesos, via the maze of underground waterways, on his way back and a fight (**paradigm #1**) almost ensued. But they patched up their quarrel—although it would eventually break out later over other matters: and then it would prove inevitable that Herakles could not forever play the winner in these contests.

Again near the Argive plain, in Arcadia, there was the **Swamp of Stymphalos**, another Entrance to the netherworld. It, too, was sacred to Artemis, but also to Hera, as the Witch or crone, the third of the three stages of the Goddess. The swamp was infested by a flock of long-necked (or phallic) 'migratory' soul birds, or actually she-birds, for they could be depicted as soul-snatching maidens with bird feet. (They had taken refuge in the Swamp to escape from a pack of wolves.) And they were poisonous (**entheogen**); their droppings, alone, blighted the lands about: and their feathers, too, were like poisoned arrows, wounding anyone on whom they fell. And even worse as an attribute, they fed on human flesh.

Athena (**anima**) helped Herakles confront this monster by giving him a rattle made by Hephaestus (**animus**): this rattle was the inspiration, the trick. Herakles stood on Artemis's Mount Kyllene (named for the Delian mountain where Artemis was born, but this was the Arcadian one which had witnessed the birth of Hermes, who was tended there by the wet nurse Kyllene); and he shook the rattle. Its chthonic sound scared the flock into flight above the Swamp. Herakles shot as many as he could with his own arrows, or with pellets of Earth hurled by a sling; but a few birds managed to escape to the 'foreign' realm at the far end of the Black Sea, where they would continue to pose a threat to future heroes who ventured into such otherworld entanglements.

The task of fetching up the watchdog **Kerberos** (Latin **Cerberus**) from the netherworld House of **Hades** pitted Herakles directly against the chthonic Queen **Persephone**. His descent this time was via the same Entrance at the southern tip of Mount Taygetos where he had injured Cheiron; and he passed all the way beneath the Peloponnesos to surface again at his father's town of Troizen, bringing back up with him also the Athenian hero **Theseus**, who had been born there.

(This episode thus also involves the city of Athens and two of its Entrances; and it attempts to accommodate the demands of shared heroism placed upon these two 'friends.' Theseus, on one of the journeys of his own career, had descended via the sacred Steps at Kolonos, just outside the city walls; and the most famous of these Entrances that Athens could lay claim to was also worked into this telling of Herakles' descent. This was the Entrance at the village of Eleusis, a neighboring town just about ten miles away that came to be administered from the city of Athens. There each year for two millennia, whole groups of people from all over the world met to be initiated into the mystery of the netherworld, and they journeyed together, as spirits, via the Eleusinian Entrance along the network of pathways that had been forged by the heroes who preceded them, to visit for themselves the House of Persephone and her consort Hades. (We will follow in their footsteps ourselves later when we come to examine this so-called **Eleusinian Mystery**.) Thus, although Herakles descended via the Taygetos Entrance, in deference to his 'friend' Theseus and his city's traditions, he was prepped, like everyone else, for the journey by undergoing the Eleusinian initiation—and he was even adopted as an honorary member of the Athenian city.)

Theseus, after entering with a 'friend' of his own (**Peirithoos**, a 'good' brother of the wild race of centaurs—although he was never portrayed with horse-like features) via the Kolonos Steps, had had the misfortune of accepting the 'hospitality' of the netherworld's couple; and he became fixed, herm-like, to a stone in the House of Hades. Herakles had rescued Theseus when he found him there in that condition, by pulling him loose.

But this rescue was to prove to be a problem eventually; for only one in a pair of heroes can ever win: not both, for someone must be the loser. If Herakles helped Theseus win—as he did —, he would inevitably have to play the role of loser, himself. And that is just what would happen to him, in one telling of his **tragic**, instead of 'successful,' career. Herakles would have to end up being the darker, befriended half of Theseus's successful career. There is no higher service a 'friend' can offer than to sacrifice himself for the benefit of the other. This is the way the story would be told in Athens, for as important as Herakles was, from the Athenian point of view, their own founding hero Theseus was the more indispensable of the two.

As for Kerberos, he was the guardian of the cattle in the bondage of Death, admitting those who belonged to his Mistress and her consort, and forbidding entrance to all others. He was a brother of the Hydra of Lerna, and he had three heads, although some tellers knew of him with fifty; and like his sister, he had multiple serpents, with bites of deadly poison, branching from his body.

Athena (as **anima**) and Hermes (as **animus**) helped Herakles through this encounter. He actually had to confront the Gorgon's head itself, but Hermes told him that it was just an apparition—for his great-grandfather Perseus had already transmuted it into the new Athena. But Herakles put his hand also to changing Athena: he found not only her Athenian favorite Theseus stuck to a stone, but also the 'Owl-man' **Askalaphos** similarly imprisoned—he was a gardener and henchman of Hades and one of the 'tattletale babblers' who had reported to his master that Persephone had eaten from the pomegranate in his orchard; it was that that made her belong henceforth to the netherworld. Herakles set Askalaphos free, also; whereupon, Persephone's mother Demeter turned him into an owl.

Then with a stone as his ultimate weapon, Herakles confronted the Queen Persephone herself and her consort in their House; and she, as a brother of Herakles (for she, too, was a child of Zeus, in this newer Olympian age), consented to relinquish the hound. Herakles leashed it, and dragged the 'tamed' beast back to the surface, plucking along with it also the toxic plant wolfsbane (aconite)—the plant that mediates between the wildness of the wolf and its tamed relative, which is the dog (**entheogen**). As with the Erymanthian boar and the Nemean lion, Herakles so terrified Eurystheus when he displayed his booty back at Mycenae, that his 'enemy' cowered from the sight by seeking refuge in his wine vat.

That was the successful version of the Kerberos episode; but there were still unresolved aspects, such as the rescue of Theseus, that would be the nucleus for the hero's eventual reversion to the darker possibility of his liminal identity. There were two stories about Herakles' wives, **Megara** and **Deianeira** (Latin **Dejanira**). Both wives independently led to his death (for there is no linear chronology in myth, just different ways of telling the same story, in essentially the same way; in fact, each of his wives was waiting for him upon the completion of his last labor, although there is no agreement about which of his many labors was actually his last—except that marriage was his ultimate downfall).

Deianeira was a marriage Herakles agreed to while in Persephone's House; and the marriage to Megara, who was the wife waiting for him at Thebes upon his return with Kerberos, ended also in disaster. In both cases, the wife was instrumental in redirecting the poisons of the beasts he had conquered back upon

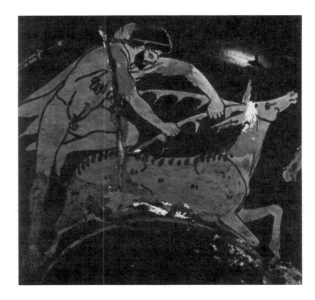

Herakles Plucking the Golden Antler of the Keryneian Hind (Red-figure vase early 5th century BC, Musée du Louvre, Paris)

(left) Herakles Leashing Kerberos, with Athena's Aid (Red-figure amphora, Musée du Louvre, Paris)
(above) Herakles Presenting Kerberos to Eurystheus (Polychrome black-figure hydria c. 530 BC, Musée du Louvre, Paris)

himself, so that his former toxic arrows now fatally intoxicated him. But before we examine the tragic problems of his marriages, let us complete the survey of the successful accomplishments of his heroic career.

The sixth labor that completes the major Peloponnesian cycle of episodes was in some ways the crowning achievement of his triumphant heroism, for it resulted in the rededication of the sanctuary of Olympia, from its former Goddess to the new Olympian Zeus. There, in the fertile plain at the base of the sacred conical hill, on the banks of the River Alpheios, he had to confront a cattle lord named **Augeias**. And Herakles' task was to clean the Stables of Augeias of all their accumulated pollution, in a single day. By doing this, he not only made the place suitable for habitation by his father Zeus, but he also purified himself of his own past pollution: for in former times, Herakles was known in that region as one of the 'digital' men who used to consort there on the bare ground with his Goddess.

Although Augeias was a son of Helios, the Sun, and had an appropriate name as the 'Radiant Man,' the cattle belonged to the netherworld herd (for Helios, as we have mentioned, spent half his time beneath the Earth, returning from the western sunset to the new day's dawning in the East); and this episode of Herakles' career on the western shore of the Peloponnesos is the theme of the hero's period of Bondage to Death. And the task of ridding the underworld of all its rotting matter is no easy challenge. If he failed, he was to serve in that job for all eternity. Herakles, however, succeeded, with the help of Athena and Iolaos: and also by the use of a trick of nature: he channeled the river through the Stables—and flushed all the manure away. Since a trick was involved, however, he had to justify his success at a trial of law, just as Hermes had with his theft of Apollo's cattle.

This episode became confused with another version of the story, in which Herakles was entertained in that region by a 'hospitable' lord named **Dexamenos**, who was a centaur. And either he or another centaur (**Eurytion**) intended to carry off Dexamenos's daughter as bride, but Herakles rescued her for himself—and her name was **Deianeira**, although this is not the more familiar story of how Herakles saved a Deianeira from a centaur and won her as his wife.

These complete the Peloponnesian adventures: the **Hydra of the Lerna Spring**, the **Lion of the Nemean Caves**, the **Boar of Mount Erymanthos**, the **Hind of Mount Keryneia**, the **Birds of the Swamp of Stymphalos**, the **Kerberos Hound of Hades**, and the **Stables of Augeias**. The canon of twelve labors that was popular at Olympia understandably presented the Augeian Stables as the twelfth and last, although the Keryneian Hind must also be involved in the dedication of the sanctuary since Herakles planted the sacred grove of olive trees upon his return from the chase that brought him to the Hyperboreans. In the story of his marriage to Megara, the Hound Kerberos was presented as his last, again, as we shall see, for thematic appropriateness—although the story was also told with the marriage problem as the reason why Herakles underwent the initiation at Eleusis as a preliminary for his descent to fetch the hound. The second cycle of six labors led Herakles further afield—supposedly, for the Keryneian Hind was hardly local to the Peloponnesos, except for the use of the particular Entrance; and ultimately, all the pathways led far afield, to a realm that was 'foreign,' but also near at hand, just beneath your feet.

By 'sailing' farther westward from the shore of the Peloponnesos, Herakles confronted the same kind of netherworld problem that his father Amphitryon had encountered with the Teleboans. Herakles had to rustle the **Cattle of Geryoneus** (or **Geryones**, Latin **Geryon**). His destination for this episode was the place where the sun set, an island called **Erytheia**, 'Red' with the glow of the last rays of light from our world of the living; and called that after the name of its nymph, Erytheia. Another **Eurytion** was the herdsman of these cattle in Bondage, and the watchdog was the two-headed **Orthos**, a brother of the Hydra and Kerberos: Orthos has a phallic name that means 'Upright-erect' and is a herm-like figure; and as for his two heads, presumably one looked forward and the other backward, like the 'trickster' pair of Prometheus and Epimetheus. The cattle themselves were purple-red, with the magical color of the animate **entheogen** that would eventually confer the rights of rulership to whoever possessed it at several of the former Minoan-Pelasgian settlements, including Mycenae and Knossos, itself. The 'sailing' to the 'Red' island, moreover, is merely a metaphor for the chthonic water journey, for Herakles, according to some tellers, sailed in the Sun's drinking cup, the same one that he nightly embarks in for his period of drunken eclipse; and the cup was piloted by the nymph Erytheia, herself, one of the Hesperides sisters who presided over the magical tree where Perseus harvested the sacred mushroom.

As for the 'king' of this herd, Geryoneus, he was another of the 'foreign' descendants of the Perseus family: it was said that he was a son of Chrysaor, and like the Teleboans, he was named for his 'Shout.' And as befits a consort of the Goddess, he had three heads, or even a body branching like a tree into a triple torso above the waist; and like Pterelaos, he was a bird-man, with wings.

The Entrance for this episode was one of the towns on the west coast of the Peloponnesos, called **Pylos**, the 'Gateway.' And the journey took him into the 'African' otherworld. In Libya, he confronted the giant **Antaios**, who is the 'Lord who Meets' you in the other realm, a son of Earth, and the consort of the Goddess, who could be named **Antaia** (like Proitos's Sthenoboia, or her sister), for the same 'hospitable' greeting. Herakles had to wrestle with him—which proved a difficult task since Antaios rose up stronger after each fall, increasing his 'strength' whenever he touched down onto mother Earth: the trick that defeated him was to drain his power by holding him up away from the ground. As with the wrestling match with the Nemean Lion, Herakles also was so exhausted that he fell into a deep slumber (**entheogen**).

The **Pygmies** or little digital 'Fist-men' were Ethiopian black brothers of Antaios and they took advantage of the hero's sleep to attack him, but he awoke and plucked them into his lionskin to bring back as booty to Eurystheus. (Presumably, Herakles had journeyed from the Libyan Antaios back to the eastern Ethiopians during his sleep in the drinking cup.)

The 'foreign' entanglements of this episode of Geryoneus's Cattle were extended and variously elaborated in different tellings, with the hero confronted by numerous other 'enemies' all the way from Spain through Italy; and even the 'Entrance' for his return was not always the same. But somewhere out there he defeated Geryoneus, his herdsman, and the dog, and stole the cattle, only to have to defend them repeatedly from several attempts to rustle them back away from him all along the way of his return.

If we follow the version that had him resurface to this world via the same Peloponnesian Gateway as his descent, the 'king' of Pylos, **Neleus**, and his sons were amongst those who tried to steal the cattle as Herakles passed back through.

(Neleus has firmly established credentials for his role as chthonic lord: his name means the 'Pitiless' and he has a 'botanic' Queen, **Chloris**, identified as **Flora**, by the Romans, but her 'floral' bouquet in those earlier days was hardly innocuous: Chloris was a daughter of Niobe and Amphion of Thebes—presumably a child who escaped the poisoned arrows of Apollo and Artemis, although she obviously belongs to the former Apolline world as a version of his Goddess; for Zephyros (or Zephyrus), the sinister west wind and lover of Hyakinthos, was also cited as a double for Neleus in the role of her consort. As for Neleus himself, he was one of a 'warring' pair of twins; and the uncle of another hero, **Iason**— Latin **Jason** —, who was sent to fetch the magical 'animate fruit,' that was called the golden fleece, from the eastern reaches of the 'foreign' lands in the netherworld.)

In the ensuing battle with Neleus and his sons at Pylos, Herakles even struck

Herakles 'Sailing' in the Drinking Cup of Helios (Red-figure vase c. 480 BC, Vatican Museum, Rome)

Hera with one of his arrows in her breast and wounded Hades, too. Some tellers knew of a version in which the champion on the Pylian side was a hallucinatory monster (the 'Famous' **Periklymenos**, a supposed son of Nestor, but really an offspring of Poseidon), who could assume various disguises, including a bee at the head of a whole Minoan swarm. It was while he was in this disguise that Herakles swatted him when he alighted on the cattle. Herakles killed the 'king' Neleus as well, and all of his sons, except for only the good and wise **Nestor**, who became the ruler of this famous city in the new Mycenaean age that Herakles was inaugurating. It may even be that Herakles enacted the whole adventure of the Cattle of Geryoneus nowhere other than at this famous palace of Nestor: for the triform bird-man Geryoneus had an eagle as his heraldic emblem: and one of the Pylian champion's disguises was also an eagle. Henceforth, the eagle was to become the special ornithological attribute of Zeus, perched atop his scepter: its high soaring flight would put to silence all the lesser 'birds,' who cower from it in fright.

The labor of the **Apples of the Hesperides** is basically another way of telling the episode of the cattle of Geryoneus (as well as that of the Keryneian Hind)— for Herakles wandered as far as that western Garden on those two other 'foreign' journeys. And even the drinking cup that took him to the 'Red' island of Ery- theia may have been his vehicle again for this 'sailing' into sleep. The Entrance was probably the cistern right beneath Mycenae—for that had served for Perseus's descent to the Garden of the Hesperides —; but more distant Gates were cited for Herakles, including the cavern from which the Po (Eridanos) flowed: there, the sisterhood of Heliades stood, as a nearer version of the western Garden: a grove of poplars, with their tears transmuted into another magical 'amber' fruit, as they wept for the death of Apollo's Phaethon. And once beneath the surface, Her- akles had to wrestle with another 'guardian' figure like Antaios: this time it was the Libyan Athena's **Triton**, himself; or even **Nereus**, the 'Watery' old man of the sea, and father of the fifty Nereid sisters. As with Neleus's champion at Pylos, Nereus, too, had many hallucinatory disguises; and Herakles had to endure the whole repertory before Nereus would let him pass.

Again, the story was variously told and greatly extended. But the gist of it was that he had to make his way through 'Africa,' with Athena (**anima**) and Hermes (**animus**) as his guides, or with the 'help' of Iolaos; and perhaps even with the 'wind' caught in the sail provided by his lionskin (**entheogen**) as the driving force for his drinking cup. Or the 'sailing' might even have involved a tour all along the world's northern edge, as well, including the Hyperboreans. And a trick was involved.

This time the herm-like role of the two-headed Orthos was played by the pair of Titans, Prometheus and Atlas: the former pillared to the mountains at the world's easternmost frontier, and the latter similarly pillared at the western boundary.

It may have been on this visit that Herakles freed **Prometheus** from the torment inflicted upon him by Zeus in retaliation for his creation of mankind: Hephaistos (or Hephaestus) had fixed him to the mountain in the Caucasus, where an eagle daily feasted upon his liver—but Prometheus couldn't die, for the liver continually regenerated itself. Herakles shot the eagle with his poisoned arrows; and then arranged for his 'friend,' the good centaur Cheiron to die at last by exchanging his own unwanted immortality for Prometheus's mortal allotment: that was the way that Cheiron finally put to rest the terrible poisoning that had afflicted him ever since Herakles 'accidently' shot him; and that was also the way that the creator of man achieved the reward of immortality. (It was the diseased livers of the two of them that functioned as the mediating organ: the liver is the human body's filter for toxins; and its bitter greenish bile associated it with botanical growths and the venom of serpents. For this reason, the liver was considered the seat of the passions or humors. When Cheiron's intoxicated, but immortal liver was transferred to Prometheus, it became no longer the cause of the centaur's wild ravings, but the seat of intellect and of those transmuted intoxications that are called prophecy: the examination of the sacrificial victim's liver became a method of divination.)

Prometheus's brother **Atlas**, the 'Enduring,' had similarly been punished for some act of trickery against the Olympians; and ever since Perseus had passed that way, Atlas had been an actual pillar of stone, as well as the mountain on the west shore of 'Africa.' It was his task to hold forever the celestial realm upon his shoulders, lifting it apart from mother Earth. The trick, perhaps divulged to Herakles by Prometheus, was that Herakles should not go himself into the sacred grove of the Hesperides—for he would forget to return —, but Atlas (as **animus**) should go in his stead.

The Golden Apples (or Flocks, for the same word means both things) grew upon a special Tree nearby, created by Earth to commemorate the spot where Hera and Zeus consummated their Sacred Marriage (**axis mundi**). It was guarded by a serpent, **Ladon**, a relative of the Hydra, Kerberos, and Orthos, and like them, he branched into many heads, like a tree himself, as he coiled about the Tree. Like the Teleboans and Geryoneus, he, too, was known for his 'shouting,' which he did in many foreign voices; and like Argos Panoptes, whom Argeiphontes killed, he never closed his eyes. And in the Garden, Atlas pastured his own special cattle. His daughters, the **Hesperides** (granddaughters of Hesperos, by Atlas's wife Hesperis) never left the Garden, but clustered about the Tree, singing songs of captivating beauty.

Atlas agreed to fetch the apples, while Herakles seconded for him as the temporary pillar of heaven. (The way that Ladon was deceived is variously told: Herakles may have intoxicated him with one of his arrows; or the Hesperides may have collaborated in putting the guardian to sleep; or many of the most famous witches in myth each contributed her special magical drink to induce the beast's slumber, including (w)oinos—which version made the whole episode into a maenadic revel.) When it was all over, some tellers claimed that, like the Heliades, the Hesperides were metamorphosed into trees, weeping.

Atlas returned with three of the apples, but Herakles had to play a trick of his own to get Atlas to resume his task of stony endurance. He agreed to let Atlas deliver the apples for him back to Eurystheus at Mycenae, if only Atlas would give him a moment of relief while he prepared a cushion to ease the weight on his shoulders. The Titan fell for it, and was stuck again, while Herakles escaped.

As for what happened to these 'apples' of the Hesperides—rumor had it that they proved too dangerous for Eurystheus to keep: they were, after all, Hera's, stolen from her own Garden; 'apples,' moreoever, were a metaphor for the breasts, and poetically a common offering of love. Ladon's fate is better known: he was transmuted into the Serpent to join the other constellations. There was, however, another Ladon that remained in this world: he was one of the rivers that snaked his way through what had originally been Hera's fertile plain at Olympia, still there even in the days after the place had been made over to Zeus. The whole episode of the Apples of the Hesperides, therefore, was another aspect of Herakles' task of making the new Olympia: the Ladon was once one of Hera's local aquatic consorts; and probably the first Entrance for the hero's 'sailing' to those interconnecting far-off lands which were really just beneath its surface. Ladon also gives us a clue as to the fruit of the Tree: he is named for one of the rockroses, the same **kisthos**, which ever since the days of Perseus hid within it the former botanic power of the Goddess's plant that the new traditions of the Mycenaeans had replaced. The poppy-like capsules of the rose's fruit were called its 'apples.'

That makes eight labors, so far, although each, as you have seen, often includes several adventures along the way, as the hero fetched whatever it was that Eurystheus this time set as his task. Nor was there common agreement as to what these other adventures were, but they were often ascribed to a particular labor because the hero had supposedly visited that particular geographic area to perform the main labor; but since ultimately the particular area is merely a metaphor for the netherworld and an Entrance sanctuary of the Goddess in this world, the adventures might be included in various tellings of each labor.

Ninth, let us look at the extensive journeys of Herakles into the eastern death-lands, the complement of his excursion to the western Hesperides. This was the labor that some told as his last: to fetch the **Golden Bodice of Hippolyta**. When he returned, he would have to face the disastrous consequences of his marriage to Deianeira.

Traditionalists, it must be admitted, would balk at the word 'bodice' here, preferring to call it the Girdle of Hippolyta, as has been the custom: a Belt or Cincture was what it really was, but sex was definitely an implied possibility; for Hippolyta was not apt to idly allow a man to untie the binding that seductively belted her gown just beneath the bosom—which, in the manner of her tribe, was usually displayed nude. And, it was rumored, they all had just a single breast, the sinister left one; for they were archers and had removed the other one so that it would not interfere with the drawn string of their bows as they shot their poisoned arrows. It was for that reason, supposedly, that they were called **Amazons** or 'Breastless.'

These Amazons, moreover, were a race of horsewomen, as witnessed by the name of their Queen **Hippolyta**, the 'Lady who Turns her Horses Loose.' And like Athena, they dressed as warrior men, but not as the helper of their male champion—but as his enemy. They were a feminist people, comprised only of females, and totally flaunted the conventions of patrilineality. They used the men of neighboring tribes for procreation, and kept only the daughters, either killing the male infants, or maiming them, or sending them back to the men to distribute randomly, with no regard for lineage, amongst themselves.

Bellerophontes had come up against these women in the course of his 'foreign' adventures. And now it was Herakles' turn. Some claimed that it was Eurystheus's daughter who wanted the bodice for herself: her name was **Admete**, the chthonic 'Indomitable' Queen; and when the whole affair was finished, the golden belting found it way to the temple of Hera, where it was displayed in later days as a relic from the past.

As to exactly how this labor was accomplished, there was a great diversity of opinion; and Herakles sometimes even took along a whole army of his own to confront them, enlisting the aid of just about every hero available at the time. The simplest pathway would be to retrace

Atlas Presents the Apples to Herakles, who Holds the Celestial Realm, with Athena and the Cushion Helping to Relieve the Burden (Metope from the Temple of Zeus, at Olympia)

the route that he would use for his return. In that case, he would have descended via the Entrance called the 'Hot Gates,' which are the complex of thermal springs that flow at Thermopylai and from the northern tip of the island of Hera that lies close off its shore, the 'Cowplace' called Euboea. This would have put him in direct communication, via the chthonic network, with the 'Hottooth' River Thermodon, that flows up out of Asia Minor into the Black Sea. It was along its banks that the Amazons lived.

The horsewomen, for obvious reasons, were happy enough to see the great hero arrive at their shore, and Hippolyta seems to have even been willing to untie her belt for him herself; but Hera sowed distrust amongst the other women, telling them that Herakles intended to abduct their Queen away from them and change the whole nature of their feminist society. A battle ensued, and Herakles had to remove the golden girdle from Hippolyta's dead body. It was just as well that way, for another hero, **Theseus**, was to have a chance to do it the other way: abduct Hippolyta and have a son by her—and the outcome was none too fortunate; but we will return to that story later when we talk of that other hero's career. (There was yet another way of telling the story, in which Herakles didn't kill Hippolyta, but gave her to his 'friend' Theseus, allowing him to carry off the burden, instead of him.)

For his own part, Herakles did not entirely escape the dominance of women while in this 'Asian' realm. He had to spend a year (or three) in Bondage to another dominant Queen, **Omphale**, the 'Lady of the Chthonic Navel.'

Such Bondage is what is thematically demanded as expiation for a lack of proper atonement or reconciliation with the 'enemy' self; for to kill one's 'enemy' is to kill oneself—a suicide, with the resultant period of servitude in Death, living out a term as the one you killed. Herakles' heroic career was always a potential threat to his brother Apollo; for it was never clear whether there was room for a thirteenth Olympian. But would he ever go so far as to murder Apollo? After all, it was the Apollo of the old labyrinth who lurks behind the figure of Eurystheus and the other lackeys of the Goddess. Well, you be the judge.

Twice Herakles came disastrously close to displacing his sibling rival. Either occasion, or both, was the reason for Herakles' period of eclipse and servitude to Omphale.

The simpler tale is that Herakles actually tried to take over the 'navel' or **omphalos** shrine of Delphi by seizing Apollo's prophetic tripod for himself. (There had been numerous such 'enemies' of Apollo at Delphi, as we have seen; but none like Herakles, who was equally a son of Zeus, and probably better at remaking the world for the newer order, since he lacked Apollo's troubled past.) Here was an evenly matched battle: Apollo with Artemis to aid him, and Herakles with Athena: a sibling pair against a sibling pair, and with the favorite daughter of Zeus to tip the balance. It was settled only by Zeus, who separated the combatants with a thunderbolt. The brothers patched up their differences by cooperating to found the city of Gytheion at the site of the Entrance on the southern coast of the Peloponnesos, which was where the pursuit and fight was concluded.

If Herakles did not presume to actually kill Apollo in this controversy over the Delphic Omphalos, he did it, at least by proxy, in the affair with **Iphitos**, who has a name ominously like another brother, his sinister twin **Iphikles**. Iphitos was a son of **Eurytos**, an 'archer's' name (like that of the centaur Eurytion, with whom Herakles had that conflict over a Deianeira near Olympia).

Eurytos was a grandson of Apollo and 'king' of Oichalia, the departure city where people 'Pass Away;' and his father was 'Black.' It was understandably a city that you might expect to find in several places; and one of them was at the Thermopylai Entrance. He was a stand-in for Apollo (one of the 'African' versions); and had even been given his poisoned bow by Apollo himself.

It was one of the famous bows in Classical myth: this bow of Iphitos (who got it from his father Eurytos); the bow of Herakles; and the bow of Apollo, himself;—and they all bear watching: Apollo's arrows will cause the death of Greeks at Troy; Iphitos's bow (in an episode of horse rustling) passes on to Odysseus, who will use it to kill his wife's suitors, on a feast-day of the Wolf-Apollo; and Herakles' bow will eventually defeat Troy. The Odysseus bow and the Herakles bow are the final rectification for Apollo's Trojan bow.

The controversy between Eurytos-Iphitos and Herakles centered upon a contest of 'archery' and the possession of an enigmatic female who is the floral toxin. She is the sibling of Iphitos, and has a name based on the ios ('poison-arrow-drug') words, as well as the plant-color that connotes the new Indo-European **entheogen**. She is **Iole**, the Lady '(V)iolet' (a female version of Apollo's Athenian son **Ion**.) Iole was the daughter of Eurytos at this 'Departure City' where people pass away down through the Hot Gates; and like Eurytion's Deianeira, she may also have been the 'king's' bride and Goddess. Exactly what happened is not clear, for it was variously narrated (since the details always tend to get murky to shield Apollo from his involvement in the events); but Herakles and Iphitos had a contest with the toxins of their poisoned bows (the one with the poisons of the 'African' Apollo; the other with the poisons he had transmuted from the deadlier times of the Goddess). And Iole was presumably the prize. But Herakles, who was entertained 'hospitably' by Eurytos at a symposium, became intoxicated—both by the drink and by his erotic desire for Iole. (For Iole had that effect upon Herakles: she could make him into her love slave.) And he killed Iphitos; and perhaps destroyed the whole city, as well—in order to abduct Iole as his bride, even though he was already married to Deianeira. (Some claimed that the murder of Iphitos actually took place at Tiryns, over a dispute about rustled Mares, the Mares of Eurytos, although we are never told that he, like Eurytion, was a centaur. In this case, Herakles pushed Iphitos from a tower, inflicting upon him the Apolline Death by Falling; and presumably Tiryns became the Entrance, instead of Oichalia-Thermopylai. And there was still another version which suggests the events took place at Olympia instead, as part of its remaking.)

To expiate for this murder of Iphitos (and for the dispute about the Omphalos), Herakles was sold into slavery to the Lady **Omphale**, in the 'Asian' lands where the Hot Gates surfaced into the eastern version of the otherworld. Like his infatuation with Iole, this was a love slavery, such as he had supposedly avoided with the Amazon Hippolyta. Herakles presented Omphale with the 'Minoan' double axe which he had taken from Hippolyta: it was such an axe that once had served to sacrifice the 'king' in Apollo's labyrinth. (The axe became the emblem of the earlier Lydian dynasty that claimed descent from her.) Not only did Herakles present her with the axe, however, but he gave her his lionskin and club to wear, while he dressed in her fine female garments. And like his 'enemy' Eurystheus, Omphale set him labors to perform, demeaning ones, like spinning wool with the other slave girls.

It was while Herakles was in 'Asia' that he also became involved in the famous controversy of Mare rustling that resulted in the 'first' Trojan War, which we have already mentioned in discussing Apollo's own Bondage to Laomedon. Like Perseus with Andromeda, Herakles rescued the 'king's' daughter Hesione, but he didn't keep her for himself. In this instance, he avoided further implications by giving her to his 'friend' Telamon, just as he may have passed Hippolyta on to Theseus. Hesione was no better news than Hippolyta, however, for she was to prove the precipitating cause of the second Trojan War.

As Herakles resurfaced back through the Hot Gates, he was waylaid by a pair of local yokels of Oichalia, the **Kerkopes** brothers, 'Tail-men,' but not simply 'digital' creatures: for these were 'black,' diminutive, and monkeys, 'African' versions of the primordial man. Their mother was the Goddess. Herakles had fallen asleep (and indeed, the whole journey may have been again a slumbering): the curative waters of these Hot Springs, through Athena's aid, were what eventually revived him. But while he was still asleep, the two Kerkopes attacked. Their mother had warned them to beware of the man who was 'Black Behind,' but Herakles was lying Face Up; so they didn't know his other half was 'African.' Herakles awoke and caught them, one in each hand; and he slung them over his shoulders on a pole Upside-down, from which position they could glimpse his Black Behind. They started laughing at their stupidity; and so did Herakles. He set them free. In this way, the 'black' brothers patched up their differences. It was as if it had all been just a dream—a (night)mare.

The remaining two labors again brought Herakles into the Apolline Deathlands. For the eleventh, it was once more a problem of mares, the Mares of Diomedes.

The route led Herakles through another of Apollo's periods of Bondage to Death, where the god was tending the herds of **Admetos**, 'king' of the Pherai sisterhood of '(Under)takers' in Thessaly; and hence the Entrance for this descent was probably the Delphic one of the Korykian Cave, the direct interconnection, as we have seen, with the magical Valley of Tempe and Apollo's northern primordial lands. Admetos 'hospitably' entertained Herakles with drink, while **Alkestis**, the Queen, was dying in place of her consort, to fulfill the terms of the agreement that Apollo had wrangled from the drunken Moirai, the Fate sisters: Admetos himself would not have to die if someone else would take his place. Herakles learned what was happening and wrestled with Death itself to rescue this exemplary wife back from the sepulchre, thus repeating what he had done in rescuing Hesione at Troy.

From Thessaly, Herakles went further north to Thrace, where **Diomedes** was 'king.' Apollo never owned up to begetting him, but Diomedes was the son of Apollo's 'African' Queen, Kyrene. And he had a sisterhood of carnivorous Mares: his chthonic 'hospitality' consisted of feeding his guests to his four Mares. Herakles was required to fetch them back for Eurystheus. His helper for this task was a turncoat, **Abderos**, a son of Hermes who was one of the henchmen of Diomedes, but who sided instead with Herakles. (This is a variant of the **animus** role that we have already seen in Herakles' twin Iphitos as a henchman of Eurystheus, while Iolaos, his son, sides with Herakles.) Abderos became proverbial of a 'simpleton.' There was a trick, and presumably it was his stupid idea: to sate the Mares' hunger with human

Herakles with the Upside-down Kerkopes (Metope from temple C at Selinunte 6th century BC, Museo Nazionale, Palermo)

flesh and thus render them tame. Herakles fed the Mares with Diomedes—which wasn't enough, and so he had to toss in Abderos, as well. To exonerate the hero, it could have all been an 'accident': there was a whole War involving the local peoples, and in the confusion Abderos, who was tending the Mares, got eaten. In any case, there was a reconciliation. Herakles (re)founded the city of Abderos, and commemorated his 'friend' with funeral games, such as were also held for the cult of Iolaos at Thebes. Herakles then rustled the Mares back to Eurystheus at Mycenae, who dedicated them to Hera. As with Pegasos, the steed of Perseus-Bellerophontes, the Mares became part of the herd on Olympus.

The twelfth labor, not in order, but to complete the cycle, was the **Bull of Minos**. This was a task that is better known from the career of another hero, **Theseus**, as part of his remaking of Delos and Athens. There were differences, however, in the telling. Theseus killed it, whereas Herakles fetched it back to Mycenae, where Eurystheus dedicated it to Hera; but it escaped and made its way to Athens, where Theseus had to kill it again—only the second killing was probably earlier than the first, and maybe there were two different bulls. But we will save the Bull for the next chapter, since it is the crowning achievement of Theseus's heroism. It was as this Bull of Minos or the Minotaur that the former Apollo and his

Goddess Artemis once presided over the human sacrifices enacted in the Minoan Labyrinth.

These were the twelve Labors: **The Hydra of the Lerna Spring; The Lion of the Nemean Caves; The Boar of Mount Erymanthos; The Hind of Mount Keryneia; The Birds of the Swamp of Stymphalos; The Kerberos Hound of Hades; The Stables of Augeias of Olympia; The Cattle of Geryoneus; The Apples of the Hesperides; The Bodice (Girdle) of Hippolyta; The Mares of Diomedes; and The Bull of Minos.**

The Sanctuary of Olympia

Herakles was credited with (re)founding the Sanctuary of Zeus at Olympia. What he had done in taming the whole world for its new order of deities, culminated in the rededication of this prime site of the Goddess (and of himself as 'digital' consort) for his Olympian Father. The commemoration of this event provided the Greeks with a chronology: the first performance of the Olympian athletic Games occurred in 776 BC, which was the beginning of historical (or written) time, and they were repeated every fourth year, so that you could date an event by Olympiads and each of the intervening three years. The lists of victors added these more recent heroes to the long mythological heritage, viewing each as a revitalization of the family's ancient ties with the divine blood lines; and poets were commissioned to celebrate the victories as festival performances (either at Olympia or back home), so that each victor might join the illustrious fame of his ancestors. Athletic contest was a ritual enactment of the same battle of equals (or self and anti-self) that we have seen as the paradigm of the hero's career.

Herakles himself, of course, was much earlier than the first Olympiad, about seven-hundred years earlier. It was he who cleared out the Stables of Augeias; and who planted the first olive of the Sacred Grove as a transmutation of the Hyperborean entheogen whose animate representation was the Golden Antler of the Hind. He also contributed his aid in ridding the region of centaurs and other 'hospitable' cow/mare lords, and in rescuing chthonic brides like Deianeira.

But he was not the first in this effort to found the new Olympia. His great-grandmother's father **Pelops**, an 'Asian' foreigner, had been there before him. Pelops had rescued an indigenous Mare-lady, **Hippodameia** (like the one that Perseus's 'enemy' Polydektes had chosen for wife): and from them would be descended the ruling dynasty of Mycenae, replacing the lineage of Perseus (with whom it was related by marriage via the female line); and the whole of the southern Greek mainland would cease to be 'Minoan-Pelasgian' and be named after him as the Peloponnesos, the 'Island of Pelops.'

We have mentioned this Pelops before, as the brother of the Theban Niobe, who was the arch-rival of Leto, the mother of Apollo and Artemis. Pelops and Niobe were children of **Tantalos**, whose background fits all the characteristics of a ruler in the primordial world. He was associated with the 'Burnt-lands' of

Phrygia and the kingdom of Lydia, where Omphale was Queen, as well as with the regions around Troy; and there were several mountains cited as the location of his tomb, most notably the same mountains of the Sipylos range above the city of Smyrna, where Niobe was transmuted into the weeping stone. But he may also have been from Argos, from the realms beneath its surface; and his tomb was there, also. The Zeus of former times was his father, and his mother was the chthonic Queen.

Tantalos was famous for a trick that he played, and like Sisyphos and the Danaids, he ended up in the netherworld, tormented by a task that he would never complete: his name was taken to mean 'Tormented Endurance.' Like the werewolf Lykaon, Tantalos tried to trick the new Olympians back into their older identities by offering them a meal of human flesh, even though he, like Prometheus, had himself been privileged to feast with them on ambrosia and nectar. Tantalos butchered his own son Pelops, cooked him, and served him up to the gods. They were not deceived by the ruse, but refrained from the banquet, except for Demeter, who was distracted at the time by thoughts of her own daughter Persephone residing in the underworld, and hence she gnawed at a bit of his shoulder. The gods restored Pelops to wholeness, replacing the missing part with a piece of ivory. This shoulder of 'African' ivory was passed on from generation to generation and was the hereditary emblem that demonstrated the divine right of the Pelopid dynasty to rule over the new Greece: they were men who had died and had come back again with something immortal from the Olympians, a race that united the old world with the new. It made Pelops so beautiful that Poseidon fell in love with him (just as Zeus had with the Trojan Ganymedes)—although it was also said that the tale of butchery was just a slander by people who were jealous that the boy was so favored. In any case, Tantalos was punished for his trick. Since he transgressed the laws of eating, he hungers eternally, with food and drink just out of reach, 'tantalized.' He stands in a pool of water which recedes as he stoops to drink; and above his head hangs the fruit of a tree, but if he reaches up to pluck it, a wind blows it away.

Pelops, the son of this Tantalos, had the very Earthy name of 'Mud-face;' and he surfaced in Greece, probably via the Argos connection, bringing up with him the magical sceptre of Peloponnesian rulership that Zeus, through Hermes, had conferred upon him. (There were even some who knew that Pelops' father was really the old Hermes.) And at Olympia, he performed the Contest with the 'enemy' (**paradigm #1**) that won over his new domains.

His opponent was **Oinomaos**, a (W)oinos-man, and he was 'king' at the sacred conical hill that rises steeply at the edge of the grove (or **Altis**) of Olympia in the plain beside the Alpheios River at its confluence with the Kladeos. The hill was the original sacred place, an Entrance where chthonic prophecy (as at the cave at Delphi) was practiced. Herakles renamed the hill Kronion, as belonging to Zeus's father Kronos—to work it into the traditions about the earlier generation of the Olympians.

Oinomaos had a team of chthonic Mares, one of them with the same name as his mother, the 'Snatcher,' so that 'centaurism' lurks in his background; the other Mare was called the 'Flea.' And like other such 'kings,' he may have been his daughter's lover, as well as her father. She was the Mare-lady **Hippodameia**; and each of her suitors had to vie with her father in a contest if he hoped to win the bride. Otherwise, he lost his head: the citadel of Oinomaos on this hill was decorated with these heads from suitors who hadn't survived the 'heady' encounter with the (W)oinos-man. There had been twelve (or thirteen) who hadn't outrun the Snatcher, before Pelops arrived.

The contest was a chariot race across the Peloponnesos, from Olympia to Isthmia (near Corinth): since that too was a famous Entrance, it is probable that the 'drunken' course took the subterranean route. Pelops won, by a trick. There was a turncoat helper involved: this was **Myrtilos**, a son of Hermes, and the charioteer of Oinomaos; he was named for the 'Myrtle,' a plant that is emblematic of 'marriage,' and hence a transmutation of the (W)oinos-man's **entheogen**. (He was also called Sphairios, the 'Ball,' since hoops and balls were similarly emblematic of sexual union.) Myrtilos sided with Pelops. He replaced the linchpins of Oinomaos's chariot with wax. In the race, the (bees)wax melted and Oinomaos was thrown to his death by his own team of Mares.

But even as a turncoat, Myrtilos was still a rival suitor for Hippodameia, and he tried to take the bride for himself; it may even be that Pelops had played a trick of his own and promised the bride to Myrtilos as a bribe for his aid. In any case, Pelops tossed Myrtilos from his chariot into the sea (off the east coast of the Peloponnesos) which was named Myrtoan after him. Hermes transmuted his son into the constellation called Auriga, the Charioteer. Pelops also tried to make amends by building the first temple to the new Hermes in the Peloponnesos.

When Herakles later rededicated the sanctuary, he erected what was supposed to be the **Tomb of Pelops**, beside the Kronion Hill; and he planted there the olive grove around it: in later times, when the Games were held, the former rites in which the suitor-contestants had died were commemorated by the young men who flagellated themselves at the tomb to offer Pelops a token spilling of their blood. The actual bones of Pelops were preserved not in the cenotaph, but in the nearby sanctuary of Artemis, where she was called by the epithet of the 'Whiplash'—as a reminder that Pelops and his men had danced a 'Rope-dance' there to celebrate his redemption from Death. There was just the sanctuary; nothing else was left of Oinomaos's town: the people who once had lived thereabouts had long since disappeared beneath the earth.

(Pelops himself had tried to make amends for the murder of Myrtilos by constructing a similar cenotaph in the hippodrome, burying beneath the marker for the race course certain secret objects: in later days, the ghost of Myrtilos, too, had to be appeased by the racers, or else he might materialize as they rounded the turn and madden their team of horses to cause their death. This terminus in the hippodrome was, of course, originally just the western limit; the race had gone all the way to Isthmia, and there another ghost used to haunt the eastern terminus: this was Glaukos, the son of Sisyphos, who had been killed and

Reconstruction of
Olympia

eaten by his team of Mares, maddened by pasturing on an **entheogen** from
the olden days, 'horse-mad' or Datura.)

Hippodameia, too, had her tomb nearby, beside the grove of Pelops' cenotaph, at the base of the Kronion Hill. Although in later days the Olympian Games
excluded females, there was still one contest for girls at a special quadrennial
Hera Festival. This was a footrace: the first maiden to win had been the 'turncoat' and 'botanic' Chloris (the only surviving child of Niobe) who would become
the mother of the similarly pivotal 'king' in the new age, **Nestor** of Pylos.

All that was left of Oinomaos's citadel on the Hill was a single pillar, labeled
by a bronze plaque.

The **Tombs of Pelops and Hippodameia** at the base of the Kronion Hill are
separated by the **Altar of Zeus**. Each day burnt offerings were made upon it;
and on a rotating basis, similar offerings were made at the altars of the other
Olympians throughout the sanctuary. The remains from all these burnings were
gathered upon the Zeus Altar, which day by day and year after year grew into
a conical mound, a rival imitating the Hill which still towers beside it, so that Herakles' initial rededication of the sanctuary was perpetually made more perfect—
until one day the Altar might equal the Hill, a mound constructed solely of the
transmuted former identities of the new Olympians. This area at the base of the
Hill was the most ancient and sacred site: beneath it are the foundations of the
buildings from the earliest period. (Nothing is left of the Tomb of Hippodameia
or the Altar; Pelops' Tomb is just a grove of trees on a mound of earth.)

The visitor today is apt to find the remains of the later Temples of Zeus and Hera
of more interest. These straddle the tomb-altar area, with Hera's closest to the Hill
and actually cutting into the slope of its base.

The **Temple of Hera** was the more ancient of the two, dating back to 600 BC
and built of wood and terra cotta tiles upon foundations a century earlier; and

the sense of its antiquity was preserved by replacing each of its original oak columns only when it became absolutely necessary, and then with a stone restoration that need not match the others, but was in whatever style was then current. The cult statue presented Hera, with Zeus standing beside her, dressed as a warrior: the head of Hera is all that survives. Of the many works of art that the temple once housed, only the famous statue of Hermes with the infant Dionysos has been found, a work of the fourth-century Praxiteles, or a copy of it. The temple also once stored several notable antiques, including what was reputed to be the original bed on which Zeus and Hera consummated their Sacred Marriage.

Further east, along the base of the Kronion Hill, stood the **Metroon**, or Temple of the Mother (of the Gods), a building of the fourth century, made over in the Roman period to the cult of Augustus Caesar. Lined up against the base of the Hill itself, extending eastward from the Temple of Hera, was the semicircular **Nymphaion Fountain** (a donation by the wealthy Athenian Herodes Atticus in the second century AD, and dedicated in the name of his wife Regilla to commemorate her service as priestess of Demeter; it was the terminus of a new aqueduct supplying water to the sanctuary; and it was also a monument to the family of Herodes, displaying statues of its members and their Roman friends); and further eastward, the line of **Treasuries**, where dedications and gear for the Games were stored for particular cities. On the slope of the Hill itself, between the Nymphaion and the first of the Treasuries, was the **Altar of Herakles**: it was later forgotten, however, whether this was the Herakles who was son of Zeus and founder of the sanctuary—or his 'digital' predecessor, a man like the Augeias-Oinomaos whom he replaced.

Parallel to the Temple of Hera, and on the other side of the Tombs of Pelops and Hippodameia, was the monumental **Temple of Olympian Zeus**, from the mid-fifth century BC. (Up to this time, Zeus had to share Hera's temple.) It lies in ruins today, shattered by an earthquake in the sixth century AD; its massive columns (of shell limestone, orginally faced with stucco) lie where they fell, strewn like wafers beside the Temple. It was the work of Libon, a local architect.

Within it was once the cult statue of Zeus, by the Athenian Pheidias, who later made the Athena of the Parthenon Temple at Athens, and like it, also constructed of ivory and gold (chryselephantine).

(The workshop where Pheidias and his artisans produced the statue is still standing, a building of the exact dimensions as the central chamber or cella of the Temple: it was later converted into a church; beside it are the houses where the workmen lived. The whole complex lies just west of the back side of the Temple, outside the sacred ground. Curiously, even the cup of Pheidias, scratched with his name, has been found. North of the workshop were the **Priests' Houses** and the buildings for the athletes to practice and socialize in before the Games (**Palaestra**, **Gymnasium**). South of the workshop was the **Leonidaion**, a fourth century hotel for distinguished visitors; it was remodeled in the Roman period as a residence for the Roman governor. West of the workshop were the hot Baths.)

Pheidias's statue presented Zeus, seated on his throne: it was so large (seven times life-size), that Zeus could not have stood in the Temple without thrusting his upper body through its roof. In his hand he held a Victory Athena, his own perfect transmutation of the Goddess that he could offer to the winners in the Games.

The sculptural groups on the Temple's pediments (or gables) conformed to the common optimistic eastward orientation of Olympian temples. (A later monument, in fact, that was intended to glorify the family of King Philip of Macedon, the **Philippeion**, off the back side of Hera's Temple, respected this symbolic orientation by being round and thus avoiding the rectilinear problem of placing an entrance either toward the optimistic east or the pessimistic west.) The Temple's eastern pediment displayed the Contest of Oinomaos and Pelops for the bride Hippodameia: standing tallest in the center was Zeus, himself, invisible to the contestants, but looking with favor toward Pelops on his right; left of Zeus was Oionomaos with his wife, while Pelops was coupled on the right with his bride Hippodameia; next on either side were the chariots and teams of four horses, that of Pelops with a boy, and a girl for Oinomaos; fitted into the lower corners of the triangle, were the charioteers, seers predicting the outcome, and finally personifications of the two rivers that join at Olympia, the Alpheios and the Kladeos. It was the work of the sculptor Paionios. He also produced the large figure of the Winged Victory which once stood on a pedestal in front of the entrance, another symbolic indication of what Zeus offered his athletes.

The western pedimental group was by Alkamenes. The marriage of Hippodameia was again its subject, but this was presumably another Mare-lady. It is the same myth that we have already seen depicted in the metope sequence of the Athenian Parthenon Temple: the centaurs became drunk and tried to abduct the bride from her husband **Peirithoos** and his friend **Theseus**; the battle is overseen by Apollo, who stands, like Zeus on the eastern pediment, in central position. Although this battle often took place in Thessaly, this is apparently a Peloponnesian version: for the centaur with Hippodameia is Eurytion, the same one who contested Herakles for his Lady, the **Deianeira** of Olympia; and the tribe of mortals (the **Lapithai** or men of the 'Stone-sisterhood') who oppose the drunken centaurs was native both to the slopes of Thessalian Mount Olympus and to the mountains in the vicinity of Olympia.

Beneath each pediment were metopes depicting the twelve labors of Herakles, the mythical prototype for the Games that the athletes would contest.

East of the Temple were the playing fields, the **Stadium** and the **Hippodrome**. The sacred ground of the Grove or **Altis** was crowded with the many dedications of various cities and commemorative representations of the victors. To earn a place in this sacred Grove was a valued honor. We have already seen how wealthy families like the Herodes and the Macedonian Philip encroached upon the prerogative by promoting themselves, without having earned it through

Contest. One of the most egregious examples of such 'bad taste' is the **House of Nero**, which was built for the Emperor's visit around 67 AD: he could not be expected to stay discretely at the Leonidaion hotel. A musical Contest was added to the Games precisely for this visit, so that the Emperor could have something to win.

South of the Temple, outside the sacred ground, were the buildings for the political administration of Olympia; and still further south, the town, not yet excavated and partially destroyed by the changing course of the river.

The Marriage to Megara

When Herakles returned from his Labors, his wives were waiting for him. There were two while he was still alive, just as there were two versions of him. Both marriages led to his death. With **Megara** of Thebes, he entered the chthonic realm, buried at Athens. With **Deianeira** of Kalydonia, he ascended to Olympus, where **Hebe** became his immortal wife, continually reviving him with her sacred drink.

The wives of the heroes were always 'turncoats.' In subduing the Queen in her many manifestations, the successful hero rescues her transmuted identity, from her chthonic past, to be his bride; and he reorganizes the queendom and its sisterhood into a Kingdom. This he did at all the Entrance sites.

We have already seen the Theban Entrance of the Thebai sisterhood: this was the Spring of Dirke, the 'horse-mad' Datura-lady, and the werewolf 'king' Lykos. At this site, the 'African' **Kadmos** (a cousin of the Danaos and Aigyptos of the Lernean Spring at Argos) had surfaced and consummated a Sacred Marriage, to beget a new sisterhood of his own daughters; these he gave in marriage to the 'digital' Sown Men or **Spartoi** to produce the first attempt to mediate the old and newer orders of civilization there. A second attempt was made with the twins **Amphion** and **Zethos**, whom Zeus begot on the 'turncoat' **Antiope**. The 'foreigner' Herakles, who was 'born' at Thebes, as we have seen, put his hand to the task, as well. In addition to the youthful Labors of his Wilderness Sojourn on the mountains of Thebes, he redeemed the city from its chthonic obligation to furnish human victims to the 'neighboring' people of the maenadic **Minyai** sisterhood (a pre-Greek people, like the Pelasgians and the Minoans: they were variously found in Arcadia of the Peloponnesos, in Thessaly, and near Thebes in Boeotia; their several towns were called Orchomenos). In payment for that redemption, Herakles won the Theban Queen **Megara**, and through her, the right to rule as her 'king'—a consort in a Queendom.

(The defeat of the Minyai involved a trick of nature. Herakles flooded their lands by letting in the sea through a labyrinth of channels dug through the mountain along the shore; and when he was finished, he drained the plain again, making it into the fertile fields of Boeotia: all that is left of the receding waters today is the swampy reclaimed marshlands of the former Lake Copais, named for the Kopai sisterhood.)

Megara was one of the females who resulted from the Kadmean mediation at Thebes: she was the daughter of **Kreon** (the 'king'), who was fifth in the line of 'digital' men that descended from the 'Serpent' Echion, through his son **Pentheus**. (Another attempted mediation would occur with her aunt **Iokaste**'s son **Oidipous**, and his sons, which would result in the great War that was fought at Thebes—to settle the place, once and for all.) Megara was named for the 'Chambers:' as 'turncoat,' these would be the the king's Palace or Throne Room, but more anciently, they would be the many cavernous Chambers of the subterranean labyrinth.

It was she who welcomed Herakles home when he surfaced again after the Labor of the Kerberos Hound. And it wasn't clear whether he had wakened into a nightmare, for in his absence, **Lykos**, a direct descendant of the aboriginal Lykos, had usurped control of the city and was planning to kill Megara, her three sons by Herakles, and Amphitryon. To avoid an unseemly and hopeless battle, Megara had agreed to let them all die, if only she could dress them appropriately for Death in funeral shrouds. And it was thus, in the guise of corpses, that Herakles found his family upon his return from the Deathlands. She meant well, but the world she had misguidedly devised for his return was dangerously precarious. Doubly precarious, as we have mentioned, was the fact that Herakles had rescued Theseus from the stone in Hades' realm and made him into a winner. You cannot have a winner without a loser. And the stone was waiting.

Herakles killed Lykos, his 'enemy'—a suicide, of sorts. Without the 'enemy' as a separate identity, Herakles would have to be both Herakles and Lykos at the same time. Hera sent the goddess of Madness, the 'She-wolf Rabies' or **Lyssa**. Through her and her pack of maenadic bitches, the poisons of the defeated beasts of his successful heroic career were turned back upon him: and infected with the wolfsbane toxin of Kerberos, Herakles now became a Wolf (a rabid hound), killing his wife and children—since the dead Lykos could no longer do it; and all the time, he hallucinated that he was destroying his 'archenemy' Eurystheus and his citadel of Tiryns.

Athena showed up just in time to prevent him from severing all ties with a mortal family by killing his father Amphitryon, as well. As the Gorgon (rather than its transmutation), she stunned him with a stone. When he woke from his trance to see what he had done, he affirmed the ties of friendship that bind together mortal families and friends, rejecting the heartless indifference of the Olympians. And now as a mortal, rather than the immortal son of Zeus, he went off to Athens with Theseus, so that Theseus could put a grave stone upon him when he died and was deposited as a 'friend' beneath the land of Athens.

In this tragic version of his liminal identity, Herakles has a mortal father, instead of Zeus. His **anima** Athena and his 'turncoat' wife have reverted to their former roles, before their transmutations, and have helped him descend into the Chambers of the chthonic realm, where he was needed more—at least for the sake of the winner, Athens and its (re)founder Theseus.

The Marriage to Deianeira

Deianeira (**Dejanira**), too, was a 'turncoat' whom Herakles rescued from a chthonic past.

Her name (like that of Perseus's Andromeda) could mean that she is 'Hostile to Men;' but transmuted, she becomes the spoils of battle, a 'Man's Booty,' won as his maiden bride, his prize from the Contest. Like Perseus and Herakles, her liminality, too, is expressed by the theme of the **two fathers**. The mortal father was a (W)oinos-man, **Oineus** of Kalydonia, the extensive swamplands in the southwestern corner of the northern Greek mainland (opposite Olympia, across the Gulf of Corinth), where the mighty **River Acheloos**, the greatest in Greece, empties into the Ionian Sea; and her mother was one of the 'floral' ladies, **Althaia**, named for the reedy swamp mallow that grows there in the marshes. She was apparently maenadic and slept with Dionysos, as well as her husband—on the same night. (Oineus was just as unfaithful as she: he slept with a 'Cow-lady,' **Periboia**, to beget his son **Tydeus**.) Oineus was a man like Megara's ancestor Pentheus, a 'king' of the olden times; and the opposition of Oineus versus Dionysos represents the evolution to the newer order: it was during the reign of Oineus that Dionysos introduced the cultivation and drinking of (w)oinos. (Oineus was one of a pair of **warring brothers**: his 'enemy' brother was Agrios, the 'Wild-man;' their father was the 'Planter;' and it was his father who discovered the first vinestock; the whole lineage is descended from the new generation inaugurated by the primordial couple, Deukalion and Pyrrha.)

We have already mentioned that Herakles' marriage to Deianeira was arranged for him in the underworld, where he was fetching the Hound Kerberos. It was suggested to him there by another of Deianeira's brothers, the dead **Meleagros** (Latin **Meleager**). Meleagros's mother Althaia had been responsible for killing him.

Like Deianeira, Meleagros also had **two fathers**, for the unfaithful Althaia had slept with Ares, too: many children were ascribed to Ares, but his paternity should not be taken too literally; Ares' children are usually the hostile creatures of the olden times, not easily assimilated into the Olympian age: Ares, himself, was the most hated of the Olympians. (Thus, for example, the serpent 'consort' of Dirke at Thebes was an offspring of Ares, and the spring was called the Spring of Ares; in transmuting its orientation, Kadmos earned the 'harmonious' Harmonia as his bride: she was the daughter of Ares and Aphrodite.) In 'accidentally' sending her son Meleagros to Hades, Althaia was helping to purge Kalydonia of its former traditions; Deianeira, as the daughter of the new Dionysos, has a similar meaning.

Meleagros was involved in the thorny problems of Artemis and Apollo: and in his death, he is another of the many fall guys for the two of them. Meleagros is named as the 'Hunter;' and hence it was inevitable that he would pose a sexual threat to Artemis. (He had another brother, **Toxeus**, the 'Archer;' and he was disposed of, too: Oineus killed him for neglecting the new vineyards.) Meleagros was destined to live only so long as a stick of wood burning on the hearth at the time of his birth remained unconsumed: Althaia removed it from the fire when she learned of this, and hid it away in a chest. (This stick was the predecessor of the vinestock; and as long as it and Meleagros remained in existence, the new vine could not sprout. Another way of telling this story involved the previous generations: the bitch of Oineus's grandfather had given birth to the stick; the next generation 'planted' it out of sight; and in the next, it sprouted into the vine.) Because of what happened on a famous 'Hunt,' Althaia replaced the stick on the hearth and caused Meleagros's death: thus getting rid of the old Apollo problem, as well as allowing the vinestock at last to sprout into the new era.

Meleagros incurred his mother's wrath because of what happened on the **Kalydonian Boar Hunt**. The Boar was sent as a plague upon the swamplands by Artemis, who often lurks in such marshy places near the sea. It was a Contest that summoned all the heroes then alive at the time, except for Herakles: he had already encountered Artemis's Boar in the Labor of the Arcadian **Boar of Mount Erymanthos**. One woman also came: this was **Atalante**, the 'Indomitable,' from—as you might expect— Arcadia; she was a proxy for Artemis herself: Atalante had been raised by a she-bear and trained as a Huntress during her Wilderness Sojourn on the Virgin Hill amidst the mountains of the central Peloponnesos; her father was variously named, but all the names indicate the chthonic realm of the old Artemis: he was either a 'Drug-man' (Iasios), a 'Cretan Hunter,' or a 'Swamp-reed man' (Schoineus). (Atalante came with another Arcadian, Ankaios: he, too, was a Hunter and dressed in a bearskin; and like Meleagros, he was destined not to live long enough to taste the wine from the new vineyard: he fell a victim to the Boar. 'Many a slip between the cup and the lip' was said about him: just as he was about to drink his first cup of wine, the Boar killed him.)

Meleagros, after much internecine strife amongst the army of heroes, succeeded in killing the Boar, but he unfortunately had also fallen in love with Atalante (-Artemis), who went about with her breasts provocatively exposed; and he presented the spoils of the hunt to her. A quarrel broke out with his uncles, Althaia's brothers, and he killed them. His mother in outrage and grief threw the stick back on the hearth. And he died. He was mourned perpetually by a sisterhood of women, who were metamorphosed into birds named after him, the Meleagridai sisters.

(Atalante is also known for another famous Contest: the **Footrace of the Golden Apples**. She had vowed to remain virgin and challenged every suitor to a footrace; the losing suitors died, shot with the toxins of her bow. An ('African') 'Black-man' **Melanion**, who was also a 'Horse-man' **Hippomenes** (and perhaps also a 'Datura-man' or the thorn apple, 'hippomanes') succeeded in winning her for his bride. He tossed some golden (thorn) apples in her course, and she was so irrepressibly possessed with love for them that she stooped to gather them, while he raced on to the finish. Atalante yielded to her victor in a place sacred to the Goddess—and Artemis got rid of the two of them, and purged herself as well from the old **entheogen**. Hippomenes and Atalante were turned into lions, doomed to chastity (for lions supposedly don't mate) and hitched to the cart of the great Goddess. This is all actually just another way of telling the story of the Kalydonian Boar Hunt: for it was also claimed that Atalante had a son, **Parthenopaios**, a matrilineal 'Son of the Virgin'—either by Hippomenes-Melanion or by Meleagros.)

Such was Deianeira's family. And when it came time for her to chose a husband, she was wooed by the River **Acheloos**, who terrified her by his chthonic courtship, as he metamorphosed into three hallucinatory monsters. Herakles arrived just in time, to fulfill his netherworld agreement with her brother Meleagros. Herakles entered the Contest with his 'enemy' (**paradigm #1**) and rescued Deianeira, winning her as his spoils. In the conflict, Herakles wrenched the bull horn from the River's forehead and transmuted it into the cornucopia, a symbol of the fertility that can flow into this world from the Deathlands (**paradigm #2**).

And unlike his marriage to Megara, with Deianeira Herakles did not make the mistake of taking up residence as consort in his wife's Queendom. But on their wedding night, as they escaped eastward from the Western Realm, they ducked down, on their way out, through the Exit-Entrance at the 'Thermal Springs' of Thermon, the sacred city of Apollo and his Kalydonian peoples, constructed high above the banks of the River Euenos, which was formerly called the Lykormas, the 'Wolf-rush.' When they surfaced, they would be at the Entrance of the 'Hot Gates' at Thermopylai. But as they made their way through the interconnected labyrinth of subterranean chambers, the centaur **Nessos**, who had survived the Erymanthian Boar Hunt, was waiting for them—and tried to steal the bride.

Herakles once again had to rescue Deianeira from a river, and a centaur, just as he had rescued the other Deianeira in the Peloponnesos from Eurytion at Olympia.

(The River Euenos, as the 'Bridled-(horse),' has a centaur's name, itself; just as the other name of the river, Lykormas, suggests Apollo's werewolf involvement in this episode of the escape from Oineus's Deathlands. There was another story that made this even clearer: Euenos, just like the Oinomaos of Olympia, used to contest the suitors for his daughter **Marpessa**, the 'Snatcher,' a maiden devotee of Artemis; the unsuccessful racers, here too, lost their heads; when Euenos finally was outrun by a great Archer, he and his horses plunged into the river; but Apollo, himself also courted the bride: she spurned him and chose the other suitor. Their daughter became the wife of Meleagros.)

Herakles rescued Deianeira by shooting Nessos with the toxins of his defeated adversaries; but as the centaur died, he gave Deianeira a few drops of his poisoned blood, for her to use, should she ever need to bind her lover irrepressibly to her and make him lose his head for love of her. Through her, the toxin would eventually return to the Archer.

Herakles, in this telling of his death, used the maenadic village of Trachis, on the mountain of Oita or 'Doom,' above Thermopylai, as a base for his remaining heroic adventures, repeatedly revisiting his wife to beget sons, whenever he returned from a task. The last labor was the servitude to Queen Omphale, on the nether side of the thermal waters. Although he worked out his period of Bondage to her, he returned enslaved by his attraction to Iole.

Deianeira, seeing herself now as the discarded 'flower,' tried to bind Herakles back again to herself, by anointing a robe with the Nessos blood to present to Herakles just as he surfaced. Once again, as with Megara, the two worlds became hopelessly confused; and Deianeira, unwittingly, had reverted to her former self: she had become another Omphale, dominating her consort.

It had been prophesied that Herakles could die only at the hands of someone dead; and this turned out now to be doubly true: for his 'enemy' Nessos was dead (just as Lykos was dead, in the Megara episode); and so was Deianeira—for she committed suicide when she learned what she had done.

In order to free himself from the maddening torment of the poison, Herakles arranged for his body to be transmuted into spirit by a funeral pyre on the top of Oita: in this death, he ascended to Olympus. But not without leaving behind the heritage of the poison for some 'friend' to bear. He required that his son **Hyllos** accept Iole as his bride; and the poisoned bow and arrows he gave to **Philoktetes**. It would prove to be the (wolfs)bane of that hero's mortal existence. But you cannot have a winner without a loser.

The Archer Philoktetes loved his poisoned heritage of the bow (**paradigm #2**) that he received from his friend Herakles: his name means just that—'Love-Possession.' Eventually his bow would find its way to the Trojan War to end the old Apollo's chthonic involvement in the Deathlands.

Winners and Losers

Herakles ultimately failed at what he had set out to do. Although he may have joined the ranks of the Olympians, it was only at the loss of his humanness. He never did manage to win Tiryns back for his exiled mortal father; nor did he ever succeed in passing a dynasty on to his male descendants. The two Zeussons, Perseus and Herakles, never established their direct lineage as rulers of the Peloponnesos; instead Mycenae would pass to the brother of Herakles' grandmother. He was a son of Pelops. This was **Atreus**; and with his two **warring** sons, **Agamemnon** and **Menelaos**, another attempt would be made to mediate the division between the masculine dominance of the immortal Olympians and the chthonic mortality of the old Goddess's realm. This time with Zeus-daughters, **Helen** and **Klytaimnestra** (**Clytaemnestra**). These two were mortal; nor were they virgin, like the Olympian Athena; or even worse, frigid, like Artemis. Klytaimnestra and Helen would marry Agamemnon and Menelaos—and finally solve their differences through the great War at Troy.

Herakles, however, had many children, both from his 'foreign' involvements and from his two wives. Those from Megara, of course, he killed. But Hyllos

Warring Brothers: Herakles and Apollo Fight for the Delphic Tripod (Red-figure vase c. 525 BC by the painter for Andokides, Pergamonmuseum, Berlin)

and the others from Deianeira were destined to die out, also. The final battle—at least so the Athenians believed—was fought at Athens.

They had sought asylum there from Eurystheus, whom Herakles had never succeeded in 'killing,' except in fantasy. Eurystheus pursued them with an army, and a War was fought, with Theseus and the Athenians as defenders. Hyllos finally managed to remove Eurystheus's head. The aged Iolaos was the companion for Hyllos, as he had been for his uncle Herakles. (It was even thought that Iolaos may have already died by this time, but that he returned from the 'foreign' lands for this encounter.) The battle could not have been won unless one of Herakles' daughters agreed to die. This was the 'Blessed-maiden' **Makaria**; where she sacrificed herself, a Spring, named after her, came into being. Alkmene was still alive, and the head of Eurystheus was presented to her; this, too, was buried in the Athenian land. And all of them made their ways to the Deathlands; they were all venerated at the Entrances.

Shortly after the completion of the Trojan War, they were thought to come back again; for the Wars hadn't really solved the problem. There was a new wave of Indo-European migrations, unassimilated people of the Dorian tribal group, associated with the tribe already inhabiting the Peloponnesos. The Greeks later remembered them as the sons of Herakles, the **Herakleidai**. This second Coming disrupted the settlements of the Mycenaean Age and plunged Greece into four-hundred years of turmoil and cultural regression, a Dark Age that they were not to emerge from until the eighth century, when the art of writing was invented again and Greece begins it historical period.

The Dorians apparently by-passed Attica, the land of Athens—perhaps because it was out of the way, protected by mountains, and of no special fertility. It also had Athena and so many pacified 'friends' from the past buried beneath its surface.

* * * *

Review

Herakles (**Hercules**) was originally a 'digital' consort of the Goddess at her many Entrance sites throughout the Greek lands. He was born anew into the Olympian age as a son of **Zeus**, from the mortal woman **Alkmene** and her husband **Amphitryon**, a grandson of **Perseus**. His heroic career pits him against the Goddess, primarily as **Hera** or **Artemis**; and like all the 'consort' figures of Artemis, inevitably he is an 'enemy' of **Apollo**.

Herakles is a liminal hero, with the typical two different ways of looking at the meaning of his name as 'Hera's Man.' And there are two versions of his former identity whom he confronts in his heroic career: his twin brother **Iphikles**, and more important, **Eurystheus** of Tiryns-Mycenae. Iphikles' son **Iolaos** often accompanies Herakles as 'helper;' **Athena** is the female version of this 'helper' role. Iolaos is a Hermes figure, and other versions of this 'stone'-helper also occur: **Theseus, Atlas, Abderos**.

The common attributes of Herakles' portrayal are: his club, his bow and poisoned arrows, and his lionskin, often worn with the gaping jaws as a headdress. All three attributes are liminal in their possibilities of meaning; Herakles' notorious eating and drinking habits are similarly ambiguous.

Twelve Labors were listed as the episodes of his heroic career. Each, however, took him to the various Deathlands, and subsumed many incidental adventures, with little complete agreement as to which ones took place where. Nor is there agreement about the order of the twelve, although the resettlement of Olympia was the culminating achievement, at least when viewed in hindsight by the Greeks as they emerged into the historical period, especially since no royal dynasty could be traced directly to his lineage. These are the Twelve in the canon of Olympia:

>   **The Lernean** (or **Lernaean**) **Hydra**
>   **The Nemean Lion**
>   **The Erymanthian Boar**
>   **The Keryneian Hind**
>   **The Stymphalian Swamp**
>   **Kerberos**
>   **The Stables of Augeias**
>   **The Cattle of Geryoneus**
>   **The Apples of the Hesperides**
>   **The Girdle of Hippolyta**
>   **The Mares of Diomedes**
>   **The Bull of Minos**

(Only one of the Labors does not require Herakles to fetch something back to Mycenae: the Stables of Augeias, although he may have fetched a Deianeira-Hippodameia maiden; the Hydra wasn't exactly fetched either, although he did take possession of its toxin.)

All of them imply a reorganization of the pattern of religion from chthonic to Olympian shamanism, and the transmutation of the sacred plants from the former to the newer traditions. These entheogens were: Datura (Dirke's **dirkaion**, the centaurs' **hippomanes** or horse-mad, Atalante's thorn apple); aconite (**lykoktonon** or wolfsbane); probably the narcotic poppy, indicated by Herakles' sleeping trances, as well as by **Ladon** or **kisthos**; Amanita; olive. At Olympia, the original 'entranced' or ecstatic shaman's rapture was replaced by 'scientific' divination by male priests, who studied omens and proclaimed their conclusion; this represents a more complete transmutation from female shamanism than that as practiced at Delphi.

The incidental adventures that accrued to the Twelve Labors include: in the

'African' Deathlands: **Contest with Bursiros**; **Contest with Antaios**; **Contest with the Pygmies**; **Contest with Triton**; in the Western Deathlands: **Contest with Atlas**; **Contest with Eurytion**; **Contest with Acheloos and Rescue of Deianeira**; in the Eastern or 'Asian' Deathlands: **Rescue of Prometheus and Death of Cheiron**; **Contest with Troy's Laomedon and Rescue of Hesione**; **Bondage to Omphale**; **Bondage to Iole**; in the Northern Deathlands: **Rescue of Alkestis**; **Discovery of the Olive**; in the Entrance Gateway: **Contest with Neleus**; **Contest with the Kerkopes**; **Contest with Nessos**; **Rescue of Theseus**; **Rescue of Askalaphos**; **Journey in the Cup of Helios**; in the Wilderness Sojourn: **Contest with Hera**; **Contest with the Theban Lion**; **Contest with Thespios and the Thespiai**; **Contest with the Minyans**.

Of his two mortal marriages, the one with **Megara** of Thebes led to his reentry into the netherworld; that with **Deianeira** of Kalydonia, led to his escape from mortality and ascension to Olympus, where he married **Hebe (Ganymede)**. The former tragic version allows another hero to be successful; the latter version, of the Olympian ascension, requires another hero to accept the burden of his relinquished mortality: **Hyllos** or **Philoktetes**: a similar pattern allows him to give **Hesione** to **Telamon**, and **Antiope-Hippolyta** to **Theseus**.

The Contest of Herakles and Eurytion for the Deianeira bride at Olympia is better known as the **Contest of Pelops and Oinomaos for Hippodameia**; it is also the same story as the **Contest of Euenos** (Apollo) **and** (the Archer) **Idas for Marpessa**.

The Labor of the Erymanthian Boar occurs, without Herakles' participation, in two other versions: **The Kalydonian Boar Hunt** and **The Footrace of the Golden Apples**. (Recall that the Boar Hunt was also part of Perseus's Contest with the Gorgon Medusa.) In both, an Artemis-like **Atalante** is the maiden; the 'consort' is **Meleagros-Hippomenes**.

For Discussion and Further Study

1. The episode of Herakles' marriage to Megara is the plot of Euripides' *Herakles* tragedy. Read it and consider:

As Euripides intended the play to be staged, the same actor, with different masks, had to impersonate the roles of both Lykos and Herakles. Is there any meaning to this doubling of roles?

2. The episode of Herakles' marriage to Deianeira is the plot of Sophocles' *Women of Trachis* tragedy. Read it and consider:

As Sophocles intended the play to be staged, the same actor, with different masks, had to impersonate the roles of both Deianeira and Herakles. Is there any meaning to this doubling of roles?

Chapter IX
Theseus: Making the New Athens

༖

Theseus, as we have seen, was a contemporary of Herakles; and like him, related, as a third generation, to the Pelopids of Mycenae: his mother **Aithra** was
of the same generation as Agamemnon and Menelaos, and their Spartan wives
Klytaimnestra and Helen: she was, moreover, a woman of Troizen, and of the
same generation as Herakles' father Amphitryon, who, you will remember, had
spent a period of 'regency' at Troizen. Theseus was no blood descendant of the Perseids, but was related only through his grandfather **Pittheus**, who was a brother of the Pelopid maiden who married Alkaios, the grandfather of Herakles.

Genealogical Chart: Theseus

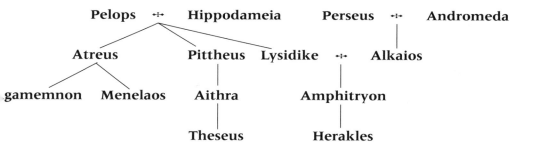

Even though Perseus, therefore, had already transmuted the Gorgon Medusa
into the new Athena in the regions of Argos, four generations before the time
of Theseus, this change had not yet taken firm hold on the city of the Athenai
sisterhood, Athens. When Theseus first came to Athens, it was still in the control of a witch, the 'Asiatic foreigner' **Medeia** (Latin **Medea**), or 'Queen,' a
name that is the same as Medusa. And children still belonged to their mother,
more than to a father, despite previous unsuccessful attempts to change the system. In the course of his heroic career, Theseus would free the city from its 'foreign' entanglements, and once again try to establish patriliny.

The main event of his career was the Contest with the Bull of Minos or the
Minotaur, an episode that had also occupied Herakles, although in a different
form; but like Herakles, Theseus, too, performed a sequence of other Labors.

This has led some people to consider him merely an Athenian imitation of the other hero: but this is probably not so, for there are major differences in their Labors. Theseus is occupied only with the sacred Entrances that are local to the lands of Athens—even the Minoan Bull had its local Entrance, as we shall see, at Marathon. And Theseus had no 'master' (or **warring brother**) like Herakles' Eurystheus or Iphikles; nor was he ever required to fetch something, like Herakles and Perseus, apart from an occasional abducted bride. And although Theseus has **Peirithoos** as an **animus** 'friend and companion,' he accompanies him on only one adventure. This lack of 'enemy' and 'friend' makes Theseus a more solitary hero; even Athena is not always with him as his **anima**.

Herakles' 'helpers,' as we have seen, often were stand-ins for Hermes or a herm-like figure. Theseus's lack of such a helper may be due to the particular nature of his own liminality: he is not a son of Zeus (for his divine potential), but of Athena's 'consort' Poseidon, and hence similar to Chrysaor-Pegasos; and he incorporates the herm or stone-fixation as part of his own identity. His name means either that he is 'Placed,' fixed to a stone, or that he 'Places,' or settles 'friends' beneath stones, as burial—to establish the legions of alliances with chthonic spirits, upon which the founding of civilization depends. As a Founder, he is like the better aspect of Apollo; and as a Trickster or Herm, he is better suited, all by himself, to confront Apollo with the tricks of nature, than is Herakles.

Although Theseus, too, like Herakles, will ultimately fall victim to a werewolf Apollo and will not succeed in establishing a dynasty of sons, the crowning achievement of his career will be the help he offers Apollo in transmuting him away from his deadly role in the Minoan Labyrinth—and replacing it with the Labyrinth Dance of the rescued victims, which constituted Theseus's reorganization of the religion at the sanctuary of Delos on the island of the god's rebirth into the Olympian age.

This was a major cultural transition, like the making of the new Olympia by Herakles. Theseus would accomplish for his own tribal group, the Ionians, what Herakles did for the Dorians. The Ionians were settled in Athens, as well as on the islands to the east in the Aegean Sea, and still further eastward on the western shore of Asia Minor; whereas the Dorians were centered in the Peloponnesos, Thebes, and the islands and shore of Asia Minor south of the Ionians. In general, the Ionians were more innovative, while the Dorians were conservative, preserving older forms of society: at Sparta there was even a dual kingship, like warring brothers; and men and women led quite separate lives.

The redemption of Apollo from his 'foreign' affairs was also enacted in the myth of the Trojan War: although Theseus and Herakles are from the next generation after Agamemnon, who led the combined troop of heroes at Troy, they appear to be a full generation earlier: Theseus's son took part in the war. And Theseus and Herakles were involved with the Trojans of the generation before Agamemnon: Herakles destroyed Laomedon's Troy and placed Priam on the throne; Priam was the father of the generation of Trojans who fought at the

War; and Theseus took part in Herakles' 'Asiatic' episode (which included the first Trojan War), as well as in the Kalydonian Boar Hunt. Both Theseus and Herakles, moreover, took part in Iason's Voyage of the Argo, another corporate endeavor of heroes which supposedly occurred in the generation before the Trojan War, although the whole adventure was over before Theseus was even conceived.

Aigeus Consulting the Delphic Priestess (Red-figure kylix c. 440-30 BC, Staatliche Museen, Berlin)

The Birth of Theseus

Aigeus (Latin **Aegeus**) was one of the 'kings' of the primordial Athens, and apparently the fifth. To judge by his name, he was a 'Goat-man.' And in that city of the Goddess's sisterhood, he was having trouble begetting a son, although there was no dearth of 'kingly' males who took their name from Pallas, the **Pallantidai**. When Aigeus, after several unsuccessful marriages, consulted Apollo at the Delphic sanctuary, the priestess gave him an enigmatic solution to his problem: do not untie the foot of your wineskin until you come to Athens.

The meaning of the riddle escaped him, although it is obvious: the wine-filled goatskin with its foot was both a metaphor for his genitals and for his satyric nature; and he was advised not to engage in a maenadic revel at an Entrance (like the Korykian Cave at Delphi) until he resurfaced back at Athens, or else he was apt to face the same trouble that Xuthos had with the Athenian Queen Kreousa, who, you will remember, pawned off Apollo's son Ion as her husband's, from an affair with a maenad at Delphi.

Aigeus apparently lost his way on his return and came up first at Poseidon's Isthmian Entrance at Corinth. There, the 'Queen' **Medeia** was the 'foreigner' in residence, fresh from the completion of the Voyage of the Argo—which had fetched her finally to the surface from the depths beneath Corinth. She explained the riddle to Aigeus (for she was notorious as a witch), in return for a safe residency at Athens, as soon as she had finished a dispute she was having with her 'consort' **Iason** (Latin **Jason**). He intended to marry a Corinthian princess named **Glauke**, the 'Owl-woman,' a primordial Gorgon Athena; and from her he wanted to beget sons, neglecting the sons that were Medeia's by him, out of wedlock. Aigeus agreed to the bargain. After he left, Medeia killed her sons—to spite Iason, and to retrieve them back into her own chthonic realm; and she fled to Athens, so that she would be waiting there for him when Aigeus got home. She also killed Glauke, poisoning her into a maenadic frenzy; the poor maiden plunged down into the Entrance that was a fountain named after her, Glauke's Well. In effect, Medeia had obstructed the transmutation of the Goddess at Corinth into the new era. And now she was ready to take on the wineskin of Aigeus, upon his return.

But again he lost his way in the labyrinthine interconnections, and surfaced this time at the Entrance of Troizen. There the 'hospitable' **Pittheus**, son of the 'horse-maiden' **Hippodameia** and **Pelops**, breached his **pithos** vat of (w)oinos and made Aigeus drunk. And in his drunken stupor, Aigeus did exactly what he had been advised not to do: he untied his wineskin and slept with the daughter of Pittheus, **Aithra**. It is clear, however, that Pittheus's intentions were sinister; for if Aigeus had, in fact, waited until he found his way to Athens, he would have had Medeia, instead of Aithra. And Aithra was a **turncoat**, named for the 'Storm-free Upper-air' that is spiritually volatile, like 'ether.'

As they slept together, Athena wakened Aithra, who swam across the narrow straits to the island offshore of Troizen to sleep with **Poseidon** also, in his temple there, so that on the same night she slept with both a mortal and a god, thus laying the basis for the liminality of the son she would conceive (**two fathers**). The island had been called Sphairia, after the Myrtilos-Sphairios who was the charioteer of Oinomaos and who was buried there, as some claimed; Aithra renamed it the 'Holy,' Hiera, and rededicated it to Athena, for Aithra would bear the child that Athena herself could never bear to her former 'consort' Poseidon (or the Goat-man 'king' of Athens).

The child was Theseus. But Aigeus did not wait for Aithra to give birth. He returned to Athens—and his Queen, the renegade Medeia. Thus it was that Theseus was born in his mother's land, and not his father's; but before Aigeus left, he deposited certain tokens beneath a stone; these would prove the identity of any son that Aithra might have conceived in their night of drunken revel: a sword and a pair of sandals. This was to be the meaning of Theseus's name. When he came of age, Aithra was to show him the stone—which only he could lift; and with these tokens, Theseus should set out for Athens in search of his father.

The Wilderness Sojourn

Although Herakles was of the same generation as Theseus, he was said to have visited Pittheus when Theseus was still a child. While being 'hospitably' entertained, Herakles happened to lay aside his lionskin. All the children took it to be a real lion and ran away in fright, except for Theseus, who grabbed an axe and bravely attacked it. Herakles interpreted this as a sign of the boy's future heroism.

When Theseus grew to puberty, he offered his hair to Apollo—and like that god, he never allowed his own beard to grow. He raised the stone, took the tokens and set off, by the subterranean route, to Athens, surfacing at each of the Entrances that are strung along the coast of the Saronic Gulf, from Troizen to Athens, which lies directly across from it on the northern shore. At each of the sites, there was an opponent who represents his own pre-Olympian role as an Apollo, Poseidon, or Hermes (**paradigm #1**). In all, there were six of these Labors.

His first 'enemy' encounter was at Epidauros, which henceforth would be sacred to Apollo and the curative powers of his mortal son, the 'druggist' or doc-

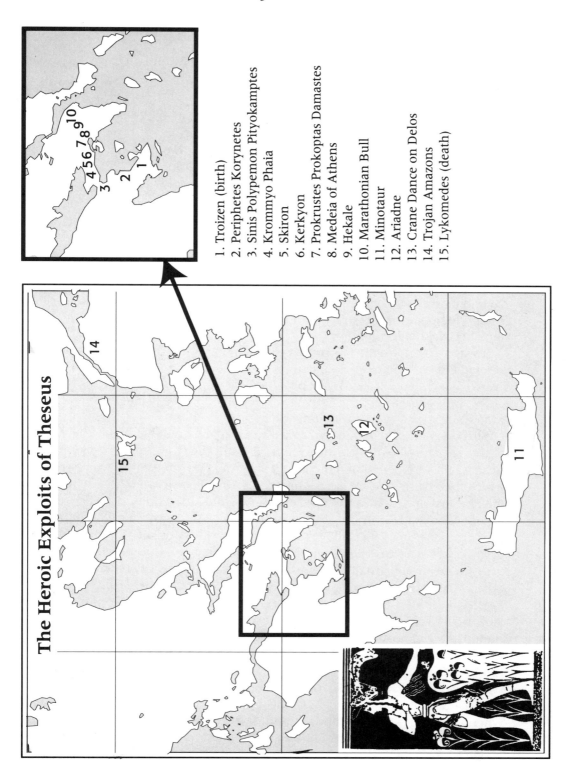

The Heroic Exploits of Theseus

1. Troizen (birth)
2. Periphetes Korynetes
3. Sinis Polypemon Pityokamptes
4. Krommyo Phaia
5. Skiron
6. Kerkyon
7. Prokrustes Prokoptas Damastes
8. Medeia of Athens
9. Hekale
10. Marathonian Bull
11. Minotaur
12. Ariadne
13. Crane Dance on Delos
14. Trojan Amazons
15. Lykomedes (death)

tor Asklepios. There Theseus met the 'Famous' **Periphetes**, a 'Club-bearer,' also called **Korynetes**, a limping offspring of Hephaistos, and a descendant of the old Hermes, as well. He customarily clubbed his 'visitors' into the Earth. Theseus stole the weapon and copied the trickster's trick: he clubbed the Famous Clubber, **Periphetes Korynetes**. This was how Theseus acquired the magical club that he often is seen carrying in his heroic career.

At the Isthmian Entrance, he found a son of Poseidon, like himself, the 'Plundering Thief' **Sinis**, who was also called **Polypemon** or 'Much Pain' and **Pityokamptes** or 'Pine-bender' because of the trick he liked to play on those he 'hospitably' entertained. Using his daughter **Perigoune** as a lure, he enticed his guests into her garden; there he bent two pine trees down to the ground, tied the visitor, one side to each, and then let the trees spring back up, to split his victim in half—to separate the liminal identities. Theseus again played the same trick on the trickster, **Sinis Polypemon Pityokamptes**. Perigoune, who was hiding from him in a thicket of asparagus and rushes, became the mother of one of his illegitimate sons, an 'African' named 'Black-horse' or **Melanippos**, who eventually was the founder of an 'Asiatic' dynasty in the region of Ethiopia: there they still held in reverence the plants that had offered Perigoune shelter. The bride herself he pawned off on someone from the Oichalia Entrance. Presumably, she made her way eastward, as well.

It was an 'Onion-witch' **Krommyo** and her ghostly 'Grey' Sow **Phaia** who greeted him when next he popped up, in the 'Onion-land' called Krommyon; despite her 'weeping eyes' as she pled for mercy, Theseus destroyed the beast—or the both of them, for the Lady was also named Phaia, like her sow—and he turned the trick against the trickster, **Krommyo Phaia**.

Skiron was his next enemy: it was later remembered that he had been one of the serpentine 'consorts' of Athena, like another Kekrops; and women in Athens still commemorated the Goddess by the Festival of the Skirophoria, in which they paraded with large white parasols (called **skira**) over the heads of the priestess of Athena and the priests of Poseidon and Helios to a place on the Acropolis called Skiron. But in the earlier days, Skiron was a thief inhabiting the narrow pathway high above the precipitous cliff along the shore; at the base of the cliff was a carnivorous Sea Turtle that carried you through this Entrance to the netherworld, just outside the labyrinthine limestone 'Chambers' of the city called Megara. Skiron's trick was to require that anyone who wished to pass by had to pause to wash his feet for him. As the traveler performed this service, Skiron would kick him over the cliff, down to his turtle. Theseus played the same trick again on the trickster, **Skiron**; and he even rode the Turtle triumphantly back down through the Entrance, to continue on his way. Later he was said to have (re)painted an effigy of Athena with white gypsum or limestone, which is called **skiras** and is abundant in these cliffs around Megara.

It was another serpent-man who met him a short way further along the coast when he surfaced at the famous Entrance of Eleusis, **Kerkyon**, the 'Tail-man,' like the Kerkopes who tried to rob Herakles at Thermopylai. Kerkyon, too, was a son of Poseidon, or Hephaistos. He challenged the traveler to a brutal wrestling match; Theseus not only won, smashing Kerkyon to the Earth, but he was said to have set the rules that henceforth made wrestling a civilized sport. Kerkyon's daughter, this time, appears to have been the trickster, the crafty 'Vixen' **Alope**; Theseus and she made love, but it was she who died: her grave can still be seen, right next to the Wrestling Ground, outside of the village of Eleusis.

Still in the plain of Eleusis, where the fig tree marks the spot where the Goddess Persephone had descended into Hades, Theseus next surfaced. Here there was a notorious 'host:' the 'Stretcher' **Prokrustes**, also called the 'Curtailer' **Prokoptas** and the 'Compeller' **Damastes**. His trick was to compel his guest to fit his bed, either stretching him longer or lopping him off shorter with his deadly hammer, until he had a perfect fit. Theseus again turned the trick on the trickster, making him fit into his own bed. (We now have the term 'Procrustean bed' for a theory or a system into which the facts are ruthlessly fitted, without regard to truth.)

(In all six of these Labors, Theseus acts alone, without **anima** or **animus**. Nothing is fetched. The plants, if any, are completely transmuted, with no indication of their former role as **entheogens**: asparagus, rushes, figs, onions; although the pine tree of Pityokamptes suggests Dionysian connotations, and the episode at Epidauros may suggest medicinal drugs; nor is there any involvement of sleepiness or trances, as was noticeable in the Labors of Herakles. It is probably significant, in this regard, that Theseus is not an 'archer,' nor does he have poisoned arrows. The sequence, unlike Herakles, is fixed, following the topographical route along the shore from Troizen to Athens: **Periphetes Korynetes**; **Sinis Polypemon Pityokamptes**; **Krommyo Phaia**; **Skiron**; **Kerkyon**; and **Prokrustes Prokoptas Damastes**. The episodes with Pityokamptes (Perigoune) and Kerkyon (Alope) involve bride stealing and 'foreign' involvements, but apart from Krommyo, Theseus's 'enemies' are male and chthonic consorts, and not the Goddess, herself.)

The Contest with Medeia

When he finally surfaced on the borders of Attica, as he made his way along the Sacred Road from Eleusis, across the Kephissos River, he was met by the sons of the man who had planted the first fig tree, which had been a gift to him from the Goddess as reward for his 'hospitality'; his name was **Phytalos**, the 'Planter,' and his 'sons' were called the Phytalidai—although they may originally have been a sisterhood. They purified Theseus, to cleanse him from the contamination of his journeys through the Deathlands: the altar still stood there in historical times, next to the river. From there, he made his way into the city. It was the eighth day of the month, the day that was sacred to his father Poseidon. But pubescent Theseus had still to establish which sex he was: some workmen constructing a Temple of Apollo even mistook him for a maiden, addressing him with compromising innuendos, until he displayed his maleness by tossing a bull right over the workmen and the roof.

Medeia was waiting for him. She even had managed to have a son of her own from Aigeus: and she had named him **Medos**, after herself, in proper matrilin-eal fashion—so Aigeus still didn't have a son. She invited Theseus to a celebra-tion at the Apollo Temple (which appears also to have been the House of Aigeus), and she poisoned Theseus's wine with wolfsbane. Just as Theseus was about to drink it, Aigeus recognized his son by the tokens, and dashed the wine cup to the ground. The spot where the wine was spilled was still shown as a relic from the past, fenced off in the Temple. (You will recall that this is the same story that we have already seen told about Ion, whom the 'Queen' Kreousa tried to poi-son at Delphi.)

Medeia clothed herself and her son in a cloud and fled to the eastern Death-lands, where she belonged. Her son became the ancestor of the Medes.

There were still the Pallantidai to contend with, those children who took the name of the old Pallas. They rose in revolt, and in a battle (or a Boar Hunt, as some claimed) Theseus and Aigeus defeated them and finally vindicated the role of the son as the father's, rather than the mother's descendant. The Pallantidai, how-ever, would remain a continual threat, a rival power group, ready to reassert themselves in this city of Pallas, in the event of Theseus's shift to the tragic ver-sion of his own liminality.

The Contest with the Minotaur

That could have been the successful completion of Theseus's heroic career. But there was another, and more famous, way of telling his story. There was still a 'Bull' that Theseus had to confront as his 'enemy.' Some people included the Bull in the Wilderness Sojourn, substituting it for one of the six Labors. This was the same Bull that belonged to 'king' Minos of the Cretan Labyrinth at Knossos, and that Herakles had fetched to Mycenae for Eurystheus: it escaped and took refuge at the Entrance in the plain of Marathon, north of Athens. Theseus set off for the adventure, and on the way he was 'hospitably' put up for the night, dur-ing a violent storm, in the hut of the good 'witch' **Hekale** (a version of the God-dess Hekate). The next day, he captured the Bull—but on his way back, he discovered that his hospitable 'friend' had died. He buried her (as he did with everyone) and founded the settlement of Hekale, which he named after her. The Bull he sacrificed to the Apollo whose Temple was the House of Aigeus (and Medeia).

But the other way of telling this story has Theseus just use the Marathon En-trance to journey all the way to the Cretan Deathlands to confront the Bull, which was still more obviously his 'enemy' contender, than the Marathonian Bull, since this one in Crete was actually part bull and part man (**paradigm #1**). This was the **Minotaur**, and before we let Theseus dispose of it, we must see where it came from.

We begin a full eight generations earlier than the time of Theseus and Herakles, back at the 'Blood-red' Phoenician shore of the 'Black' Ethiopian Deathlands, at the Port of Ioppe, famous for its sightings of the Cow Goddess Io; and with a Phoenician Queen who was the granddaughter of Libya, and a cousin of the

'Egyptian' Aigyptos and his brother Danaos (when the Perseid dynasty was first emerging from the Lerna Springs): this Queen was the sister of their cousin Kadmos (back in the days when the Kadmeans of Thebes were just beginning to show up out of the Minyan Swamplands of the Boeotian 'Cow-country' and Dirke's Spring). (The Pelopids wouldn't come up from the Trojan lands until five generations later.) It was back in those days that the newly surfacing 'foreigners' were attempting to reconcile their differences and inaugurate the Olympian era. (See Genealogical Chart: Perseus.) But we are not talking of linear time, but mythic; for it will take us only two generations of reckoning forward to catch up again with the age of The-

Rape of Europa (Metope from the Temple of Hera mid-6th century BC, Selinunte, Museo Nazionale, Palermo)

seus: for it was the daughter-in-law of this Queen who gave birth to the Minotaur. This Queen was the Lady 'Broad-face,' **Europa**, who would lend her name to the whole continent of the new world. The breadth of her appearance would become the wide domains of Europe, but back in Phoenicia, her consort was a Bull, and her broad face probably resembled the Gorgon Medusa. As Europa walked with her sisterhood along the shore, amongst the cows of her father's herd, she took particular notice of an extraordinary Bull. The Bull was Zeus, and as they played together, he breathed into her the magical scent of the flowers he had been grazing upon. She was entranced by their hypnotic perfumes. Enraptured, they took off, the two of them, for the new world (**entheogen**).

When they came ashore on the island of Crete, Europa bore three sons: **Minos**, **Rhadamanthys**, and **Sarpedon**. (Sarpedon and Minos were **warring brothers**. After a dispute over the 'kingship' of Crete, Sarpedon fled and eventually became an ally of Priam and the Trojans in the great War; Rhadamanthys and Minos, after they died, joined **Aiakos**, the grandfather of the Greek hero Achilleus, to become the three judges in the underworld—that is to say, presuming that Crete in the days of Minos was ever above ground. Rhadamanthys was always the more just of the two: he had the same problem as Amphitryon: he 'accidently' murdered a kinsman and went into exile: there he ended up marrying Alkmene, Herakles' mother, although this may have occurred not only after Amphitryon died, but she as well.) But while they were still alive, Minos was 'king' of Knossos and the Cretan Labyrinth.

His wife was **Pasiphae**, the aunt of Medeia, and a sister of the 'witch' **Kirke** (Latin **Circe**), who tried to turn Odysseus into a Boar. (Pasiphae, Kirke, and

(right) Daidalos Presents the
Cow to Pasiphae (Roman bas-
relief, Palazzo Spada, Rome)

(below) Capture of the Bull,
with the Cow as Decoy (Gold
cup from tholos tomb at
Vapheio c. 1450 BC National
Museum, Athens)

their brother **Aietes**, the father of Medeia, were all children of the Sun, **Helios**.
Their mother was Perse—back in the pre-Olympian days, before Perse became
Persephone, the 'Killer of Perse.' They were the offspring of the Sun's nocturnal
voyages through the subterranean waters, and originally they were probably
'black'—for even in this world, the heat of the Sun turns all men black. Pasiphae

is named as the Lady who 'Shines on All,' a shining from the depths of her father's realm, beckoning to us all to take the plunge down; Minos, her husband—and his two brothers—have names that are pre-Greek, although Minos might be related to Minyan.)

Pasiphae had the misfortune to suffer from the same passion as her husband's mother, Europa. She fell madly in love with a special Bull in her husband's herd. The Bull was the old pre-Olympian Poseidon, and Minos had neglected to offer it in sacrifice—which would have helped change its nature. The son Pasiphae bore to it was thus a half-brother to Theseus: a rival claimant to his heroic identity. But at first the Bull would pay no attention to the desperate longings of Pasiphae.

To seduce it, she had to enlist the aid of the Athenian craftsman **Daidalos** (Latin **Daedalus**), the 'Crafty:' we have the term 'Daedalian' in English to describe the ingenious artistry of such craftsmen. Daidalos was a descendant of Erechtheus, and he was temporarily down in Crete for a period of Bondage to work off his own 'suicide,' which was enacted through the murder of his nephew **Talos**, who, like the other Erechtheids, was a serpent, and had given promise of rivaling his uncle's skills: Daidalos pushed Talos off the roof of Athena's Temple on the Arcopolis. Daidalos's solution to Pasiphae's dilemma was one of those fiendishly clever devices that are characteristic of the mechanical wizardry from the chthonic realm: he constructed an artificial, and 'souless' cow: souless, at least, until Pasiphae put it on, for disguised as a Cow, she was mounted by the Bull. The child she bore was the **Minotaur** (or 'Minos Bull')—half Bull and half man, and the product of the Athenian Daidalos's trick of nature to begin the long process of mediation.

(A gold cup found in a 'Beehive' tomb at Vapheio in the Peloponnesos, illustrates Daidalos's trick: a Cow in oestrus is being used as a decoy to attract a bull for capture by its hunters.)

Daidalos also constructed the Labyrinth. The Minotaur was housed in the courtyard at its center. The one whose ruins we can visit today above ground at Knossos is just a physical replica of the original, which was a metaphor for the Entrance. In it, the Dance with Death was performed. As the Bull lunged, the dancers attempted to grasp the bull's horns, to somersault over its back to salvation, landing upright on their feet behind it. At the time of Theseus, the Athenians sent a troupe of twice seven, youths and maidens, to perform for the Lord and Mistress of the Labyrinth.

(As for Diadalos, he eventually managed to escape from the Labyrinth, where, like the Minotaur, he was being kept prisoner. He made another device—this time mechanical wings, so that he could turn himself and his son **Ikaros** (Latin **Icarus**) into birds. Talos, his nephew had himself been turned into a bird, a partridge, after his murder. Ikaros, despite his father's warnings, however, flew too near the Sun, and the heat melted the (bees)wax that bound the feathers of his artificial wings: he fell to his Death into the western sea, the Icarian, which was named after him. Daidalos surfaced in safety at the Italian Entrance of Cumae. There he built a Temple to Apollo in thanksgiving for his deliverance.)

Genealogical Chart: Minotaur

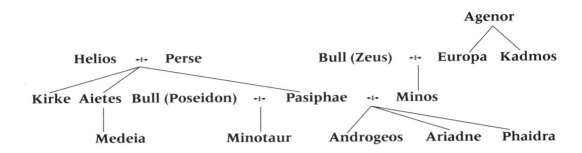

It was later claimed that Theseus boldly offered, despite the pleadings of his father Aigeus, to be enlisted as one of the fourteen victims to set sail for the Labyrinth and its deadly Dance: the ship was still preserved as a sacred relic in Classical times. Or it could have been some plot by Medeia to get rid of him. But it ultimately was the Marathonian Bull that was responsible; for when Theseus killed it, a son of Minos—somehow—was also disposed of: this wasn't—supposedly—the Minotaur, but Minos's son by Pasiphae, **Androgeos** or 'Earth-man.' Once again, in Androgeos, it is easy to see the same 'enemy' double who appears in the Marathonian Bull and the Minos Bull or Minotaur; Androgeos was a 'foreign' ally of the Pallantidai. And in 'murdering' Androgeos, Theseus, like Daidalos, incurred the obligatory Bondage in the Labyrinth.

By some accounts, Minos himself was in Athens at the time, and he, too, went down to Crete with Theseus and the Dancers; and the ship itself was like a Dream, piloted by the same 'Shining' Phaiax whose people (the Phaeacians) later lent Odysseus the dream-ship that allowed him to wake up back home after the Trojan War. Minos was the 'enemy' on the voyage; and it was an uneasy truce that let Theseus and him sail together (**paradigms #1** 'enemy' **& 3** 'helper companion' as transmuted enemy). On the way, Minos tried to rape one of the 'cow' maidens in the troupe, Periboia, who later became the mother of the hero **Aias** (Latin **Ajax**); but Theseus warned him to keep his hands off of her. And then again, as they approached the shore, Minos, who was a son of Zeus, challenged Theseus, who claimed to be a son of Poseidon, to a duel. Minos requested, and received, a sign from his own divine father, a flash of lightning, to confirm his Olympian heritage. Then he tossed a ring into the sea and dared Theseus to plunge—still farther—down into the depths to retrieve it, if his father would let him. There Theseus was 'hospitably' received by the old 'black' Athena and her consort, now called Triton and Amphitrite; and he resurfaced resplendent, and with the ring, as proof. Rings were tokens of union and friendship, binding together, in this case, Theseus and his 'enemy' Minos (**paradigm #2** 'reconciliation').

But the more common telling of the story let Theseus go ashore with the Dancers, to confront not just his dangerous companion Minos, but the true opposite identity, the Minos Bull, of which Minos was the transmutation. There, it was the Princess **Ariadne**, a daughter of Minos and Pasiphae, and a sister of Androgeos—and the Minotaur, who 'hospitably' received him. It was she who was the **turncoat**. She was called in Cretan Greek the 'Holy Lady,' and also the 'Shining;' and she is a thinly disguised version of the terrible Artemis of the Labyrinth. Ariadne showed Theseus the trick. When Theseus went down to her, Ariadne was spinning, like the old Arachne image of Athena as a Fate Goddess. Instead of playing her more sinister role as a spinstress of his Death, she lent him her spindle and ball of spun yarn. One end she held; the other was his to hold as he traveled through the confusing maze of the Labyrinth. The thread was like an umbilical cord attaching him to her as he wandered into the Labyrinth. It was at this point that Theseus appears to have ended his solitary heroism: up to now, he was either alone, or had only the hostile Minos as companion; now Athena was to join him as his **anima**. (She apparently wasn't available to him until the transmutation of Ariadne.) And after killing the Minotaur 'sleeping' at its center, with Athena at his side, he found his way back out of the womb-like enclosure, to claim Ariadne as his bride; for he had redeemed her from her chthonic role: she had betrayed her own brother, the Minotaur—supposedly her mother's child and not her father's—and cast her lot for a male who was not a kinsman of her blood.

Or Ariadne, as some told the story, may have entered the Labyrinth herself with Theseus as his **anima**, lighting his way with her 'shining' crown. When they emerged, the crown was transmuted into Ariadne's Garland and set amongst the constellations.

Theseus fled from Crete with Ariadne and the rescued Dancers, but somewhere along the return he lost her. There was a parting of their ways as they wakened and emerged, and she was reclaimed by the Earth. Several places were venerated as her burial site, and sometimes it was Artemis herself who summoned her back down; but the most popular telling located the Entrance on Naxos, near the island of Delos.

Wherever it occurred, Theseus was

Theseus in the Waters off Knossos: Athena Introduces the Hero to her Aquatic Other, Amphitrite, with Triton Buoying him up (Red-figure vase by Euphronios c. 500 BC, Musée du Louvre, Paris)

wakened from his sleep with Ariadne by his 'helper' Athena. Even redeemed, Ariadne, with such a family background, was not an appropriate mate for the founder of the new Athens—and certainly not a sleeping Ariadne, drugged by **Hypnos**, the god of 'Sleep:' we often see him, a winged creature, sitting on her head and ministering his narcotics to her eyes, as Athena summons the hero away from their bed. It was as if it had all been just a dream, and Theseus, through Athena's aid, totally forgot the nightmare with Ariadne and fled. Abandoned on Naxos, Ariadne was claimed by Dionysos as his bride. They celebrated their Sacred Marriage there; and she descended with him and his maenadic entourage, to become his Queen in the netherworld.

From Naxos, Theseus and the Dancers sailed north, up toward Delos, and went ashore, with a sacred effigy of Ariadne that they had rescued from Crete. And there they celebrated their redemption with sacrifices to the newly reborn Apollo and Artemis and by imitating the windings of the Labyrinth in a line dance, with joined hands: the dance was danced in memory of Ariadne (and her Wet Nurse witch, **Koryne** or 'Plant Bud'—Queens, apparently, are inseparable from their chthonic support system). They danced in front of her statue; and it was called the Crane Dance, after the long-necked birds whose migratory pathway brings them repeatedly into the 'black' Ethiopian Deathlands. Each year thereafter, the Dance was danced again—with the spirit of Ariadne still in attendance; and in memory of the victims who used to be offered in the Labyrinth, the dancers still were flogged as they wound their way through their steps. And in commemoration of the more sinister sacred plants of Koryne and her former times, they bit the trunk of Apollo's olive tree—which like the one on the Athenian Acropolis, or the ones that Herakles transplanted for the Altis at Olympia, was the first to appear in our world, the oldest olive in existence. It marked the inauguration of the new era, with the coming of the Indo-Europeans: and each year at the celebration of the Dance, the entheogen of their homeland, which had become the olive now after its transmutation, was honored by the presentation at the Delian sanctuary of a secret botanical specimen that was supposedly sent from the Hyperboreans.

The Contest with Aigeus

As the returning Dancers showed up off the coast of Attica, Athena helped Theseus out with another bout of forgetfulness. Theseus was supposed to have changed the sails from black to white, to signal to his human father that the expedition against the Minotaur had been successful. But he forgot, and when Aigeus saw the sails still black, as he watched anxiously from the Acropolis, he assumed that his son was dead: and he jumped to his death, offering his own body to the winds and to the old Apollo. Thus Theseus was responsible for the 'accidental' murder of Aigeus—just as Perseus had 'accidentally' killed his grandfather Akrisios. As with Ariadne, Aigeus, too, belonged to the old chthonic order: he was not an appropriate father for the successful hero. Aigeus gave his name to the Aegean Sea, the waters surrounding Delos, the eastern sea that counter-balances the Icarian on the west, where Ikaros similarly 'Fell.'

The Marriage to Phaidra

It might have been better if Theseus had ever taken the time to marry the **turncoat** Amazon Queen **Antiope-Hippolyta** ('Opposite-face Horsewoman'), but whether he abducted her all by himself, or merely took her off of Herakles' hands as the result of a joint venture that the two undertook to the 'Asiatic' Deathlands, the truth is that he never did marry her. And the son he had by her, **Hippolytos**, was both a bastard and named with his mother Hippolyta's name—a totally unsuitable offspring for Theseus, as the founder of patriliny, to have as his own.

The Amazons were notorious adherents to the old worship of Artemis, and they had 'risen up' right outside the walls of Athens to reclaim their Queen. And just as Theseus had gotten rid of Medeia, the Athenians, under his leadership, now disposed of the Amazons. A great War was fought; and if you were to try to find an Amazon today, you couldn't: for every last one of those terrible horsewomen was destroyed there at Athens; their graves were pointed out in Attica and its sur-roundings. Other cities similarly had traditions that the race was annihilated outside their own cities, at the beginning of the new era. And always, the remains were deposited back where they belonged—and venerated.

But Antiope wasn't Theseus's only marital indiscretion. After abandoning the turncoat Ariadne to her chthonic fate on Naxos, he took up with her 'Shining' sister **Phaidra** (Latin **Phaedra**)—how, we don't know, but presumably he had stolen her also from the Labyrinth, along with Ariadne and Koryne.

Although Theseus did marry Phaidra, and even had two sons by her, she, too, was ultimately unsuitable—as unsuitable as Ariadne (Artemis) herself. The marriage ended fortunately in his 'accidentally' being relieved of both Phaidra and Hippolytos.

The Pallantidai had again 'risen up' in revolt; and again Theseus had mur-dered them—and had to pay the penalty for this 'suicide' of his other self: the pe-riod of Bondage in exile. This was served out at Troizen, the Entrance that was his Motherland. And while he was 'down' there, he had left Phaidra alone with his family in that town where the Goddess had her 'Triple Throne.' Hippolytos lived up to his (mother's) name as a horseman, and he and Artemis were hav-ing a fatal infatuation, racing their horses together and hunting, in a sacred 'gar-den.' It was a completely chaste affair (Hippolytos was still a virgin and found sex unappealing; he even mortified the flesh by adhering to a vegetarian diet), but nevertheless, any 'consorting' with Artemis was apt to trigger remembrances of her former identity.

Aphrodite was explicitly excluded from Hippolytos's attentions; and in anger, she caused Phaidra to be afflicted with an uncontrollable passion for Theseus's bastard son by the Amazon. It was not a matter of incest (for Phaidra wasn't his mother), but of oestrual madness. Phaidra, too, sought relief in the mortification of the flesh: she yearned to chastely 'consort' as a horsewoman herself with this favorite of Artemis; and since she couldn't, she had determined to die, by starving her body, in order to master her passion—which she realized was a resurgence of her heritage from the Labyrinth, and from Pasiphae, her mother, and Ariadne, her sister.

But her old Wet Nurse intervened to save her 'Shining' Queen, reminding her about the 'shining' that beckons from the depths of Earth. The Nurse offered a cure: a witch's potion, a secret drug—but she was speaking only metaphorically to mislead her Queen into accepting a return to the old order, with an **entheogen** as 'consort.' Hippolytos was the curative salve to apply for the physical alleviation of her yearnings. And she acted as a go-between to arrange a sexual liaison, divulging to Hippolytos the Queen's passion. Hippolytos openly rejected Phaidra; and she, in order to preserve her name—and the inheritance of her legitimate sons—, committed suicide, leaving a note accusing Hippolytos of rape (just as the horseman Bellerophon's Sthenoboia had done with her husband Proitos at Tiryns).

When Theseus returned (or came back up), he found his wife dead, read the note, and cursed Hippolytos, with one of the three curses he had been given by his divine father Poseidon. The curse was granted, ratifying the fact that of the hero's **two fathers**, the one who presided over his successful heroism was the identifying factor for this phase of his liminality; a Bull rose from the sea, by the Troizenian sanctuary of Artemis, and Hippolytos was dragged to his death by his own maddened team of (night)mares, as he left Troizen on the same pathway that the pubescent Theseus had used when he departed for the first of his heroic Labors at the sanctuary of Asklepios (Apollo) at Epidauros.

As he died, he was forgiven and reconciled with his beloved Artemis, and with his father Theseus, who agreed to bury his body—which again ratifies this successful phase of Theseus's heroism: of his **two names**, he is (like the colonizer Apollo) the 'settler,' rather than the 'settled.' Artemis discretely withdrew before having to witness Hippolytos's actual death, thus avoiding any chthonic contamination which might trigger her own regression from her new Olympian identity. (As we have already mentioned, she did inveigle Apollo's son Asklepios into recalling Hippolytos temporarily back from death; but this led to Apollo's losing his son, too: the loving son becomes the recipient of the father's tragic potential. The same paradigm was seen in the role of Hyllos in Herakles' ascension to Olympus.)

The grave of Hippolytos was venerated in Athens: it was the chthonic foundation for the Temple of Aphrodite on Hippolytos. And Hippolytos himself was honored by a ritual: maidens made offerings to the dead hero at the time that they reached puberty and had to relinquish their innocent consorting with their virgin male companion and enter into the throes of sexual maturity, governed by the irreconcilable opposition of Artemis and Aphrodite.

This return of Theseus at Troizen relieved him of his inappropriate wife from the Labyrinth and his unsuitable son from the Amazon. It is, from the tragic point of view, a terrible burden to be successful: it isolates you from humanity—as Hera had ironically demonstrated with Herakles in his madness: the final Labor, if that's what you want, is to lose your mortal affiliations.

The Marriage to Helen

Another way of telling this story about Theseus's marriage lets us know what he was doing in the Deathlands beneath the surface of Troizen. This is the episode that ended by his coming up there, after his rescue by Herakles from the House of Persephone, where he had become permanently 'settled' himself to a stone, rather than the 'settler' that he would prove to be when he offered to bury the polluted Herakles beneath Athens, after the murder of Megara.

Helen, the daughter of Zeus and the woman for whom the Trojan War was fought, had a 'handful' of lovers—five, to be exact; and Theseus was one of them. He had entered into a compact with his 'friend' **Peirithoos**: they each wanted to abduct a daughter of Zeus. (You couldn't do much better than that if you wanted to avoid the problems of ambiguity that we've seen in wives like Megara or Deianeira or Phaidra.) You never can be sure what you're getting, however: Theseus chose Helen—as the first of her 'digital' consorts; and Peirithoos chose Persephone, who although a daughter of Zeus, was Queen of Hades. Or it may have been merely the luck of the draw that ascribed the two brides that way.

Peirithoos and Theseus, as a pair of heroes, are 'enemy' 'friends,' like Herakles and Iolaos; only these two are reversible, and either of them can play the hero, to the other's supporting role as **animus**. We have already seen one episode of their heroism as the subject for the metope sequence on the Parthenon Temple at Athens and for the eastern pedimental sculptures of the Temple of Zeus at Olympia: the marriage of Peirithoos to the Mare-lady Hippodameia, at which the drunken centaurs tried to abduct the bride.

Helen herself had a pair of brothers who exhibited a similar kind of shared heroism, and they, too, became implicated in the scheme of Theseus's involvement with Helen. These brothers were the **Dioskouroi** (Latin **Dioscuri**) or the 'Zeus-boys:' **Kastor** (Latin **Castor**) and his twin **Polydeukes** (Latin **Pollux**). They were sons of Zeus (or at least one of them was), but although only one of them was immortal, they shared that destiny by both being immortal on alternate days, while dying together on each intervening day. (We will come to the fuller story of their birth—and of Helen's and her sister Klytaimnestra's—later.) The Dioskouroi, as similar dissimilars, are the theme of the **warring brothers**, and they are a common occurrence in the stories about how a place was (re)settled for the new order.

Helen was Queen at Sparta in the Peloponnesos, but Theseus apparently didn't take the overland route from Athens to fetch her: he may have dredged her up from beneath the surface of the Athenian lands at the village of the

Aphidnai sisterhood. Nor was his 'friend' Peirithoos always a foreigner from Thessaly; for he, too, could be found just beneath the surface thereabouts. In these local versions of their 'foreignness,' Helen and Peirithoos occupy the same topography as the Marathonian Bull—which we have seen was a local version of the Labyrinth of Knossos, and of Ariadne, Phaidra, and Minos. It was, in fact, on an episode of cow rustling in this region that Theseus and Peirithoos first made the other's acquaintance.

For their marital escapade, the two heroes pledged their 'friendship' at Kolonos, just outside the walls of Athens, and descended by that famous 'horseman's' Entrance, where the steps down were paved with bronze.

Theseus and Peirithoos stole Helen, while she was dancing as a still virgin maiden in the sanctuary of Artemis; and her brothers, the Dioskouroi took off in hot pursuit to rescue her back—the two of them were apparently in their chthonic day.

(Or was it Persephone that the two friends found down there? In that case, Theseus and Peirithoos were initially rooted to their thrones in the underworld, and Theseus couldn't flee until Herakles yanked him free: Peirithoos, unfortunately was not so successful and he was stuck there for good, becoming the losing half for Theseus's escape and resurfacing—although some people thought that it was Theseus who became fixed there forever. (The power of these thrones to imprison their occupants was said to be that they cast a trance of forgetfulness on whoever sat in them, like a deadly narcotic.) In this way, Theseus left a 'friend' underground—just as he would have to 'help' Herakles, too, go underground, after he and his replacement for Peirithoos got back up here. Theseus himself was 'purified' of his other half by the experience; and some people claimed that he even left part of his own backside stuck to the throne when he awakened.)

Theseus deposited Helen with his mother Aithra, who was supposedly now making Aphidnai her motherland. The Dioskouroi emerged there in pursuit and reclaimed Helen (who was still 'black' back in those days), taking Aithra as hostage, to serve as Helen's slave—but not before Helen was delivered of a daughter to Theseus: this was an Artemis look-alike, **Iphigeneia**, better known as a daughter of Helen's sister Klytaimnestra. Helen took Aithra to Troy when she ran away there with her lover Paris. At Troy, Aithra served as the Wet Nurse for her grandson, the child that Theseus's son **Akamas** secretly begot on a sister of Paris.

The second of Theseus's sons by Phaidra, a certain **Demophoon**, (or, as some said, by the Amazon Hippolyta) eventually took part in the Trojan War, and the aged Aithra was finally rescued from the burning city and brought back home.

The Death of Theseus

It may be, as some claimed, that Theseus never separated from his other half on the descent to Persephone's House, but stayed fixed in his bout of forgetfulness on the Throne. That was, in any case, ultimately to be his fate—to live out the more sinister potential of his name as the 'settled.'

The more popular version of his death, however, involves another 'uprising' of the Pallantidai lineage. **Menestheus** ('Abiding Strength'), who was a descendant of Erechtheus and the 'digital' men at Athens, sided with the Dioskouroi when they came up to reclaim their sister Helen; and he cemented their 'friendship' by allowing them free access to the city via the sacred Eleusinian Entrance. It was Menestheus who would usurp the 'kingship' from the sons of Theseus and be the leader of the Athenian contingent at the Trojan War.

Theseus was forced to flee into 'foreign' exile; and on his way down to the Cretan Labyrinth, where he had been offered asylum, he was 'blown' off course to the island of Skyros in the northern Aegean. (This, too, was a Deathland: it was here that the aquatic nymph **Thetis** tried to disguise her son **Achilleus** as a woman in a sisterhood in order to keep him from going to his heroic destiny at the Trojan War.) The 'king' of Skyros was a son of Apollo and a 'Virgin,' Parthenope: this was **Lykomedes**, the 'Wolf-lord,' another 'foreign' ally of Menestheus. He 'hospitably' received Theseus, who intended to 'settle' there on lands that he claimed were his inheritance. In a dispute over the boundaries, Lykomedes got Theseus 'drunk' and pushed him off a cliff, making him into an offering to the Apolline 'Fall' and the winds.

In the year 473 BC, the bones of Theseus were discovered on Skyros; and after eight-hundred years, they were finally returned to Athens. And Theseus, who had successfully buried so many chthonic 'friends' in Attica, was himself at last deposited beneath the soil of Athens and venerated in his Theseus Shrine, near the Acropolis.

* * * *

Review

Theseus has the typical **two fathers**: the 'tragic' potential of his identity associates him with **Aigeus** (and his 'foreign' Queen **Medeia**), and with the Entrance of his mother **Aithra**, daughter of **Pittheus**, at **Troizen**; his 'triumphant' identity associates him with **Poseidon**, whom he replaces as the new Athena's favorite (as was also the case with Perseus and the Gorgon Medusa, who was Poseidon's Queen). The two aspects of his liminal identity are described by the ambiguity of his name: he is either the 'settled' beneath a stone, or the 'settler' of the stone; the name has connotations of both Hermes and Apollo, the colonizer.

It is perhaps his own herm-like nature that is responsible for his lack of the customary **animus**: this role is fulfilled by his 'friend' **Peirithoos**, but he is involved only in the episodes of the **Marriage of Hippodameia**, the **Abduction of Persephone-Helen**, and the **cow rustling at Marathon**; the hostile 'friendship' of **Minos** on the journey to the **Minotaur** is another example. Theseus also lacks the aid of **Athena** as **anima** until he meets the transmuted **Ariadne** (who is the Cretan **Artemis**); it is apparently his own Apolline nature that makes him too unstable to have the customary **anima** in his other exploits. Ultimately, his task was to rescue and redo the sinister aspects of the Apollo-Artemis couple.

This he did as his major achievement: the **Combat with the Minotaur** in the Labyrinth of Knossos, the **Abandonment of Ariadne** to become the bride of Dionysos on Naxos, and the **Dancing of the Labyrinth** on Delos, the island of the twins' rebirth into their Olympian identities. The Cretan **Bull of Marathon** is another version of this same story. In the **Abduction of Persephone-Helen**, the Marathonian Entrance (at Aphidnai) became a double for his motherland of Troizen. Although Theseus is often considered an imitation of **Herakles**, the similarities are probably archetypal; and the differences are significant and the result of Theseus's own characteristics: he is an Ionian, and not Dorian; and he is not an 'opponent' of Hera; and he is often solitary. Since the source for much of our knowledge of Greek myth is Athenian tragedy, Theseus appears more consistently 'triumphant,' betraying the Athenian bias: as the (re)founder of Athens, he repeatedly welcomes his 'tragic' heroic 'friends' into burial sites beneath the soil of Attica.

The other of his exploits occurred in his **Wilderness Sojourn** as he traveled along the shore from Troizen to Athens, surfacing at six places that were sacred to the old religion: **Periphetes Korynetes** at Epidauros; **Sinis Polypemon Pityokamptes** at the Corinthian Isthmus; **Krommyo Phaia** at Krommyon; **Skiron** at Megara; **Kerkyon** and **Prokrustes Prokoptas Damastes** at Eleusis. He also took part in the joint ventures with other heroes: the first War at Troy with Herakles (and the abduction of the Amazon Queen **Antiope Hippolyta**); the **Kalydonian Boar Hunt**; and the **Voyage of the Argo**.

For Discussion and Further Study

The story of Theseus's marriage to Phaidra is the plot of Euripides' *Hippolytus* tragedy. Read it and consider the following:

As Euripides intended the play to be staged, the same actor would have impersonated the roles of Aphrodite, Artemis, and Phaidra. Would this add or detract from your appreciation of the play?

Chapter X
The 'Foreign' Legions

᛭

Sometimes, as we have seen, the heroic venture was a corporate event, involving the careers of everyone who was available at the time. The Kalydonian Boar Hunt was an adventure of that kind, although it really is the story of Meleagros and Atalante. Similarly, no one of that generation refused to sign on as a sailor for the **Voyage of the Argo**, but that, too, was primarily just the story of a single hero and his Lady, **Iason** (Latin **Jason**) and **Medeia** (Latin **Medea**).

Two other events had similar broad appeal, but did not center upon a single hero. The problem of (re)settling Thebes required eventually a whole War, in which the sons of **Oidipous** (Latin **Oedipus**) faced off at the Seven Gates of that troubled city: **Eteokles** (Latin **Eteocles**), with his Theban forces, against his **warring brother Polyneikes** (Latin **Polynices**), who had mustered a legion of 'foreign' allies. The **Seven Against Thebes** was only the most famous of these local Wars, where a city had to confront a legion of 'foreigners' who rose up to reassert their aboriginal rights; it was fought, for example, also at Athens, several times: when the Amazons came is one example, but it happened as well with the uprising of the Dioskouroi to reclaim their sister Helen, and on other occasions when the troops emerged from the Deathlands through the Eleusinian Entrance and had to be met in dubious battle along the Sacred Way to Athens.

Even more famous than the War of the Seven, was the venture that enlisted the lives of all the heroes of the next generation. This was the **Trojan War**, and again it centered upon reclaiming Helen; but this time it was the heroes who banded together as the legion that brought the battle down to the 'foreigner's' homeland, to settle the matter definitively, once and for all. That epic story will be the subject of our next chapter. In the next few generations, the race of heroes became insignificant and tended to die out—although their descendants today are still proud to assert their relationship, whenever they do anything themselves of note.

* * * *

The Voyage of the Argo

We have already found the 'witch' **Medeia** at Corinth (where some people knew that she was the kind of 'foreigner' that is aboriginal) and at Athens (where her aboriginal identity is masked as Pallas and Medousa or Kreousa): she is the

'Queen' and was apt to pop up as a 'foreigner' in many an old city out of its aquatic substructure. But from the Pelasgian town of Iolkos (modern Volos) near the foot of Mount Pelion, at the coastal end of the plain of Thessaly (which was one of Apollo's beloved Deathlands), **Iason** had to travel all the way to the eastern ends of the world to bring her up, nor was he fortunate enough to desert her, as Theseus had his Ariadne, before it was too late.

The Birth of Iason

Like the Danaids and their Perseid dynasty, and like the descendants of their Pelopid in-laws, the lineage of **Iason** began in the eastern 'African' Deathlands. **Salmoneus** was his great-grandfather, a brother-in-law of Perseus's daughter Gorgophone (which is Iason's only family connection to the Perseids, although he had an aunt **Chloris** whom we have already met as the surviving daughter of Niobe, and hence a Pelopid); Salmoneus was one of the many brothers who claimed the wind Aiolos as their sire—which made him a brother of Sisyphos, and hence an uncle of **Odysseus**, one of the heroes of the Trojan War; but in the chronology of his own family, his great-grandson Iason (two generations later than Odysseus) lived in the generation before the heroes of the War at Troy. Salmoneus has a non-Greek name that we have seen before in Salmakis, the aquatic nymph who joined her body to Hermaphroditos—to make him a male-female. Salmoneus is called for the Goddess in that 'Asiatic' land, where the enervating waters of her spring were said to deprive a man of his maleness.

Not only was Salmoneus a Goddess's man in that other world, but he set himself up as a chthonic rival to Zeus, at the very source of the rivers that flowed through the lands that would eventually be reclaimed as the sanctuary of Olympia. He went so far as to impersonate Zeus himself, imitating the god's thunder and lightning, from down under (by tossing firebrands into the air and dragging brazen kettledrums behind his chariot)—until Zeus finally put down the impostor and his impudent Peloponnesian settlement of Salmonia, with the real thunderbolt, hurled from the skies. (Salmoneus had surfaced there, via the connection that often linked Arcadia with his Apolline Deathlands in Thessaly, where he had settled after deserting the 'Asiatic' version of Apollo's homeland.)

His daughter was the **turncoat** from whom the hero would be descended. She was **Tyro**, who still bore the name of her Tyrian homeland in the east, and the city of Tyre in Phoenicia. (Her descendants would eventually carry their people to Italy, to surface on the banks of the Tiber River: there they became the ancestors of the Etruscans, who were called Tyrrheni, and who remembered traditions that they had all come originally from Asia Minor: they were the pre-Indo-European inhabitants that the Latin-speaking Romans assimilated.) And typical of the fate of such turncoats, every effort was made to keep Tyro from bringing about the change to the new order in Peloponnesian Salmonia and Thessalian Iolkos. Like Antiope with her twins Amphion and Zethos at Thebes, she too was persecuted by the 'Queen' and even confined underground, until she was ultimately rescued by the **warring brothers** she bore as her sons.

Tyro slept with the 'thundering' river that rose in her father's Salmonian colony, and under cover of the waters, it was actually Poseidon who was her mate: she had fallen asleep and Poseidon overwhelmed her in the shape of a monstrous wave, purple-crimson in color, like the dye for which Tyre and the 'Bloody' Phoenicians were famous in Asia Minor. She gave birth to twins, **Neleus** and **Pelias**; but she did not dare to keep them, for she had a cruel and evil step-mother, the 'Iron Lady' **Sidero**, who had replaced her good mother as mate of Salmoneus. Instead, Tyro set them adrift on the river in a hollowed-out log—disguising them as a plant (**entheogen**); when they floated ashore, a herd of (night)mares rescued them. Neleus, the 'Pitiless,' was suckled by a bitch, whose nature was responsible for his cruel name; and his brother was nursed by a mare, who accidentally stepped on his face with her hoof and left a dark scar—for which reason he was named Pelias or 'Muddy' (a name with the same metaphor as Pelops or 'Mud-face'). Like Antiope's twins, the two of them were tended through the time of their **wilderness sojourn** amongst the flocks of herdsmen.

Now, in the meantime, the Tyrrhenian Tyro was being cruelly mistreated by her stepmother Sidero: she did everything she could to keep Tyro 'black' and true to her 'Asiatic' ancestry: even though this Tyro had a 'milk white' face like 'Cheese' (or **tyros**)—the new meaning for the turncoat's name—, Sidero made it black and crimson-blue (like the Phoenician dye) from her repeated blows, and she imprisoned her in a dungeon.

When the twins had grown to maturity, they chanced upon Tyro while she

Genealogical Chart: Iason (Jason)

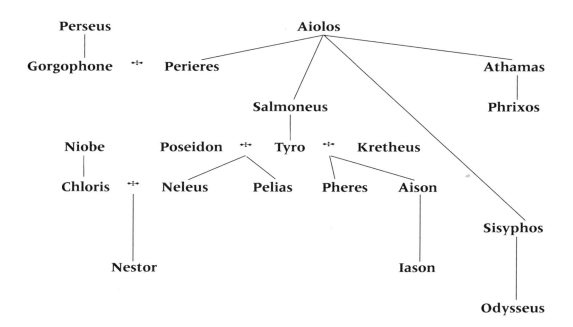

was fetching water. The mother and sons recognized each other—and the herdsmen produced the original log as proof. Sidero fled to a temple of Hera, where
she was killed by Pelias, while Neleus drove Salmoneus away. (In the underworld, Salmoneus continues to drive madly about, vainly imitating the noise
of thunder—joining Tantalos, Sisyphos, and Ixion—and the Danaids—in futile
repetitions of his sin for all eternity.)

The **warring twins** then parted ways over a dispute for the sovereignty of
Iolkos, and Pelias drove Neleus down to preside over the Entrance at Pylos on
the south-western shore of the Peloponnesos. Neleus married **Chloris**, the only surviving daughter of Pelops' sister Niobe, but all of their children, except for
Nestor, were destroyed by Herakles when he resettled the Entrance: the 'good'
Nestor was famous for his role in the Trojan War; and hence the whole family
takes its name from his father, as the Neleids.

Now, Tyro became the grandmother of Iason. She married Salmoneus's brother **Kretheus**; and from him she bore **Aison** (Latin **Aeson**), who was Iason's father. Another of her sons was **Pheres**, whom we have already met as the 'king'
of the Pherai sisterhood of '(Under)takers.'

The Wilderness Sojourn

However, Pelias, her son by Poseidon, (again) seized the kingship of Iolkos,
and considered Aison and his lineage a threat to his own continued sovereignty. (Pelias and Aison repeat the theme of the **warring brothers** that was already played out with Pelias and Neleus; and Pelias as the 'wicked' uncle of the
hero Iason is the same theme that we have seen in the relationship of Perseus
and Proitos: Pelias is the chthonic 'enemy' claimant to Iason's heroic career, a variant of the **two fathers** theme.)

When Iason was born, his parents pretended that he had died, and they sent
him into his **wilderness sojourn**, to protect him from his cruel uncle.

(Aison's wife was variously named, but she is a version of the 'Queen,' another
Medousa or Medeia: **Polymede** 'Much-Queen' or **Alkimede** 'Strong-Queen,'
or still other names of the same sort. And in (only) pretending to celebrate the
funeral of her son, she is fulfilling her role as **turncoat**.)

On the slopes of neighboring Mount Pelion (named with the same 'Muddy'
name as the chthonic Pelias), Iason grew to maturity, under the tutelage of the
'good' centaur Cheiron (the 'Hand-man'), who taught him the skill of archery
and trained him in the lore of magical plants: it was Cheiron who first named
him 'Drug-man' or Iason. (Before that, his name was **Diomedes** or 'Zeus-lord;'
the **two names** express the liminality of his heroic identity: Iason is the chthonic name of his Pelion sojourn, and 'botanic,' like the log that rescued his uncles
Pelias and Neleus; while Diomedes identifies him as the master of the Goddess,
like another Zeus with Hera.)

As Iason embarked on his return from Mount Pelion, he had to cross a river
(usually the one in Thessaly, but sometimes it bears the same name as the one
in the Peloponnesos, where Tyro conceived Poseidon's twins). On the banks

there was a 'witch-like' crone who demanded to be carried across: she was the goddess Hera in disguise. Iason offered her his help—and lost one of his sandals (**maimed hero**) to the muddy waters of the river. In return, he won the favor of Hera: Iason was to have Hera, as well as Athena, as **anima** 'helpers' for his ensuing career.

(The river-crossing finalized Iason's role as the 'enemy' equal of his 'Muddy' uncle, who had usurped the 'kingdom.' From the wilderness sojourn, he returned as another Pelias. Or actually, as another Pelias and Neleus, combined, for he wasn't a pair of warring twins, but a single person, with a sandal in both worlds, and with the nature of the new 'drug' that allowed him to mediate between them: nor was he the nurseling of a bitch or a mare, but of the 'good' centaur. There were other ways of telling the story, but the meaning is the same: he may not have lost his sandal to the mud of the river, but, as some said, he removed it himself in order to get a better grip with the bare foot upon the slippery mud; and then he 'forgot' to put it back on after he carried Hera across—as if the encounter with her had some effect upon his mind. Or it may have been the way that people ordinarily dressed on Mount Pelion—to wear just a single sandal, because of the Mud on Mud Mountain. The river-crossing, moreover, associates Iason with Poseidon and symbolically lends him the second of his **two fathers**: Aison, the mortal; and Poseidon, the divine—who up to this point had been the father of his 'enemy' twins.)

(Iason realized that it was actually Hera who was disguised as the crone, when she grew increasingly heavier as he carried her across the river, with her weight pushing him into the Mud. This 'Mud' or clay (**pelos**) is the substance that his ancestor Prometheus, seven generations earlier, had taken from earth and animated with fire to create the first man of the new era. It represents the chthonic material from which humans were formed, and suggests that figures like Pelias and Pelops still bear traces of their origins in the 'blackness' that hasn't yet quite bleached out totally through their stay here above ground, away from the darkening effect of the chthonic Helios. Whereas Pelias had murdered Sidero in Hera's temple, Iason befriended the Goddess and received the Muddy foot as an emblem of her favor.)

The Contest with Pelias

When Iason showed up in Iolkos, Pelias immediately recognized him as the 'enemy' who was destined to supplant him—the single sandal (and the muddy foot) were the sign: Pelias had learned from an oracle that this would be the man who would kill him (**paradigm #1**). Pelias was engaged in performing a sacrifice to his father Poseidon at the time of Iason's arrival. And he inquired who the stranger was; and Iason told him straight-out both his new name, Iason, and his old, Diomedes, and that he was the son of Aison.

"What would you do to the man who would kill you?" Pelias asked; and Iason replied, "Send him to fetch the Golden Fleece."

"Then, that is your task!" was Pelias's response.

Thus it was Iason who sentenced himself to perform his 'enemy's' bidding.

(Or Pelias, as some claimed, may have agreed to transfer the sovereignty back to Aison, keeping the 'herds' for himself—on condition that Iason first put to rest a troubling ghost that came to him from the netherworld: it was Iason's cousin **Phrixos**, demanding to be brought back home, with the **Golden Fleece**.)

This Fleece was now down(east) in the House of **Aietes**, where the Sun Helios spent the night. Aietes was a Man of Aia, or 'Earth's Man,' and a brother of the 'witch' Kirke and the Cretan Pasiphae—all children of Helios and the 'Destructive' Queen **Perse**, begotten during his nightly visits to the Deathlands; and Aietes was the father of **Medeia**.

The Marriage to Medeia

Just as Herakles had two 'shadow' figures or 'enemies' to contend with (his twin Iphikles and his father's cousin Eurystheus), Iason had a second other self in the dead Phrixos. Like Neleus-Pelias, Phrixos had an evil 'Iron Lady' for stepmother; and he was paired with a sibling, his sister **Helle**. And like them, the two of them also were raised by herdsmen. And like all the others, Phrixos and Helle also were sent into Death, but saved by a trick of their turncoat mother. All of them, moreover, were rescued through the mediation of a botanical agent—which for Phrixos was the Golden Fleece.

The father of Phrixos and Helle was **Athamas**, a 'Loner' and a Wanderer; like Salmoneus, Kretheus, and Sisyphos, he was an Aiolid, one of the 'wind' brotherhood. His wife was the 'Cloud Lady' **Nephele**: she was the hallucinatory likeness of Hera, and as such, she could be either 'bad,' as in former times, or, more recently, like a turncoat, 'good.' In the earlier days, she had deceived Ixion into sleeping with her, thinking she was Hera; and on her, he begot **Kentauros**, who then mated with the (night)mares of Pelion to produce the whole race of centaurs. But with Athamas, Nephele was the **turncoat** mother of Phrixos and Helle; and sometimes she even had the name of **Themisto**, the 'Righteous.' It may even have been Hera herself who arranged the marriage to Athamas, in order to get the troublesome Nephele out of Olympus and off her hands.

Athamas, however, had a second wife, the Strong and 'Sinewy' **Ino**, through whom, as with Sidero (the 'Iron' stepmother of Pelias and Neleus, and the tormentor of Tyro), Hera's more wrathful nature was displayed. The locale for this drama was twofold: just as Salmoneus was located both in the Thessalian Deathlands and at Salmonia at the headwaters of Peloponnesian Olympia, Athamas belonged both to Thebes (where Ino was a daughter of Kadmos, and one of the maenadic sisters of Semele, the mother of Dionysos) in Boeotia and to Thessaly, where he founded the city of 'Loners' or Athamanes at the place of 'wandering' called Halos.

There are two ways of telling the story; one centers on Nephele; the other on Ino. In both cases there was a drought that was caused ultimately by Hera, on behalf either of Nephele or Ino. In the case of Nephele, the 'Cloud Lady' may have been jealous that Athamas had taken up with Ino. The Delphic oracle pre-

scribed a human sacrifice as the only remedy: such sacrifices were frequently re-
sorted to in order to offer the Deathlands a victim and thus incorporate them
back into appeased familial relationships: to have a 'friend' in the other world.
The victim demanded was Phrixos, Nephele's own son by Athamas—or perhaps
Helle as well, for she was included in the sacrifice. (Even in later times, the
Athamanes of Halos maintained the custom of sacrificing the 'king's' son to the
'Gluttonous' Zeus Laphystios, to commemorate the former days when Zeus—
and his Hera—had not yet been assimilated to Olympus, but was still a carnivorous nether god, like the one that Tantalos had tempted with the feast upon his
own butchered son Pelops; although, by those later times amongst the
Athamanes, the victim had only to avoid ever stepping into a certain prohibit-
ed building, to avoid being sacrificed.) It was, moreover, endemic amongst these
Hera turncoats to express their dissatisfaction with the way that things were
'turning' out by packing up their children and taking them back home to their
mother's Deathlands—or at least, to pretend to.

Therefore, on Mount Laphystium in the Pelion range of Thessaly, Athamas prepared to offer up his children, who up until this point had been tended like animals in the 'king's' herd. But at the last moment, a miraculous Ram with Golden
Fleece (like Pegasos, an offspring of Poseidon) appeared. Phrixos (or 'Bristle,'
like the Fleece itself, or like 'Rilled' waters, for such is the meaning of his name)
hopped aboard, as the Ram commanded, together with his sister Helle (or 'Greek
girl,' named after her great-grandfather Hellenos: a turncoat name, like Danae).
The Ram was sent by either Hera or Zeus (in their better natures) as a gift to
Nephele; and it had the power of human speech. On its back, the brother and
sister escaped.

But as they crossed over into the Deathlands, passing the Entrance at the
narrow channel that separates the peninsula of Gallipoli in Europe from Troy in
Asia across the waters, Helle fell as a bride into the waiting embrace of Poseidon;
thereafter the straits were called the Hellespont, which means the 'Greek Sea,'
or the Sea of Helle, which today is named the Dardanelles. (Did Phrixos push her?
No one remembered, but 'loving' siblings never got along that well together.)
Phrixos continued on to the far end of the 'Hospitable Sea' or Euxine, also now
known as the Black Sea. There he surfaced at the Phasis River, which flows
down from the mountains which border on the Hyperborean homeland. Here
was the House of Aietes, where the Sun slept until it waked at dawn.

Phrixos completed the sacrifice by slaughtering the Ram, and hanging its
Fleece on a Tree, where it would remain, guarded by a Serpent, until Iason
would come to fetch it back. As for Phrixos, he married Aietes' 'black' daughter
'Bronze-face' **Chalkiope**, a sister of Medeia, who would be the one waiting
when Iason finally arrived for her—and the Fleece. This Fleece, that talked and
offered transport between the worlds, would be the object of Iason's quest, an **entheogen** in the eastern Garden that was the counterpoise to the Golden 'Apples'
that Perseus and Herakles had sought in the western Garden of the Hesperides,
where the Sun began its nightly sleep. And when he brought it back, with the
turncoat Medeia's aid, it will have had its nature transmuted from a plant of the

old traditions of shamanism, to the Indo-European import, that signified the new age of Olympians: the new Zeus and Hera.

When, on the other hand, Ino is the center of the story, there are two pairs of children: Nephele's and her own, **Melikertes** and **Leukon** or **Learchos**; and Ino, instead of Nephele, is the jealous wife. In this version, it was Ino herself who caused the drought by convincing the women to roast the seeds before planting them (cooking what shouldn't be cooked); and then she bribed the messengers from Delphi to say that Nephele's children should be sacrificed, in order to assure the sovereignty for her own sons. Again, Hera intervened with the Fleece, and Phrixos and Helle escaped.

But there was still another way of telling the story (nor are the details of one always separate from any of the others). In this version, Hera is Ino's enemy; and the infant Dionysos is substituted for Nephele's children. Ino has assumed the job of 'wet nurse' for her dead sister Semele's baby, whom she has disguised as a girl; and Hera is the jealous one. To take out her rage, she makes Athamas mad, so that he slaughters Learchos; and he would have completed the sacrifice with Melikertes, had not Dionysos blinded him, so that he attacked a she-Ram (or Ewe) instead. In the confusion, Ino snatched up her other son, Melikertes, and fled. At the cliff where Theseus encountered the brigand Skiron, outside of Megara, she plunged through the Entrance down into the sea. By rescuing her son into the Deathlands, she (and Hera) transmuted their identity to its better nature: Ino (like Helle) this time became the sea maiden; and she changed her name to the 'White Goddess' **Leukothea**, who was a friendly 'helper' for heroes in the sea. Melikertes also changed his name: his tomb was across the Saronic Gulf, at the Isthmian Entrance, where he had surfaced on the back of a dolphin; there, he was known as **Palaimon**, the 'Wrestler,' and his spirit presided over the athletic Contests at the sanctuary of Isthmia in future times, as the one contender embraced its 'enemy' equal in hostile play: where, in bygone days, Sinis Pityokamptes used to split heroes, like Theseus, in two: dividing one half from it equal other. Learchos, the brother of Melikertes-Palaimon, had a chthonic name, which means the 'Ruler of People;' but he, too had another name: **Leukon**, the 'White.' And in grief for his death (either by sacrificial slaughter, or some other cause), Athamas began his wanderings, which would take him eventually to Halos in Thessaly, where he founded the city of the Athamanes. In this manner, two 'Whites' were taken to the Deathlands, as mediation. (This version has the same meaning, showing a transmutation to the newer traditions of shamanism. Ino and Athamas, as caretakers of the infant Dionysos, are playing the same role as the silens and maenads of Nysa, tending the baby god through the period of his wilderness sojourn, before his discovery of the (w)oinos drink for the coming era. **Melikertes**, the 'Honey boy,' belongs to the former traditions, associated with the Bear Goddess Artemis and the Bee symbolism of Minoan (Pelasgian and Minyan) times. Even in the Classical period, as we have seen, the common word for 'drunk' implied the 'honey drink.')

There was still another way of telling this story, in which the 'white'-'black' dichotomy again figures. In this version, Ino has gone out Hunting and become involved in a maenadic revel; her blood-stained clothing convinces Athamas that she is dead; and he marries **Themisto** as his second wife. From her, he has a second pair of sons. But then Ino returns alive, and without Themisto's knowledge, Ino is employed as 'wet nurse' for the new sons. Themisto learns the truth and plots to play the wicked step-mother to Ino's former sons. She tells Ino to dress her predecessor's sons in 'black' so that they can mourn for their dead mother; and to dress her own two sons in 'white.' She then directs her henchmen to kill the 'black' boys and to spare the 'white.' But Ino reverses the sign, so that Themisto's sons are the ones who are slaughtered; thus Themisto 'accidentally' kills her own sons, through the agency of Ino.

This Fleece that Iason sentenced himself to fetch is the best documented of the various prizes that the heroes sought to retrieve from the Deathlands (or at least until the next generation, when Helen would be the prize, and the heroes would cooperate in the Trojan War to fetch her back); and the task that confronted Iason, ultimately, was no less than that of turning Hera, herself, around—of making the former 'Black' Ladies (Tyro, Sidero, Ino, Chalkiope) into 'White' (Tyro, Leukothea), or at least of so confusing the distinctions of 'black and white' and 'kind and cruel' that she was brought into the family of the new age. (Perseus and, of course, Herakles had come up against Hera in their careers, too, but Iason's would be the definitive settlement.) This Fleece, as we have seen, was the animal-human sacrificial victim (Neleus-Pelias, Iason, Melikertes-Leukon-Palaimon, Phrixos-Helle), sent to the Deathlands by its mother, stepmother, wet

Iason, Fetching the Golden Fleece from the Tree Guarded by the Serpent, with Athena and an Argonaut as 'Helpers' (Red-figure vase c. 470-60 BC, Metropolitan Museum, New York)

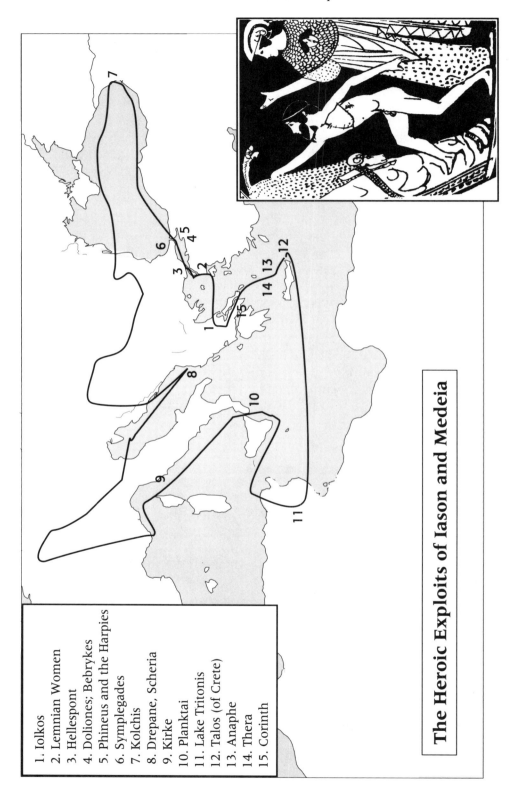

1. Iolkos
2. Lemnian Women
3. Hellespont
4. Doliones; Bebrykes
5. Phineus and the Harpies
6. Symplegades
7. Kolchis
8. Drepane, Scheria
9. Kirke
10. Planktai
11. Lake Tritonis
12. Talos (of Crete)
13. Anaphe
14. Thera
15. Corinth

The Heroic Exploits of Iason and Medeia

nurse, witch; and it had botanical associations with the Nysian Dionysos, and like him, its return would signify the transition to the 'civilized' era of sacred plants.

The ship that would undertake this voyage down to where the Sun spent the night through in drunken slumber in the easternmost House of his 'landed' son Aietes, was, like the Fleece that had preceded it, a magical transport. It was called **Argo**, the 'Bright-white,' and it was named after the craftsman who built it with Athena's aid: he was **Argos**, like the one whom Hermes Argeiphontes killed. It was reputedly the first ship ever constructed; and, like the Ram of the Fleece, it, too, had the gift of human speech—or superhuman speech, inspired speech: for Athena herself fitted a timber from Zeus's oracular oaks from Dodona into its magical prow (**entheogen**).

And as 'helpers' for the journey, every hero then alive came along to second Iason's effort (**animus**); for it was his journey, and they were his helpers: they were named together as the **Argonauts**, the 'Sailors of the White Ship.' The exact list varies, but there were supposedly fifty of them, and amongst them were many a chthonic ally. The most famous were Herakles, Theseus (and Peirithoos), **Peleus** (the father of Achilleus), Kastor and Polydeukes (the Dioskouroi), Nauplios, Meleagros (with his Atalante), and **Orpheus**, the inspired poet and singer (who is better known from his other descent into the netherworld to attempt to bring up his own bride, **Eurydike**).

Down they all went, but they followed the overland route that would take them through all the Entrances that lay on the way from Iolkos in Thessaly to the Deathlands of the River **Phasis** (named for an aquatic son of Apollo), that flows through the land of **Kolchis** (Latin **Colchis**).

First, there were the **Lemnian Women** to contend with. (The island of Lemnos is a volcanic Entrance, and was famous for its Mystery religion which in later times reintroduced its initiates to their own chthonic brothers, the **Kabeiroi**, from the primordial days; it was here that Hephaistos had fallen to earth when Zeus hurled him down from Olympus, and within the volcano's molten core, he maintained his subterranean blacksmith's forge.) The women of this island were a fierce sisterhood, inimical to men, like the Danaids and the Amazons. Their Queen, who presided over this Entrance, was the Lady 'High Gate,' **Hypsipyle**. As one might expect of women who inhabited the Deathlands, their bodies gave off a noisome stench that had driven away all the men of their race, to seek more suitable company elsewhere; and in retaliation, the women had attacked the men and their new mates, killing them all, except one. Like the Danaid Hypermnestra, Hypsipyle spared her own father by setting him adrift in a chest upon the sea: this was the 'king' **Thoas**, a son of Dionysos.

When the Argonauts arrived, this was the situation that greeted them: a whole race of women without men; and like Amazons, they even dressed like men in order to ward off all invaders. The Queen's 'wet nurse,' however, warned them that their race was doomed for extinction, unless some remedy was found. She advised a union between Hypsipyle and Iason—which would also cure the stench. (Her name was the 'Big Itch,' **Polyxo**.) Thus the men were welcomed into their city of **Myrine**, named for the 'myrtle,' which was a plant that was emblematic of weddings (**entheogen**).

Iason had to satisfy Hypsipyle (and her women, with the help of the Argonauts) in a drunken marriage celebration that lasted days, months, or even years. And finally like Theseus with Ariadne, he had to desert the Queen—but he left behind a new era on the island: the civilization there had been turned around, and now included both males and females, with many family ties, through this legion of heroes, to the people in our world; there were even twin sons that Iason left behind. Even its Dionysian heritage had moved on to our times: Iason's sons were Euneus (named for the marriage 'Bed') and a new Thoas; Euneus became king and supplied the Greek troops with wine during the Trojan War. (As for the former Thoas: he came ashore in his chest in an Apolline Deathlands in Thrace, where he became 'king'of the 'Bull People,' the **Taurians**, who were still performing human sacrifice a generation later.)

As the Argonauts resumed their course toward Kolchis, they took advantage of the cover of night to slip past the 'Lord' Laomedon, whose city of Troy guarded the Entrance into the Hellespont (and thus they were able to avoid repeating the first Trojan War, which had been one of Herakles' episodes).

Their next adventure (beyond the Hellespont, and on into the Propontus, which today is called the Sea of Marmara) involved the 'friendly' **Doliones**, whose name means the 'Tricksters.' It was a hallucinatory land that they inhabited, a place where 'friend' and 'enemy' were easily confused (**paradigms #1, 2, & 3**: 'enemy;' reconciliation; 'helpers'). **Kyzikos** was their 'king;' and their city on the promontory of the 'Bear Fountain,' at the foot of Mount Dindymon, was named after him. He had been warned to welcome a legion of heroes 'hospitably,' should one ever arrive; and he interrupted the consummation of his own marriage in order to invite the newcomers to the festivities. But the Doliones had relatives in the neighborhood who were less civilized than they; and, like the centaurs at Peirithoos's wedding, these six-armed monstrous giants descended from the slopes of Mount Dindymon and attacked. The Argonauts, however, defeated them and killed them all.

The Argonauts then sailed off, but the winds were against them and they lost their way: they were driven back in the night, without knowing it, to the same promontory. This time their 'friend' Kyzikos thought they were 'enemies;' and again he interrupted the consummation of his marriage bed, for battle. Both sides fought without recognizing the other, until dawn, when the truth was discovered: Iason had 'accidentally' killed Kyzikos. The 'king's' chthonic bride (the 'Famous Lady' **Kleite**) hanged herself in grief, and the tears of her lamenting sisterhood became the Fountain. The Argonauts could not sail on until they had appeased the Goddess, after whom the mountain was named. This they did by climbing Mount Dindymon, the former home of the giants whom (like the Doliones) they had killed; and there they discovered a miraculous wild vine stock (**entheogen**) which they incorporated into the new era that they were inaugurating by their voyage: Argos carved an effigy of the Goddess from its wood—

in the likeness of Rhea, the mother of Zeus. And to Athena, they dedicated the anchor stone that they had used to stop there amongst the Doliones. (It was still on view in her temple there in later times.) The Argonauts replaced it with another stone that they took from that land, thus exchanging the old for the new.

They next beached their ship on the Propontic shore of Mysia: on their way there, they had engaged in a Contest of rowing, in which finally only Iason and his 'friend' Herakles were left competing—until Iason at last had fallen asleep from exhaustion, just as Herakles had broken his oar: otherwise, Herakles would have won; but fortunately, the **Contest (between Iason and Herakles)** ended in a draw. Herakles went inland to find a suitable tree from which to carve a replacement for his broken oar (**entheogen**).

This is where Iason (and the Argonauts) lost Herakles; as with Kyzikos, there is no higher 'help' a 'friend' can offer than to become the losing half of the heroic duo. (Imagine, for example, what would have happened if both Iason and Herakles had reached Medeia's Garden and the Tree with the Fleece together.)

So this is how Iason lost Herakles—and no one was to blame. When Herakles returned to the campsite, with the huge fir tree that he had uprooted, intending to carve it into his new oar, he discovered that his own personal 'friend and helper' was missing. This was **Hylas** or 'Woodsman' (not the same person as his son **Hyllos** by Deianeira, but destined to play the same role as 'loser'). Like Hyakinthos, whom Apollo loved and 'accidentally' killed, Hylas was a beautiful boy, the beloved companion of Herakles. He was someone with ties to the old chthonic world: he may have come from Oichalia (the 'Pass-away' city of Iole), or from Argos, or, more probably, from the 'Oak-people' or **Dryopes** (like Druids) of what is today Albania. He was someone that Herakles eventually would have to get rid of somehow, and fortunately, in losing Hylas, Herakles ended up, himself, being lost to Iason and the Argonauts. It couldn't have turned out better.

While Herakles had been out picking his Tree, Hylas had gone to fetch water from the spring of the 'Fountain Sisterhood.' And as Hylas reached down to draw the water, the sisters seductively pulled him down into their depths, clutching him for their consort. Herakles went in search of his 'friend,' but found only the deserted pitcher, beside the spring. Herakles, however, refused to give up the search, and he wandered off, disconsolate, throughout the Deathlands, calling for his beloved companion. It was as though his erotic passion for the 'Woodsman' were a drug that made him forget the expedition of the Argo: he deserted them all. Meanwhile, Iason resumed course toward Kolchis, without waiting for Herakles' return: even though the Argonauts accused him of abandoning his 'friend' to get back at him for the Contest in rowing

There were two more **Contests** as the Argonauts approached the final Entrance into the realm of Kolchis; and these encounters explore other ways of resolving the dilemma of the hero's double (or liminal) identity. The Argo next touched base at the island of the **Bebrykes**, another one of those chthonic peoples who were noted as 'Shouters' (like their 'western' counterpoint, the Teleboans). Their 'king' was a 'Bull-bellower' **Amykos** and a famous boxer. His 'hospitality' consisted in challenging his guests to a match, and the loser was tossed off a cliff into the sea. Fortunately, the crew of the Argo listed a pair of boxers, the 'inseparable twins:' the **Dioskouroi**, **Kastor** and **Polydeukes**. And instead of engaging each other in their usual 'friendly' combat, Polydeukes entered the ring alone—to contest Amykos. Polydeukes won; and Amykos lost.

Another pair of twins were involved in the next encounter, as well. These were the Athenians, **Kalais** and **Zetes**. This time, they both won together—although they both were to die, together, later on the expedition.

The 'host' for this episode was **Phineus**, a figure with good credentials as a 'black' man: a son of Poseidon, although he is otherwise known as an Ethiopian, a son of Agenor (who was father of the 'Phoenician' Phoinix and the Theban Kadmos; and who was the brother of the 'Egyptian' Belos, from whom the Danaids and the Perseid line was descended); you will remember that a Phineus had been Perseus's rival for Andromeda. This time, Phineus was found in Thrace, on the European shore of the Sea of Marmara, with a nether Queen as wife, either Chthonia or Erichtho, although she was also known as Kleopatra, a woman 'Famous for her father.'

Phineus was the final guardian for the passage to Kolchis; it was from him that you might learn the secret of how to go there—and come back again. He lived in a realm of darkness, for he had renounced the lands above, where the sun's rays gave light; and he was himself blind, but with a blindness that let him pierce through the darkness with prophetic sight. As a guardian and prophet, he stood at the **limen** or doorway between two worlds, belonging to neither, totally; and hence, he found the environment of the Deathlands not to his liking—in particular, the dilemma of eating, in a place where the natural state of food is unpalatable and rotten. Whenever his meal was served, a sisterhood of (usually three) 'Soul-snatchers,' the **Harpies**, part vulture and part women, flew in to snatch it away, between his hand and his mouth; and what was left on the table, they defiled with their excrement, rendering it disgusting from its stench. From lack of nutriment, he had withered like a corpse, but he could not die: just grow forever older, and more filthy. (The 'Witherer' is a possible meaning for his name.)

(The reason for his torment was variously cited: perhaps it was his punishment for having let Phrixos pass by with the Fleece into the Deathlands; or it may have been because he had blinded his own sons—because of their wicked stepmother, Idaia, 'Lady of Cretan Mount Ida,' another Hera double and Queen like Sidero and Ino; or he may have revealed too much in his prophecies.)

The Harpies were robbing Phineus of his food just as the Argonauts landed; and the old man knew that they were destined to rid him of his curse, but as he rose to greet them, the exertion was too much for his feeble, withered body, and he collapsed into unconsciousness before them.

Zetes (the 'Seeker') and Kalais (the color 'Cyanic-blue-and-purple-to-turquoise'), the Athenian twins who were his wife's brothers, rescued him. Like the Harpies, they too were winged.

(They were the Athenian version of the **warring brothers** theme, like the

Dioskouroi or Amphion and Zethos of Thebes; Zetes and Zethos are, in fact, both 'Seekers,' and Zetes is also called **Zethes**, and **Zethos** is known also as **Zetos**: the 'seeking' makes them mediators, looking for lost relatives, usually sisters, in the Darklands. Kalais and Zetes were the children born from their mother **Oreithyia**, the 'Mountain-maenad' and her abducting consort, the wind Boreas, while she was gathering magical plants with her sisterhood of 'Druggists,' one of whom had the name of Pharmakeia. The name of Kalais, like that of the Athenian Ion, suggests the color of the violet sacred 'flower.')

When the Harpies swooped down upon the food that the starving Phineus was trying to eat, Kalais and Zetes, attacked them. The Harpies fled, with the flying twins in hot pursuit—as far as the 'Islands of Turning', called the Strophades. There, the twins turned back; and the Harpies forever after took up residence beneath the Labyrinth of Knossos on Crete. (Some claimed that the twins also rescued their blinded nephews from their cruel stepmother.)

As the twins—both—traveled back, Phineus at last feasted, offering his 'hospitality' to the Argonauts. He revealed to them the secret of the final Entrance: the cyanic-purple **Symplegades** or 'Clashing Rocks,' which were also called **Kyaniai** for their color. They were twin Rocks, on opposite shores, just where the Sea of Marmara narrows to only a few hundred feet. (The place is known as the Bosporos or Bosphoros, where the city of Istanbul, the former Constantinople and Byzantium, now stands: the name of the strait means the 'Cow Crossing:' it commemorates the crossing by the Cow Io on her tour of the Deathlands.) Each day, through the gap of these Symplegades, a sisterhood of doves flew, bringing ambrosia (**entheogen**) to the gods on Olympus, the 'immortal' food that was their nourishment; and as the birds passed through, the Rocks clashed together: but always, too late to catch any but the last dove in the flock. The Argonauts were to imitate the flight of these doves; Phineus told them to race through the gap, just after the Rocks had reopened after clashing upon a dove that they had sent on ahead of them: this they did, losing only the tip of the ship's stern in the passage; the dove ahead of them had similarly lost only its tail feathers. Ever since that passage, these Rocks have stood apart and the way through the Bosporos has remained open. (It was sometimes claimed that Athena herself had 'helped' by holding the Rocks apart, while she pushed the ship through.)

Thus, the sailors passed on into the Black Sea. As they continued their Tour, they met Apollo himself, in the period of his own liminality, as he traveled between his two homes in the Deathlands, from the 'Wolf-people' of Lykia to the Hyperboreans: the time was the transitional hour we call twilight, but the Greeks knew as the 'wolf-light;' and some people thought that this was the Entrance that had been used when Herakles had fetched up the dog Kerberos and the plant wolfsbane.

There were further adventures on the Tour, and other of the 'foreign' peoples were observed, as they passed. (In actual fact, many of these foreigners who had settled on the shores of the Black Sea were distantly related to them as branches of the Indo-European migrations.) These 'foreigners' often did things

Iason Disgorged Unconscious by the Serpent, with Athena, and Fleece Hanging on the Tree (Red-figure kylix c. 480-470 BC, Vatican Museum, Rome)

backwards, from the way they are done in our world: sometimes, for example, they do in public the acts that should be performed only in private; or it is the men who lie in for the birthing, groaning in labor. They even lost a couple of other sailors from their crew (notably **Idmon**, their prophet, and **Tiphys**, their pilot), and they took on some 'foreigners' to replace them. In one instance, the 'foreigners' turned out actually to be close relatives, the sons of Phrixos, by his 'dark-faced' wife Chalkiope, the daughter of Aietes of Kolchis.

Finally, at the eastern end of the Black Sea of 'Hospitality,' the Argonauts, this crew of related 'enemies' and 'friends,' landed at Kolchis. Aietes had been warned that he should be wary of relatives; and already his grandsons were enlisted on the other side, and eventually his brother would aid the cause of the newcomers, but he had no idea that he was to be betrayed by a turncoat so closely related as his own daughter **Medeia**—the granddaughter of Helios, and sister of the 'dark-faced' Chalkiope, and niece of the Cretan Pasiphae and the 'witch' Kirke. As to what exactly happened, the story is variously told; but all accounts agree upon this one point: it was she who turned on her own father.

The Fleece was hung upon the Tree (**axis mundi**) in this Garden where the Sun slept through his nightly bout of drunkenness, and like its western counterpart, the Tree of the Golden Apples in the keeping of the Hesperides sisters, it was guarded by a Serpent. Some people knew a version of the story in which Iason was actually swallowed into the labyrinthine pathway of the Serpent's gullet (like another Theseus entering the Labyrinth of the Cretan Bull); the trip rendered him unconscious (like Herakles' descent into the tunneling lair of the Nemean Lion), and only with Athena and Medeia's help was he revived when he reemerged. There could be no more total merging of identities of hero and 'enemy' (**paradigm #1**) than this journey into the maw that gaped wide enough, as some said, to engulf the entire ship Argo and its crew.

Others knew that there were three tasks that Iason had to perform to win the Fleece (for the Goddess herself was always triple), and the journey into the gullet of the Serpent was only the first. For all of them, however, Medeia's help (**anima**) was indispensable. His divine 'helpers' Athena and Hera (**paradigm #3**) had contrived to make Medeia drunk (or drugged)—but with love for Iason. She could not help but help him. Eros shot her with his toxic bow, and she was poisoned uncontrollably in his favor.

The second task was a Contest with Aietes. Each had to plow a furrow, but the danger was that the plow was to be pulled by a team of ferocious fire-breathing Bulls, 'black' with the brazen darkness of their owner Helios. Medeia (who had already used her magical herbs to revive Iason from his slumbering encounter with the Serpent) now anointed Iason with a magical drug (and thereby for a second time ratified the meaning of the name that had first been given him by the centaur Cheiron: Iason is the **ios**-man or 'Drug-man'). The drug she used was the plant that lent its name to Kolchis, a plant that was later identified with the autumn Crocus or meadow saffron (Colchicum), a poisonous bulb from whose purple flowers the saffron dye is extracted. (This plant of Kolchis completes the gamut of the sacred spectrum that defines the **entheogen**: its colors were already seen in the purple Clashing Rocks and in the twins who guided the Argo through its passage, as well as in the tawny Fleece.) In Medeia's Garden, it grew from the blood of the tormented Prometheus, and when she plucked it, the Titan himself groaned with pain on the nearby mountain. It was for this outcome that Prometheus had been offered in sacrifice; and anointed with his plant, Iason was invulnerable on this day of his heroism, a second Prometheus, forging a role for humankind in the opposing realms of Earth and Sky.

The third task was the mediation (**paradigm #2**). A crop of new men had to be planted for the coming age. The toxic nature of the Serpent had to be returned by Iason to the earth as seed for the people born into the Olympian era. The seeds were the Serpent's fangs. It is the same task that Kadmos faced in resettling Thebes, and the two episodes became intertwined, so that some claimed that it was not Medeia's Serpent, but the Theban Dirke's, whose teeth were sown (or half of them, at least, a gift from Athena) at Kolchis. A battle ensued amongst the creatures who sprouted.

And Iason escaped with Medeia—and the Fleece: Iason picked it from the Tree, while Medeia drugged the Serpent to sleep. So fervently did she side with Iason, that she turned upon her own blood lines, in favor of his 'alien' lineage—as does any woman who marries. She butchered her own brother **Apsyrtos** and strew the path of their escape with his remains, so that Aietes was forced to delay his pursuit, while he gathered them up for burial, catching them as they 'Washed Away' (which is the meaning of Apsyrtos) in the wake of the Argo.

The return took the Argo on a Tour of the Deathlands. As with Herakles' Tour, such travels can prove extensive, and there were various ways of embellishing the story. By most accounts, they departed the Black Sea by sailing up the Danube. Some claimed that it was here that Apsyrtos was butchered and washed away; others said that Iason killed him instead, in a battle there, in the same place where Herakles had tracked down the Keryneian Hind of Artemis, and plucked its Golden branching antler; and that Medeia deceived her brother into an ambush at the Temple of Artemis. From the Danube, they sailed south into the Ionian Sea (with which the Danube was supposed to afford a passage via a connecting river). As they passed the island of Corfu, the ship itself spoke and advised them to seek out the island of Kirke, so that the 'witch' (who was Medeia's relative) could bless the union by purifying them of blood guilt in the slaughter of Apsyrtos; so they headed north again, up the Po-Eridanos and across the Italian peninsula, north into Europe via a supposed connection to the Rhine, and then south (again via an assumed link with the Rhone) into the Tyrrhenian Sea. After Kirke—wherever she was to be found, on her enchanted island of 'Lamentation,' called Aiaia: later located as Monte Circello—, they sailed south through the strait that separates Sicily from the southern tip of Italy: this was a narrow passage like the Symplegades, but here it was characterized as the 'Wandering Rocks' or **Planktai**; and the monsters **Skylla** and **Charybdis** lurked in wait, a 'Bitch' and a 'Whirlpool.'.

Somewhere along the way, Medeia lost her virginity, if this had not already happened, as some thought, back in Kolchis; but some tellers had it finally take place on the magical island of the Phaiakians (where Odysseus 'later' had his affair with the princess Nausikaa on his return after the Trojan War). The Fleece was spread upon the bed where they consummated their marriage: the island's name was the 'Reaping-hook,' Drepane (like the instrument that Perseus had used to reap the Gorgon's head and the Apples of the Hesperides); the island was also known as **Scheria**, and was later located as Corfu, although with Iason's journey, we are in the wrong sea.

From Drepane, they journeyed to Libya, across the dangerous 'Washed' sands of the Syrtis's shallow banks, and into 'Africa.' There, three weird sisters advised them to treat the ship Argo as they had been treated by their own mothers in the womb: they must carry it. So overland they went, south into the Motherland, with the ship in portage, through the desert: to Lake Tritonis (origin of Athena Tritogeneia), where they met the Hesperides, just the day after Herakles had killed the Serpent Ladon. Triton himself pushed them back to the sea, after entrusting a clod of 'African' soil to them to transplant in the next world.

After that, they began turning up at various Entrances up in the Greek lands; and everywhere they went, the sites were reoriented, and made over to the newer versions of Athena or Hera, but more especially, of Artemis and Apollo. Crete was first to be pacified by their passage. This time, it was not the Minotaur (Theseus's 'enemy') that they encountered, but another Bull-man, **Talos**, a henchman of Minos, and dark and made of bronze, invincible, except for his ankle; he guarded the island, throwing rocks at any ships that approached. Medeia bewitched him with drugs (or just with her glance, like another Medousa); and unstoppered the plug in his ankle and allowed his life force to flow out of him; or, as some told the story, the 'Herb-man' Poias, who was one of the Argonauts, shot him in the ankle with a poisoned arrow. The sailors then erected a temple to the Minoan Athena.

But Crete was not the only place that they resurfaced to put down the Minoan ways. On the island of Anaphe, north of Crete, Apollo himself greeted them on their return (as he had on their entrance into the Deathlands)—standing upon one of the two cliffs, the so-called 'Black Rocks' of the island. Anaphe means 'Re-ignition;' and here, Iason, who had been anointed with the Promethean herb, lit the first fire of the new world. It was the first performance of what would become an annual festival of Apollo on the island; and it commemorated the new order of sacrifice, in which human victims were no longer offered, but only a sham of what would have happened in former times.

As they were leaving the island of Anaphe, **Battos**, the 'Stutterer' (one of the Argonauts), who was also called **Euphemos**, the 'Well-spoken' (for he was about to be cured of his infirmity), threw the clod of Africa into the caldera of the volcano that lay beneath the waters of the sea; and from it grew the island of Kalliste (the 'Most Beautiful,' an overly optimistic name for the Death Goddess); which was also called Thera (named 'Beasts' as one of the Hunting preserves of Artemis); and which is today called Santorini (after Saint Irene or 'Peace,' who still later replaced the ancient Goddess). In actual fact, the Thera volcano exploded just about the time the Argonauts would have got there, leaving the remnants that comprise the island today; its destruction is generally recognized as one of the reasons for the demise of Minoan culture. The descendants of Battos, who no longer babbled in foreign tongues, formed the new peoples of the island.

They turned up elsewhere—including Corinth (where it was later remembered that Medeia had always been, lurking just beneath the surface); it was there that Iason would have his 'tragic' identity. But ultimately they had to come up at Iolkos, for the successful completion of the task that had been set them by Pelias, the uncle of Iason.

Aison, his father, was so old by now that he could not join in the celebration of the heroes' return (or, as some said, he was already dead, murdered by his warring brother); but Medeia rejuvenated him, as a demonstration of the power of the new Artemis of Anaphe. Pelias, too, was very old (if he was not already dead, as some told the story); and Medeia deceived the sisterhood of his daughters into attempting to rejuvenate him, as well: either by the example of Aison, or by butchering and cooking a Fleeced Ram with magical herbs, so that it emerged whole and young from the cauldron (or perhaps, it wasn't a cauldron, but actually a hollow image of the Anaphe Artemis that she used as her cooking pot, as some versions claimed). This second attempt failed miserably, since Medeia substituted different herbs for the spice of life; and thus Pelias was indeed destined to fall to his nephew Iason. (As might be expected, Alkestis was the only daughter in the Pherai sisterhood of '(Under)takers' who refused to join with the others in this ruse of attempted rejuvenation.)

The Death of Iason

The murder of Iason's other self, of course, was a suicide: Iason had to enter the Bondage of Death to expiate for what had happened to Pelias. Just as Theseus retired to his motherland of Troizen upon the death of the Pallantidai, Iason turned up in Corinth, while Pelias's son, the 'Impure' **Akastos** (who had journeyed as a 'helper' turncoat with the Argonauts) took over control of Iolkos.

Corinth was Medeia's ancestral home. It was there that Helios had begotten her father Aietes, by the Corinthian 'turn-face' Antiope. The high mountain that looms over the city of Corinth to form its Acropolis (the so-called Akrokorinthos) was Aietes' inheritance, where he was associated with the goddess Aphrodite (whose erotic madness had turned Medeia in Iason's favor) and with

Hera: she was known there as Bounia, the 'Hill-Lady,' and her consort was the 'king' Bounos. At Corinth, it was this Hera who presided over the old Death ritual, like Artemis at the Labyrinth of Knossos. Each year, twice seven, a group of boys and girls, was sent to Hera's Temple on Akrokorinthos to serve the Goddess; they were mourned, as if they had died, but in these later times, they no longer did, for the Goddess had turned merciful, and they all returned unharmed at the end of the year. It was Medeia originally (this granddaughter of the turn-face bride of the nether Sun) who had turned Hera around at Corinth: for Zeus had courted Medeia, but she refused to betray Hera; and as reward for upholding the sanctity of Hera's matrimony, Hera granted Medeia's children immortality: the feigned death each year of the sacrificial victims commemorated that change of face. In the Temple, Medeia performed her rejuvenation routine on each of the victims.

Iason, however, didn't fit in at Corinth: he was a 'foreigner.' As to exactly what happened, there were different ways of telling the story. He may have spied on the secret ritual, as often happened in such cases, and not understood it, thinking that she was killing his children—all fourteen of them, boys and girls (doing with them what she had done to Pelias, rather than what she had done with Aison). Or the Corinthians themselves, in these later times, may have forgotten their own subterranean past and looked upon her as a 'foreigner' and been repulsed by her strange ways, which they no longer understood—thinking her a murderess.

The Athenian way of telling the story, however, is the one that became popular ever since. Iason had made the mistake of trying to become 'king' by marrying into the dynasty at Corinth, as if the place were still a Queendom. He has decided to reject the (supposed) 'foreigner' Medeia (his former turncoat 'helper'); and marry the 'Ruler' **Kreon**'s daughter, the 'Owl-lady' **Glauke** (not the Athena—and Hera—who had 'helped' him, but their pre-Olympian precedent). (He might as well have taken up residence at Kolchis, and never returned from his voyage on the Argo to the Deathlands.)

(This was the situation at Corinth when Theseus's father Aigeus arrived; and after it all was finished at Corinth, Medeia, as we have seen, turned up at Athens as his bride. There were also people who claimed that she popped up at Thebes and had an affair with Herakles first.)

Medeia sent Glauke a poisoned robe and crown for the wedding, using her own children as messengers; and when the bride put them on, she—and her father, and perhaps all the wedding guests as well—went mad: Glauke tried to escape the torment of her burning oestrual heat (for such was the nature of the poison) by jumping into the so-called Spring of Glauke, which was named after her, near the marketplace of Corinth. And the messengers were put to death: either by the angered Corinthians, in retaliation, or, as Euripides told the story, by Medeia herself, proving that children belong to the mother, instead of their father. It was left for Theseus to sort out the problem of the Medousa Queen Medeia and *glaukopis* Glauke-Athena at Athens.

Such was the Corinth that Medeia left to Iason, when she escaped to her new refuge with Aigeus in Athens: a Corinth that had regressed to the 'foreign' matrilineal ways of olden days. And Iason, at the Isthmian Entrance, nearby to the city of Corinth, where he had first dedicated his ship Argo, died, struck on the head by one of its decaying—and formerly magical—timbers. (Or alternatively, it was in the Hera Temple that he died, the place where he had once dedicated the ship's prophetic figurehead, carved from the sacred oak.) In either version, whether it was the timber or the figurehead that knocked out his brains, it was the **entheogen** of his former heroism that had turned against him, so that he never left Corinth, but descended into the Deathlands as the losing half of the liminal pair, leaving success to some other hero in that band of Argonauts.

* * * *

The War at Thebes

The city of the Thebai sisterhood (Thebes) has already figured in our discussion of the birth of Dionysos, and the contest of Apollo and Artemis with Niobe, and the birth and madness of Herakles; but it is time now to review the story of its (re)settlement from the beginning, in view of our expanded repertory of mythical themes.

Anyone visiting Thebes today would hardly guess that this was the place where all those events happened, so squarely does the modern city sit atop its ancient foundations, defying all who would delve into the past that lies beneath it: little remains of its famous Acropolis citadel, the Kadmeia, protected by the surrounding fortification walls with their magical Seven Gates. The ancient city, however, underwent repeated attempts to turn it around to the new Olympian era. The first was the arrival of **Kadmos** (Latin **Cadmus**), who came up from the East out of 'Africa' to Thebes, via the swamplands of what would later become the fertile plain of the Cow-land **Boeotia**, on whose former shores the Minyans had already settled, at sites like the 'Pass-away' towns of Orchomenos. In those days, Kadmos was still 'black' from his Phoenician homeland (for he was a brother of **Phoinix**, and of the **Kilix** who gave his name to the Cilicians who lived in the lands south of Troy), and 'muddy' from the muck at the bottom of the Boeotian Lake Copais, where prior to his emergence, he had ruled over his people of eels; and still small, a 'digital' dwarfish little Kadmos or **Kadmilos**, a phallic beloved other self of Hermes.

He was one of those 'Seekers,' looking for his lost sister; for he was also the brother of that **Europa** who had been abducted by the Zeus Bull to Minoan Crete; his cousins were **Danaos** and **Aigyptos**, who surfaced at the Lerna Springs of Argos, at the start of the Perseid lineage. And Kadmos, himself, came up many times at various Entrances on his wandering Tour of the Deathlands as he looked for his sister: one of his more famous sightings was on the island of Samothrace, where he was recognized as the leader of the 'black' **Kabeiroi** brotherhood of primordial men. Just before showing up at the sacred Spring of

Kadmos, Contesting the Serpent and the Spring Lady, with Athena's Help, and Harmonia, Watching from the Skies (South-Italian red-figure krater, Museo Nazionale, Naples).

Thebes, he had emerged through the labyrinth of the Korykian Cave of Apollo's Delphi, to ask for guidance in his quest. The old grey-haired oracle told him not directly where his sister was, but simply to follow a Cow with a lunar cresent on its flank: where it lay down, he was to found a city. The Cow led him to the site of Thebes, and to her former herdsman, the 'Mud-born' **Pelagon (paradigm #1)**.

The place was already inhabited. The 'Datura-lady' **Dirke** was there, with her eel-like Serpent, Kadmos's natural 'enemy.' (The Lady of the Spring had other names as well; and as Dirke, she reappears later in the genealogies: she was also **Thebe**, of the Thebai sisterhood—but under that name, she was to become a bride of Zeus, although by family background, she belonged to the Stymphalian Swamp and the 'Rockrose' River Ladon, the Serpent of the Hesperides.) As Kadmos attempted to fetch water, he Contested the Serpent—and won, with Athena's 'help.' The toxic fangs (or teeth) of the beast he planted as the first 'cultivated' crop of the new era: for Kadmos was seen as the great civilizer, even bringing with him the Phoenician symbols which were to become the Greek alphabet and the beginning of history. Men sprouted from the Earth. He tossed a stone amidst them, which elicited a war, in which they all killed each other, except for a 'digital' five, the 'Sown-men' or **Spartoi**, from whom the future aristocracy of Thebes was all descended, like the **Erechtheids** at Athens (and like them, all born supposedly with a hereditary birthmark as proof). The internecine strife of the Spartoi was the first of the Fraternal Wars that would culminate eventually several generations later when a pair of **warring brothers** faced off with their counterbalanced legions of heroes at the Seven Gates of Thebes.

By his victory, like Iason with Medeia, Kadmos won the Lady as his bride, transmuted into the new era as **Harmonia**, the daughter of Ares by his illicit affair with Aphrodite—although formerly she was known as a witch and a 'foreigner.' (And as might be expected, Kadmos was required to spend a period of 'exile' in Bondage to expiate for the suicidal murder of the Serpent.) The new union was so auspicious that the Olympian gods and goddesses all attended the wedding celebration, each conferring a special gift: the most famous, although it was to prove the most potentially dangerous, was Aphrodite's—a necklace made by her husband Hephaistos, which had formerly been given by Zeus to Europa, and which like a drug made its wearer irresistibly attractive. Possession of this **entheogen** conferred rulership at Thebes.

Kadmos and Harmonia had many daughters and a single son. Five of the girls, probably—although we can be certain only of the one whose name we know—, were married off to the Spartoi to produce the new populace of Thebes: amongst these was **Agave**, the mother of **Pentheus**. A second group were the three daughters who were instrumental in the transmutation of the older forms of Bakchos, Apollo, Artemis, and Hera. These were: **Semele**, who became mother of **Dionysos**; **Autonoe**, who was the mother of **Aktaion**, by the 'African' **Aristaios**, son of Apollo; and **Ino**, who became the 'White Goddess' **Leukothea**. (The genealogical relationships of the descendants of Kadmos should not be taken too literally, since they were later regularized by historians who tried to make patrilineal sense of the mythical traditions, or by the ruling families who tried to justify their aristocratic privileges; the significant pattern, as usual, is the several occurrences of disjunction, and the apparent difficulty of begetting male heirs. Eventually the lineage of his female and male descendants will come together to produce **Oidipous**—the Latin **Oedipus**—, whose right to rule comes to him, unfortunately, both through his mother, whom he marries, and his father, whom he killed. This is the tragic version of Oidipous's heroism, and it has come to overshadow his great achievement as one of the founders of Thebes.)

It was while Kadmos, the 'civilizer' of Thebes, was in one of his periods of

Genealogical Chart: Oidipous

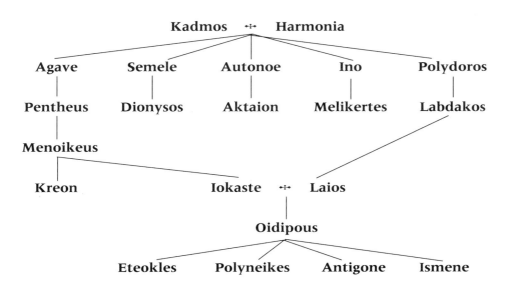

eclipse (explained as a recurrence of the problem of the suicidal murder of the Serpent, and because he was in need of rejuvenation) that he resigned the 'king-ship' to his grandson Pentheus, his daughter's son, even though he had male heirs of his own (or at least, he was later assumed to have had them). When Pentheus was killed by his mother Agave and the maenadic sisterhood, the foundation of Thebes became undone, and Kadmos reverted to his primordial serpentine identity. He and Harmonia (who also turned into a snake) drove away from Thebes, in a way that inverted the manner of his triumphant arrival: in a cart drawn by heifers. They went into exile in the northwestern Death-lands, where on the coast of the Adriatic at a place called 'Swift Cow' (Bouthoe: named for the running heifers of their cart) they gave birth to a 'foreign' heir, Il-lyrios, who became the ancestor of the Illyrian peoples, and the tribe of the 'Eel-men' or Encheleis, like the men Kadmos had formerly ruled over beneath the Copaic Lake of Thebes. His descendants were destined to return again, genera-tions later, as a legion of 'foreigners,' attacking the foundations of many Greek cities, rising up as enemy spirits through their tombs and graves, until they fi-nally would be put down again when they came against Delphi—which was an event that was thought to have actually taken place in historical times at the beginning of the fifth century.

After Pentheus (Kadmos's grandson by Agave), **Labdakos**, who had the same relationship, but by the son **Polydoros**, instead of the daughter Agave, took a try at controlling Thebes; but he was no more successful, although it was he who would lend his name to the family: the **Labdakidai** or **Labdacids**. What exactly happened is not clear, but he appears to have failed by doing the same thing as Pentheus—namely, refusing to mediate between the old ways and the new. He left a single son as heir, **Laios** (Latin **Laius**).

Laios did not immediately inherit the 'kingship,' but there was a reversion to a male descendant of the female lineage, from another of the 'digital' Spar-toi, **Chthonios**, the 'Chthonic-man': his son may or may not be a Kadmean, for the wife is never mentioned. (The disjunction was glossed over by assuming that Laios was too young to inherit.) Instead, the son of Chthonios's unnamed wife took control. This was the 'werewolf' **Lykos**, whose mate was **Dirke**, the 'Datura-lady.' Lykos and she are another version of the Serpent and the Spring-lady; and in their rulership, a second attempt was made at (re)founding Thebes.

This second remaking of Thebes was the episode of **Amphion** and his 'Seek-er' twin **Zethos**: these were the **warring brothers** whose Fraternal Strife would be reconciled in the building of the city's outer walls to the harmonious ac-companiment of Amphion's lyre, a gift to him from Hermes. The twins were the children of the 'turn-face' **Antiope** and Zeus, in a second infusion of Olympian lineage. Antiope was the good mother, who with her sons was per-secuted by the wicked stepmother Dirke; simply put: Antiope is the transmuta-tion of Dirke (although the genealogists reckoned her as the wife of Lykos's **warring brother**, **Nykteus**, the 'Night-man;' she had a sister **Nykteis**, who was the wife of Polydoros and the mother of Labdakos, and hence a bridge back to the male Kadmean lineage.) And Amphion and Zethos similarly shared the two versions of the Spring-lady in the next generation: Zethos took the Spring **Thebe** as wife, and Amphion took the ill-fortuned 'foreigner' **Niobe**, whose children fell to the arrows of Apollo and Artemis and who turned into a Spring (and a mountain) in the eastern Deathlands from which she and her brother **Pelops** had come. One daughter of Niobe may have survived: **Chloris**, who would become the good mother of **Nestor** and the new (re)foundation of Pylos, in the time of Herakles.

This settlement of Thebes also came undone, although the details are vague: the episode is similar to the fall of Pentheus (and Labdakos). Antiope went mad, and like Agave and Kadmos and Harmonia, she, too, went into a wandering Tour of the Deathlands, an exile, where she became the ancestor of a 'foreign' peoples, the Phocians, who dwelt around Delphi: their descendants in later times, like the Illyrian uprising of Kadmos's relatives, would actually attempt each year to steal earth from the Theban graves of Amphion and Zethos to add it to hers and her Phocian mate's, as a magic to insure their crops' success. Amphion, himself, had apparently shared Niobe's fate: he may even have been killed by Apollo as he attempted to storm the Delphic sanctuary; and he and his brother Zethos shared a common tomb at Thebes; for Zethos, too, had proved unfortunate. His wife had 'accidentally' killed his son **Itylos**, and in her grief she became an eternally weeping 'Nighingale,' an **Aedon**, as was the meaning of her name; she had intended to kill not her own son, but her sister-in-law's: and Zethos, like Iason, died in grief. Threnody, or the song of eternal lament for the loss of someone related by blood, is another of the bonds that bridge the gap between the worlds.

(This story is better known in the Athenian version that we mentioned earlier. The two women are sisters, **Prokne** and **Philomela**, daughters of the 'king' **Pandion**. The sisters are interchangeable in their roles, for either one can play the part of the child's lamenting mother, but Philomela is the one whose name means she 'Loves the Song.' One of the girls was married off to a 'foreigner,' **Tereus**, who had cropped up as an ally in a War at the Megarian Entrance. She went to live with her husband, and her sister joined them as a guest. Tereus raped the sister and then tore out her tongue, making her mute like a corpse, so that she could not tell her sister what happened. But she contrived to employ her Spinstress arts to weave the story in a tapestry, and show it to her sister. The women got back at Tereus by butchering his and the mother's son, **Itys**, and serving him up as food to the father—who only too late discovered that he, like the grave of his realm, had swallowed down his own son. All three were transformed into birds: Tereus, as a hoopoe—which is named 'epops' for its cry, a sound that means 'Seeker' or 'Overseer' in Greek—, forever pursues the fleeing sisters, one of whom became the lamenting nightingale, a bird that sings its sobbing song in the night; the other, having regained the use of her tongue, became an eternally chattering swallow. The boy's name is what they forever call, Itys, which in Greek means the 'Round' of a wheel or a shield, a common pictograph of the Indo-European **entheogen**.)

Meanwhile, Laios grew up underground, in hiding, an exile dependent upon the kindness of 'foreign' strangers, at the Entrance of Olympia (or Nemea, or perhaps even Thebes, downstairs), with **Pelops** and **Hippodameia** (or their predecessors) in residence. It was there that Laios committed the error that would lie upon his family of Labdacids like a curse: instead of mediating between the sexes, he excluded the female and fell in love with someone of his own sex.

(Now, we should be clear that the error was a failure as mediator, and is not a condemnation of homosexuality, which, as we have already seen, was expected behavior, and especially amongst the Dorian tribes to which the Thebans belonged. Pelops, himself, by some accounts, had been abducted by Poseidon; as had Ganymedes from Troy by Zeus: these abductions signify redemption from the chthonic Motherlands. Perseus did the same sort of thing in rescuing the horse Pegasos from the body of the horse-lady Medousa; and even Theseus had begotten a horseman Hippolytos out of the Amazon Hippolyta.)

Not surprisingly, Hippodameia had a horse-boy in her household. In that dark place where the Sun is eclipsed, Laios fell in love with the boy called 'Golden-horse' or **Chrysippos**, and stole him away. Hippodameia, the 'Horse-lady' may have been his mother—in former times, but by now, with Pelops, she appears to have become only his step-mother. As to what happened exactly, again there were various accounts. Pelops' sons, **Atreus** and **Thyestes**, may have killed the alien boy in Fraternal Strife, and thus incurred a curse also upon the Pelopid family; or Hippodameia may have committed the murder, herself, when she found the boy in bed with her 'guest' Laios; Laios may have been accused of the murder and acquitted, and Pelops, as some claimed, even divorced Hippodameia and drove her into banishment. Or the murder may have taken place at Thebes, where the boy's story becomes confused with another Queen's son: for both Laios and his Theban wife **Iokasta** (Latin **Jocasta**) conspired to kill Oidipous.

The Birth of Oidipous

Laios, this deficient mediator (who may have been still living with his beloved Chrysippos), had trouble begetting a son when he became 'king' of Thebes, even though he took to wife a great-granddaughter of Agave, a Kadmean on the female side, just as he was himself a Kadmean of male descent. This wife was the turncoat who could be expected to produce the hero who might turn Thebes around: Iokasta was 'Io, the Pure;' she was also known as **Epikasta**, which means simply 'Over-again Pure.' Laios had been warned by Apollo at Delphi that if he continued in his attempts, the son he begot would be his death (as Theseus had proved to be for Aigeus, and Perseus for his grandfather Akrisios). But Laios, the herm-like 'Stone-man' (for such is the meaning of his name), got drunk, and like Aigeus, in his drunken stupor, he begot a son, who was Oidipous. Laios and Iokasta tried to remedy their error by refusing to acknowledge the son: instead, as was the custom with unwanted offspring, they exposed it on Mount Kithairon to die—of natural causes, thus incurring no taint of blood guilt. (The exposure took place amidst the winter snows on the mountain, the season when the maenads from Thebes conducted their ceremonies; and the child, whose hair had the tawny color of the new sacred **entheogen**, was left to die in an earthenware pot, like a divine plant, such as they might have gathered. The exact spot was known as the Meadow of Hera, the same place where Herakles began his Wilderness Sojourn as a picked nurseling of the Goddess, through Athena's intervention.) To insure that the boy would not be raised by someone else, perhaps to be a slave—as also often happened—, Iokasta maimed the boy's foot to make him lame and not worth the raising: she may have even maimed both his feet, piercing them together with her brooch, so that he had only a single foot—like a plant—and he would have to crawl, if he survived, like an infant on all fours forever. They named him Oidipous for this 'Swollen Foot,' although some people remembered that the 'foot' and the 'limping gait' were the common metaphors: the boy was an erect 'digital' little herm, with the name Oidyphallos or 'Swollen Phallos,' one of the 'black' Kabeiroi brethren.

The infant was found by a herdsman called **Euphorbos**: his occupation (as with the twins of Tyro, Pelias and Neleus) suggests that the child may have been an animal, and his name may even suggest a horse, for Euphorbos means 'Good Horse-Fodder.' He gave the infant to a herdsman from a neighboring 'foreign' realm, who conveyed it to his 'king' and Queen to raise as their own, replacing one they had recently lost; or perhaps, they, too, had not been able to beget a son. The couple had bovine names: **Polybos**, the king, was 'Many Cows,' which is pretty much also what the Queen **Periboia** means; she was also sometimes one of the 'Bee-ladies,' with the name of **Merope**. Polybos was a son of Hermes, and his realm was Corinth, or thereabouts: Sikyon, the former 'Poppy-town' of Mekone (where Antiope had found 'foreign' allies), or Anthedon, the 'Place of Flowers'.

It was sometimes claimed that the exposure occurred not on the mountain, but that the infant (like Perseus) was placed in a chest and set adrift upon the sea, in the unpredictably reversing tides of the strait that separates the 'Cow-lands' of Boeotia and the island Euboea; and thus he made it to the Deathlands, where Periboia fetched him ashore as she washed her clothing. Unless, as some said, it wasn't Periboia, but none other than Hippodameia at the Olympian Entrance who adopted him when he washed up in the river—so that he became a foster brother of Chrysippos, and for that reason, like her other sons, Oidipous, too, was an enemy of Laios, in support of their mother's rights.

However the story was told, Oidipous had **two fathers**, like any liminal hero: both Laios and Polybos. It was upon the hero's return from his Wilderness Sojourn down under, that he, who had been named for his Swollen Foot, would earn the more optimistic potential for the **two names** of his heroic career.

The Contest with the Sphinx

Hera had sent the Sphinx up from the 'African' Deathlands of Ethiopia as a plague upon the Thebes of Greece, for she was angered that Laios preferred his

Oidipous, as an Ithyphallic Daktyl, Confronts the Sphinx on her Pillar (Museum of Fine Arts, Boston)

boy-love to his Queen and wife. The Sphinx was a female monster, a woman with various bestial parts, usually lioness and bird and serpent. (The Sphinxes of Egypt were male: their existence, however, would have confirmed the 'African' origin of the Theban Sphinx; as also did the fortuitous coincidence of a city called Thebes upstream on the Nile.) And she sat upon a hill or upon a herm-pillar in the city's marketplace, posing a riddle to the men of Thebes: she was a Singer, an Enchantress, a (Spell)-'binder,' this last being the meaning of her name. Whoever lacked the insight to solve it, she sexually assaulted and abducted down to the Deathlands as her consort.

The riddle was: What is it that has two feet, or sometimes three feet, or sometimes four; and when it has four, it is weakest?

Oidipous, with his own problem of feet, was obviously destined to solve it: the answer was Man, who walks on two feet when adult, three feet in old age, with the assistance of a stick, and four, as an infant, crawling. Three feet is also the condition of the consort, propped up on his erection. By his success, Oidipous earned the heroic meaning of his name, as the 'Know-foot,' although there lurked still further riddles in the answer, that he had yet to know.

Oidipous had grown up with his 'foreign' parents, thinking them his own. But a drunken 'foreigner' sowed the seed of suspicion, and Oipidous traveled to Delphi to gain confirmation of his parentage. There, the oracle drove him away as a patricide, destined to kill his father and marry his own mother as replacement. To avoid this, Oidipous vowed never to return to his supposed parents—and journeyed instead to Thebes, killing a man on the way, who turned out to have been his father.

He solved the riddle and liberated the city from the Sphinx, winning Iokasta and the 'kingship' as his reward: a role that was rightfully his, both as the male inheritor of his unknown father Laios, and as the consort of the Queen, his unknown mother; a 'foreigner' who, unbeknownst to him, had a double tie of kinship through blood.

The Marriage to Iokasta

Since linear chronology does not dominate in myth, there is some confusion as to exactly what happened, but all agree that Oidipous did 'accidentally' kill his 'enemy' and prove to be a patricide, closer to his mother than his father—in fact, too close to his mother, from whom he begot four children, a pair of **warring brothers**, **Eteokles** and **Polyneikes**, and a similar pair of dissimilar daughters, **Antigone** and her sister **Ismene**.

It all seems to have taken place at once, although it can be stretched out to make a story. As Oidipous journeyed into exile from his 'foreign' homeland, on the road from Delphi to Thebes, he met Laios—and perhaps Iokasta as well—, at a parting of the pathway: such forks in the road afford a traveler the opportunity to change direction; and since it is always possible to shift into a vertical journey there, each was considered an Entrance (**limen**), and was under the jurisdiction of the terrible nether goddess **Hekate**, who represented all three aspects of the Queen, together in one body, as Maiden, Mother, and Witch. The exact spot is still pointed out to tourists today, as the mountain pass called 'Divide' or 'Three Roads.' When Oidipous, returning from his 'Foreign' Sojourn, came up to Laios at the divide, the 'king' was riding (with Iokasta) in a horse-drawn chariot, driven by his henchman **Polyphontes**, the 'Serial Killer.' There was room for travelers in only one direction at a time; and Laios plunged forward, driving his chariot right over Oidipous's foot (as if this were still the moment of the infant's maiming and exposure), and he even treated the 'foreigner' like a horse, striking him on the head with his goad as he drove down by. As to why the father and son met at this pass, opinions differed. Perhaps Iokasta and Laios were (again) on their way to Delphi to inquire about their childlessness; or as some knew, Oidipous was actually out on the mountain to rustle horses—and get a bride. Most tellers agreed, in any case, that the Contest was a moment of madness (**entheogen**), on the part of both father and son.

Oidipous retaliated by killing Laios and his 'Serial Killer,' making the sacrificers into their own victims. (Remember that this all took place on the road to Delphi, to and fro, and up and down, where the old Apollo maintained a slaughterous henchman called the 'Knife.') And then Oidipous took possession of the Queen, perhaps right there on the spot, as she raged in maenadic grief on the mountainside; or perhaps only later, after he got to Thebes and had won her as his prize for Contesting the Sphinx: for Iokasta was the Sphinx—transmuted: she had two other names, as well: the happy one of 'Widespread Cheer' or **Euryganeia** (a name perhaps too optimistically cheerful not to imply just the opposite), and the more ominous one of the 'City's Medusa' or **Astymedousa**. (Even the Athenian tragedian Sophocles, in his famous telling of the tale, allowed no time to lapse between the murder of Laios, and the murder of the Sphinx, which resulted immediately in the marriage to Iokasta and the birth of the four children.)

It was thus that Oidipous, the triumphant victor over the Sphinx, unwittingly became the tragic version of himself. The city that he might have claimed (like a Theseus) as his father's son, became his as the Queen's 'king' and his maternal inheritance.

The failure to mediate resulted (immediately) in a Plague of sterility upon all the lands and peoples of Thebes (although in linear chronology, there had been enough time for Oidipous to beget his pairs of sons and daughters). Again, the hero undertook to save Thebes. From Apollo he learned that the murder of Laios demanded expiation.

Oidipous dutifully cursed the unknown murderer, his 'enemy' (**paradigm #1**), banishing him into the Bondage of Death and making him the sole recipient of the pollution that was now shared by the entire city. And then he set out (again) to solve the riddle, namely to find himself.

The Contest with Apollo

He declared himself the ally, the 'helper' (**animus**) of the god; together they would rescue the city. There was much he shared with Apollo (**paradigm #1**): they both were Lords, and both possessed the insight of seercraft. But unfortunately, Oidipous was also the god's 'enemy:' for Apollo had foreseen that Laios would be killed by his son; and if the murdered Laios had not been killed by his son, then Apollo and the whole sanctuary of Delphi would come undone and prove worthless. The only way to 'help' Apollo would be for Oidipous, who comes to suspect that he may have killed Laios (or some such 'kingly' person at the divide), to also be Laios's son—which would also mean that he has married his own mother, Iokasta.

This is the truth that Oidipous uncovers, through confrontations with proxies for the god (for you cannot enter into direct rebuttal with Apollo). As stand-in for another version of himself as temporal Lord, he cross-examines Lord **Kreon** (whose name means 'Lord'), Iokasta's brother; and as spiritual Lord, he confronts the Lord **Teiresias**, the blind seer who sees the same things as the Lord Apollo: all three, along with Oipidous, share the same titled rank of Lord in Greek, for ultimately Oidipous must play the role of 'enemy' to his 'ally' Apollo (**paradigm #1**). (Teiresias is the same famous Theban prophet who was already an old man at the time of Pentheus, three generations earlier, and a contemporary of Kadmos, the founder of Thebes.) By tracking down the footprints of the old murder, Oidipous discovers himself. (Iokasta figures it out before him, and like the Sphinx that is her latent potential, she again attempts to keep the riddle to herself.)

The awful (or awesome) truth that Oidipous sees, as the last sight that will blind his eyes to the piecemeal sights of this world, is that his role of 'helper' for Apollo is to become the Sacrifical Victim, the god's other self, losing—so that the god can win.

As to what happened after the blinding, opinions differed. Oidipous may have tried to kill Iokasta, only to find that she had already hanged herself, in their bridal chamber: as with the Sphinx, solving the riddle destroyed her. Or he may have gone on living—underground—with Iokasta at Thebes right up to the time of the great War at the Seven Gates. Or he may have gone into a Wandering exile, like the 'enemy' he had cursed, to die as somebody else's friend in a foreign land.

Brotherly Warring

After Oidipous, the rulership of Thebes passed to Kreon, until the sons of Oidipous could take control. They were appropriate inheritors since they, like their father, were descended from Kadmos on both the male and female sides; and as males, they were better than their sisters for turning Thebes around to the new order. But there were two of them, and unlike the Dioskouroi twins, who alternately shared the other's lot of mortality and immortality together, day after day, the sons of Oidipous warred with each other as they attempted to share the 'kingship,' alternating year by year. (During this time, they tried to befriend their father, feeding him with food and drink in his subterranean lodging; but he did not find their manner of tending him to his liking, and instead of an ally down under, they had an enemy.)

Eteokles (Latin **Eteocles**) had the good name of 'True-fame,' and it was he who took the first stint of ruling for the year; while his bad brother **Polyneikes** (Latin **Polynices**), the 'Quarrelsome,' went into exile amongst foreigners—taking with him the talisman of Harmonia's necklace and the maddening robe. Clearly, Polyneikes had a strong claim upon Thebes when, at the end of the year's term, his brother refused to relinquish control to him. And, moreover, from exile, Polyneikes had contracted for a powerful legion of foreign allies to support his claim.

Polyneikes had taken up residence down in Argos, where he had managed to marry into the lineage and even to get a friendly brother-in-law, to replace his own hostile brother. The 'king' of Argos was **Adrastos**, the 'Inescapable;' and it was he who had brought the new alliance of brothers(-in-law) together, by marrying off to each of them, one of his two, much-courted daughters: the Ladies of the underworld were always much sought after by suitors. Polyneikes got **Argeia** herself, the 'Maiden of Argos,' as wife. And with the power that the necklace conferred to impose harmony amongst dissident allies, a mighty force of heroes had been assembled for an uprising against the Thebes of Eteokles.

(Adrastos was not a Perseid, but was descended from the brother of the 'Black-foot' **Melampous**, who had cured the madness of the Proitid sisters, in return for two-thirds of the 'kingdom;' Melampous and his 'Forceful' brother **Bias** traced their lineage back to Iolkos, as sons of still another of Tyro's children, along with Pheres and Iason's father Aison. Melampous and his brother Bias were recent new arrivals from the Egyptian Blacklands. Melampous, himself, was a cattle rustler down at the Gate-city of Pylos, and a prophet; he had discovered a redeeming new **entheogen** called 'rust,' a fungal surrogate for Amanita, by taking the rust that had grown upon the sacrificial knife as it lodged in a sacred tree or **axis mundi** and using it to cure the impotence of the 'king's' son and intended victim. We will have more to say about 'rust' later, when we investigate the goddess Demeter. At Argos, Melampous and Bias took over, leaving one-third of the 'kingdom' to Proitos's son **Megapenthes**. Adrastos was the third generation after Bias. In the Theban lands, the tomb of Bias was the connecting Entrance to the lands of the Argolid: it was located at the port town of Aigosthena, far down the precipitous southern slopes of Mount Kithairon; and he was honored there with an annual festival.)

Adrastos's other daughter was **Deipyle**, the 'Hostile Gate.' And Adrastos gave her to Polyneikes' new brotherly ally: this was **Tydeus**, the 'Smiter.' Like Polyneikes, Tydeus had come to Adrastos as an exile and foreigner. While Polyneikes, as we have seen, was his mother's son by her own son, Tydeus was his father's son by his own daughter: this was Gorge, the Gorgon daughter of Oineus of Kalydon (whom we already know as the father of Deianeira, the wife of Herakles).

Both Polyneikes and Tydeus had arrived at Adrastos's palace on the same night (while the Sun was in his drunken period); both of them, hated and banished by their fathers; and both of them, their own brothers' enemies, for the 'dwarfish' Tydeus (who was half-brother of the unfortunate Meleagros) had accidentally killed his brother, the 'Black Horse' **Melanippos**, while they were out together on one of those notorious Kalydonian Hunts in the Deathlands; and Tydeus and Polyneikes, the two future friends and brothers-in-law, had immediately engaged each other as enemies in a fight at the citadel's Gates. Adrastos had been warned by an oracle to award his daughters as brides to a lion and a boar, and when he awoke to the din of battle, he realized that the quarrelsome pair must be what was meant. He promised, on the basis of their relationship to him as sons-in-law, to assemble a legion of allies to return each to their countries, against their fathers' wishes.

Adrastos recruited a 'handful' of Argive heroes for the uprising. The most difficult, and most essential, was his own brother-in-law, **Amphiaraos**, with whom he had a double tie of lineage, both through marriage and by blood—a double curse, or 'Ambi-damned,' as is the meaning of his name: for Amphiaraos and Adrastos were both third generation descendants of the **(warring) brothers** Melampous and Bias. And they had managed only recently to patch up their quarrelsomeness, by the marriage of Amphiaraos to Adrastos's sister, **Eriphyle** or 'Family Feud.' It was she who had brought the men back together. Before that, Amphiaraos had driven Adrastos from the 'kingship' and murdered the father of his own future in-laws. Amphiaraos took after his 'black' and herbalist ancestor, for he, too, was a prophet; and he foresaw that the uprising was doomed to failure: and that everyone (on both sides), except for Adrastos, would die in the battle at Thebes' Seven Gates: and the battle was the way that Adrastos would 'accidentally' get rid of him and solve the family's feud. (As for Amphiaraos, himself, he didn't quite totally die at Thebes: **paradigm #2**; for he alone, of the fourteen warriors, was swallowed up alive by the earth, with his team of horses, to become a helpful friend in the underworld: for there was another way of interpreting his name, as the 'Ambi-sacred.')

Since he foresaw the outcome, Amphiaraos had to be forced to enlist, against his will; and the ploy that bound him, like all the other recruits, into the expedition, was the maddening allure of Harmonia's necklace. Adrastos connived with his new sons-in-law, Polyneikes and Tydeus, to offer the talisman to Eriphyle; and it was her irresistible beauty that tied the dissident fraternal band together and imposed harmony amongst them all. It was this legion of 'foreigners' that would crop up at Thebes, to Contest the descendants of the surviving 'digital' crop of Spartoi (**paradigm #1**). It was a War all fought for a woman's sake, and a repetition of the original attempt at settlement, when the Spartoi became pacified as in-laws of Kadmos and Harmonia. (When it was all over, Eriphyle was murdered by her sons, on behalf of their dead father: so that Amphiaraos became pivotal in resolving the dispute of patriliny.)

The other recruits were the 'Charioteer' **Kapaneus** (a Perseid, as grandson of Megapenthes); 'True-fame' **Eteoklos** (whose name resembles Eteokles, not surprisingly, since a similar band was being assembled to counter them up at Thebes); the 'Horse-lord' **Hippomedon**; and the matrilineal 'Woman's-son' **Parthenopaios** (the 'foreign' brother of Tydeus, as his sister-in-law Atalante's son).

As the band was passing up through the labyrinthine caverns of the Nemean Entrance, they 'accidentally' lost someone. (Up at Thebes, a similar offering was being made: they had been advised by Teiresias that a family member had to join the other side, so that they would have another ally in the Deathlands; Kreon's young son, who was named 'Household Foundation' or **Menoikeus**, after his grandfather who had done the same thing, volunteered himself as a sacrificial victim.) At Nemea, it was the 'Helpful' child **Opheltes**, whose name was changed to the 'Beginning of Death' or **Archemoros**. (His funeral was commemorated in the athletic Contests that were celebrated there in later times—like Pelops at Olympia and Palaimon at Isthmia.)

Opheltes was a 'foreigner' (and the son of the Wolf 'king' of Nemea) when the Argive band came upon him; his wet nurse was none other than the 'good' Amazon Queen **Hypsipyle** or 'High Gate,' who alone had spared her father's life; (it was she who had conceived twins by Iason when the Argonauts passed through Lemnos). She had been told never to let the infant touch ground, until he could walk (which was probably—never, since a serpent, or eel, is not apt to ever acquire the feet of a man); but in her eagerness to 'help' the heroes through this Gateway, she set him down in a bed of what would soon become celery (but up to this event was probably still the more deadly hemlock **entheogen** of Nemea), while she showed them her Spring of Adrastos. The Serpent there that guarded it devoured him, making the two of them into one body; and the heroes could do nothing but honor him with burial—after they killed the Adrastos Serpent—and whatever remained of the 'boy.' (Thus they gained both High Gate and the commemorated 'loser' named Helpful as their final guides: **anima/ animus**. Eventually, Hypsipyle, who was a tormented slave of the 'king' and his Queen at Nemea, had a story like that of Antiope of Thebes: she was recognized and saved by her twin sons that she'd had by Iason back in Lemnos.)

These victors over the Adrastos Serpent and its Lady Adrasteia of the Spring were the new crop of Kadmeans who came up, one at each of the city's Seven Gates. And Eteokles had arranged to counter each with his perfect match, ending with himself against his own brother Polyneikes at the seventh Gate (**paradigm #1**).

Tydeus was pitted against a **Melanippos** (supposedly not the same 'Black Horse' as the brother he had 'accidentally' killed on the Hunt, but a watery version from the Poseidonian depths of the sea, the son of 'Lobster' or Astakos). Melanippos, who was fatally wounded, managed to reciprocate with a fatal wound on his opponent; but as Tydeus lay dying, he commanded Amphiaraos to toss him his victim's head: Athena was already running up to 'help' Tydeus revive with a magical drug, but he drank down the brains of Melanippos's severed head, instead; and in disgust (at her former self), Athena let her hero die. As a prophet, Amphiaraos had, of course, foreseen the outcome, but he let it happen.

On both sides, everyone died in the War, except for Adrastos, who wasn't directly assigned to one of the Gates. The Thebans refused to allow the other side to bury their corpses, until the mothers of the dead, led by Adrastos, beseeched the Athenian Theseus to intervene. He invaded Thebes and brought them back for burial at the sanctuary of the Entrance at Eleusis, which lies in the Athenian lands: their six tombs can be seen there today, six only, for Amphiaraos's body was never found, although several places claimed to be the spot where the earth opened up for him. As with the tragic career of Herakles, the Athenian land, and its own ascendant hero Theseus, was strengthened by these additional 'foreigners' from Thebes, who joined Herakles (and Eurystheus, too) in the legion of allies placed beneath its surface. The 'good' wife of Kapaneus met her end at Eleusis, too: this was **Euadne**, the 'Good Flower;' she was descended (as daughter) from the 'king' who had imprisoned Melampous, three generations earlier, but she demonstrated the strength of the bond to her married mate, by leaping upon his funeral pyre. Euadne's voluntary immolation was seen as a rectification of the Family Feud caused by Eriphyle: Euadne was the turncoat daughter of the sacrificer and 'Jailor' **Phylakos** of the 'Gate' City of Pylos, where the new 'rust' **entheogen** had freed the pathways between the Realms. (Or perhaps she was that other Euadne, who had cropped up more locally in Arcadia; it was she who gave birth, by Apollo, to a divine serpent violet flower boy, named for the curative and prophetic 'drug' as **Iamos**: his descendants provided the hereditary family of prophets at Olympia.)

A generation later, the War occurred yet again, the so-called War of the 'Descendants' or **Epigonoi**. The sons of the heroes of the previous generation again met in Contest at the Gates of Thebes; and again it was Harmonia's talisman that maddened them together into a legion of dissident brothers. This time, it was Polyneikes's son **Thersandros**, the 'Bold Man,' who bribed Eriphyle (with the robe, since she already had the necklace from the previous time)—before she was killed by her own son. The son of Eteokles, **Laodamas**, was now in control of Thebes, ten years later.

In this second uprising, the invaders were successful; only the son of Adrastos, who had himself been the only one to survive the first assault, died this time. And some claimed that the city of Thebes was completely destroyed. Many of the veterans from this War, the victorious sons of the former losers, would go on to take part in the great War that was already getting under way at Troy— in particular, **Diomedes**, the son of Tydeus.

(In actual fact, the city of Thebes was leveled to the ground eight-and-a-half centuries later, in 335 BC, when an alliance of 'foreigners,' who were distant relatives, under the command of the Macedonian Alexander, the Great, came against it. Only the house of the poet Pindar was spared, in commemoration for what he had said about Alexander's mythical ancestors: for the family of Alexander's mother claimed descent from one of the greatest heroes of the Trojan War; although, more recently, Alexander himself, like another Herakles, was supposedly a son of Zeus. As to his mother's husband, she had met the 'king' Philip, the 'Horseman,' at one of those Entrances where the reunion with the Kadmean primordial peoples was celebrated as a 'Mystery,' on the island of Samothrace. It was Alexander who was destined to inaugurate another New Age, when he led his legion of dissident Greek brothers across the Hellespont, through Troy, and still further on into a Tour of the old Deathlands. In the deserts of Egypt, he even conversed with the 'African' Zeus, who had begotten him, when his mother Olympias took a Serpent to her bed.)

Sisterly Loving

As valuable as were the corpses of the six ('losers' or) heroes that Theseus retrieved from the Gates of Thebes, a still more priceless acquisition for Athens was his burial of Oidipous at the Entrance of Kolonos, just outside the gates of Athens. This was the Entrance that Theseus had used himself to descend to the Deathlands with his 'friend' Peirithoos; and just as he left him behind upon his ascendant return with Herakles, Oidipous, too, would be 'placed' as a friend and ally underground, another triumphant enactment of Theseus's own ascendant version of his liminal identity.

Oidipous had become a Wanderer after the discovery of his own darker identity, a self-imposed exile that was seconded by the verdict of the god at Delphi. During this time, while his sons warred over control of Thebes, he was sustained by the care of his daughters Ismene and Antigone, daughters who were more than daughters to him: for they were a sisterhood of his own sisters, as well, fathered by a father of their mother's blood (just as his warring sons were also his brothers, cursed brothers with whom he, too, warred). While Ismene (the 'Knowledgeable One,' who was named for an Apolline River of Thebes, and hence had the darker identity of the two girls) shuttled back and forth (or up and down) to Delphi to keep her father in constant accord with the god's wishes, the other daughter, Antigone, had taken upon herself the task of nurturing her aged and blind father and brother, who had become like a 'helpless' baby to her, helpless but for her; it was her feeding alone that Oidipous would accept, instead of the rejected attempt that his sons had made, in his underground dungeon at Thebes. Antigone was the **turncoat** replacement for Iokasta as his 'mother' and maenadic bride; her name means something like 'Reverse Birthing:' she would forever prefer the closeness of her own family's bloodlines, to any marriage with alien blood.

As the legions assembled at the Gates of Thebes, Oidipous and his sisters arrived at Kolonos, a rocky outcropping like a 'Column' or herm pillar, named like a grave stele for the 'horseman' of former times who lay buried there. This was the place that he knew, through Ismene and the god, that he was destined to die: it was sacred to the infernal sisterhood of the **Erinyes** or avenging 'Furies,' three ancient, terrible and awesome goddesses, but terrible only to those who did not respect the power of the Goddess; at Athens, they had been assuaged and given their appropriate rights—but underground: it was a mediation that had marked the transition to patriliny at Athens; and at Athens, the sisters were called by a different and optimistic name: the 'Kind Ladies' or **Eumenides**. These are the new sisterhood that will take over (as **anima** or transmuted enemy) from his daughters. Oidipous enters into a contract with Theseus, promising that Athens will have an eternal friend and ally, even against his native Thebes, so long as the city tends his grave, and feeds him, beneath its surface. Theseus then escorted Oidipous to the Entrance, to the Steps paved with bronze that led down to the Deathlands. The final moment, as the 'friends' parted, was a Mystery; all that was seen by those watching from the distance was a blinding flash of light that seemed to unite the celestial and earthen realms.

When the War at Thebes was over, Kreon, unlike Theseus, lacked the knowledge that an 'enemy' was your 'friend.' He decreed that only Eteokles and his legion be given burial, while Polyneikes (and his allies) were left to rot, unburied—a noisome pestilence above ground that could only breed a plague upon his city, turning the upper world into a tomb.

Antigone and her sister Ismene divided (or warred) on this point; although both wanted to honor both of their brothers, only Antigone had the courage to oppose Kreon and bury Polyneikes—just as she had already, despite Kreon's wishes, brought Oidipous to his grave in Athens. At the moment of the decree, Antigone was about to marry Kreon's son **Haimon**, who was named as 'Blood.' But he was alien blood (although related, through the female line), from whom she would have had to share in the begetting of sons; instead she chose the more closely kindred and irreplaceable male lineage of blood from her own 'quarrelsome' brother Polyneikes; and she buried him. It was a burial, as some told the story, that not only Antigone performed; but she was seconded by Nature herself, in the form of a sandstorm, in natural revulsion for the stench of corpses, squandered and left to decay uselessly in the wrong world.

For disobeying the decree, Kreon perversely buried Antigone—alive; and when her bridegroom Haimon went down to bring her back, he found her already dead: in grief, he killed himself, in a pool of his own (rejected) blood. The failure of Haimon's marital alliance is the sign of Thebes' final undoing and destruction: it reverses the ties that should have been established through the immolation of his 'founding' brother Menoikeus, as the troops had marshalled outside the city's Gates.

* * * *

Review

A city quite literally is built upon the rubble of former times, leveled anew to form the foundation of its future. Its past lies directly beneath it. Its whole mode of civilization rests upon a **liminal** surface, a vertical threshold beyond which lies an archaeology of its former way of life. Similarly, the enclosure of its citadel walls is a another frontier, horizontal this time, defending its institutions and society from the wilderness that lies outside, beyond its Gates, and from its sometimes hostile neighbors. Down or outward are the points of contact with the Cities of the foreign world: some real and easily seen; others, only heard about— usually—from visitors, but no doubt just as real. Each opening to the other worlds is a potential threat, requiring political contracts, rituals, and treaties of mediation. Each must be properly tended, constantly guarded. These are the places like the sacred caves and labyrinths, the wells, the rivers and fountains, flowing from subterranean reservoirs, the temples and sanctuaries, tombs, gateways: in short, the many Entrances, within the city or the boundaries of its lands. For each, a legion of allies is enlisted for its defense, sometimes far off in the Deathlands, but always no further away than these more near-at-hand openings of interconnection. The whole city, like the heroes who journey on its behalf, is liminal, a reflection of its 'enemy' and opposite on the other sides (**paradigm #1**), requiring acknowledgement, acceptance, and mediation (**paradigm #2**). The Entrances provide access to the Deathlands, which lie just beyond the **limen**, simultaneously right there on the other side, and in the many far-flung distant lands joined together through the long wandering pathways of the Labyrinth. It is at that dividing surface that the 'enemy' is confronted; and it is there, both near and far, that the 'helpers' are stationed.

Amongst the legions of the city's allies (**paradigm #3**), are the foreign, but befriended outsiders, like Oidipous, or Polyneikes and his men, and Herakles, and so on; and even Eurystheus—all of whom were awarded grave sites in Athens and the Attic lands, enrolled as honorary citizens through burial, to reinforce the troops of the city's own ancestors, whose tombs were placed strategically near the Gates, in cemeteries usually just beyond, or at the other Entrances, where they could be called upon to return or mediate with the other world.

In addition to these new 'friends,' there were the ties of family relationship that had been established by intermarriage with the foreigners: sometimes, by the heroes, during their Wilderness Sojourns or on a Tour of the Deathlands; sometimes, and in particular, at moments of crisis, through the immolation of a special emissary, like **Menoikeus**, or **Phrixos** and **Helle**.

It is at the Entrances, too, that the Goddess is found, near and far, both of olden times and transmuted, so that it is hard to tell which is there: the maiden, the mother, or the crone, and for each, whether 'friend' and ally, or 'enemy.'

They are places where the vast foreign realms are but a hair's breadth away, just in another dimension.

In establishing these alliances, the turncoat mother, in the stories told, often is enslaved or pulled back into a 'blackening' subterranean imprisonment; and opposed by a wicked stepmother: and the immolation of the emissaries (or their dispatch into the Sojourn) can be blamed on the 'bad' mother (who is not of the same blood, anyway), instead of the 'good.' Such was the 'milk-white' **Tyro**, whose twins **Pelias** and **Neleus** were tormented by her own 'iron-like' stepmother **Sidero**, the wife of **Salmoneus**. Or the 'turn-face' **Antiope**, whose twins **Amphion** and **Zethos** were opposed by the 'Datura-lady' **Dirke**, the wife of the 'Wolf' king **Lykos**. More ambiguous in the roles of 'good' and 'bad' was the enslaved foreign Queen **Hypsipyle**, who 'accidentally' killed the 'wolf-king's' child with the twinned (and 'warring') names of **Opheltes** and **Archemoros** ('helper' and 'death-start'), despite her careful tending as wet nurse— a child who was not her own, although no one could call her a wicked stepmother.

Still more confusing were **Nephele**, that 'nebulous-cloud' who was a look-alike for Hera (but wasn't) and the 'sinewy' **Ino**: **Helle** and **Phrixos**, Ino's children by **Athamas**, were rejected by his new wife Nephele and dispatched on the sacrificed Golden Fleece to Kolchis: where Phrixos intermarried into the 'black' solar family of the 'bronze' **Chalkiope**, sister of **Medeia** and daughter of **Aietes**; while the 'accidentally' murdered Helle took up residence to bridge the crossing at the Hellespont Entrance. Unless it was the other way around: and Phrixos and Helle were Nephele's children, and Ino managed to get them sacrificed, in preference to her own sons, the 'honey-boy' **Melikertes** and the 'white' **Leukon** (or **Learchos**). Or maybe it was Hera, herself, who was the stepmother—of Dionysos, whose witchlike but good wet nurse Ino now is; and Athamas 'accidentally' (in madness) murdered the 'white-boy;' while Ino 'accidentally' (by jumping into the sea) carried Melikertes to his death: where he took up residence to guard the Isthmian Entrance as the 'wrestler' **Palaimon**, while she became the good 'white goddess' **Leukothea**. Unless it was the 'lawful' **Themisto** whose sons were nursed by Ino, the former and presumed dead wife of Athamas: and by reversing the 'black' and 'white' clothing of the two sets of sons, Ino managed to make Themisto 'accidentally' kill her own sons, instead of the ones whose stepmother, only, she was.

The dispatch of the emissaries often involves the former entheogen (honey, Datura, pre-viticultural (w)oinos, hemlock, opium); after the establishment of familiar relationships in the Deathlands, with the possible begetting of turncoats to help, the entheogen comes back transmuted (wine, Amanita, rockrose, celery, 'rust') upon the hero's return. This is another way of enlisting the Entrances in the defensive structure of alliances: for Entrances can go in either direction.

The theme of warring twins is another way of establishing alliances: one son seizes the city, while the other takes up residence in exile and makes new 'friends' there out of enemies. The outcome will be decided by a War at the Entrances and the final disposition of the corpses in burial.

In the case of **Iason (-Diomedes)**: his father **Aison** and his uncle **Pelias** (who are half-brothers, both sons of Tyro) warred for control of Iolkos. And Iason, himself, is almost the half-brother of the 'black' Pelias, as well: for Iason and Pelias are both related to Tyro in the generation after Salmoneus, although one is her son and the other her grandson. Iason was first dispatched to his Wilderness Sojourn on Mount Pelion by his turncoat mother who only 'pretended' that he had died—in order to prevent Pelias and his 'Queen' from killing him. He returned with the witchy Hera now as his 'friend' and with the drug-knowledge of the centaur **Cheiron**. The second dispatch was to the Deathlands, from which he returned with the 'Queen' **Medeia** as his 'helper' and wife, and with the transmuted entheogen of the Golden Fleece.

The voyage of the 'white' **Argo** took him and his alliance of helpers on a Tour of the Deathlands that pacified each of the Entrances that they passed through: the **Lemnian Women** (and their turncoat Queen of the Gateway **Hypsipyle**); the 'tricky' **Doliones** and their 'king' **Kyzikos**; the Contest of rowing that resulted in the loss of Herakles and the Dryopian 'woodsman' **Hylas** in the fountain of Mysia; the Contest of boxing between **Polydeukes (-Kastor)** and the Bebrykian 'king' **Amykos**; the rescue of **Phineus** from the **Harpies** by **Kalais** and **Zetes** at the Bosphorus' **Symplegades**; the 'kingdom' of **Aietes**, and his daughter **Medeia**, with the loss of her brother **Apsyrtos**; the **Keryneian Hind** of Artemis; the **Planktai** (**Skylla** and **Charybdis**); the island of **Scheria-Drepane**; the **Syrtis** sandbar and the African journey to **Lake Tritonis**; the Minoan **Talos** of Crete; the island of **Anaphe**; Iolkos and the 'rejuvenation' of Aison and Pelias; Corinth and the stationing of **Glauke** in the well.

In the case of **Oidipous**: the War at Thebes pitted his two sons (and brothers) **Eteokles** and **Polyneikes** against each other at the Gates of the city, in an attempt to resolve the problems that were endemic in the original founding of Thebes by the chthonic 'foreigner' **Kadmos**. The myths involved are: the Wandering of Kadmos to Thebes; the Contest with the Serpent; the sowing of the **Spartoi**; the Marriage to **Harmonia**; **Pentheus**; **Aktaion**; **Amphion** and **Zethos**; **Prokne**, **Philomela**, **Tereus**, and **Itys**; (or **Thebe**, **Aedon**, **Zethos**, and **Itylos**); **Laios** and **Chrysippos**; the birth and Wilderness Sojourn of Oidipous with **Polybos** and **Periboia** (**Merope**); the Contest with the **Sphinx**; the murder of **Laios** (and **Polyphontes**) and marriage to **Iokasta** (**Epikasta**, **Euryganeia**, **Astymedousa**); the Contest with Apollo (and **Teiresias** and **Kreon**); **Melampous** and **Bias**; the quarrel of **Polyneikes** and **Eteokles**; Polyneikes and **Tydeus**, and their father-in-law **Adrastos**; the bribing of **Eriphyle** (wife of **Amphiaraos**); **Opheltes** of Nemea; the War at Thebes and the burial of the corpses at Eleusis, with the immolation of **Euadne**, the wife of **Kapaneus**; the burial of Oidipous by Theseus at Kolonos in the grove of the **Eumenides** (**Erinyes**); the quarrel of **Antigone** and **Ismene**; the War of the **Epigonoi**.

For Discussion and Further Study

1. The Oidipous myth was very popular in later antiquity, largely because the philosopher Aristotle considered one of its tellings the most perfect tragedy, at least in terms of his own philosophical criteria: Sophocles' *Oidipous Tyrannos* (or *Oedipus Rex*). Summarize Aristotle's definition of a tragic hero (from his *Poetica*, or 'On Poetry'). How does it compare to what you have learned about 'heroism' in studying Mythology? Apply both Aristotle's definition and the mythopoetic definition to Sophocles' play.

2. Sophocles dealt with the Oedipal 'sisterly loving' in two other tragedies: *Antigone* and *Oedipus Coloneus* (or 'Oedipus at Kolonos'). Compare the role of Kreon in the two plays.

3. Euripides dealt with the same theme in his *Phoinissai* (or 'Phoenician Women'). What does it add to your understanding of Antigone?

4. Aeschylus treated the war of the brothers Eteokles and Polyneikes in his *Seven Against Thebes*. Study and discuss the emblems of the opposing native and 'foreign' heroes who are stationed at each of the seven Gates.

5. The myth of Iason was the subject of a literary epic in later antiquity (3rd century BC) by Apollonius of Rhodes, the *Argonautica*. What events in addition to what you have learned does he include; and what do you think they mean?

6. The burial at Eleusis of the 'foreign' contingent from the Theban War was the subject of Euripides' *Hiketides* (or 'Suppliants'). Compare Theseus's role in that play to his role in the *Coloneus*.

Chapter XI
The Last 'Foreign' Engagement: Troy

⚕

After the War at Troy (which was the old Apollo's 'foreign' city of the Troia trinity, settled near the southern shore of the Hellespontine crossing of the Sea of Marmara at the Entrance to the Asiatic Deathlands), the age of heroes came to an end. Tradition remembered that this city of **Priam** and his Queen **Hekabe** (Latin **Hecuba**) was destroyed in the year 1184 BC, after a lengthy struggle that lasted a full decade. None of the many Greek heroes who joined forces for the War left descendants of any great renown that persisted beyond the next generation. In fact, like the Theban War of the Seven, the Trojan controversy took a second generation of heroes to be finalized: the War was ended only after **Neoptolemos** (or 'New War') joined the troops, after the death of his father **Achilleus** (Latin **Achilles**), who was a member of the original expedition. As to why the heroes disappeared after that: it may be that the task of making the new world had finally and definitively been accomplished; or it may be that the old conflict between the rival traditions of matrilineal and patrilineal cultures had become irrelevant, in view of the new crisis that was being posed by the arrival of still another wave of Indo-European immigrants who had to be assimilated. They disrupted the centers of civilization, destroyed the bureaucracies of government, and plunged the Greek cities into a period of turmoil that would last for four-hundred years (the so-called Greek Dark Age), after which history began anew, in the sense of written records in the Greek alphabet, and a system of chronology, dating by Olympiads.

It was then, in the eighth century, that the oral accounts of the War at Troy were at last committed to writing, and ascribed to the authorship of its traditional poetic persona, named **Homer**, the 'Hostage.' Homer was all the tellers of the story who, like their legendary namesake, were taken hostage by the Muse, their minds taken over and possessed by her inspiration: through them, she passed on the burden of the oral history from generation to generation over the centuries, using a special language (that no one spoke in common usage) to retell and sing (and perform) the old story, exactly as it had always been told, supposedly; but since there was no writing during all that time to act as a factual check, it was only the special language, and the apparent proof it offered of authentic Homeric inspiration, that could validate each new telling as what was accepted as a verbatim recitation.

(This Homeric language retained words of great antiquity, and was a melange of various tribal dialects, the tongue not of one locality or people; and it was structured in whole melodic phrases and generic themes that could be manipulated and varied, as the story was retold, or actually made up anew, through the technique of **formulaic oral recomposition**.)

Inevitably the story continually changed and underwent evolution, to keep pace with the interests of its audience; just as the special language that was used for encoding the story had been used before, to tell of many events that had occurred long before the fall of Troy, events even that had happened before the peoples whose language was becoming Greek, in their new places of settlement in the Greek lands, had separated from their Indo-European brethren in the Hyperborean homeland and embarked upon their long migrations.

When these accounts of Troy finally were committed to writing, in the eighth century, the text served to stabilize the versions of the new retellings by the latest singers, who styled themselves as a brotherhood of the 'sons of Homer' or Homeridai. The common heritage of myth embodied in these **epic** songs gave the Greek peoples a cultural and ethnic identity that transcended the local traditions of heroism: the Trojan War was to a large extent the story of the remaking of Greece itself. Of the several texts that once existed, two have survived. One, the *Iliad*, tells of an event that happened during the long War; the other, the *Odyssey*, tells of just one of the many journeys home.

(Neither Achilleus nor Odysseus, who are the main heroes of these songs, came from cities of importance in the older stories of heroism: they both came from the northern fringe of the earlier centers of settlement: Achilleus from Thessaly, and Odysseus from the western island of Ithaka in the Ionian Sea, although both had ancestral ties to the Peloponnesos, and were rather like 'foreign' allies of the **warring brothers** who were their overlords at Troy; these were the Pelopid brothers who were the continuators of the original Perseid dynasty: **Agamemnon** of Mycenae, and **Menelaos** of Sparta.)

Several shorter songs, the *Homeric Hymns*, also have survived: these use the special authenticating language of the Homeric tradition to tell of various events, not part of the War. They, too, were all ascribed to Homer.

The Birth of Helen

Helen, the Queen of Sparta, was the cause of the War. The controversy centered upon whether her marriage vows to Menelaos (Latin **Menelaus**) bound her to a single mate, or whether she might regress at will to the older polyandrous traditions of the Goddess and her multiple consorts.

Helen (Latin Helena) was a name for the Goddess from one of the pre-Greek languages and has no known etymology, although she was associated with a sacred tree; the name has no relationship to Helle, the 'Greek' sister of Phrixos who lent her name to the Hellespont and the Hellenic peoples. Like many of the heroes, Helen had **two fathers**.

Her mortal foster-father was **Tyndareus**, a grandson of Perseus, by his daughter Gorgophone and a 'Hunter' (Kynortas) with a pack of hounds (like Artemis's Aktaion), who was a brother of Hyakinthos in Laconia, the land of Sparta in the central Peloponnesos, at the eastern foot of Mount Taygetos. He had been established there as 'king' by Herakles, in one of his numerous acts of reorganizing the former world: (just as he had similarly established Nestor in the kingship of Pylos, on his way back from the eastern Deathlands); Tyndareus had warred with his own 'Horseman' half-brother (Hippokoon), who drove him into exile; but Herakles had restored him to the kingship. He took to wife a Lady of the old school, as yet unreclaimed: the 'Rockrose' Queen **Leda** (of the sacred 'Kisthos basket,' like the Medousa's Graiai sisterhood), whom he had met while in 'foreign' exile in the Aetolian Deathlands: she came from the famous family of the Kalydonian Boar Hunt: a sister of the mother of Meleagros and Deianeira, or perhaps only a half-sister, for her father may have been the 'Owl-man' Glaukos, a son of Sisyphos.

But by most accounts, Tyndareus did not beget Helen himself; instead, it was Zeus who was her father. In the disguise of a swan, he possessed Leda by the banks of the River Eurotas, on the same night, as some claim, that she (like Herakles' mother Alkmene) had lain with her husband Tyndareus. (Leda with the swan, like Europa with the bull, is another instance of Zeus's consorting with the old Goddess of Minoan traditions, in his attempt to beget the world of the new order.) From this union with Zeus, Leda produced an egg (or some said, two), the sacred hyacinth in color: it could still be seen at Sparta, where it was kept, a thousand years later. From the egg (or eggs) were hatched dissimilar pairs of warring siblings: four, in all, (the complete quartet of **liminal** possibilities, like the children of Oidipous), two girls and two boys: **Helen** and her sister **Klytaimnestra** (Latin **Clytemnestra**); and the **Dioskouroi** (Latin **Dioscuri**) or 'Sons of Zeus,' **Kastor** (Latin **Castor**) and **Polydeukes** (Latin **Pollux**). These latter two, the sons, were to wear the eggshell halves that were the mark of their birth throughout their lives, as (mushroom) caps, the 'pilos;' and when they died, they ascended to the Zodiac as the Twins, **Gemini**. Only one of them was immortal, originally, and the other mortal; but they had vowed to share their dissimilarity by dying and living together, on alternate days. Similarly, Klytaimnestra, by most accounts, turned out bad—so bad, that no one would ever assert that she was Zeus's daughter, although she came from the same egg as her sister, or even her brothers; and Helen

Leda and the Swan, with her Hatched Eggs: Kastor, Polydeukes, Helen, and Klytaimnestra (Copy of a lost painting by da Vinci, formerly Spiridon Collection, Rome)

supposedly was her opposite—although this beloved daughter of Zeus could be very troublesome, too.

The Marriage(s) of Helen

Theseus, as we have seen, was the first to claim Helen, as soon as she surfaced at the Marathonian Entrance. There were even some people who knew that it was there that Zeus had possessed Leda—although in those regions, she had a more terrible name: **Nemesis** or 'Vengeance.' Others said that Nemesis was the one who had actually laid the egg, or eggs, and then merely entrusted them to Leda in Sparta to hatch as stepmother.

But as Zeus's daughter, Helen was the most beautiful woman ever to surface from the black depths, and she cast her erotic spell on many men, so that everyone was her suitor—as must also have been the case with her more sinister sister Klytaimnestra, whose name means that she was 'Famous for her Wooing.'

The two sisters were lodged securely in matrimony, by Tyndareus, to two **warring brothers**, the sons of Pelops, **Agamemnon** and **Menelaos.** And some explained the willingness of all the Greek heroes to participate later in the Trojan War under the leadership of Agamemnon, by claiming that Tyndareus had exacted a pledge from Helen's suitors to uphold the sanctity of her marriage to Menelaos and to see to it that she would remain faithfully monogamous—which, obviously, was not going to be easy.

The Pelopid 'Kingdom' of Mycenae

The Pelopids were related to the Perseid family, before the double marriage to the Tyndarid sisters, only via the marriage of two sons of Perseus to two daughters of Pelops and Hippodameia: which was the union that resulted in the Heraclid family, and its archenemy, Eurystheus. (Another Pelopid son produced the Theseids; the Labdacids were related only via the affair of Laios with Chrysippos, and via Pelops' sister Niobe, who had married, however, into the pre-Kadmean line; while the Neleids, or the family of Iason, were related to the Pelopids only via Niobe's daughter Chloris, although Salmoneus was a brother-in-law of the Perseid Gorgophone.)

After the death of Eurystheus, the Heraclids, who should have inherited the Perseid dynasty of Mycenae, did not return immediately from exile. Instead, Mycenae was taken over by **Atreus**, the 'Fearless,' a son of Pelops and Hippodameia. It was he alone, and for the first time in Hellenic history, who was granted the right of sovereignty over all of Greece. As a pledge of this power, Zeus conferred upon Atreus a sceptre and a golden ram.

(Like Iason's Golden Fleece which had rescued Nephele's Phrixos from being sacrificed, and like the ram with which Medeia rejuvenated Aison—and sacrificed Pelias, the Ram was a sign of the transition from the traditions of the earlier religion and from the times of human sacrifice offered to the old Artemis and Apollo. The Ram was originally the substitute for Pelops himself, in his Contest with Oinomaos for Hippodameia of Olympia. And still earlier, before he came to Greece from the Asiatic Deathlands, Pelops had survived a similar sacrifice at the hands of his own father Tantalos, as a sign of Zeus's special role for him in turning the world around: all the Pelopids inherited the ivory shoulder bone that commemorated Pelops' rejuvenation, after the new Olympians refused to feast upon his butchered flesh.)

Unfortunately, Atreus had a **warring brother, Thyestes,** the 'Sacrificer and Pestle' or drug-man, who connived with the nebulous and Nephele-like wife of Atreus, **Aerope** or 'Misty-face,' to steal the Ram and the 'kingdom.' She was a granddaughter of Minos, of the Cretan Labyrinth, (where her grandmother Pasiphae had become enraptured by the Bull in her husband's herd to beget the Minotaur). Aerope kept the ram's Golden Fleece in a chest, and like her second-cousin Medeia, she could give it to whomever she pleased. She fell in love with her brother-in-law Thyestes, and gave it to him, and with it, transferred control of the 'kingdom,' thereby forcing her husband into exile (down in Sparta with Tyndareus).

That was not the way that Zeus had intended, in turning the world about; and he signaled his displeasure by reversing the whole course of the sun and the heavenly bodies, so that Mycenae returned to Atreus, and his brother became the exile.

Atreus then sacrificed the Sacrificer Thyestes' two sons, the illegitimate twins born to him, out of wedlock, by Atreus's own wife Aerope. And like his and Thyestes' grandfather Tantalos, he butchered and cooked the flesh, and served it up to his brother, the twins' own father, as a feast to celebrate their supposed reconciliation. Only after Thyestes had eaten of his own sons' flesh, did Atreus reveal what manner of animals he had butchered.

Genealogical Chart: The Pelopid Family

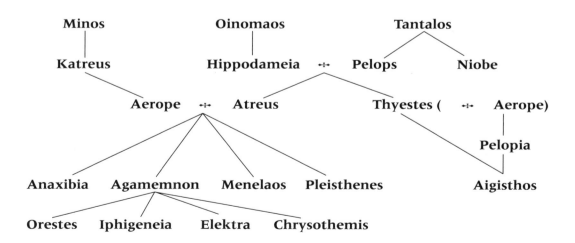

Zeus was no better pleased with this event; and again the course of the sun was reversed. It would require another generation, that of the brothers Agamemnon and Menelaos (and the Tyndarid sisters), to sort out the problems involved in turning Mycenae around to the ways of the new order of Olympians.

Thyestes had also begotten a single daughter (Pelopia, the one still black with the 'Mud' of her chthonic origins;) and from her, he begot one more son, who survived, uneaten. This was **Aigisthos**, the 'Goat-boy' (Latin **Aegisthus**), who received that name to commemorate his **wilderness sojourn** in the old 'Opium-town' of Sikyon (Mekone, where Prometheus first devised the rules for sacrifice). For Pelopia abandoned the infant at the banks of the river where her father Thyestes had assaulted her, still stained with the blood of the sacrificial victim she and her sisterhood of maidens had just offered; and the boy was raised instead by a nanny goat.

(Atreus had two more children, siblings of Agamemnon and Menelaos. One, a girl, Anaxibia, united the Pelopids with the Neleids of Pylos, by marrying Nestor. The other was a boy, Pleisthenes. Now, some tellers knew that the brothers Atreus and Thyestes had enlisted their sons Pleisthenes and Aigisthos in their war against each other: Atreus thought that Aigisthos was his own son, since he, too, had slept with Pelopia; and he tried to use Aigisthos to murder Thyestes; and Thyestes did the same thing with Pleisthenes, whom he had raised as his own son, but Atreus 'accidentally' killed him.)

Thyestes and Aigisthos (and Aerope-Pelopia) represent the recidivist strain in the Mycenaean dynasty. While Agamemnon is away for the War at Troy, his sinister wife Klytaimnestra will turn Mycenae back into a Queendom, by taking Aigisthos as her consort, to replace her absent husband.

The Priamid 'Kingdom' of Troy (Troia)

Meanwhile, as Aigisthos was still growing to manhood in the care of the she-goat in the wilds at the Sikyon Entrance, another recidivist consort was being made ready to challenge the marital stability of the other Tyndarid sister, through a **wilderness sojourn** of his own, down across the waters, in the Trojan Deathlands: he was to surface eventually at Sparta as the third husband for Klytaimnestra's twin sister Helen. This was **Paris**, the son of Troy's 'king' **Priam** and the Queen **Hekabe**.

Priam, like Tyndareus, had been established by Herakles as the ruler of a supposedly reformed city; but Hekabe was not a fortunate choice for wife, since her name is the same as the Goddess **Hekate**, the great Queen who unites in one identity the three aspects of the sisterhood, as maiden, mother, and witch. Her first son, **Hektor** (Latin **Hector**) was the optimistic possibility; but her second, **Paris**, was his brother's **liminal** complement. Before she bore him, she had dreamed that he was to be a flaming torch that would set all of Troy afire; and her own prophetic daughters had advised her to get rid of him. So when Paris was born, Priam left him on the mountainside for his **wilderness sojourn**, hopefully to die there.

The Apple of Discord

Paris was the third to claim Helen as bride (in line after Theseus and Menelaos). On Mount Ida, the Trojan mountain with the same name as the sacred one near the Minoan Labyrinth on Crete, the infant Paris was made ready for his role in unsettling the new realm of Zeus. He was prepared metaphorically to be a consort, as in the earlier times of the Goddess. He was suckled by a bear (like a darling of the Artemis of old); and raised like an animal by shepherds (who named him Paris for the 'Wallet' in which he lay hidden—like the **kisthos** that hid away the Gorgon's head from sight); and he was befriended, like an equal—which he was—, by a bull; and he was even tended by maenads, like a Dionysos of former times, and took a (W)oinos-maiden (Oinone) for wife, while he was there in the wilds. But when it came time for the boy to come back to the civilized world, he faced the familiar problem that a hero always had in choosing an appropriate mate for the role he would play in the ensuing world. In his case, the story was told as the **Judgement of Paris**.

Three goddesses all laid claim to the enticing 'golden apple' (an **entheogen**, perhaps, as some claimed, the same one that Perseus and Herakles had picked in the Garden of the Hesperides, but this time, it was called the **Apple of Discord**); it was labeled with the word Kalliste, the 'Fairest' (that overly optimistic name, as we have seen, for the sinister Artemis); and Paris had to settle their dispute by awarding it to only one of them.

The dispute had arisen at one of those Marriages that were meant to stabilize the world into its new Olympian order. (Not Helen's this time, nor that of the Theban Kadmos and Harmonia, but the marriage of **Peleus** to **Thetis**, from whom the great hero of the Trojan War, **Achilleus**, would be born—but we will come to that story later.) Only Discord was excluded from the list of invited guests, which should have ensured the couple's marital bliss, but she showed up anyway, uninvited, and cast the apple in the midst of the other assembled goddesses; Hera, Athena, and Aphrodite each claimed it for herself. Zeus commanded Hermes to escort the three down to Paris in his wilderness sojourn; and left it for the Trojan prince to decide.

Each offered the herdsman a bribe, to bind his will: sovereignty from Hera; warriorhood from Athena; but from Aphrodite, none of those newer Olympian transmutations: just plain erotic passion, still unmitigated by mediation. The fool chose the last—to serve a woman; for he could not judge rationally, but was deluded by Aphrodite's exceptional physical charms. His reward was Helen, Zeus's own overwhelmingly beautiful daughter, even though she was already given by now as wife to Menelaos and had borne him their only child, a daughter **Hermione**, who was named as a female version of a Hermes.

Paris surfaced, after the watery crossing, at the ancient city of the Amyklai sisterhood (where the 'flower' Hyakinthos had yielded, via the 'accidental' murder, to the newer Apollo), just outside of Sparta. His cousin **Aineas** (Latin **Aeneas**, the hero of Vergil's *Aeneid* epic poem), who was a son of Aphrodite herself, seconded him on the expedition (and some even claimed that the other, more famous son of Aphrodite, Eros or Cupid, himself, led the way); and as they came up, they were met by Helen's brothers, the Dioskouroi (who were always alternating back and forth); and then finally by Menelaos up at Sparta (although Paris and he had already met just recently when the Spartan 'king' was down in Troy to offer sacrificial victims to cleanse his land of a plague). The pretext for this visit by Paris and Aineas supposedly was to reclaim Hesione, the sister of Priam who had been stolen away by Herakles in the destruction of the former city of Troy and given as wife to Telamon, his companion in that exploit. But it appears there was another reason, as well: for Troy, no less than Sparta, was suffering from plague (or trouble with their Apollo); and Paris also had arranged, on their previous meeting, that Menelaos would cleanse him for his own 'accidental' murder of a cousin: this was the 'flower' Antheus, son of Priam's counselor **Antenor** (the reversal 'Turn-man:' Antenor would side with the Greeks in the coming War).

Paris and Helen fell desperately in love; for she, too, lost her will. They went back down to Troy together, setting sail from the port of Hermione, on the eastern shore of the Peloponnesos: their route was through the chasm outside the town, famous as the shortest Entrance to the Deathlands. (They took advantage of Menelaos's absence: he had been suddenly summoned down to the Labyrinth in Crete to attend the funeral of a Minoan ancestor.) This third marriage of Helen was consummated on a 'Rocky' island on their way across; and, despite the previous marriage still in effect, it was officially formalized when the lovers showed up in Troy; there she cast the spell of her beauty upon the whole infatuated city, so that there was not a single Trojan who would have agreed willingly to relinquish her back.

The only tie to her other life was the herm-like daughter she had abandoned, to live a life as her father's child, instead of a mother's;—and the Entrance that bridged the two worlds of her existence.

The Birth of Achilleus

With the affairs above and below the Peloponnesos in such a balanced state of deadlock, it was left for a 'foreign' outsider to tip the scales back toward the realm of Zeus—through the tragic offering of his own chance at immortality. When the former suitors of Helen prepared to honor their pledge, Menelaos learned from **Nestor** (the last of the surviving Neleids, whom Herakles had established at the pacified Entrance of Pylos) that the hero **Achilleus** was essential to their endeavor, even though he had not himself been a suitor. (He would become the fifth husband of Helen, but only after his death, in line after a brother of Paris.) He would have been the greatest of the Olympians, displacing not Apollo (like Herakles) from the select family of twelve, but Zeus himself; and hence he was destined to be a loser, since winning would have inflicted upon the world exactly the opposite of what should have been the successful hero's task: instead of further stabilizing the Olympian hierarchy, he would have ushered in an age to replace it. Achilleus almost was born as Zeus's best son, but instead Zeus had to forgo begetting him; and in the process, become reconciled at last with humankind and man's creator, Prometheus. This would-be son of Zeus had to be sacrificed to redeem Zeus's daughter Helen back from Troy.

Although Zeus knew that one of his sons might replace him (as he had supplanted his own father Kronos, and as Kronos had with his father Ouranos), it was only Prometheus (or his mother Themis) who knew the identity of the woman whose son was destined to surpass his father. Despite his continuing hatred for Zeus, Prometheus traded that knowledge to secure his own release from the never-ending torment Zeus had inflicted upon him in retaliation for the creation of Man. The woman was the sea-goddess **Thetis** (one of the aquatic Nereid sisterhood), whom both Zeus and his brother Poseidon were courting at the time. To avoid the otherwise inevitable outcome, Zeus gave Thetis in marriage to **Peleus**, so that when Achilleus was born, he had only Peleus for father, instead of Zeus (or Poseidon) as the other of his **two fathers**. Achilleus was thus doomed to lose, done in by both the Olympian and (through Prometheus) the chthonic sides in the controversy—for he was to be the ultimate sacrifice needed to stabilize the world and humankind's role as mediator in it.

Peleus had a name (like Pelops) descriptive of his 'Muddy' dark origins, a mortal who by background was something less than mortal. His family traced its origins back to the island of Aegina (Aigina, sacred to the old Minoan Artemis, and in olden times called Oinone, like the maenadic bride of Paris), and its subterranean bridge to the old Apollo's lands in Thessaly. Zeus had begotten Peleus's father **Aiakos** (Latin **Aeacus**) on Aigina herself (a twin sister of Thebe, of the Theban sisterhood): she was named as a 'goat' goddess (like the aegis of Pallas, or Aigeus of Athens); and her son Aiakos was named after her as a piece of 'Earth' (or 'Aia's Man'). And to beget his own son Peleus, Aiakos had consorted with a Queen in the infernal sisterhood that had for father the brigand Skiron, whom Theseus had defeated on the mainland, just north of Aigina, on the shore of the Entrance at Megara. And upon his death, Aiakos was entrusted with the keys of Hades and became one of the three great Judges in the underworld (joining the Minoan 'kings' Rhadamanthys and Minos, who were also sons of Zeus), as compensation and reward for his role in taking on the burden of being Achilleus's grandfather.

Under his 'kingship' on Oinone-Aigina, Zeus had repeopled the island for him with **Myrmidons**, a race of 'Ants,' which are chthonic queen-dominated insects, but which were transmuted for the reign of Aiakos: for these ant people had climbed an oak tree (**entheogen**) on the island, that grew from an acorn planted from Zeus's sacred grove at Dodona: the ants carried kernels of grain, and then fell from above, like acorns, back to earth as men. These Myrmidons would be the troops that Achilleus brought to the war at Troy.

To claim Thetis as his bride, Peleus, this son of the Aeginetan Aiakos, showed up in Thessaly, on Mount Pelion, named for the same 'Muddy' complexion as the bridegroom: there were even those who claimed that the Myrmidons who

Courtship of Peleus and Thetis (Red-figure kylix early 5th century BC, Staatliche Museen, Berlin)

came up with him were not 'foreigners' at all, but actually autochthonous or indigenous to Thessaly. Peleus took possession of Thetis at Cape Sepia by the shore of the sea at the base of the mountain—for she was an aquatic nymph. And as she wrestled to free herself from his embrace, she rapidly began to change shape, shifting through a whole repertory of hallucinatory metamorphoses, until she finally subsided into her last, as a cuttle-fish, that squirted him in the face: so that the lovers consummated their union in a cloud of the black sepia ink that gives this fish its name in Greek as 'Putrid,' with its connotation of the dark rotten matter in the Deathlands.

The Marriage was solemnized by all the gods and goddesses, in attendance—except for Discord, as we have already mentioned. And when Achilleus was born, he, too, was sent off for a **wilderness sojourn**: on Mount Pelion, where he was entrusted to the tutelage of the good centaur **Cheiron**, who taught him archery and the toxins for arrows.

His mother never willingly acquiesced in her son's fore-ordained tragic end; and she did her best to make him invincible by dunking him in the waters of the underworld, except for his heel, which she held onto, so that it remained his one spot of vulnerability (**maimed hero**): his 'Achilles tendon,' as we now call that part of our bodies in English. Actually, as some told the story, Achilleus may have been her seventh son; and the first six, she burnt in a fire (or cooked in a cauldron) to destroy the mortal flesh they had inherited from their father, anointing their remains with ambrosia; and she was in the process of doing the same with her seventh, but Peleus intervened before all but a single ankle had been consumed. In either case, whether it was his mother or his father's error, the heel was the part that the parent refused to relinquish, either down to the dreadful waters, or up to the Olympian empyrean. (Peleus and his wife parted ways over this dispute about their son, and never shared a married life in concord.)

It was this son, an outsider amongst the Greeks, and a 'foreigner,' raised in the Thessalian wilds of Mount Pelion, who was the essential counterpoise needed to rectify the marital discord that would be caused by that other 'foreigner' from Troy, whose fate mirrored his own across the waters, and who was at this same time being raised in the sojourn on Mount Ida (**paradigm #1**). Paris would eventually shoot Achilleus in his heel, so that he died before the end of the War, never fulfilling the other, more successful of his **liminal** potentials; and Neoptolemos, his son, finally would bring the affair to a close by enlisting another outsider, **Philoktetes**: who would fatally shoot Paris in his heel, with the bow and poisoned arrows that Herakles had left behind when he ascended to Olympus to claim his inheritance as Zeus's best son, the role that had been denied Achilleus.

When Helen's former suitors were being drafted for the expedition against Troy, Thetis again tried to keep her son from his inevitable death. She disguised him as one of the girls in the sisterhood on the island of Skyros, where Lykomedes, the murderer of Theseus, was 'king.' It was while he was there, disguised as the maiden **Pyrrha** (or 'Flame-red'), that he begot his son Neoptolemos on one of the maidens in the sisterhood: Neoptolemos was also named **Pyrrhos**, in matrilineal fashion, after his mother, who was actually his father. It was this torch that would bring to pass the fearful conflagration in the dream that Hekabe and Priam had tried to avoid by exposing Paris on the Trojan mountainside. (Pyrrha is a name you have already encountered as the wife of Deukalion, the fire-bringer Prometheus's son: they, too, many generations earlier had ushered in the first new age, after the Great Flood.)

The Tricks of Nature

But none of this could have happened without the help (**animus**) of **Odysseus** (English **Ulysses**; Latin **Ulixes**), a descendant of Hermes and another outsider, who was the other great hero of the Greeks in the War. It would take the two of them, not just the loss of Achilleus, but the tricks of Odysseus as well, to end the whole affair. It was he who was sent to Skyros to fetch both Achilleus for the original expedition, and then later his son Neoptolemos ('New War'), who like Odysseus's own son **Telemachos** (or 'Final Battle'), had been still an infant when his father left for Troy: so that both boys knew only their mothers at first, and had to learn to be their fathers' sons later.

It was a trick that allowed Odysseus to uncover Achilleus' disguise amongst the daughters of Lykomedes. He arrived in Skyros with a chest full of trinkets as gifts for the girls; and hidden amongst the things that would delight a woman, was a sword, which Achilleus was tricked into selecting for himself, throwing off his female robes and thus inadvertently exposing himself as the male member of the sisterhood.

There were some who claimed that Odysseus himself had been tricked into joining the War, even though he was the first of Helen's suitors, and had even devised the oath that would trick all the other suitors into defending her precarious marriage to Menelaos. Instead of Helen, however, Odysseus had chosen her cousin **Penelope** for his own wife, a daughter of **Ikarios**, who was a brother of Tyndareus; but instead of taking up residence as consort in his wife's native Sparta (as Menelaos did), he had insisted, against her father's wishes, on removing her to his own island of Ithaka, off the north-western shore of the Peloponnesos. When Menelaos later showed up with **Palamedes** to draft him for the War, Odysseus (who had been warned that he would spend ten years fighting at Troy, and ten more coming home) pretended to be too crazy to be of any use to the other Greeks: he feigned not to recognize his visitors, and devoted his sole attention to ploughing in a bizarre manner, yoking an ass and an ox, and sowing salt in the land, and dressed with a mushroom cap that made him resemble a 'digital' man from the chthonic realm. But this Palamedes or 'Hand-lord' was a 'digital' man himself and notoriously clever enough to be a perfect match for Odysseus (**paradigm #1**). He placed the infant Telemachos, as if he were just a plant, in the path of the oncoming plough: Odysseus was thus tricked into revealing that his insanity was just a chthonic disguise (like Achilleus amongst the maidens) when he swerved aside to avoid running the furrow through his own son.

This trick earned Palamedes the unrelenting hatred of Odysseus. At the War, Odysseus retaliated by falsely implicating him as a traitor and turncoat to the Trojan side; and one way or another—for the story is variously told—, he managed to thrust Palamedes back down into the chthonic realm: either drowning him or burying him in a well or having him stoned to death by the other Greeks. But the hatred lived on, now from the other direction: for Palamedes was the son of the 'Helmsman' **Oiax** and the brother of a **Nauplios** or 'Sailor;' and this father and brother of Palamedes controlled the portal Entrance back up from Troy, through the sanctuary of Artemis at Aulis, at the southern tip of the island of Euboea: these two 'navigators' assured that the Return would be hazardous for the Greeks by lighting the treacherous coastal passage with deceptive and misleading beacon fires.

Hatred was, in fact, Odysseus's legacy from his maternal grandfather, the cattle rustler **Autolykos** (the 'Very Wolf'), who was himself a son of the thieving Hermes. (We have already told how Odysseus was begotten by **Sisyphos** on the **turncoat Antikleia** or 'Reverse Fame', who was the daughter of Sisyphos's neighbor Autolykos. It was a notorious episode of reciprocal theiving: Autolykos had stolen the cattle of Sisyphos, who retaliated by stealing Antikleia; and in both instances, Sisyphos played a trick that would incriminate the thief: first Autolykos, by putting telltale markings on the hooves of the cows that were being stolen from him by his neighbor; and then himself, by leaving his neighbor's daughter with a note that acknowledged his own complicity in her pregnancy.) When Autolykos was visiting his daughter and her newborn infant in the house of **Laertes**, who passed as the other of the **two fathers** for the hero Odysseus, the parents asked the grandfather to name the baby. 'Odysseus' was his choice, naming him for the 'Hatred' that everyone directed toward Autolykos himself: but he promised that when the child had grown and came to visit him in his own estates at the Delphic sanctuary he would reward him for all the hatred he would have to endure. Odysseus eventually claimed his reward—although he returned from the visit to Mount Parnassos **maimed** with a scar on his thigh from a Boar Hunt there. Such was the lot of all those who entered into a pact of friendship, to further the transmutation of Apollo.

At the War, Odysseus played a famous trick that helped redeem Apollo from his old ways. It was the only battle that occurred at night. **Dolon**, whose name means 'Trick,' set out as a spy from the Trojan side, having disguised himself as a Wolf; but Odysseus intercepted him (at the sacred plant or **entheogen** of the Trojan Apollo: thymbra, the 'smoke herb' or savory), forced him to betray his own side by revealing the password, which was Phoibos (Apollo), and then killed Dolon, stealing his disguise. With Dolon's wolfskin now donned as his own trick, he stole past the Trojan sentries, misleading them with the stolen password, and killed a newly arrived ally of the Trojans, **Rhesos**, before his horses had had a chance to graze on the plants of Troy—which would have assured that the Greeks would lose the War: as his reward for joining the War, Rhesos, in turn, had been promised the immortal pair of horses that belonged to Achilleus—but because of the trick, he did not live to claim it. Athena helped (**anima**) Odysseus by playing a trick of her own in the exploit: after telling Odysseus about the imminent arrival of Rhesos and his horses, she misled Paris by disguising herself as his beloved Aphrodite.

It was Odysseus also who contributed the final trick that led to the fall of Troy: this was the ruse of the **Trojan Horse**, in which Athena again demonstrated which side she really supported—at least in her Olympian transmutation, rather than her former persona. The Greeks built a large wooden horse, dedicated to Athena (as the old horse-goddess); and after hiding a contingent of heroes in its hollow belly, the others pretended to sail away back home. One of them was left behind to play the role of traitor: this was the 'Bandit' **Sinon**, a full son of Sisyphos (whereas Odysseus was only the putative son). He pretended that he had been betrayed by Odysseus, and hence had turned against his fellow Greeks; and accordingly, he divulged that Troy would be victorious only if it welcomed the Horse within its city walls. The Trojans were thus tricked into dragging it into Troy, destroying the fortifications of the Gateway to make room for it as it passed within.

There were some Trojans who had opposed this decision, notably two children of Priam and Hekabe: **Kassandra** (Latin **Cassandra**; also called **Alexandra**, the female version of **Alexandros-Paris**); and **Laokoon** (Latin **Laocoon**). Kassandra was a prophetess of Apollo, but she had been cursed by the god for refusing to be his bride; and although she could foretell the future,

Laokoon and his Sons, Wrestling with the Serpents of Apollo (Hellenistic sculpture by Hagesandros, Polydoros, and Athanadoros 2nd-1st century BC, Vatican Museum, Rome)

she was never believed—or even understood, in her jumbled babbling. Laokoon similarly was a seer, and a priest of the old Thymbraian (**entheogen**) Apollo; but as he attempted to prevent the entrance of the Horse into Troy, two serpents came from the offshore islands where the departed Greeks lurked in hiding, and killed him and his twin sons. (These sons bore names that indicate their **liminal** dichotomous natures as representatives of the god their father served: one was called **Thymbraios**, for the plant associated with the Trojan god, and was also named 'Black Flower' or **Melanthos**, for the entheogen that thymbra replaced; the other was named **Antiphas** or 'Reverse Name.')

Troy had just recently been made vulnerable by another trick that Odysseus had played. Troy was deemed impregnable so long as it possessed its **Palladion**: this was the ancient idol of Athena, as the goat-goddess **Pallas**, portrayed as she looked before the artistic innovations that would transmute her image away from its primordial nature as the Gorgon Medusa. To safeguard their sacred talisman, the Trojans had multiplied the idol into a whole sisterhood of copies. Odysseus had entered the city through the Labyrinth of its sewer system and stolen it away—with the complicity of Hekabe and Helen (who was now married to her fourth husband, **Deiphobos**, a brother of Paris): for the Troia Queens were now ready to change sides.

In this and his other exploits, Odysseus was accompanied by his traditional **animus** companion, **Diomedes**, the son of Tydeus (who was Polyneikes' rival and then ally in the War at Thebes), and, like Odysseus, especially close to the goddess Athena. Therein lies a problem, however. It is an uneasy truce that binds the hero and the befriended 'enemy' companion; and especially so, if they must share the same **anima**: so that she might be compelled to play a double role, as 'enemy' or befriended ally. Athena inevitably would have to choose, as she did between Troy and the Greeks, for only one side could wield the transmuted power of the goddess. In the Theft of the Palladion, Odysseus turned on his 'friend' (**paradigms #1&3**) and 'almost' (**paradigm #2**) killed him, attacking him from behind as he carried the Palladion, strapped to his back; in just the nick of time, Diomedes defended himself, for he had glimpsed the shadow of his 'friend' cast forward by the light of the full moon. This may have been the end of the their friendship, although some claim that they patched up their difference to fetch Philoktetes and the poisoned arrows of Herakles' bow.

(Athena, as we have seen, had similarly turned against Diomedes' father Tydeus in the War at Thebes, despite her devoted patronage of him. As he lay dying from the wound inflicted by Melanippos or 'Black Horse' at the Theban Gate, she was about to revive him with an Olympian potion or entheogen, but he drank instead the brains of his 'enemy' Melanippos; and she abandoned him in revulsion and let him die. This Melanippos was also known as the brother that Tydeus had 'accidentally' killed back home in Kalydon, before he went into exile and joined the foreign legions with Polyneikes: for Melanippos, it was claimed, was destined to cause his brother's death, just as with Polyneikes and his brother Eteokles.)

Some tellers of the story knew that the Theft of the Palladion had involved still another trick. Odysseus had arranged to have Diomedes flog him, so that Odysseus pretended, like Sinon, to be a traitor to the Greek cause, and thus gained entrance to Troy: it was the welts on his bloodied back that earned him the compassion of the Trojan Queens.

On the night that Troy fell to the Greeks who emerged from the belly of the Horse, Kassandra sought asylum at the Athena idol that replaced the stolen Palladion, but the copy had no efficacy to save her, and she was dragged away, still clutching it, eventually to die back in Greece. The hero who stole this substitute was another traditional 'enemy' of the hateful Odysseus: **Aias** (Latin **Ajax**: there are two heroes with this name, although they are similarly paired with Odysseus's 'friendly' hatred; in this story, it is the one called the Lesser Aias who is involved; we will come to the story about the Greater Aias, later). For a thousand years after this violation of asylum, the kinsmen of Aias who lived on the northeastern slopes of Apollo's Mount Parnassos were required to atone for what happened to his priestess at Troy. Each year, they sent two maidens as sacrificial offerings to the Trojan Athena, but the goddess usually relented, as long as they escaped detection by sneaking into the sanctuary through the same subterranean Labyrinth that Odysseus had used for the original theft.

The Contest with Artemis (Iphigeneia)

When the War was all over, Artemis, too, tended to become more merciful, and to relent, when humans were offered to her for sacrifice at her sanctuary at Brauron: she was satisfied in later times if the victim received only a superficial scratch, just enough to draw blood. But right across the straits from Brauron, at Aulis on the island of Euboea, the Greeks in former times had been required by her to slaughter a maiden in order to gain access to her Entrance for the journey to the War at Troy: this victim was Agamemnon's daughter **Iphigeneia**. And similarly, as they came back up on their return after the War was all over, they had again been forced to offer another maiden: this time it was Priam's daughter **Polyxena**. But as a result of the War, the old idol of Artemis, too, was redeemed from its earlier image as the slaughterer, and the Olympian goddess ordinarily could be satisfied with merely symbolic deaths.

For both the journey out to Troy and the return, the Greek troops were stalled for lack of a Wind. To catch a Wind (or 'inspiration:' **entheogen**), a maiden had to be given over as bride to the chthonic realm; and on the strength of this new marital alliance, the others would sail, calling upon the now befriended alien kinsman for their transport: for Winds, it was thought, flowed (like Rivers) to and fro, back and forth through the Entrances, from cavernous sources deep within in the subterranean Labyrinth. It was Achilleus who was the nominal bridegroom in both cases, although it was only a ruse with Iphigeneia (since he was still alive at the time); but Polyxena, at the end of the War, was offered on his tomb.

(None less than Zeus himself, as we shall see in the next chapter, had set the precedent for such an alliance. He had arranged to give over his own daughter Persephone (against the wishes of her mother Demeter, who was also his sister), in order to reconfirm ties of kinship with his own chthonic brother Hades, and thus divide the Goddess between the two houses, as mother on Olympus and maiden in the underworld. For the War at Troy, however, neither Klytaimnestra nor Hekabe was ever reconciled for the loss of their daughters; and both of them were to take their wrath with them down into the chthonic realm when they died.)

As to how Agamemnon could bring himself to kill his own daughter (just to get his sister-in-law back for his brother), the story was variously told. Helen's daughter Hermione might have seemed a more fitting offering, but she was the mother's one tie back to Sparta; and the girl couldn't get married until after the mother returned—which was the whole point of the venture at Troy. And besides, Agamemnon and Klytaimnestra had the perfect offering for Artemis, for the girl was named after the goddess, with one of her common bynames: as Iphigeneia ('Strong in her Birthing'), or, as some knew her, **Iphianassa** ('Strong in her Ruling'). These were names like the Minoan Ariadne and Diktynna that were merely ways of calling Artemis, as was also Polyxena, the 'Foreign Friend and Hostess.' The only problem was whether Iphigeneia was really her father's child to offer, or whether the mother still could lay claim to her, as in the traditions of matriliny. (Some tellers of the story even knew of her as Helen's daughter, by Theseus, and hence no blood kin to Agamemnon at all.)

Agamemnon, it was said, had angered Artemis by hunting in the goddess's sanctuary at Aulis, as the Greeks awaited the favoring Wind; and he had shot an antlered hind, the animal that was the goddess's familiar. When the story later was told, no one could figure out why this so angered Artemis, that she demanded compensation in the form of Agamemnon's daughter, surely a more grievous offering: but the sacrifice of the hind implies that the old goddess had already mended her ways, before the War at Troy had even been fought; and it was a human victim, not an animal surrogate, that in those days was still required. This is what the prophet **Kalchas** (Latin **Calchas**) advised.

(Kalchas, the great prophet of the Trojan War, was a **turncoat** from the other side, sent originally by Priam for a consultation with the Pythoness at Delphi concerning the approaching War. She had reassigned him and ordered him to join the Greeks to assure their unswerving perseverance through to the completion of the War, which would ultimately redeem Apollo from his 'foreign' involvements. He is one of the chthonic 'Bronze' men (which is the meaning of his name), an 'African,' and a descendant of the 'black' Apollo. By some accounts, it was his inspired vision that allowed the Greeks to find their way down to Troy.)

It was Odysseus who devised the trick that would lure Iphigeneia to her death at Aulis: she was summoned, with her mother, as a bride for Achilleus. When the wedding party arrived, Odysseus and Diomedes carried her to the altar, and Kalchas solemnized the rite.

There was, however, another way of telling what actually happened. At the last moment, Artemis may have relented and replaced the maiden with one of her familiars (a hind, a she-bear, or even a witch), and transported Iphigeneia herself to the **Taurians** or 'Bull-people' of the Crimean peninsula, on the northern shores of the Black Sea, in the Deathlands. (Their 'king' was **Thoas**, the 'Swift Darter,' a netherworld son of Dionysos and Ariadne, and the father of the Lemnian Hypsipyle, whom Iason encountered in his tour of the Deathlands with the Argonauts—although that would have been a Thoas of four generations earlier. Thoas has the same 'swiftness' of foot that traditionally characterized the 'swift-footed' Achilleus, the intended husband of Iphigeneia: hence, amongst the Taurians, Iphigeneia has consummated the same union with Thoas that had begun as a fatal marriage to Achilleus.) There it was the maiden's task to sacrifice all hapless Greeks who chanced to wash ashore, offering them to the old idol of the Artemis goddess, who amongst the Taurians was simply called the 'Maiden.' Eventually her own brother **Orestes** and his 'friend' **Pylades** washed in: their mission was to rescue the idol; Orestes himself had 'almost' been killed at Delphi, and he was still in his maddened state, which would only be resolved when it finally was decided whether a child was a mother's child or a father's. Iphigeneia-Artemis 'almost' sacrificed the two of them, but at the last moment the 'foreigners' recognized each other and sibling love prevailed. The sanctuary of Delphi had been on the brink of reverting to its old ways: dream hallucinations were beginning to emerge from the cavernous Labyrinth on Apollo's Mt. Parnassos, but the reconciliation of the siblings (both Orestes and Iphigeneia, and their divine counterparts: Apollo and Artemis) righted the world back toward its Olympian transmutation. The rescued idol of Artemis was reinstalled at the Birthing sanctuary at Brauron, and henceforth it would suffice to offer the human victims only in sham.

The Contest with Apollo (Thymbraios)

But the main bout of the War at Troy was the Contest with Apollo; and it wouldn't be resolved until both Achilleus fell, killed by an Apollo disguised as Paris, down in the temple of the Trojan Thymbraios; and then his son Neoptolemos, as well, in a battle fought up at Delphi, where he fell victim to the official named **Machaireus**, the 'Butcher,' who wielded his sacrificial knife against him, instead of a beast, in a dispute over offerings to the god (— although some said that Orestes either instigated the murder or actually accomplished it, because both claimed the right to marry Helen's daughter Hermione). Neoptolemos was buried at Delphi, taking up residence there, beneath the sanctuary, as the final victim of the old Apollo (**paradigms #1&2**), for such was the tragic role assigned to Achilleus and his lineage in the remaking of the Hellenic world. Achilleus is a figure like Dionysos's 'enemy' Pentheus, born to suffer and die, so that another, more essential, may thrive and win. Suffering was the essential nature of Achilleus, and 'Grief' was the very meaning of his name. And from the very beginning, he was not only a potential threat to Zeus, but an 'enemy' both of Apollo and of the Pelopids, and in particular of Agamemnon, and then in the next generation through his son Neoptolemos, an enemy of Orestes. (Nor was he ever close to Odysseus, whose tricks would finally help win the War, although there was a distant link between their families: Odysseus's (other) father Sisyphos had tattled on Zeus, in the affair with Aigina, that begot Achilleus' grandfather Aiakos; in retaliation, Zeus had confined Sisyphos in the underworld.)

At Troy, in the version of the events as told by the reciters of the tradition that was recorded eventually as the Homeric *Iliad* (which takes its name from Ilion, an earlier name for Troia), we glimpse the glory that might have been, and even for that fleeting moment of success, Achilleus had first to die in the persona of his 'friend' **Patroklos.** The story of Achilleus is a tour de force: how to tell of the victory of a hero who could never be allowed to win.

It all began as a squabble over chthonic maidens, in the tenth year: with a Contest with Agamemnon, that was itself only the prelude to the Contest with Apollo. When the maidens who had been captured in the recent battles with the Trojans and their allies from the Deathlands were divided amongst the Greek victors, **Briseis** fell to Achilleus: she is named merely as the daughter of her father **Briseus**, the 'Weighty,' which is an epithet of Dionysos: there was another maiden with this epithet who was said to be a daughter of Kalchas that he hadn't managed to drag up with him when he surfaced at Delphi to be reassigned; she was known in later traditions as **Cressida**, the 'Golden.' Agamemnon's booty was the maiden **Chryseis**, the daughter of **Chryses**, the 'Golden,' who was a priest of Apollo on the island of Chryse (which was once offshore of Lemnos, but has since sunk beneath the sea: it is named for the Trojan priestess of Pallas, who was the guardian of the idols of the old religion). When Agamemnon refused to accept the father's ransom for the return of his captured daughter, Chryses invoked the aid of his god Apollo; and Apollo began to shoot his poisoned arrows up from the deadly island at the Greeks, who became afflicted with a plague. The cure was obvious, but Achilleus had the misfortune to suggest it: return the Apolline maiden Chryseis. Agamemnon bowed to necessity, but retaliated by confiscating Achilleus' Dionysian maiden Briseis for himself. This insult to the reluctant ally of the Pelopids, earned him the hatred of Achilleus, who turned against the Greeks and withdrew from the War, so that, although the plague was now lifted, his own absence from the fighting became the new source of plague. As the Greeks died in the ensuing unsuccessful battles, Achilleus now, instead of Apollo, became the 'enemy.'

Finally, after many encounters, which are like a roster of all the available heroes of that time (each enacting versions of the typical paradigms), Patroklos takes pity on his fellow Greeks and begs Achilleus to allow him to put on the other's armor and enter the War, disguised as his friend.

As to who Patroklos was, there were various accounts, other than the general agreement that he was a relative and the best 'friend' (**animus**) of Achilleus. He is named as a person 'Famous for his Father,' although it was really Achilleus who 'almost' had the most famous father of all, Zeus. Patroklos's lineage is, however, on the darker side, from the chthonic dynasties of Thessaly. He had 'accidentally' killed a man with a 'Famous Name,' **Kleitonymos**, in a game of dice; and (like Polyneikes' ally Tydeus), this mysterious stranger had shown up seeking 'hospitality' in the house of Achilleus's father Peleus, and thus became his friend's companion, and some claimed, even lover.

(Achilleus had come to Troy with another chthonic companion. This was **Phoinix**, named as one of the 'Bloody' men from the Phoenician Deathlands, although he, too, had surfaced into the Thessalian house of Peleus from closer to home, right up from the native region of Phthia or 'Wasting Decay:' Phoinix had had an illicit erotic involvement with the local nymph who bore that unfortunate name. His father had cursed him with blindness, but the centaur Cheiron had restored his sight; and Peleus had assigned him to Achilleus as a tutor and second father. But even Phoinix had failed to dissuade Achilleus from his wrath against the Greeks.)

Once Patroklos had put on the heraldry of Achilleus's armour, he appeared to be Achilleus himself. In this guise, this friend of Achilleus entered the War as his own friend; and attacked the citadel of Troy, engaging Apollo, no less than three times, and then a second three times, until Apollo, in hand to hand combat, coming at him in the night and attacking his backside, struck the armor of Achilleus off of him: and thus was he revealed for who he was. **Euphorbos**, who was a priest of the Trojan Apollo (although his father had been stolen down from the sanctuary of Delphi), and who had been the first to kill a Greek when the foreigners had come ashore nine years earlier, threw a spear at Patroklos and wounded him; and then Hektor killed him.

(You have already met a Euphorbos before: he was the 'Fodder-man' who found the baby Oidipous. It is a name appropriate for a herdsman or a centaur, the sort of creature you might expect to encounter in the **wilderness sojourn**. The heroic paradigm, as we have seen, involves a return to that primordial world. At Troy, the first Greek ashore, who was the man Euphorbos killed, was named **Protesilaos**, or 'First-people.' He was a maternal uncle of Iason, from Thessaly; his wife **Laodameia** or 'People-queen,' killed herself when she learned of his death.)

Now that Achilleus symbolically had died in the persona of his friend Patroklos, he reentered the War for his moment of glory, knowing in advance that once he had killed Hektor, his own death would not be far off. But before he could come against his archenemy, the killer of Patroklos, he would need a new suit of armor, a heraldry to replace that which Hektor had stripped from the corpse of the dead Patroklos. This his mother Thetis commissioned for him, forged in the watery netherworld by Hephaistos and his brotherhood of Kyklopes: emblazoned on his new shield was a scene of humans, engaged in the rhythmic cycle of human activities. With this new and chthonic emblem of humanity— to replace the shield lost to Hektor, under whose sign he could never be allowed to win—, Achilleus rejoined the War.

He killed so many of the enemy forces that the rivers of Troy became clogged with corpses, and the rising waters inundated the land. Achilleus continued the carnage, and was nearly overwhelmed himself by the flood, as the battle evolved into an elemental Contest of the forces of Nature, with water fighting fire: for Hera directed Hephaistos to set fire to the land, and the Winds were summoned to dry off the waters. The Trojans sought refuge in the citadel; but even then, Achilleus would have brought the War to its end, had not Apollo distracted him by deceiving him with a hallucination, that was himself disguised as a Trojan enemy, elusively fleeing just beyond his grasp.

Hektor took up the challenge, despite the pleas of his parents, and came out to meet Achilleus, one on one. And Achilleus killed him: the dying Hektor had one final glimpse of his beloved Apollo as the Trojan god departed him.

Achilleus then dragged the corpse around the city, binding its ankles together and mutilating it within sight of the grieving Hekabe, who watched from the battlements of the citadel.

Achilleus lodged the corpse of Hektor unburied in his tent (although Apollo protected it from corruption), and arranged for the burial of the dead Patroklos: offering on the pyre twelve Trojans as human victims. But nothing could assuage his grief: neither the mutilating of his enemy, nor the honors given to his dead friend.

In the night, Priam went out to the tent, to ransom back his son's body for burial. And Achilleus and the father of the hero he had killed were reconciled. The *Iliad* ends with the funeral of Hektor.

The Contests with Troy's Allies

Other tellers of the story record that on the twelfth day, at the completion of Hektor's funeral, there was an uprising of Amazons who came to the defense of their ally, Troy; but Achilleus put them down, too, engaging their Queen **Penthesileia** (who like himself was named as 'Grief') in a duel; and when he stripped the armor from her corpse, he was said to have wept as he saw the beauty he had killed (**paradigms #1&2**). **Thersites**, who (despite his name as the 'Bold') was the ugliest and most deformed of the Greeks at the War, a dwarfish 'digital' miscreant, and the most hateful and hated—especially to Odysseus and Achilleus,—mocked his grief; and was repaid by a fatal blow from Achilleus, which finally put an end to his despicable life (**paradigm #3**: substitute loser). Some later tellers claimed that he was a kinsman of Odysseus's 'friend' Diomedes, although the Homeric tradition left him without any kindred, in this world.

And then still another ally for the defense of Troy came up to confront Achilleus: this was **Memnon**, a 'black' man from the Ethiopian Deathlands, and a son of the Dawn goddess, **Eos** (who like Thetis had wedded a mortal, **Tithonos**, a brother of Priam: she made him immortal, but neglected to grant him eternal youth, as an immortal; so that he grew ever more old and decrepit, until all that was left of him was a chirping grasshopper). Memnon, too, like Penthesileia, was a creature of extraordinary physical beauty, and like Achilleus, protected by armor that was the fiendish workmanship of Hephaistos (**paradigm #1**).

Memnon killed Nestor's son **Antilochos**, who was a special protege of Achilleus: it was Antilochos who had told Achilleus of the death of Patroklos.

The Greeks had chosen the Greater **Aias** as the fitting hero to oppose this newcomer, but when Achilleus learned of the death of Antilochos, he rushed into battle and pushed him aside. Zeus was just then weighing the outcome of the Contest in the two pans of a scale, and Memnon's fate proved to be the heavier. Achilleus, instead of Aias, however, thus dealt the fatal blow: if Memnon had weighed in against Achilleus, the outcome this time might have been different from the Contest with Hektor. Memnon's black head was offered to the funeral pyre of Antilochos; his body was buried at Troy on the shore of the Sea of Marmara, and his Ethiopian troops were changed into birds (as was he also) that each year migrate back to honor his tomb, which, they say, is still there to see today. And one of the two colossal black effigies at Egyptian Thebes, which was supposed to emit a sound as the Dawn struck it, was a statue of Apollo-Memnon.

The Contest with Aias

This Aias, the so-called Greater, was by most accounts the greatest hero at Troy after Achilleus. And it was he who should have inherited the armor of Achilleus, after Achilleus died—as he did, shortly after the death of Memnon, fighting with Apollo Thymbraios, or Paris, at the Western Gate of the citadel. But the Greeks decided to award the armor to Odysseus, instead.

Like Patroklos, Aias, too, was a 'cousin' of Achilleus, although in this case, the Famous Father was not anonymous: Aias was the son of Peleus's own brother, **Telamon** (the 'Bearer' or 'Endurer'), although like the shady background of Patroklos, Telamon's 'endurance' suggests family ties with the darker chthonic realm: for Telamon married first a primitive Athena type (named Glauke, the 'Owl-lady' of Salamis, which is the supposedly serpent-infested island adjacent to Peleus's own island, and grandmother, Aigina), and then, as his second wife, a bovine Queen (named Periboia, of Skiron's Labyrinth Entrance on the nearby mainland coast at Megara). It was from this second marital connection with Periboia that Aias was born. He also had a bastard brother, the archer 'Marksman' **Teukros** (Latin **Teucer**), from Telamon's involvement with Priam's sister Hesione (whose abduction to Greece had been the pretext for Paris's original visit up to Sparta and the ensuing retaliatory abduction of Helen to Troy). Teukros bore the same name as the Apolline figure that some counted as the first 'king' of Troy, after whom the Trojans could also be called **Teucrians**.

And like his cousin Achilleus, Aias was 'almost' another Zeus. When Herakles visited Telamon to draft him for his own earlier expedition against Laomedon's Troy, Periboia was already then pregnant with her son Aias; and Herakles suggested the name for the child that would be born: he asked for an omen from his

Genealogical Chart: Achilleus

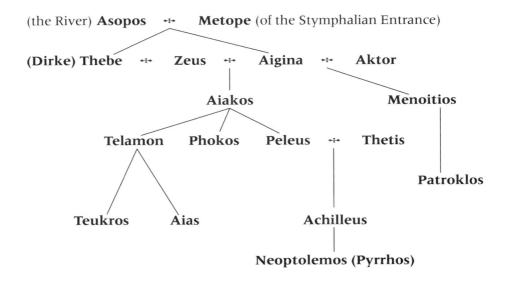

own divine father Zeus; and Zeus sent an eagle (or **aietos**) into flight, after which Olympian **totemic** bird Aias supposedly was named, although really there were **two names** for him as a **liminal** hero. Like the darker version of Herakles' own name, Aias is really mother Aia's (or mother Earth's) man. And like Achilleus, his lot was to be Grief: for **aiai** is the cry of Lamentation; he even shares with his cousin the fate of invincibility, except for a single spot: when the child was born, Herakles wrapped it in his Nemean lion skin, which touched all but his armpit, where alone he remained vulnerable.

(In addition to Telamon and Peleus, Aiakos fathered a bastard son, **Phokos**, the 'Seal': his mother, like Thetis, was another of the Nereid sisterhood, **Psamathe**, the 'Sandy Shore'; and a Seal—an aquatic mammal, like the dolphin, which is **totemic** of Apollo—was the last of her metamorphoses as she attempted to elude her involvement with Aiakos. Because of his two half-brothers' jealous animosity, Phokos emigrated with some colonists from Aigina to the so-called Phocian lands in the regions around Apollo's Delphi, although the place was supposedly named not for him, but his namesake, the Phokos who cured the Theban Antiope of the madness that Dirke had inflicted her with; and he took her to wife, and was buried with her in a common grave. But just as the Pelopids, Atreus and Thyestes, with their half-brother Chrysippos, had done, the Aeacid brothers Telamon and Peleus also plotted to 'accidentally' murder Phokos in an athletic Contest—to preserve their right of patrilineal inheritance. Aiakos, however, discovered the corpse and drove Telamon into exile at Salamis, allowing him to plead his case, unsuccessfully, only from a boat offshore, without setting foot ever again on Aigina; and Peleus was driven out to Thessaly.

Phokos was buried, near his father, on Aigina.)

Now, although Achilleus was the particular favorite of the new Athena (as his **anima**) at Troy, Aias was just the opposite. He shares with his Lesser namesake, the Locrian Aias (who was termed the son of **Oileus**), the special implacable animosity of her older Palladian manifestation; and both were similarly recipients of Odysseus's 'friendly' hatred.

When the Greeks at Troy awarded the dead Achilleus' armor to Odysseus instead of Aias, the latter tried to retaliate by doing what Apollo had not yet managed to accomplish in the War: namely, to slaughter the entire alliance of heroes that had come down against the citadel: but Athena drove him mad, so that he mistook her for his 'friendly' helper, instead of his 'enemy.' This madness, that reversed his vision, was something he 'harvested' as an **entheogen**: the plant called horse-mad, which is also called Dirke or the drug Datura, associated with the old

Suicide of Aias (Black-figure amphora by Exekias c. 540 BC, Musée Bologne-sur-Mer)

Apollo. And thinking, like Herakles in his wolfsbane madness, that he was doing one thing, he was actually doing another: he thought he was slaughtering Greeks, but Athena had substituted the newer form of victim; and he was slaughtering only cattle instead. Athena had used him as a pawn, to redeem her brother Apollo from his pre-Olympian ways, so that Aias was the loser, and not the winner: the 'lamented' 'earthling,' and not the eagle's inheritor.

When he came out of his madness (if he ever did: for it remained unclear even then whether he did what he actually intended), he slaughtered himself, impaling himself on the sword that was a gift of 'friendship' that he had received from his Trojan 'enemy' Hektor. In such offerings of sacrifice, it was always the Knife that was deemed guilty of the murder, even when it was just an animal that was the victim, thus exonerating the Slaughterer from blame.

And then came the reconciliation (**paradigm #2**). His concubine **Tekmessa** (who is named as the fateful 'Ordainer,' like the Arachne-Athena) and his Trojan half-brother, the archer Teukros, arranged for his burial, with the 'help' of Hermes' hated descendant Odysseus, who although he now wore Achilleus' armor and had Athena as his 'friend,' realized that the fall of Aias could have just as easily been reserved for him. Instead of Achilleus' armor for protection, Aias is covered first by a veil spun by the Spinstress Tekmessa; then by the bastard son he had by her (a mother's child, and not the father's), **Eurysakes** or 'Broad-shield,' who was named for the armor of his dead father; and finally by Teukros, who used to share his brother's shield when they entered battle together (**paradigm #1**). Now Odysseus (**paradigm #3**) joined with him to convince the hateful Atreid brothers that the man who intended to slaughter them should be allowed a decent covering of earth; as for Aias, he took his unflinching hatred with him into the netherworld, and never relented, not even when Odysseus visited him there. Nor did Telamon ever forgive Teukros for returning home without his brother, but drove him into exile in the Deathlands.

The Contest with Philoktetes

Odysseus also 'helped' in reconciling the hateful **Philoktetes**, whose archery was essential if Troy was ever to fall to the Greeks. This Philoktetes, as you have seen, had inherited the bow and poisoned arrows of Herakles, and he was named as the man who 'Loved his Property,' although possessing it caused him more suffering than joy: for until he was brought to the War, he was intoxicated by the very toxins of his own archery. Troy offered him the opportunity to shoot an 'enemy' and rid himself of his madness.

Philoktetes is a shadowy figure, another stand-in for the old Apollo. He is reckoned as the son of **Poias**, a Thessalian herdsman who is named as the 'Herbman' for the plants his herds graze upon; and supposedly another Poias had a **Thaumakos**, or 'Wonder-worker' for father and was counted one of the Argonauts.

Although a member of the original expedition to Troy, Philoktetes didn't arrive together with the others, but had spent the first ten years of the War in the Labyrinth cave of Apollo's offshore island of Lemnos, adjacent to the now no longer existent Chryse. After descending through Aulis for the journey to Troy, the Greek forces resurfaced into the Deathlands first through Chryse, at another sacred Entrance of Artemis, who was here called the 'Golden.' And there, the goddess's serpent had bitten Philoktetes on his foot, **maiming** him with the old **entheogen**, that poisoned his body, so that it festered and rotted with a noisome other-worldly stench that made him a repulsive companion for the other heroes, and that subjected him to recurrent fits of madness and unconscious trances, making him an unsuitable partner in their otherwise civilized drinking and conviviality. As a result, they had abandoned him on Lemnos, where he had spent the duration of the War living as a primitive man in the cave, and having as food only the birds he managed to shoot with his arrows, food which inevitably merely recycled the poisons of the primordial world (that Herakles once had tamed and aimed against the former gods) back into his own body.

Although Philoktetes represents the Apollo of the old religion, he had a cousin who was the just opposite. This was the **Protesilaos** that the Apolline herdsman Euphorbos killed, as the first Greek to come ashore at Troy. His father **Iphiklos**— a name like Herakles' twin Iphikles—had been able to beget this (patrilineal) son of his, as we have mentioned, only after he was cured of his impotence by drinking a potion of 'rust' from a knife embedded in the sacred oak tree, where it had lain ever since he as a boy had fearfully mistaken what his own father (another Apolline herder, named **Phylakos**, the 'Jailor Guardian') intended to do with it: Iphiklos had thought that Phylakos was going to sacrifice him, instead of one of the animals in his herd. The man who devised this new **entheogen** to cure the old ways of religion was the 'Black-foot' **Melampous**, the same figure that we have already met as the brother of the Argive Bias and the man who cured the Proitid sisterhood of their bovine delusions at Tiryns. It was later claimed that Protesilaos even initiated the ancient founders of Troy into the new religion, but that must have occurred as the final outcome of the War.

Throughout the War, the abandoned Philoktetes had directed his hatred toward his fellow Greeks, lurking on the island from which the Trojan Apollo shoots his deadly plague of arrows. And only in the tenth year did the alliance of Greeks learn that this War that had begun with the offering of Protesilaos (and the defeat of the new ways) would never end, unless the polluted other, his cousin, was appeased and reconciled into the coalition of forces, led by the 'New War' Neoptolemos, who had to be summoned as well, from his own Apolline island of Lykomedes' Skyros (**paradigm #2**).

Some claimed that it was Odysseus's friendly enemy Diomedes (**paradigm #3**) who was paired with him for the embassy to Lemnos; others, that it was Neoptolemos, and that he was almost swayed by Odysseus's thieving trickery into dishonestly stealing the bow, without its Archer, until Herakles himself appeared to rectify the error: both the bow and the Archer had to be brought to Troy—and for a second time, Troy would fall to Herakles. And even the two ways of heroism, the tragic and the tricks of comedy, had to be reconciled. Odysseus shared Achilleus' armor with Neoptolemos, and finally, in that guise, the New War shot the Old, poisoning Paris in his heel, while Philoktetes was at last relieved of the toxins festering in his own foot, by the surgery of the 'Knifeman' **Machaon**, a disciple of the new Apolline discipline of the medical arts devised by Apollo's own mortal son **Asklepios.**

The Homecoming of Odysseus

The return from Troy was never easy for the heroes, since like Herakles' confusing return up from Hades to Thebes and his wife Megara, the world they had left behind tended to relapse back into its old ways in their absence. As a theme, the 'homecoming' in Greek is called the **nostos**, which really means the 'awakening' or the return to the mind of conscious perceptions (**nous**). They all had journeyed into the sacred realm of dreams, and nothing would have been accomplished unless it, too, was reconciled with wakening. Of all the Homecom-

Penelope, with Telemachos, at her Loom (Red-figure vase from Chiusi mid-5th century BC, Clusium)

ings, the most famous was that of Odysseus, which lasted ten years and took him on a whole tour of the Deathlands, before he finally woke up miraculously back in Ithaka. It was the subject of the *Odyssey*, the other epic poem still extant from the Homeric tradition of storytelling.

After the Greeks set sail from Troy on the Wind they had seduced by the offering of Hekabe's maiden daughter Polyxena as a victim to the tomb of Achilleus, a violent storm dispersed the fleet and scattered the heroes throughout the Labyrinth to find their separate wandering pathways home. Odysseus's Tour took the longest, although most of the time was spent with the subterranean goddess **Kalypso** (Latin **Calypso**), the 'Lady who Hides,' on her island of Ogygia, which was located at the 'navel' or omphalos of the sea, apparently somewhere in the aquatic substructure directly beneath the Entrance of Dirke's spring at Thebes, down beneath Mount Parnassos, and the chthonic counterpart to the omphalos that marks the resettlement of the new Apollo above it at the sanctuary of Delphi. (One of the seven Gates of the Theban city bore this name, the Ogygian Gate, after its primordial 'king,' in whose reign the city had sunk beneath the waters of the Great Flood that destroyed the ways of former times.) Odysseus had ended up there shipwrecked and alone, after the loss of his entire crew, who had incurred the Sun's wrath by rustling cattle from the nocturnal herd he tended in his netherworld flock. With Kalypso, Odysseus dallied, seduced by her with promises of immortality, to remain down there as the man in her Queendom.

Meanwhile, his native island of Ithaka was in danger of reverting to the same old ways; for in his absence, his wife Penelope was being courted by many suitors, each vying to gain the kingdom through his marriage to the Queen. Like the other wives of heroes, Penelope could easily have played the role of such a Queen, reversing the transmutation that had suited her for the Olympian era. By name, she was a 'bird-lady,' like Athena, but not the owl Glaukopis: Penelope was an aquatic fowl, the duck or *penelops*. (Her name had formerly been Arnaia, a 'Goat-girl' like Pallas, but her father Ikarios renamed her after he ordered her tossed into the sea to die, but a flock of ducks had nursed and rescued her. The discredited Arnaia ended up being the name of the detested male Arnaios, who was a beggar in the house of Odysseus and who served the interests of the suitors.) Penelope was also notorious as a Spinstress: it was even possible to discern the 'pene' of the 'spun web' in her name. And her weaving could have sinister consequences, but for the transmutation: for from the very beginning of her relationship with Odysseus, the concealing web that she (like Kalypso, or Tekmessa) might spin was done in the service of her husband. When Ikarios refused to let her leave Sparta to live in the patriarchy of Odysseus, she had concealed her face with a veil, and her father had relented. Now in Ithaka, she had devised a ruse to put off the suitors, telling them that she could choose one of them only after she had finished weaving a shroud to hide the corpse of Odysseus's mortal father Laertes: presumably, he would die once she did; but each night she unwove what she had woven, and thus postponed her decision. Meanwhile, she had a son Telemachos, who was named for the final battle of the distant War, but who did not know his father.

With the two homes of the hero thus stalled in balance, the Olympians had to provide an impetus. Athena urged Zeus to take advantage of Poseidon's temporary absence amongst his 'black' people in the African Deathlands of Ethiopia, and he sent Hermes (as **animus**) down to Ogygia to release Odysseus from Kalypso, and Athena (as **anima**) to Ithaka to prod Telemachos to learn more about his father. She disguised herself as **Mentor**, his mentor or 'mind-man,' and advised him to go down through the Gate of Pylos to look for Odysseus. In this way, father and son simultaneously journey toward each other, down and up, a journey that will culminate at last back in Ithaka when Odysseus wakes up, and after meeting his son and wife, finally like someone resurrected from the dead, goes out to find his own aged father Laertes, still living, in the orchard/vineyard he had planted for his young son. Instead of the immortality offered by Kalypso, Odysseus's heroism poses no threat to the gods, but moves instead toward the reunion of mortal sons and fathers, like the tragic version of Herakles' liminal identities, with his father Amphitryon.

Through Pylos, where Telemachos was 'hospitably' entertained by the good 'king' Nestor (who was back from the War and still living, although it was a full generation ago that Herakles had put him in charge of that resettled Entrance), he traveled on to his maternal homeland of Sparta, with the companion and guide (**animus**) he had acquired: Nestor's son **Peisistratos**, the 'Persuader for the Expedition;' and there Telemachos learned of the other homecomings and was entertained by Menelaos and Helen, whose 'hospitality' included the wine she laced with her special 'African' opiate called **nepenthe**, which is an **entheogen** that makes one forget all suffering. There Telemachos pleasurably dallied, until Athena at last came to prod him again to start back Home. And again, as he passed through Pylos and dropped off Peisistratos, he just barely managed to evade the garrulous old Nestor's grasping 'hospitality.'

Meanwhile, Odysseus, too, was dallying in a pleasurable place, another netherworld paradise that could never be his Home, if he was ever to resurface in Itha-ka and successfully rectify his tottering patriarchy. Once again, he was ship-wrecked, this time with the beguiling maiden of the 'Ship Afire,' **Nausikaa** (Latin **Nausicaa**), on her magical island of **Scheria**, the same place where Ia-son and Medeia had put in on their own homeward Tour of the Deathlands.

For after parting from Kalypso and setting sail from her Ogygia on a makeshift raft, Odysseus had encountered rough seas again and his old archenemy Posei-don, who was returning from the Burnt Lands of Ethiopia. Poseidon had singled out Odysseus for his particular hatred ever since the **Contest with Polyphe-mos**. This had been the third episode on his Tour, near the very beginning of the homecoming, when he still had a crew.

Although nominally a son of Poseidon, Polyphemos is really a stand-in for the old Apollo. And if it were not for Odysseus's new relationship to Apollo, he and his crew would never have survived the ordeal; but the hero, as the first episode of his Tour, had befriended the hostile Trojan god, and had even been entrust-ed with his new **entheogen,** a drug that was to prove essential in saving him from Polyphemos. (Odysseus is unique as the only hero who can count on Apol-lo for help as **animus**, for his heroism does not endanger the superiority of the other. Oidipous's alliance with Apollo is similar, but Oidipous was deluded, and the ultimate outcome was not what he intended. Odysseus's homecoming was the final solution, rendering the continuance of the age of heroism irrelevant.)

This is how Apollo, the former 'enemy' became Odysseus's secret sponsor (**paradigm #3**). At the end of the War as they fought their way through, back up out of Troy, Odysseus and his men had attacked the Thracian tribe of **Kikones**, a people notorious for their worship of the old Dionysos (who, as often, gets blamed for his Olympian brother's misconduct); but Odysseus had respected and spared their priest of Apollo and his family: **Maron**, the '**Smar**t,' who was the son of 'Flowering' **Euanthes**, and who had even instructed Bakchos-Dionysos in the old days of Nysa, before the invention of wine, about a plant that would later become Centaury, the centaur Cheiron's herb (which was also known as Maron's plant), after its transmutation to later times. In gratitude, Maron had re-paid Odysseus with a goatskin of a secret wine laced with the old herb (that Centaury, and the Trojan Savory, symbolically replaced), a wine so potent that even twenty-fold dilution with water barely tamed its power.

This gift Odysseus had ready for his Contest with Polyphemos, to use, as the heroes always did, as his weapon to turn the toxin of the old world back upon itself. And since Polyphemos was nominally Poseidon's son, Apollo wasn't really involved.

But Polyphemos was a herdsman, which Poseidon wasn't; and his name has Apolline connotations as well. Polyphemos is the 'Famous' or the 'Fame-grantor,' and more the latter than the former: for he is really a Nonentity, except for the Fame he acquired by contesting the Famed Odysseus, whose story is perpetu-ated by the myth-telling that Apollo and his sisterhood of Muses inspires, in their newer Olympian function. Meanwhile, back in Ithaka, there was just such an Apolline lyre-playing myth-teller named **Phemios**, the 'Famed Fame-grantor,' who was being forced to amuse the suitors with his stories. Upon his return, Odysseus almost murders Phemios, but at the last moment relents and is reconciled with him (**paradigm #2**).

Polyphemos was a perfect exemplar of everything that is primitive, chthonic, and representative of the former, pre-Olympian world. He was a primordial giant and a **Kyklops** (Latin **Cyclops**), a member of that whole brotherhood of Kyklopes who serve Hephaistos in his devilish mechanical wizardry in the subterranean volcanic forge, and whose single-eye (which is supposedly the meaning of their name) has connotations of different or altered (in)sight, like the eye of the Graiai sisterhood of witches. They were all lawless primitive men, living in caves,

The Blinding of Polyphemos (Black-figure amphora 520 BC, Museo di Villa Giulia, Rome)

as isolated families, with no common government or society (neither matriarchal nor partriarchal—but the zero-point of culture), and devoid of all the arts of civilization and agriculture; but instead, plants grew naturally, by themselves, and even the grapes of the vineyard required no fermentation to yield what passed, amongst them, for a natural wine, like the wild growths of Nysa. Nor do they cook their food, or know the correct manners for table and animal sacrifice.

The first landfall of Odysseus and his crew amongst the Kyklopes had been on a nearby island, just opposite the harbor of their island, a totally wild, natural, and deserted place, but rich, as the enterprising Odysseus notes, with every advantage for development, if the Kyklopes had not been so backward; and on the next day, Odysseus and a contingent of his men crossed over to explore.

Leaving all but twelve on the shore by the ship, Odysseus led the way inland, up to the cave of Polyphemos: he was absent with his flocks at the time, although his cave had other animals in their pens, and abundant milk and cheese. They helped themselves to dinner and awaited the return of their host, who did not notice his guests hiding in the Labyrinthine recesses of the cave, until he had prepared his own evening meal, blocking their escape, as was his custom, with a huge rock as a door to close off the mouth of the cave. Odysseus introduced himself and his companions, and boasted of their 'fame,' but he lyingly told

Odysseus Escaping from the Cave Disguised as a Ram
(Black figure lekythos 6th century BC, Staatliche
Antikensammlungen und Glyptothek, Munich)

Polyphemos that his name was No-body. Polyphemos, however, despised the ways of the new Zeus and of civilized hospitality; instead he was a cannibal (like the Werewolf creatures of pre-Olympian times) and he proposed to eat them, two by two, slaughtering them as victims, instead of his beasts (as in the newer form of sacrificial meal), and devouring them raw, followed by a monstrous draught of milk.

Odysseus devised the ruse, the trick of Nature, that saved him and the men who survived the first meal. He introduced Polyphemos to Maron's wine, which induced a drunken stupor; and they took advantage of the opportunity to blind the Kyklops by ramming a burning log into his single eye, thus changing his sight to the blindness characteristic of Apolline inspired insight. When Polyphemos summoned help from his fellow tribesmen, they gathered at the locked entrance to his cave, but then dispersed, satisfied that nothing was amiss, since Polyphemos shouted that Nobody was harming him.

This zero-point of culture is a **limen**, a threshold between the hero's two identities: as he passes from one to the other, there is a moment when he is No-body (neither Famed nor Fame-granting), a stage that is typically encountered in rites of passage. Nor is he human, rather than beast. A second ruse tricked Polyphemos into letting them escape, for they were trapped in the Cave by the rock across its Entrance-Gate. The men disguised themselves as sheep in the herdsman's herd by tying themselves beneath their bellies, and when the blind Polyphemos groped at their upper sides as he let them out to pasture, he mistook the **liminal** men for animals.

When they were out of reach, Odysseus called back his true name and Fame; and then the ram that had saved him, he slaughtered to Olympian Zeus, as a proper sacrificial meal. And Polyphemos at last gained insight: he had been told that an Odysseus would put out his sight, but he been on the lookout for somebody of importance, and had never suspected it would be a Nobody like this enemy; but he called upon his father Poseidon to avenge him, foretelling the difficult homecoming that he wished upon Odysseus.

(You will recall that Apollo himself killed the Kyklopes, in retaliation for their role in the death of his son Asklepios, and had then been forced to expiate the murder by his period in the Bondage of Death, serving as herdsman for 'king' Admetos of the Pherai 'Undertaker' sisterhood in Thessaly.)

(As for Polyphemos, he never did manage to become somebody of importance, except for his Contest with Odysseus. It was later told how he tried to impress the 'Milk White' maiden **Galateia** with his fame, but she rejected him as a monster, preferring the beauty of his rival **Akis**. 'Milk White' is also known as the idealized love of the sculptor **Pygmalion**, one of the 'digital' 'Fist-men,' like the dwarfish pygmies of black Ethiopia.)

As Poseidon journeyed back up toward Olympus from his Ethiopian visit, he caught sight of Odysseus from the Trojan lands coming up from Kalypso's Ogygia, and overtook him just as he was within sight of Nausikaa's Scheria; and he roused a storm that again left Odysseus shipwrecked. And the hero would have perished, but for the help (**anima**) of Hera: the 'black' Ino appeared to him as the 'White Goddess' **Leukothea** and gave him a veil, and on this cloth of fine Spinning he was sustained until he could make landfall on the island, where he swam upriver, where seawater turns fresh, as counseled by Athena (**anima**), and crept ashore, naked, to fall into a sleep, poured like an opiate by her, in the protection of a thicket of her olive (**entheogen**), the one wild, the other the cultivated (**limen, axis mundi**): his life reduced to a single ember of fire, awaiting the day to be rekindled into Flame, to awake with the arrival of the 'burning' Nausikaa and her sisterhood, and their load of spun clothes (for the women of the island were noted for their Spinning), but these linens were soiled and in need of washing, since the maiden was ready for marriage. Such are the metaphors, at least, that were remembered in the Homeric telling of the story, even if they were no longer understood.

Scheria lay somewhere still in the Labyrinth, in the aquifer just beneath the surface, accessible through the Cave of the watery sisterhood, where Odysseus would eventually rise into consciousness, next to an olive tree, to Reenter back up home in Ithaka. But Scheria was a beguiling false Awakening: he would not be truly Home until he climbed into the bed he had fashioned for himself and Penelope, with one leg of it still rooted and immovable in the fundament of his house, made from an olive tree rising, as it had grown, right through the center and into their bed chamber on its second floor, where he had cut and pruned it for this purpose: the secret knowledge of this bed, where he can eventually fall safely back to sleep, will be Penelope's final proof that her returned husband is who he appears to be, and not just a hallucination. For Scheria is the land of the 'Best' Queen, named **Arete**, with her 'king' **Alkinoos**, the lord of 'Strong Conscious Perception' or **nous**, both of them too optimistic as names not to mask their opposites. (All the while up in Ithaka, the 'Opposite Perception' or unconscious **nous** called **Antinoos**, the son of the 'Persuasive' **Eupeithes**, is the chief of the suitors for Penelope.) The island itself has a name that is not Greek, although someone remembered that it meant the 'Shore.' It was also called Drepane or the 'Pruning Hook' (which is the 'Knife' wielded as the implement to mediate between the wild, natural growths of olden times, and the cultivated evolutions that would replace them in the newer era). Its inhabitants, too, were probably not Greek, but took their name after their founder **Phaiax** and were called Phaeacians (which could be interpreted as the 'Shining,' but probably in its netherworld phase, glimmering up from the depths: for he was otherwise remembered as the inventor of the sewer, whose labyrinthine subterranean pathways could be similarly called Phaeacians). Later explorers who mistakenly

Awakening of Odysseus on Scheria: Athena
Introduces the Hero to Nausikaa (Red-figure vase 5th
century BC, Staatliche Antikensammlungen und
Glyptothek, Munich)

looked for Scheria on the topographical surface tended to identify
it with the island of Kerkyra (Cor-
cyra, Corfu), conveniently nearby,
just to the north of Ithaka, because
Phaiax was reckoned a son of Poseidon, from his affair with Korkyra, but
that must have been in the days before she rose up (blossoming like a
new flower into this world, as often
happened with the islands, after their
love affairs in the dark, watery
depths).

Odysseus woke to the sounds of
Nausikaa, playing like an Artemis
with her sisterhood of maidens, as
the washed clothing dried by the
riverbank; and covering his naked-
ness with branches plucked from the
thicket of olives, he made his presence known to the princess: she re-
minds him, as he tells her, of the
young palm he had seen once on Delos, sprouting beside the very altar of
Apollo, the tree that was called Phoenician and was sacred to the Goddess, and
to Leto, as mother of the twins; he had gone there with a troop of companions,
apparently to dance the dangerous Crane Dance of the Labyrinth. She offered
him clothing (of which fortuitously—and because of Athena's helpful intervention—she had quite a bit, her own and her family's, all washed in anticipation of her immanent wedding); Nausikaa and the maidens—so unlike the
ordinary Artemis at her bath—then cleansed his body; and finally she discretely arranges to introduce him, as a 'stranger,' to the parents she hopes will become
his in-laws. Although he is a Nobody to them, they entertain him hospitably, even
offering him their daughter for wife, should he wish to stay; but they do accept
that he must go Home, and promise him the aid of their own renowned ships
and crew. Still Nameless to them (these kindly hosts who are actually kinsmen
of Polyphemos, although the Kyklopes are their traditional enemy), Odysseus
is further entertained by a telling of his own Fame at Troy: the insightful, but blind
Phaeacian bard, **Demodokos** of 'local renown,' by chance, has chosen to tell
of an episode, the quarrel between Odysseus and Achilleus, that the Delphic
Apollo had predicted would mark the turning point in the War; and then as the
'hospitality' turns to sporting, the guest is challenged to a Contest, which he ac-
complishes with unsuspected skill. Heaped with gifts and ready for departure,
he takes his leave of his Phaeacian hosts, but one final telling of his Fame at

Troy moves him to tears—the Ruse of the Trojan Horse; and he reveals at last who he is: Odysseus, and he himself now, instead of the bard, narrates the rest of his own story, the famed events of his Deathlands Tour. It is a narration (to Nausikaa, before Awakening) that he will recapitulate, in abbreviated form, once more back in Ithaka, just as he falls asleep with his true wife Penelope in their bed, rooted to the trunk of the old, pruned tree of olive.

After the episode with Maron and the Thracian Kikones (where the drunken crew had dallied dangerously too long), Odysseus and his sailors had been driven off course, down to Africa and the land of the **Lotophagoi** or 'Lotos-Eaters,' who also kindly entertain their foreign visitors with an opiate, the sweet fruit of the Lotos Tree (supposedly the stinging nettle tree): everyone who tastes of it loses all desire ever to return Home. (Later tellers thought the tree grew somewhere on the banks of the waters in the underworld; and some knew that it had once, like Daphne, been a maiden who changed into the Tree to avoid an amorous involvement. Before its transplanting up into this world and the newer era, the Lotos was probably still Apollo's old Datura or thorn apple, so named because of its fruit encased in nettles, like the nettle tree.) Odysseus himself refrained from tasting the fruit, and forcibly removed those who had become addicted back to the ships in chains.

After the **Contest with Polyphemos**, the crew sailed on to the floating island of **Aiolos** (Latin **Aeolus**), the 'Shifting' lord of the Winds; there they were again hospitably entertained for an entire month, while Odysseus himself told the story of the Famed events at Troy and of the homeward returns of the heroes. His host rewarded him with the windy spirits for his own return, all the Winds confined in a sack tied with a silver cord, except for the gentle West Wind, which would waft him peacefully back up to Ithaka, reanimated; but when they were already within sight of home, Odysseus fell asleep, and his men, jealous of what they imagined the sack contained, released the other spirits, causing a storm that drove them back to the island of Aiolos, who this time refused to 'help' them further.

The next landfall was amongst the **Laistrygones**, where time seems to cease: for it is the zero-point in the Sun's netherworld passage, the nadir of its descent, like the zenith of noon here above, and evening there borders on dawn, with no intervening night; an enterprising man amongst them could earn a double wage. Odysseus sent scouts ashore. They met the princess drawing water from a spring, and she directed them to the palace. Within was a gigantic mountain of a female, with a monstrous appetite for human flesh. (She was later named as the Bogey-woman Lamia.) Her 'king' **Antiphates** was nothing but her 'Spokesman.' He immediately ate one of the men, raw. Two others escaped back to the ships, but the Laistrygones rushed to the cliffs above the shore, throwing down rocks and fishing in men to eat. Odysseus was left with only a single ship after the ordeal.

He came ashore next in **Aiaia**, an island of 'Lamentation,' where the witch **Kirke** (Latin **Circe**) was Queen: she was a sister of Medeia's father Aietes, and

An 'African' Kirke Presents her Black Magic Potion to a 'Dwarfish' and 'Digital' Odysseus (Black-figure Kabeiroi vase, British Museum, London)

of Pasiphae, who was wife of Minos, the lord of the Cretan Labyrinth: all three of them, children of the Sun, from his subterranean dalliance with the Lady **Perse**. Odysseus divided his crew into two groups, placing himself in charge of one, and **Eurylochos** of the other. By lot, it fell to the latter to investigate the island. With both groups in tears, in this land of Lamentation, they parted.

The woods surrounding Kirke's palace were haunted by wolves and lions that the sorceress had charmed with evil drugs to walk upright like men, and to fawn upon her visitors like dogs. She herself was inside, a Spinstress tending her loom, and singing. She offered them hospitality, all but Eurylochos, who remained outside, suspecting a trap or 'Ambush,' which is the meaning of his name; but the others she gave a potion, in which she had mixed her evil herbs, to make them forget their Home. They turned into swinemen, the lascivious animals that belong to the Goddess as her mate, and she confined them in her sty.

Eurylochos managed to report back what had happened; and Odysseus, alone, now went inland. Just before he reached the palace, Hermes appeared and 'helped' him, pointing out the **entheogen** that would counteract the poisons of Kirke's potion, the plant called **molu** (or moly), a root that is black, with a flower white like milk. Moly is what the Olympians call it: later speculation as to what it actually was ranged from the innocuous (although apotropaic) garlic to the hypnotic nightshade, with its poison strychnine, or the hallucinatory Peganum harmala. (What is significant is that moly belongs to the Greek linguistic tradition, rather than the pre-Greek: it signifies merely drug-plant, and it is related to words that mean 'alleviate' and is cognate with 'mollify' in English; moly is the antidote in the new era to Kirke's black magic. Its black root, which is difficult to pull, and its white flower make it a good mediator between the two realms.)

Nor was it the old herm-like Hermes who helped Odysseus, but Hermes disguised as a young boy, pubescent, actually; and with Odysseus's own mature passionate nature mollified by the moly (for such is also the effect of this 'softening' and emasculating antidote), he was able to withstand Kirke's charms—and safely acquiesce to her bed, as Hermes had advised (**paradigm #3**)!

In this way, a less than ardent Odysseus won the affection of the hospitable Kirke, without succumbing totally to her porcine eroticism; and she even transformed her swine back into men by the use of the antidote, that acted as a counter-charm: they all ended up spending a full year there, safely mollified, in an orgy with the goddess and her sisterhood; and Odysseus had at least one son by her, who mirrors Penelope's son and will one day, too, go looking for a father, although with the opposite result: for **Telegonos** or 'Final Birth' will eventually show up in Ithaka, according to some accounts, and 'accidentally' kill Odysseus—and marry Penelope.

Odysseus, however, had his common problem on Kirke's island with underlings, the second-in-command who, like Diomedes, was treated like an 'enemy.' When Odysseus had first gone back to the ship to invite the other group of his men to join the former swine-men in the orgy, their tears of Lamentation had turned to joy, as if they had actually managed to come Home in Ithaka; but Eurylochos alone, of course, still suspected an Ambush, and held back, pleading with them not to go. Odysseus 'almost' killed him out of irrational rage; but they left him behind at the ship—although he followed along, after them, anyway.

When they did finally leave Aiaia, this paradisiacal Island of Lamentation, with Kirke's blessing, they again left someone behind, and were required to return one last time: for one could not depart in joy, without the Lamentation of a proper funeral. This time it was **Elpenor**, the 'Optimistic' counterpoise to Eurylochos's suspicious nature. He got drunk just a few days before departure and fell to his death from the roof of Kirke's house; but in the commotion of departure, no one noticed his absence. The next stop on the Tour was straight on down to Persephone's House—as instructed by Kirke, and just riding with the Wind; and there Odysseus found Elpenor's ghost, still unburied: and they all had to go back up to Aiaia to perform the tearful ritual: for Odysseus could not leave Kirke's island without offering at least a token victim (this 'accidental' death) to the goddess who had so kindly mended the older ways of the slaughtering Artemis: nor was anyone responsible for Elpenor's death, neither Odysseus nor Kirke, for the Optimist, unlike Eurylochos, never even suspected an Ambush; like a cemetery, Aiaia serves as Entrance to the realms below. (Similarly, when Odysseus finally takes his leave of Nausikaa and the Phaeacians to go up to Ithaka, he is wrapped in a shroud and escorted to the ship with Lamentation; he will have definitively renounced another paradise, to die up and out of their world toward Awakening.)

In Persephone's house, Odysseus saw his own mother **Antikleia** (Latin **Anticlea**), like a dream image, as she herself explains, and a parade of the great Ladies of former times, as well as many of the dead heroes; but the purpose of the descent was for insight: to consult the Theban seer Teiresias, who advised him on his Return and foretold his death. (In the Homeric telling, he will have a gentle death, from the sea, perhaps still at the hands of Telegonos; but first he will travel so far inland that the people mistake his oar for a winnowing fan: and there he will plant it as a marker, the complement to the oar he will plant at the seaside grave of his 'companion' Elpenor on Aiaia, the shadow underling of his other self that he leaves with Kirke, in addition to the fatal son Telegonos.) In fact, from this time on, Odysseus knows where he is going; for back up in Aiaia, Kirke gives him still further advice, as he passes back through on his ascent: adding to the growing chorus of Apolline prophecies predicting his Return. The sorceress, who was his former enemy, has gone full 'Circle' (the meaning of her name, if

Greek—although it may be a version of Dirke, and her plant) and is now his in-sightful sponsor (**anima**). (The Greek etymology of her name perhaps implies the spoked 'circle' of the Datura flower: the 'horse-mad' that is responsible for the lascivious nature of the centaurs, and the eternally whirling wheel of **Ixion**, who fathered them by his affair with the Cloud he mistook for the goddess Hera; and the horse-maddened Aias, the Lamentable hero who bears the name of her island.)

It was Kirke, the singing goddess of Aiaia, who taught Odysseus the trick that would allow him to hear the enchanting singing of the spell 'Binder' **Sirens** as he passed by their island without losing his way back Home. These were a sis-terhood (usually of three) bird-maidens, who enticed him with 'knowledge' (such as he already had through the kindness of Kirke); and this he heard, and yet did not stay, but passed on by: for he had stoppered the ears of his crewmen with (bees)wax, so that they were deaf to the song, which he alone heard, tied with Bindings, at his own command, to the mast, as they rowed on by.

After them, was the dangerous narrow passage between **Charybdis** and **Skylla**: the former was a monstrous voracious woman in the form of a Whirlpool, constantly gulping down the waters and spewing them out again; the latter, a Bitch, who had once been a beautiful rival of Kirke, but the sorceress had dis-figured all but her head with her poisonous herbs. To avoid Charybdis, Odysseus sailed too close to Skylla, and lost six men to her gluttonous appetite. (There was an alternate route, through the Symplegades, which Iason had taken with the Argonauts; but Odysseus chose the other.)

From there, they sailed up to **Thrinakia**, the 'Trident' (later identified topo-graphically as the island of Sicily, probably merely because of its coincidentally triangular shape, although its volcanic Mount Aetna was a convenient Gate-way; this identification led to the locating of Skylla and Charybdis at the straits between Sicily and mainland Italy, although the alternate route of the Symple-gades would supposedly have been through the Bosporos, hardly nearby—on the surface). Here, despite the express prohibition of Teiresias and Kirke, and the direct command of Odysseus, his crew rustled cattle from the Sun to as-suage their hunger.

This led to the great storm in which Odysseus lost the rest of his men, and passed back down, Circling again through Skylla and Charybdis, and on to Ka-lypso; from there, he passed through Scheria on his way back Home.

He Awoke in Ithaka, amidst the preparations for a festival of the archer Apol-lo: the time was the 'Wolf-walk,' when the moon is new and sheds no light, the liminal period between eras, like the similar 'Wolf-light' which marks the tran-sitional times of twilight and dawn. What follows is a progressive sequence of recognitions and testings, to sort dream from reality. First Odysseus and Telema-chos, who has just then also returned, recognize each other in the hut of the Swineherd **Eumaios**, the 'Good-birther,' as if they were born into, or from, his Sty: they plot to reverse the direction of the kingdom, which is now at a critical moment since Penelope has been forced to complete Laertes' shroud. Next his old dog **Argos** (who is named after the 'enemy' herdsman that Hermes Argeiphontes killed) instinctively recognized his master—and died, 'accidentally,' for joy. Then his old birthing wet nurse, the 'Famous' (or perhaps too famous) **Eurykleia**, recognized him by his **maimed** leg, the scar he had received years ago in the boar hunt on Apollo's Mount Parnassos, where he had gone to visit his mother's father, the 'Very-wolf' Autolykos, and to claim his promised inheritance: to be the 'hated' other—to Apollo, who is now his 'friend.'

As on Scheria amongst the Phaiakians, here, too, Odysseus will be nameless, without Fame, mocked and reviled, a guest of his hosts, until the Contest, this time with the suitors. Penelope has declared she will marry whoever can string the bow of Odysseus. (This is the famous bow that **Iphitos**, whom Herakles later killed, had given Odysseus, when the two met, each looking for their rustled herds.) None but he could even string it: Odysseus shot its poisoned arrow straight on through the empty sockets of twelve double-edged axe blades— dead center, safely through the whole gauntlet of sacrificial Knives (such as would once have served for the Slaughterer), to complete a full year's worth of new moons, the Wolf-walk, and usher in the Olympian era. His Return vindicates the validity of the new Delphic Apollo's prophetic voice. And then Odysseus took upon himself, with good effect, the task of the hated Wolf, and directed the toxin upon the suitors, slaughtering these enemies who were his rivals at Apollo's Feast, sending them chattering as ghosts down to the House from which he had risen.

But even then, Penelope cautiously required one final test—which was the Ruse of the Bed, as they fell asleep. Still ahead the next day was his meeting with his mortal father Laertes; and finally, one last War with the kinsmen of the suitors: to impose his restored kingship upon his people, who had fallen into older ways.

The Homecoming of Menelaos

The homeward Tour of Menelaos took him down through the Labyrinth at Crete, where he was shipwrecked; and on to Cyprus, Phoenicia, Egypt, and Libya; but it is only what happened in Egypt that is remembered. There he was stalled on the offshore island of Pharos, at one of the mouths of the Nile delta, unable to rouse a wind to carry him further away from Egypt, until he chanced upon the 'help' of a **turncoat** maiden, **Eidothea** or 'Godly Vision.' She was the daughter of the 'First-in-Command' **Proteus**, who was the herdsman in charge of the 'African' Poseidon's pod of seals, the so-called Old Man of the Sea, with a stench as rank as the animals he tended; he was also 'king' of the Egyptian lands—and a prophet. Eidothea instructed Menelaos how to get the old man to give him advice for his return; for Proteus was a repulsive and slippery creature, shifting shape as you tried to interrogate him—protean, as the English word is, in his repertory of hallucinatory appearances. Menelaos and three of his men had to disguise themselves in the repugnant sealskins she provided (although she kindly deadened their sense of smell with ambrosia); and then they were to masquerade as animals in his herd (like Odysseus with Polyphemos), until the unsuspecting Old Man came and slept amongst them. Then Menelaos had to grab him, as he lay dreaming, and wrestle with him (like Peleus with Thetis), holding on through the whole repertory of metamorphoses, until he at last would acquiesce, returning to the human shape he had assumed when he first fell asleep. Then, when he was constrained to stay in the same reality, he would answer whatever question you put to him. Menelaos learned that he could not get Home until he circled back to Egypt, supposedly to appease the hostile gods with (animal) sacrifice. (The Homeric tradition is squeamish about the ways of the older gods, and tends to gloss over their more nasty habits.)

Other tellers of the tale, however, knew that, like Odysseus's circle back to Ogygia, Menelaos would be required to offer a token burial of himself in the Deathlands, before he would be allowed to surface. For the Helen that he had with him on his ship was not the real Helen, but only a godly vision, a ghostly impostor (or **eidolon**) who had unfairly and deceptively impersonated his profligate and faithless wife at Troy. All the while, the real Helen (the daughter of Zeus, not the other one who was her **liminal** complement) had abided, chaste and loving, in Egypt.

By this telling, Proteus had been Helen's trusted protector; but upon his death, his son had assumed command, the 'Godly-spoken' **Theoklymenos**; and unlike his good father, he intended to mate with his beautiful foreign guest. (The Homeric tellers knew the protean Egyptian host who was first-in-command as **Thon**, whose Queen was probably really in charge: **Polydamna**, the powerful 'Mistress' who subdues all; it is from her that Helen learned all about drugs.) This Theoklymenos (who is otherwise known, both at Pylos and on Ithaka, as an 'African' prophet, the son of the 'black-foot' Melampous) has a sister in Egypt who is prophetic. She used to be called **Eido** or 'Appearance,' but when she reached puberty, like an Artemis look-alike, her name was changed to **Theonoe** or 'Godly Perception.'

And indeed, Egypt is a confusing place of shifting appearances. Just before Menelaos circled back, Teukros had passed through, on his way to found a sister city of the Salamis back home, from which his father had exiled him for returning from Troy without his half-brother Aias: and Helen had cautioned him that Reality isn't necessarily what you see, but what you make of it with your conscious Perception. When Menelaos gets there, shipwrecked, and becomes convinced of his error about the mistaken identity at Troy, Helen and he plot their escape: the ruse is that Menelaos is dead, and she will agree now to marry Theoklymenos, but only after she has borrowed a ship to offer her deceased husband the honor of a cenotaph at sea. The only problem is that they could never deceive the prophetic Theonoe, for she has the inspired perception to pierce through deceptive appearances; and if she sides with them, she will get in trouble with her brother.

But that is exactly what she does do. The world is at its liminal moment, with the gods equally divided. It is up to her to use her Godly Perception to choose what is right, rather than her own self-interest. She deceives her brother and allows the ruse to go forward, inaugurating a newer ethical era. Menelaos dies without dying, and escapes with Helen back up at last, after all the circling, home to Sparta. Theoklymenos is about to vent his rage upon his self-sacrificing sister, but the Dioskouroi, Helen's twin brothers (on one of their dead days, obviously), show up to save Theonoe and ratify this new, ethical way of finding truth in appearances.

The Homecoming of Agamemnon

No telling of the Homecomings was complete without at least a mention, for comparison, of what happened to Agamemnon. He, too, awoke to a world of deceptive appearances; but his wife, Klytaimnestra, the twin sister of Helen, had orchestrated the confusion to snare him in her trap. For when he came up to Mykenai, she had managed, through her sinister network of henchmen, to light his own city afire with the very flames he had lit at Troy to destroy the vanquished citadel; and then she enticed him to walk, just like another Priam, into the palace, treading underfoot the tapestry, a fine piece of Spinning, that she had laid before him as a carpet. For she had taken offense at the slaughter of Iphigeneia, the daughter who was hers, and not his alone to dispose of; nor did she take kindly to his arrival with the prophetic concubine **Kassandra**, even though she herself had reverted to the older premarital traditions, and was ruling now at Mykenai as Queen, with his archrival as paramour and 'king:' the 'Goat-man' **Aigisthos**, who was son of the 'Sacrificer' **Thyestes** (whose other sons had been sacrificed by Atreus and fed to their father). Once inside, Klytaimnestra threw a net on her husband, and slaughtered him at his bath; and then (or before, as some said) she did the same with his Trojan girlfriend, whose prophetic voice Apollo had so muddled that no one could ever sort out the truth from it, until it was too late.

Here was a dilemma, like the War at Troy itself, that would require yet another generation to solve. **Orestes**, the son of Agamemnon and Klytaimnestra, was in his **wilderness sojourn** at the time of the murder, being hospitably entertained by the 'Circler' **Strophios** in his high mountainous lands around Apollo's Delphic sanctuary on Parnassos: Orestes is named for that visit as the 'Mountaineer.' It was there that he 'befriended' his helper and (usually silent) constant companion, the 'Gateman' **Pylades**, who was Strophios's son. While he dallied with these two agents of Apollo, his only link back home to Mykenai was his sister

Klytaimnestra Wields the Double-ax to Slaughter Kassandra (Red-figure kylix c. 425 BC, Museo Archeologico, Ferrara)

Elektra, who like the sacrificed Iphigeneia was named for the Goddess (whether as 'Virgin,' or more probably, as the 'Shining' one, with the luster of amber, the electrifying stone-like exudation of a magical tree; and the precious metallic alloys, such as the mixture of gold and silver, that resemble it in color). Elektra was a **turncoat** and had sided with her dead father and against her mother Klytaimnestra.

Pylades and Elektra stand in for Apollo and his sister, to prod Orestes to commit the matricidal act that will move the world forward to the newer ways. Orestes must choose whether he is his father's son or his mother's. He circles back, by his father's tomb, to Mykenai, claiming that he himself had died in a Contest at Delphi, and even carrying the empty urn that is supposed to contain his own funeral ashes. This is the ruse, the trick whereby the final Slaughtering can be stolen, and moral Righteousness at last prevail. At the last moment, as he hesitates to slay his mother, Pylades breaks his silence and reiterates Apollo's Delphic decree: and Klytaimnestra and Aigisthos fall victim.

(Another way of telling the story provides Elektra with a cowardly and indecisive sister—like Antigone and Ismene—named **Chrysothemis** or 'Golden Righteousness,' named after the Goddess **Themis** who was transitional in the transfer of Delphi from the old ways of Earth to the new Apollo. And Elektra and Klytaimnestra vie with each other to enlist Chrysothemis on their side, but although she agrees that Elektra is right, she is too terrified of her mother to act with the courage of conviction that Theonoe displayed.)

(Still another way provides the Virgin Elektra with a morganatic and unconsummated marriage. Condemned by her hostile mother to Poverty, Elektra, nevertheless, insists on hospitably entertaining her as yet unrecognized brother and his 'friend' in her hovel; but to enrich it sufficiently for the task, she sends to the mountain to summon her dead father's old tutor to bring down some provisions for them. He arrives with the pivotal **entheogen**, a goatskin of the old centaur drug that she can use to fortify the wine: he stopped along the way by the tomb of Agamemnon to offer it a bit, also. Although Elektra and her brother have hovered, unbearably long, just on the brink of recognition up to this point, the tutor, who traditionally has good 'horse sense,' immediately recognizes Orestes as the child he once conveyed to his wilderness sojourn. Now that Elektra is reunited with her brother, she presides over a specially enriched hovel: she and he contrive a ruse to (in)hospitably entertain the mother who had fatally welcomed their father home: the Virgin pretends to have given birth, and when Klytaimnestra rushes out to visit, in order to slay the child, the Queen who would have slaughtered someone, if he had existed, is herself instead the victim, to her own son. As is Aigisthos, who hasn't managed to have a son by Klytaimnestra, although he has been trying; but the Virgin did it first, with the imaginary pregnancy. The pattern is the familiar one: to turn the tables against the enemy, and use its own toxic weapon to put it back in its place, in the old world.)

Once again the Dioskouroi come down to ratify what is right, this time with their other, less than divine sister: Helen—the real one—and Menelaos at this very moment have just surfaced from Egypt through the 'African' Gateway at Lerna; and they will see to burying Klytaimnestra, whose death was necessary, although her twin brothers can hardly sanction Apollo's role in her murder. And they direct Elektra to marry anew, this time to Pylades; and to circle back with both husbands to Strophios's lands, to replace Poverty with Wealth—and eventually to give birth to another Strophios.)

By all accounts, however, Orestes was hounded by his dead mother's ghost and her sisterhood of Gorgonian Furies or Erinyes, and he Wandered far and wide, pursued and demented—perhaps even as far as the Taurians, to rescue Iphigeneia and the effigy of the Slaughtering Artemis. Apollo and Artemis could not solve the problem themselves, even when Orestes fled to the Delphic sanctuary for their help. Apollo needed the 'help' of his sister Athena to put the matter finally to rest.

Orestes showed up at last in Athens, along with the host of other revenant spirits rising from their graves, just as the Athenians were celebrating their communal banqueting with the dead at the Anthesteria Festival for the new wine. (The special drinking ceremony employed at that festival was supposedly invented to accommodate their unexpected and insane guest.) His crime of matricide was put on trial in the sacral court that met on the Hill of Ares (the Areopagos), just below the entrance to the Acropolis. The jurors, who were the citizens of Athens, were deadlocked, equally divided, until Athena herself intervened to cast the deciding vote: on the basis of her own motherless birth, she declared that fatherhood was the more essential parentage, over the claims of motherhood: thus Athena, as the woman with the characteristics of a man, rectified the perversion of such dominance in a Queen like Klytaimnestra. And then, just as she long ago had commemorated the defeat of the Gorgon Medousa by donning the Gorgon head as her emblem, Athena again pacified the furious sisterhood of spirits by offering them an honored domicile in the Labyrinth beneath the city of Athens. Thus Orestes finalized the Contest that had first been fought by his distant Mycenaean relative Perseus, four generations earlier.

(But there was another way of telling the story of this famous legal debate, although it took place in another city, and from the Athenian point of view, it was, of course, risible. Klytaimnestra, however, did, after all, have her Rights; and the other of her **two fathers**, the mortal one, Tyndareus, who was son of Perseus's 'Gorgon-killer' daughter Gorgophone, was determined to press charges against Orestes in a court of law at Argos-Mykenai, upholding the rights of his dead daughter and her matrilocal ties to his 'kingdom' of Sparta. Even though the jurors were about to find Orestes guilty of matricide, Menelaos, his own father's brother, refused to support his insane and persecuted nephew, choosing instead to side with his father-in-law, who was no blood kin of his, but merely the less optimistic of the two fathers for his wife Helen, who really should be Zeus's daughter, now that he had sorted out the dilemma in Egypt. Pylades 'helped' Orestes by advising him to take Helen hostage, and to kill her, too, this other sister of Klytaimnestra, to get back at Menelaos. But just in the nick of time, Helen disappeared, saved by Apollo, who brought her up to Olympus. So Elektra proposed that they do the same thing with Helen's daughter Hermione, namely, Slaughter her now, instead of Helen; and when Menelaos attacked the palace, they threatened to set it afire and let everyone die. Apollo showed up just in time to set things right himself. Elektra was to marry Pylades, and Orestes would marry Hermione—after being cured of his delusions by the trial at Athens; and then rule in Argos.)

Upon the death of Menelaos, who never managed to beget anything but bastard sons, Orestes was invited to assume the leadership of Sparta. He died in Arcadia, of snake bite, at the town he had founded, named after him; and he was buried at Tegea, secretly: his bones were rediscovered only later, in response to a Delphic oracle; and like Theseus's reinterment at Athens, Orestes was finally buried again at Sparta.

The Homecoming of Neoptolemos

The final event was for the victorious Neoptolemos to fall victim, like his father Achilleus, to Apollo, but only after he had got back successfully up to Greece, instead of at Troy; and the mad Orestes, whom the Delphic god favored, turned out the winner in the Contest.

Neoptolemos (Pyrrhos) took **Andromache**, the wife of his father's archrival Hektor, as his concubine at the end of the War, and traveled with her back Home, without incident, avoiding the disasterous Storm that had scattered the others throughout the labyrinthine byways of the return, since he alone had the 'help' of a Trojan **turncoat**: this was **Helenos** (the same name as Helen, only masculine), who was the twin of Kassandra and the only one of Priam's sons to survive the War: it was he who had divulged the three secrets which led to the fall of his city (namely, the Palladion, Philoktetes, and the enlisting of Neoptolemos). For like his sister, he was a prophet of Apollo, but his 'help' was not misleading, like her accursed, futile and incomprehensible warnings to Orestes' father Agamemnon.

(Or, as some told the story, Andromache may have been given as concubine to Helenos, for his reward as turncoat, instead of to Neoptolemos as the victor; Neoptolemos, as the 'enemy' of the old Apollo, and Helenos, as the advocate of the new, are an interchangeable pair of 'companions:' for the turncoat was destined to end up more fortunate than the hero he 'helped.' And it was Neoptolemos at Troy who had taken up the sinister ways of the old god, throwing Andromache's son **Astyanax** to his Apolline death, 'falling' from the walls of the city; and he who wielded the Slaughterer's knife for the sacrifice of Polyxena; he, too, who slaughtered Priam on the very altar of Zeus, by which sacrilege he had revealed himself as the same kind of potential threat that his father had posed to the stability of the Olympian deities: Zeus could never forgive him for that; Neoptolemos became the 'enemy' of Zeus, in addition now to being Apollo's.)

When Neoptolemos surfaced from the Labyrinth with Helenos and Andromache, after finding their way through the extensive interconnections of the great Cave that underlay Zeus's oracular sanctuary at Dodona, up through its Entrance into Epiros in northern Greece, either Neoptolemos, or more probably Helenos (for there were two ways of telling the story), had a son by Andromache: **Molossos**, who became the founder of a newly reformed and resurgent 'Troy' town there and its race of Molossian people. And for this more optimistic Olympian era, Zeus now commemorated the bygone days by adding his pre-Greek name to his own, so that he was thereafter known there as Zeus Molossos.

But when Neoptolemos next came up from the Labyrinth through its Parnassian Entrance at Delphi, he finally had to pay his debt to Apollo, and to Zeus, as well. He accused Apollo of having murdered his father, and like the other traditional 'enemies' (and former identities) of this newcomer son of Zeus at Delphi, he plundered and burned the sanctuary; and meandering on still further through the linkage of subterranean chambers, he even popped up next in Sparta, where he laid claim to Hermione, rescinding Apollo's declared intention to assign her to Orestes, and siding with Tyndareus and Menelaos, who, he asserted, had previously betrothed her to him; but when he failed to beget a son on her, he foolishly sought advice back up at the blackened and smoldering sanctuary of Delphi: there he ran into Orestes, who was still Wandering himself, trying to shake off the pursuit of the maddening Furies. Orestes 'almost' Slaughtered him at the altar; but instead, it was the Delphic official whose job it was who 'Butchered' him: **Machaireus**, as they disputed over the sacrificial victims: the Slaughter was later excused as a misunderstanding, that Neoptolemos simply didn't understand the local customs. (Andromache was there at the time, and she, too, was 'almost' Slaughtered by Hermione, but instead was dispatched back to the Molossians and Helenos, to complete the peopling of the new era up there.) Neoptolemos was buried in the sanctuary, although this 'enemy' wasn't fully appreciated until he was sighted much later as an revenant ally, fighting alongside the Hyperborean ghosts who had Wandered to the surface from the far-distant olden times through the Entrance Cave, to defend the sanctuary from the attacking Gauls in 279 BC; after that date, his grave was more carefully tended, since he had proven his worth against the foreign threat.

As for Orestes and Hermione: they had a son, **Tisamenes**, the 'Vengeance;' his descendants went on to recolonize the old Deathlands of Asia, as did many of the restive and disruptive elements in the continually evolving society, both mythical and historical, who no longer fit in the newer times, but went abroad to found colonies of Hellenic civilization in the midst of foreign peoples. (Thus also, the son of Aigeus by Medeia, Medos, went abroad to become the ancestor of the Medes; and Perseus's son by Andromeda, Perses, founded the Persian race. So, too, had many of the heroes dropped off sons on their Tours of the Deathlands.)

Aeneas Fleeing Troy, with Anchises and Ascanius
(Bernini, Museo Borghese, Rome)

The 'Homecoming' of Aeneas (Aineas)

The most famous of these migrants was **Aeneas**, who would be credited with recolonizing the former Deathlands peninsula of Italy and founding the Roman World, which would eventually inherit and replace the Greek. His story, based on local traditions and family histories (including the belief that the Etruscans had migrated from Asia Minor), rose to prominence through the Latin poet Vergil's telling of it in the *Aeneid*, which, unlike the Greek Homeric epics, is a written and consciously manipulated reformulation of myth, with an intended message: to authenticate the new nationhood of Rome as the worthy political and cultural heir to Hellenism, and to grant its former traditional enemy, Troy, the franchise to rule the world as its empire.

Unlike the Greek heroes, with their two liminal fathers, Aeneas's divine lineage is on his mother's side, a throwback to the heroes of the older type, from the times of the Goddess, and like the darker potential of a Herakles and the others, destined to a future of self-sacrifice. His mother, as we saw, was Aphrodite (Venus): but it would be hard to imagine a figure less like his brother Eros (Cupid) than the Roman version of Aeneas, a joyless hero, bound by a sense of duty, and whose main characteristic is Piety. And unlike his lascivious brother, Aeneas does have a definitely known father. To humble Aphrodite, Zeus made her fall in love with a mortal, the Trojan grandson of Tros, **Anchises** (so that she thereafter might not mock the other gods and goddesses for their amorous affairs with mortals).

Aeneas escaped from the fallen Troy, with his father and **Ascanius** (later called **Iulus** or **Ilus**, after the fourth 'king' of Troy), the son he had by the 'Queen' **Creusa** (a daughter of Priam and Hecuba), who did not survive the War. It was thus a very patrilineal grouping of three generations of males who left the motherland of Troy to found the Roman fatherland.

The Deathlands Tour (which except for the actual final descent and resurfacing at the Cumae Entrance of the Apolline Sibyl on the Italian peninsula near Naples, is for Vergil an entirely surface phenomenon) passed down through Thrace and on to Apollo's birthplace on the island of Delos: there the oracle told Aeneas to seek the land of his ancestors, which he at first thought was the Cretan Labyrinth; but his followers encountered pestilence there, and in a vision, his family gods told him that his ancestor Dardanus had come originally from Italy. They set sail, encountering the Harpies at the 'Circling' islands of the Strophades and passing through Dodona in Epirus: where he saw Helenus and the new Trojan resettlement, and received still further directions, and other prophecies; for the entire Tour was made under divine auspices, whose guidance the pious and almost impersonal hero was simply compelled to follow, so that the eventual founding of Rome could be seen to have been inevitable, the result of divine sanction. When they reached Sicily, where **Acestes**, a former ally of Troy had settled, Anchises died, at the ripe old age of eighty, and was buried.

Upon leaving Sicily, Juno roused a Storm that drove them down to Africa. There Aeneas dallied with **Dido**, the amorous Queen of Carthage (Rome's historical enemy, ever since the invasion of Hannibal in the Punic Wars, nearly a millennium later). Her desperate love for Aeneas was inflicted upon her by his mother Venus; and when he finally deserts her, driven onward, solely, by Jupiter and his Roman destiny, Dido commits suicide, laying the mythical cause for the future enmity between the two nations.

Back at Sicily, Aeneas, as a piously patrilineal and devoted son of his father, pauses to celebrate the anniversary of Anchises' death, while the women in his troop, forever a problem for male dominance, go mad, because of Juno's hatred for him, and burn half his ships. The next landfall is Cumae, to consult the Sibyl: she foretells the future and directs him to descend, with the aid of the entheogen of the golden bough, into the Labyrinth of the lower world to receive the final orders from his dead father, whose vision encompasses all of Roman history, up to the time of Vergil and his political sponsor Augustus, whose Julian family boasted their descent from Iulus-Ascanius.

At the future site of Laurentium, two of the prophecies are fulfilled, and Aeneas contracts a peaceful relationship with the king **Latinus** (supposedly a son of Odysseus and Circe, in that region), who has been told by an oracle to betroth his daughter **Lavinia** to a foreigner. Accordingly, Latinus offers her hospitably to Aeneas. But **Amata**, his 'Beloved' wife, prefers the local suitor, the 'Roundly Turned and Circular' **Turnus**, who was only partly Italian, and hence also a foreigner. The Contest develops into a War (which is Vergil's redoing of the War at Troy). Both sides have allies. Turnus is supported by the sinister and godless **Mezentius**, while the Etruscan **Tarchon** (who has been advised, also by an oracle, to make a foreign alliance) joins Latinus and Aeneas, as also does the 'Manly' **Euander**, a Greek who had migrated to Italy and settled at the future site of Rome. In single hand-to-hand Contest, Aeneas kills Turnus, who had killed his ally **Pallas** (Euander's son), and marries Lavinia.

* * * *

Review

The Trojan War was the final assimilation of Apollo and the olden times into the evolving Hellenic world, and by the time it was fought, there had already been so much intermingling of ideas and peoples that the sides are difficult to keep separate, what with the alliances and resettled colonies that bridged the two worlds, both here and now, and with the revenant and metaphysical past. After the War, the traditional tasks of the heroes became immaterial, and they passed away within a few generations, except for the noble families that clung to the memories of their traditional ancestors. The War (of rivaling cities and their allies) would continue to be fought, although its participants, for the most part, will have emerged from the oral reformulations into history, until a foreign people insidiously usurped and espoused the same Myth to turn it against its originators, as the legitimate successors to their World and its reality.

The outcome of the Trojan War was the last making of the Peloponnesos, with the new Pelopid dynasty at Mykenai and the resettlement of Sparta. (Athens and Thebes played only marginal roles; their evolutions had been set firmly underway a generation earlier, with Theseus and the Labdakids.) The Pelopid family of Tantalos, originally from the Troylands, (one branch of which had already been involved in the transmutation at Thebes) succeeded to the Perseids and Heraklids of Argos: **Pelops** and **Hippodameia** (of Olympia and Pisa), whose sons **Atreus** and **Thyestes** continued quarreling into the next generation, with their sons: the Atreids **Agamemnon** and **Menelaos**; and Thyestes' son **Aigisthos**. The Atreid brothers married into the Perseid lineage, with an alliance to the Spartan **Tyndareus** and his liminal (and potentially Zeus begotten) daughters and sons, by his wife **Nemesis Leda**: **Helen** and **Klytaimnestra**; and the **Dioskouroi** brothers: **Kastor** and **Polydeukes. Elektra, Iphigeneia, Chyrsothemis**, and **Orestes** (**Pylades Strophios**) finalized the settlement with **Hermione** in the next generation.

As terms of the settlement, the foreign Trojan alliance was at last sanctified by marriage: **Andromache**, the wife of the dead **Hektor** and the daughter-inlaw of **Priam** and **Hekabe**, was established with **Helenos** over the **Molossians** at Zeus's reorganized prophetic sanctuary at Dodona; and **Neoptolemos**, the son of **Achilleus** (the man who had killed her husband) and who had now, at the end of the War, become her mate, was given as the final offering to Apollo at the prophetic sanctuary of Delphi, thus linking the two mouths of the Labyrinth.

As for Apollo's troublesome twin sister, Artemis (Kalliste), the whole Contest had begun with the birth of **Alexandros Paris** at Troy, who intruded upon the matrimonial stability of Menelaos's union with Helen, when he showed up to claim her as his reward for deciding the Discord between the three rival goddesses who each (in lieu of its true claimant, Artemis) aspired to the title of Kalliste: Athena, Hera, and Aphrodite. This disruption of the marital fidelity that had been imposed upon Zeus's latest and most ravishing daughter Helen could be traced back to another exemplary marriage, that of **Peleus** and **Thetis**, which similarly was supposed to have imposed the ultimate stability upon the Olympian era, this time by condemning Achilleus (the would-be son of Zeus) to a career of heroism that was destined to end tragically in his dying, as a loser to the Apollo that he and his son Neoptolemos would 'help' to reform. (Both Helen and Achilleus, as 'children' of Zeus, were thus ascribed subservient roles: she as monogamous wife, instead of the polyandrous Goddess; he, as a mortal with no claim on the Olympian patrimony, such as a Herakles (optimistically) 'might' have had. And suitably, these two—each the 'best' of what they were, woman and man—would eventually lodge together for eternity, once they died.)

Apollo, however, could not be reformed solely through Contests with his 'enemies;' he required the same kind of 'help' that his trickster brother Hermes once had provided by rustling away his cattle, backwards. The other 'best' of the Greeks was his descendant, **Odysseus**. It was he, aided by Athena, who contributed the tricks that would turn the world around. Essential to his stratagems was the old technique of usurping the 'enemy's' weaponry and using it as his own. Thus he stole away the Palladion, leaving Troy with only the replicas of his 'friend' Athena. And he enlisted the poisoned arrows of Herakles and the maddened, putrefying **Philoktetes**, who had inherited them in this next generation, as the antitoxin to the Trojan Apollo (whose deadly drug was remembered later only by what came to be innocuously substituted for it, the Savory or fragrant 'fume-herb' of Thymbraios Apollo.) And finally the Trojan Horse of Athena, pregnant with heroes, just like her former identity, the Gorgon Medousa, with her transcendent offsprings, Pegasos and Chrysaor. As reward for these winning tricks, Odysseus was accorded the mantle of the dead Achilleus, his armor—he, instead of **Aias**. Odysseus could play the tricks, whereas Aias refused all 'help,' and in particular, that of Athena. But helping is a reciprocal phenomenon, and if Athena could not help Aias, he could not help her. Neither of them could become their better selves: for him, she was still a Gorgon; and he, the lamentable offering. He was still intent upon Slaughtering: until Athena 'helped' Odysseus, instead of him; and Aias, infected with the horse-mad herb, the Datura of the old Apollo (before it yielded to its transmuted substitute), was deluded into rustling cattle and sparing Odysseus and the other heroes, whom he all the while thought he was Slaughtering.

But for all the heroes, the War was a confusing experience. As Menelaos discovered in Egypt with **Proteus**, the real Helen may not even have gone to Troy; and the way back required that you appease the Slaughterer by dying, if only in mock pretense, or by substitute offering. Agamemnon was actually slaughtered by Klytaimnestra when he returned, in retaliation for his offering of Iphigeneia to Artemis.

The fullest account of these homeward Awakenings is that of Odysseus's return to Ithaka as the successful heir to Apollo's hateful former identity. This was the ultimate 'help' he would afford to the god who was Hermes' troubled brother, shooting the poisoned arrow straight through a full year's Wolf-walk of

Slaughterer's axe blades. He triumphantly claims the rank of man, instead of god, a 'wily man,' as he was called, in a patriarchy that his good wife **Penelope** (**Ikarios's** daughter) has preserved for him, and reunited with his son **Telemachos** and his mortal (instead of immortal) father **Laertes.** And Odysseus, unlike an ordinary man, has not forgotten the dream experience, or become hopelessly lost along the way; he awakes laden with knowledge: for he has profited from his Tour of the Deathlands, from all the Circling and Wandering, like the revenants scattered throughout the Labyrinth. His itinerary brought him to: the **Kikones** (where he won Apollo's gratitude and the use of his 'Centaury' Datura as his weapon); the Lotos-eating **Lotophagoi** (where he avoided their addiction to the 'thorn-apple' Datura of the nettle tree); the **Kyklops Polyphemos** (where he used the poison and earned his Fame); the visit to **Aiolos** (where be began re-circling with the Winds); the landfall amongst the cannibalistic **Laistrygones**; the visit and circle back to **Kirke** on **Aiaia** (where he acquired the 'mollifying' moly from Hermes, which was the antidote to Kirke's Dirke herb, and buried the accidental death, a token of himself, **Elpenor**—and didn't slaughter **Eurylochos**); the visit to **Persephone's House** (where he consulted Teiresias, and discovered his own mother **Antikleia**, a personal mother, instead of the all inclusive totality of mother Nature and the great Ladies of the past); the passage through the **Sirens** (whose song of Home he heard, without becoming addicted to the wrong reality); the passage and re-passage through **Charybdis** and **Skylla** (the evil rival of Kirke); the visit to **Thrinakia** (where his men rustled cattle from the netherworld's herd); the long dalliance with **Kalypso** (on **Ogygia**, straight down below Dirke, the former Datura spring at Thebes); and finally (with the help of the formerly 'black' **Leukothea** of Thebes, the wet nurse of the Dionysos of olden times) landfall on the 'Shore' of **Scheria**, which was the utopian island of the **Phaiakians** in the sewer Labyrinth, and the Artemis maiden **Nausikaa**, who could have 'burned his ships'—but didn't, so that he could die instead, not downward, but up, to his awakening back Home.

For Discussion and Further Study

1. The story of Agamemnon's homecoming is told in Aeschylus's *Oresteia* trilogy: *Agamemnon*, *Choephoroe*, and *Eumenides*. Read it and consider the following:

What techniques in production might be used to convey the Athenian bias, that Mykenai's evolution can be completed only at Athens? Consider, in particular: what role(s) did the Athena actor impersonate earlier in the trilogy? What masks would the chorus of Erinyes-Furies wear as Bogey Women?

How does Klytaimnestra symbolically remake Mykenai (Argos) into Troy for Agamemnon's Awakening?

What is the significance of the wet nurse's role?

Why has Klytaimnestra yielded power to Aigisthos as ruler in the second play of the trilogy?

2. The reunion of Elektra and Orestes-Pylades is told in Aeschylus's *Choephoroe*. Two other tragedies tell the same story: Sophocles' *Electra* and Euripides' *Electra*. (The same story as told by each of the three most prominent tragedians, one from each successive generation, spanning the Classical Age: they were preserved, after the passing of the Classical Age, to serve as subjects of study for the newer generations, as they tried to maintain their cultural roots to their past history and traditions.) Compare and contrast the way that the recognition of brother and sister is managed in these three plays. In each, what meaning is given to the delayed recognitions?

3. Orestes's other sister Iphigeneia also has trouble recognizing him in Euripides' *Iphigenia in Tauris* (Amongst the Taurians). How is the recognition managed and what does it mean? (Consider that Iphigeneia is named 'after' Artemis, and that Orestes-Pylades have connotations of Apollo's Delphic sanctuary: what significance does their recognition have for another pair of siblings, Apollo and Artemis?)

4. Menelaos and Helen have the same difficulty in Euripides' *Helen*. What themes are involved in the recognition? Pay particular attention to the (prophetic) pair of siblings, the brother Theoklymenos and his sister Eido-Theonoe.

5. Odysseus wakes up in Ithaka in book 13 of the *Odyssey*. From that point on until the end of the epic, trace the successive stages in his recognition and reintegration into his Home. What does each mean? (Consider that Odysseus returns, with Apollo's 'help,' to claim his Delphic heritage.)

6. The 'wrath of Achilleus' begins as the subject of the first book of the *Iliad*. Why is Achilleus(-Neoptolemos) the appropriate mythopoetic configuration to play the role of Apollo Thymbraios? Trace their involvement in abductions: Iphigeneia, Chryseis-Briseis, Polyxena, Andromache, Hermione-Helen. Consider also their conjoined role in their mythopoetic relationships to Zeus.

7. Zeus's best son was (probably) Apollo—unless it was Herakles (who was perhaps the thirteenth Olympian: but only after Philoktetes inherited the poisonous bow and arrows). The story of Philoktetes' reenlistment for the War is told in Sophocles' *Philoctetes*. Discuss the role Philoktetes plays mythopoetically in regard to Apollo and to Herakles; and also to Odysseus and Neoptolemos.

8. The cattle rustling of Aias is the subject of Sophocles' *Ajax*. Consider the parallel roles of Athena and Tekmessa, who are impersonated by the same actor: one pretends to be his 'helper,' while the other, in trying to 'help' him precipitates his failure—by doing the same thing as the other, but inadvertently. How is the suicide staged? (Is the Aias actor left lying dead onstage, or is he used to impersonate another role, after his suicide?) Compare the different relationship of Athena to Odysseus and to Aias.

Part IV
Liminal Heroines

Heroes were born to die, to die and be buried, honored in this world for their accomplishments in remaking Hellenic civilization, and ultimately taking up residence in the other, adding to the ever growing alliance of friendly revenants who had resettled there, in the netherworld. Anything less—or more—would destabilize the delicate balance that maintained the Olympians in control. There wasn't room for a man (perhaps not even for a Herakles) to become a god, without threatening to displace one already established there. Humans, and their whole array of cultural institutions, were essential to perpetuate the Olympian era; and the final, and most demanding, task of the liminal hero was, at the end, to step back, to accept the awesome burden of his 'friendship' with divinity.

Heroines, too, are liminal, even as the former Goddesses, now transmuted to Olympian status: for an Athena, when crossed, might revert to the Gorgon Medousa; nor was it ever safe, as Hippolytos learned, to get too close to an Artemis. Typically, the great Ladies of Classical myth have a hidden side, unknown, usually, even to themselves: like the docile Deianeira, puzzling over the old Lernean (and centaur's) poison, unaware that she is toying with the power of an Omphale; or Tekmessa, unwittingly repeating the very act that will condemn Aias to his grave.

But they were not all loving and docile. Klytaimnestra knew what she was doing, and even could claim it Rightful; as did Medeia, for it wasn't right that she be so mistreated, after all the 'help' she'd given Iason. These willful women differ from the ones who merely stumble upon their latent power. Suffering has made them mad, and they demand the return of their Rights.

Suffering, in fact, may be naturally a woman's lot, even apart from the deprivation and subservience imposed upon them in a society that is dominated by males. All humans are born from women, nourished by the material substance of their flesh, inevitably while still within the womb: a demanding and expanding fetal nucleus which, if not attended to, will threaten the mother's depleted life; as it does again at the, at least potentially, painful crisis of its birthing. And then, still further, the continued task of tending the dependent and demanding child through its sojourn in infancy, even if the mother is supported by a sympathetic (and empathetic) communal sisterhood: this task, too, restricts and limits a woman's activity and life. These joys of motherhood—for they are that, too (the bonding with other women, the triumph of creation)— these are what lie for women across the limen, the threshold of puberty: not the same exuberant life of freedom as a man, physically unrestricted even in a female dominant society, but still less so for women when males control the power.

The limen, itself, moreover, is, at best, for a female more psychologically confusing. Puberty for the male is liberating and ultimately pleasurable, but menstruation, with its disturbing regularity and unpredictable shifts in mood, ties the woman closer to nature, and to other women, all in step together with the periodicity of the moon, and the ebb and flow of the seas. Nor was it proper even, in polite society, for conception to be anything more than a duty demanded of the females in a patriarchy, where ideally the father, with previous sexual experience, took to wife a girl, younger and still naive about eroticism, a girl who would henceforth live in his house, dominated by him, and by the older women of his household.

The maiden phase (the **kore**) and motherhood (the **meter**) thus are bridged through suffering; and motherhood, too, for all its rewards, is still further suffering. But two joyously pathetic personae do not complete the female archetype, as it does for the liminal hero. There is no clear age at which ejaculation definitely ceases, but for the woman there lies ahead the trauma of menopause, an additional physiological limen, liberating, perhaps, but with more suffering from nature and uncontrollable moodiness.

To survive it all, to endure was not easy, nor certain: what with the frequent, hazardous birthings (and often sorrowful, as well, with the unwanted female babies, her own dishonored daughters, discarded, left to die, or to be reared by someone else for a slavish life outside the citizenry). But this was a woman's lot—and her pathway to ascendancy: in the household, she might eventually replace her mother-in-law and become the new female power there; and in nature, the reward was to profit at last from a life of suffering that had been lived so near the edge and close to nature, to be wise now, and frightfully so, in the tricks of Nature: to use her now as one's weapon. Across the second limen was a third persona that reunited all together as a fearsome triad, the power of the crone (the 'drug-woman' **pharmakis** or witch, and the 'nurturer' **trophos** or wet nurse), who through suffering has ascended to the old knowledge and power of the Goddess, to do knowingly what a Deianeira merely inadvertently stumbled upon.

These are the three personae that join to form the sisterhoods; **kore, meter**, and **pharmakis-trophos**: as in the groupings for the maenadic celebration, utopian where honored, but terrible if denied. In myth, they are the three con-joined goddesses of the Eleusinian Mystery: **Persephone**, **Demeter**, and **Hekate** (who in herself has three bodies; the 'Willful' chthonic goddess—as is the ety-mology, probably fanciful, of her name; Hekate, the patroness of witchcraft and of wet nurses, the fearful goddess who can be found wherever three roads meet, and whose proper Offering is a dog, left to rot; Hekate, whose name is best not mentioned, when one speaks of the benevolence of the other two).

Priam's wife Hekabe discovered this sorrowful pathway to righteous, willful power. When Troy fell, she was confiscated as booty, along with the other women of the city, by the victors. As they awaited the wind for the return, she discov-ered that her young 'Gifted' son **Polydoros** had been stolen, murdered by her supposed foreign ally in Thrace, the greedy 'Wise Counselor' **Polymestor**; and this, just after she had lost her daughter, the 'Foreign Friend' **Polyxena** as the Slaughtered offering to Achilleus' tomb. She had tried to get Odysseus to inter-cede on her behalf, as repayment for her own role as turncoat in helping him steal the Palladion, but he had refused, and even justified it as his Right: the debt was owed to her, and not to her daughter. As she sorrowfully prepared to bury the corpses of her two dead children, she hits upon an unscrupulous way of get-ting her will. She uses her prophetic daughter Kassandra as a ploy to curry fa-vor with her captor Agamemnon. (Only the two Apolline prophets, Kassandra and Helenos now survive of all her twelve daughters and fifty sons.) She begs Agamemnon to allow her to wreak her vengeance on his ally Polymestor, telling her daughter's abductor (and her quasi son-in-law) that Kassandra will be more compliant in his bed, out of gratitude for this kindness to her mother: in effect, to use the suffering of the **kore** as her base of power, to enact a **meter**'s retali-ation for her maternal suffering.

Then, as they all await the wind, she entices her enemy Polymestor and his two sons into her tent, using his own greediness for still more Gifts as her lure. There the captive women, the ones who are still maiden (**kore**), effusively fawn over Polymestor, admiring the handicraft of his clothing: inverting their pathetic persona and seducing him, until he realizes that he has become confined in this woven web of his wife's Spinning. Then the others, the women who have already suffered childbirth (**meter**), equally enact an inversion of their persona of moth-erhood: they deceptively fondle the children, until, with the father now im-prisoned, they slaughter them in his sight, just before they put out his eyes. The last thing Polymestor sees in the tent is this nightmare that these two groups of females have enacted: the same nightmare that Hekabe had earlier had as a prophetic dream in this same tent, a dream of a mother deprived of her chil-dren, but now it is a dream of her own making.

And finally there is a second trial; and this time Hekabe, who earlier lacked the skill to counter Odysseus's oratory, justifies her Will as Right. On the voyage Home, Hekabe was metamorphosed into a Bitch and she joined the sisterhood of Furies in the netherworld, a dog in the pack that attends the Willful Hekate, as she tracks down those who offend her Rights.

Chapter XII
The Two Worlds Of Persephone

⚶

A good day's walk outside of Athens, across the low pass over the ridge of mountains that forms the western boundary to the plain of Attica, lies the village of Eleusis, which was originally independent, but from the seventh century on, it had fallen under the administration of its more powerful neighbor. There, amidst the surrounding fertile grainlands, each year, ever since Mycenaean times, increasingly large numbers of men and women, from all walks of life, both Greeks and others (provided only that they could understand the Greek language, and the Myth), had gathered for the opportunity to experience anew for themselves, firsthand, the old alliance of friendship that the Hellenic world had forged with the past that lay pacified beneath it in the Deathlands. They would assemble together at evening, after the overland procession from Athens, in the cavernous great hall that had been built right into the slope of the Eleusinian Acropolis; and then, like the mythical heroes before them, they would file on through the narrow corridor of the Entrance, down into the branching Labyrinth, into the House of Persephone. And when they Awoke back up in the hall of the sanctuary, they could anticipate that their own visit with friends down there might be reciprocated, someday; that they and the foreigners below were forever now bound together on terms of easy familiarity and shared hospitality. Death, himself, who could be called the 'Bountiful' lord **Plouton**, might be expected to show up with his blessings as a frequent guest in their very own homes. This journey was known as the Eleusinian Mystery, itself only the most famous and universal of the other, similar Mysteries, journeying down to the re-settled past through the other Entrances in the Classical world: all of them Mysteries, so-called, because the travelers were required to respect a vow of secrecy about what exactly they saw.

At Eleusis, what they saw was **Persephone**, the 'Killer of Perse,' as she was now called, now that she had become a daughter of Zeus, although, like Dionysos, she was never more than just a welcome guest amongst her relatives in the Olympian family, which included her own mother **Demeter** (Latin **Ceres**), her father's sister. And, moreover, they saw this Persephone, who could also be called the **Kore** or maiden, at the precise moment that she returned to visit her mother Demeter: as a mother or **meter**, herself, upon the birth of her 'Dreadful' son, who was named in the old matrilineal fashion still after her, as **Brimos**, the son of the 'Dreadful' **Brimo**—although, like her, he had many other names, as well, depending upon how you thought of Death: some good, like Plouton (Latin **Pluto**), some bad. And for this reunion of mother and daughter, with the Dreadful son, inevitably there came along as well, the boy's wet nurse Hekate, the **pharmakis-trophos**. Persephone never visited thereafter without her, although she wasn't numbered in the sacred 'Duo' of goddesses, the two **Theo**, to whom the sanctuary at Eleusis was dedicated: the Kore and the Mother; and there was no need to mention, at least directly, the lurking presence of the Willful third.

The Marriage to Hades

Although by heritage Persephone should have been an Olympian (as the only offspring, apart from Ares, of parents who were both themselves Olympians—unless you accept the Homeric version that made Hephaistos a son of Zeus, instead of only Hera), it was her marriage to Hades (who played the darker third to Zeus and his other Olympian brother Poseidon) that brought her back into the family as a foreigner, a visiting outsider. And in a sense, it brought him, too, up to date for the newer era: for the union of Persephone and Hades hadn't begun as a marriage, but as an abduction, against her mother's wishes, although with the connivance of Earth herself with Zeus and his chthonic brother: for all three of them conspired together, Earth, Zeus, and Hades, in order to convert the Olympian daughter into an in-law, married to her old chthonic realm, where formerly she was known as Perse, before she was transmuted and pacified into a Persephone. The story was often told, but the best known version is the *Hymn* (in the Homeric style of language) that was presumably composed and performed, for some occasion, at the Eleusinian sanctuary, but not for the Mystery, itself.

The myth begins at the frontier of this World, amidst wild and poisonous plants, and culminates in the centers of civilization, with the cultivating of the basic foodstuff of humankind, the edible grains, and in particular, barley. Persephone, like so many other maidens ripe for the maenadic abduction, was plucking flowers, with the Oceanid sisterhood (all daughters of Okeanos or Ocean, the great river that encircles the habitable land), when her eye caught sight of the delightful bauble that would snare her, the holy flower called **narkissos**, blooming from its single root into a hundred, fragrant heads: a full 'hundred' or **hekaton** of them, with its pun perhaps upon Hekate. Narkissos was what it was called in the pre-Greek language, in the rituals of Minoan times; and the effect of this **entheogen** (which later was identified as the Narcissus) was narcosis, the narcotic stupor that was considered sacred, as the access to the realm of the Goddess. The place where this all occurred was Nysa, the old Dionysian wilderness. And as she reached to pick the plant, the earth yawned open before her, and Hades rose to abduct her down, away through the waters on his chariot drawn by horses. As she struggled against him and cried to her father Zeus for help (even though, unknown to her, he was privy to the plot), no one heeded her screams: no one, except for Hekate (in her cave), the Sun Helios, and then finally—but too late—her mother Demeter.

For nine days, Demeter Wandered, searching for her; and on the tenth, she came upon Hekate, similarly Wandering; and the two of them then joined their search, both carrying torches to light their way through the darkness of the interconnecting bypaths. And they came at last to Helios, who alone had witnessed the abduction. He revealed what had happened, and divulged that Zeus was behind it all.

Abduction of Persephone (Votive plaque 460 BC, Museo Nazionale, Taranto)

The Hospitality at Eleusis

Demeter at first refused to accept this separation from her supposedly Olympian daughter. She disguised herself in the appearance of an old woman and a wet nurse (the next stage in her life, as **pharmakis-trophos** or Hekate); and arrived at Eleusis, at the House of the 'king' **Keleos** and his Queen **Metaneira** (Latin Celeus and Metanira or Meganira). There, she paused by the Well, that was known as the 'Maiden's Well' and as the 'Well of Flowers.' Down through this narrow passageway, beyond the reflecting boundary of water, like a mirror of herself, lay the subterranean aquifer and Persephone; but this was as close as the Olympian Demeter could approach her daughter, except by impersonation: she, too, becomes involved in a sisterhood of water maidens, and offers them a false story of her own abduction. She is approached by the daughters of Metaneira who have come to draw water from the well; and she tells them that she had been abducted across the waters from Crete by pirates, but had escaped when they came ashore: in her wanderings, she had come upon them.

They offer the old woman, as she appears to them, a suitable employment in their house: that of wet nurse for their brother **Demophoon** (after whom Theseus's son was named), who was the sixth and last born son of their mother. Metaneira enthusiastically hires the old woman, who promises to nurture the child, warding him from malignant witchery with an antidote more powerful than any herb.

What she intends is to prepare him for the immaterial and spiritual existence of an immortal Olympian, the heritage that should have been her daughter Persephone's. This she did by denying him the nourishment from her breast; but instead, she anointed him daily with ambrosia, and breathed the spirit of her breath upon him. And by night, she placed him in the fire, to burn away his mortal flesh and transmute him into the smoke of air. Day after day, Demophoon grew marvelously more and more like an Olympian.

Metaneira, however, cannot accept this good witchery that would steal her son away from her. She lay in wait one night and spied upon Demeter as she burnt

The Enthroned Demeter Welcomes Back Persephone, Returning with Torches from the Dark Lands (Bas-relief 5th century BC, National Museum, Eleusis)

off the boy's mortal ties to her family. But Metaneira could hardly be blamed for objecting to the same, although inverse, severance that Demeter was experiencing from her daughter Persephone. Neither mother could be expected to accept the total loss of her child.

Demeter, thwarted and angry, removed the boy from the hearth and left him to a human life such as the heroes had, of death—with glory: of mediation between the realms.

Which was also to be the lot for Persephone. Demeter ordered the people of Eleusis to build the sanctuary and promised to impart to them the ritual of the Mystery. Both mothers would have to compromise; both would have to sacrifice a child (a son and a daughter), although only partially, to the other's realm.

Demeter sat a full year apart from her fellow Olympians, enthroned in her new temple at Eleusis; and she played a terrible trick of nature. The seed planted in the earth refused to sprout: humankind was faced with extinction, and without them and the ritual they performed of the sacrificial meal, the forward evolution of the Olympian era itself was threatened by the possibility of regressing to the past of primordial times. (There was to be no mediation between the realms of spirit and earthy matter.) Her whole family of Olympians approached her, one after another, with bribes, begging her to return amongst them, but the angry and grieving goddess refused them all, stubbornly persisting in her vigil, enthroned at the Eleusinian Entrance.

Finally Zeus sent Hermes down into the House of Hades to summon Persephone back. And he, who was now her husband, relinquished his wife and Queen for a visit up in his brother's House. But first he made sure that she could not stay there forever, by playing a trick of his own: he contaminated her ethereal nature with earthy matter. He gave her the seed of pomegranate to eat (whereas formerly as an Olympian, she had eaten only ambrosia and drunk nectar, or breathed in the smoke from sacrificial victims); and he planted, as well, the seed of himself, her own son, within her body: so that she, too, just like Earth, had seed about to sprout.

This child that he planted was the one known as Brimos at the Mystery, Brimo's son, the chthonic grandson and nephew of the Olympian Zeus and

Demeter. He was a son that Demeter herself (who as an Olympian was son-less) would never have, except by proxy through her Kore, and in her role as foster mother and wet nurse, another Demophoon for her to nurture. He was a child, that is to say, worthy of the triple goddess Hekate, adding maleness as the final attribute to the trinity of females, and reestablishing the Goddess as hermaphrodite, male, as well as female. (The pomegranate, itself, first came into being from the blood that Gaia shed when she separated maleness from herself.)

The Mission of Triptolemos

Metaneira had another son; and Demeter taught this one the Mystery. He was **Triptolemos**, the 'Triple Warrior.' There were other, more secret, versions of who his parents were: like Hekate, his trinity unites him with the transcendent phase of the Goddess. He is the divine Koros, as Persephone is her Kore. (Some knew him as the son of Gaia herself, by Ouranos, a generation earlier than Zeus; others claimed that this was the child of Metaneira that Demeter succeeded in nourishing as wet nurse, but with her milk, the mediating role she had denied to Demophoon.)

To him (who ultimately, amongst his identities, was probably Brimos, this child that sprouted): to him, Demeter, relenting, imparted the antidote for the sterility she had placed upon the fields of planted seed. She sent him upon a mission throughout the world, teaching humankind the art of agriculture, and in particular, the growing of barley. As with the cultivation of the vine and the manufacture of the (w)oinos drink, it involves the art of compromise and mediation, nourishing mortal life upon the proper transmutation of the chthonic past and death.

Just as the vine had the ivy (kissos) as its poisonous wild ancestor, the edible grains were seen as civilized hybrids of inedible avatars, which, to some extent, is botanically true. The primitive version of barley (krithe) was supposedly the grass called Lolium temulentum (aira, in Greek): 'drunken Lolium' as the botanical Latin name means, because of the intoxicating and poisonous ef-

The Mother and the Kore with Triptolemos (Bas-relief 5th century BC from Eleusis, National Museum, Athens)

The Dry and the Liquid Foodstuffs: Dionysos with the Grapevine and Wine Cup, and Demeter with a Sheaf of Barley (Terra-cotta votive plaque from Locri c. 450 BC, Museo Nazionale, Reggio Calabria)

fect it has upon those who eat it, and affecting, in particular, the eyesight. (In English, it is called darnel, because it makes you 'dizzy;' and tares, because it makes you a 'fool;' it is also known as cockle; and as ivray, because it makes you 'drunk.')

Surprisingly, the plant itself has none of these effects. It is, however, commonly the host for a fungus or ergot which does, Claviceps purpurea or 'purple club-head,' which is also known as 'rust' (in English, as well as in Greek: erysibe) from its reddening color that spreads, like rust on iron, corrupting the grain (enlarging the infected club-like kernels) and returning it to its useless origins, like the manufactured metal back into its ore. (This is the 'rust,'—from the sacrificial knife—that the seer Melampous used to cure the impotence of Iphiklos, and his fear of death.) Lolium is a common weed in fields of grain, and not only is its useless growth a threat to the tended crop, but its corrupting fungus spreads its poisonous contamination to the other grains. Grain infested with ergot produces delusions in those who eat it, a painful gangrenous rash on the skin, with club-like mummification of the extremities (called the sacred fire or Saint Anthony's fire, after the religious order that tended to the afflicted); and uncontrollable convulsive movement, the dancing fever and death (that is called Saint Vitus, after the third-century Christian who was martyred as a child and invoked by those who suffered from the malady). Barley, itself, it was thought, would revert to this apparently ecstatic and deadly Lolium, without the art that Demeter had imparted to her disciple Triptolemos. (In later Christian times, the deposed pagan deities typically became demonic: ergot was known as 'Mother-corn,' and the Goddess was blamed for the infested kernels, which were her wolf children: although even in Greek antiquity, 'Rust' was one of the names of Demeter, and she had other, more sinister, black manifestations as a Mare.)

The Sacred Drink of Eleusis

When Demeter accepted hospitality, and employment, in the House of Metaneira, the Queen offered her a drink of (specifically) red wine, but the goddess refused it, saying that it was not Right for her to drink it: presumably because in the division of foodstuffs, hers was the dry, whereas Dionysos was the liquid; but perhaps also because of the wine's maenadic implications of the narkissos and the Nysian abduction of Persephone (for which some even blamed Dionysos).

Instead, Demeter specified a new sacred mixture, the 'stirred' potion or **kykeon** (just as (w)oinos, too, was always a 'mixture'), a drink, however, that was symbolic of the dry foodstuffs: it was drunk thereafter at the Mystery as the **entheogen**. It contained barley and mint (pennyroyal or Mentha pulegium, called 'blechon' in Greek), mixed in water. The two plants represent the opposites that are reconciled. Barley is the cultivated foodstuff; mint represents the wild herb, whose (sweet and supposedly soporific) fragrance connotes (like all such perfumes) the illicit abduction at Nysa: the plant itself was said to have once been the concubine of Hades, and Demeter transformed her into the plant when first she learned of Persephone's forced concubinage to the nether lord, who would later, as terms of the settlement, be her wedded husband.

Neither plant, however, could have induced the visionary experience, the 'seeing' that was, by all reports, the central experience of the Mystery. Nor could either have been involved as the drug in the profane recreational use of the drink at symposiums, as it was discovered was happening, in the notorious scandal of the Profanation of the Mystery that came to light toward the end of the Fifth Century in Athens: even the nephew of Perikles, Alkibiades, was implicated, and his mentor Sokrates, by association. It is also unlikely that the entheogen would be openly named.

Ergot, however, is an ideal secret mediator: between the primitive and cultivated grains, and between the experiences of deadly ecstatic convulsive rapture (Persephone's Nysian abduction) and visionary sight (Persephone's birth of the Brimos child); and between the opiate shamanism of the chthonic Goddess and the fungal traditions of the Indo-Europeans. Amongst the several, and variable, alkaloid toxins contained in ergot, only two are soluble in water: the one commonly known as LSD; and ergonovine, a drug of use in midwifery, to induce the birthing contractions in the uterus.

Instead of narcosis, wakeful vision. Instead of seed that would not sprout, birth. Death was the ingredient in the cup; and life, its outcome. And even the wildness of Amanita, seedless and evading cultivation, was tamed and incorporated into the era of Olympian civilization: for the red club-like kernels (which are the sclerotic mycelia or mass of fungal root-like fibers) resemble enlarged seeds of grain; from them when planted sprout the fruiting bodies of mushroom.

(Furthermore, just as the manufacture of wine involved the tended growth of fungal yeasts and the controlled putrefaction that reversed rotting matter into spirit and food, that same transmutation was true of Demeter's dry foodstuff: for grain, too, is a medium for fungal growth: the dough, sour and evil smelling, is undergoing the leavening that will lighten it with spirit to produce bread.)

And as with the hero Perseus (Perse's man), who hid away the former religion of the Gorgon Medousa in the kisthos or rockrose and in the wallet of Hades

(above) Demeter and Kore, with Flower and Wallet (Bas-relief 5th century BC, Musée du Louvre, Paris) (top right) Caryatid from the Smaller Gateway, Bearing Cista Hamper with Kykeon and Rose-Poppies (National Museum, Eleusis) (right) Baubo Figurines (Terra-cotta 2nd century BC from Priene, Museum für Völkerunde, Berlin)

(when he converted Mykenai to the Olympian era), the Cista or hamper basket (of woven twigs, decorated with the kykeon chalice for the drink and with rose-like flowers of poppy) and the wallet-bag were emblematic of the Eleusinian Mystery, concealing certain secret objects from profane view.

The kykeon was apparently prepared for Demeter by Metaneira's servant, **Iambe** (who was also known as **Baubo**), a dwarfish 'digital' female. She also cheered the grieving goddess with her scurrilous jesting: by the former name, she is called for the iambic verses which were the traditional form for such songs; by the latter, we may surmise the nature of her 'obscenity,' for the *baubon* is the female's phallus. She was depicted as a pregnant woman, in the overall shape of a penis, with her face in her belly, and sometimes playing the lyre to accompany her singing jest. Some claimed that her obscenity consisted of her revealing her hermaphroditism to the goddess; others, that she was about to give birth— to the Brimos child. She was the final configuration given to the doubled trinity of female and male for the Mystery, a vision of the transcendent chthonic Goddess.

(Perhaps, too, they all were dwarfs such as she in Metaneira's House: Demeter had trouble making herself small enough to cross the threshold, and her head reached up to the roof. The Eleusinian Mystery was merely the most famous of these religions, which characteristically reestablished bonds of friendship with the primordial little people.)

The Sanctuary of Eleusis

There actually were two levels to the Mystery, the Lesser and the Greater. The former took place in late winter in Athens: there was some kind of secret ceremony (of which we known a little): maenadic, like Persephone's abduction; and the woman who was called Queen (a hereditary title for the wife of the man who as 'king' performed the sacred tasks for the city) was prepared by her sisterhood of witches and united, in a Sacred Marriage, to Dionysos, in the Bull Stable: like the mythical Kreousa, Ion's mother, in the Labyrinth beneath the Acropolis. This was a secret ceremony and probably did not involve the hordes of initiates who would participate in the later Mystery in the sanctuary at Eleusis.

For the Greater Mystery, the initiates (eventually, as the fame of the religion spread, coming from all parts of the Classical world) would convene upon Athens in the autumn for their final preparations, which included about a week of specific sacrifices and dietary prohibitions. Then on the day of the initiation, they gathered at the western gate of the city, which was its ceremonial entrance, near the Potters' Quarters or Kerameikos, just beyond the Marketplace or Agora, below the north slopes of the Arcropolis. This was the beginning of the Sacred Road, that led out of the city, past the Cemetery, toward the village of Eleusis.

Reconstructed
Model of Eleusis

They formed a processional parade and journeyed out for the long walk over the mountain ridge, and down into the neighboring Rharian plain (or Rarian, named after one of the presumed fathers of Triptolemos, Raros, the 'Belly-man,' in the pre-Greek language), a once fertile grainland, in which, beside a low hill-like acropolis, lay the village. At the top of the ridge, they paused to rest, at the place called Daphnai, after its thicket of laurels, sacred to Apollo (but now known for the Byzantine monastery that the Christians later imposed there upon its pagan sanctity). And then, after their descent, at the base of the ridge, they crossed a pond, of supposedly subterranean waters, on a purposely narrow bridge, which is still visible today, beneath the surface. The journey was meant to imitate the Journey that they would finally take that night, down the Eleusinian Entrance. It would be a difficult passage, in which they all, rich and poor alike, would be equal: and as they approached the village, across a stream through the plain, the villagers greeted them at the bridge, lining its narrow way, and hurling scurrilous and abusive comments, like Iambe, at them as they squeezed past. Just beneath the high citadel walls that hid the sanctuary from profane view, and beside its gate of entry, they found the Well, where Demeter, before them, had once come. And in front of it, a plaza, with its temple of Artemis, who once was mistress of this Labyrinth. Here they danced, further testing their powers of endurance: for they had walked all day, nor had they eaten, for they had to prepare for the experience by a day-long fasting.

Finally, the great gate was rolled open, and they passed within, through its two portals, the larger and then the smaller with the two caryatids, parading past the cave, with its temple of Hades, behind which lay the actual Entrance. They proceeded on the Road, up a slight incline, past the so-called Laugh-less Rock, where Demeter had once sat in her grief, commemorating the simple stool she had chosen to sit on when she accepted hospitality in Metaneira's House, as she awaited Iambe's cheering jest and refreshment. Just beyond, was the great hall of initiation, the Telesterion or 'Place of Completion.'

This was a cavernous hall, cut on three sides right out of the stone hill of the acropolis: like an architectural version of a cave itself. (It was not a temple, although by the Classical age, an ornamental portico of columns had been added on its southern facade, although the initiates filed in through doors on its eastern flank.) Inside, was another smaller building, encased in the surrounding hall, built upon the ancient foundations of the original, much smaller edifice of Minoan times. High above, in the center of a roof supported by ranks of interior columns, was a lantern of windows, which alone admitted light down into the hall. But this was night now, and the illumination was supplied by torches. And it would be Torches, too, that would light their final way, led for them in procession down into the darkness by the Torch-bearer, one of the hereditary priesthoods for the Mystery, as they Shouted out the mystical name of Dionysos, **Iakchos**, who was the very personification of their call. They sat, each with their (animus) guides, on the tiers of steps, carved out of the bedrock, that lined each wall, and watched the ceremonies that they were forbidden ever to describe, under penalty of death. A little, over the nearly two millennia of its per-

(left) Ex Voto of the Blind Eukrates for the Gift of Vision (From Eleusis, National Museum, Athens)

(right) Death, Portrayed as the Koros (Personification of the Triple Conspiracy: Eubouleus) (From the cave at Eleusis 4th century BC perhaps by Praxiteles, National Museum, Athens)

formance, leaked out to the profane. The Cista hamper was opened and the sacred objects were handled. The sisterhood of priestesses danced through the hall, with the ancient **kernos** vessels, which were a symbolic display of seeds, both plant and eggs: a vessel (of joined cups) going back to the days of the Cretan Labyrinth. And the kykeon potion was prepared and drunk, the midwife's poisonous birthing remedy.

Perhaps only the more fortunate managed to go the whole way. But in the darkened chamber, there was, by all reports, a Great Illumination. The hereditary priest who held the title of Hierophant, the one who 'Showed the Sacred,' opened the door, beside his high-backed throne, on the old little building; and in a falsetto voice, to mimic a woman, he announced the Mystery: Brimo had returned with Brimos. This is what the initiates Saw. Even a blind man once saw it, and left us a votive plaque of the ascending Goddess to commemorate his Sighting.

Those who had gone the whole Journey not only knew, but had experienced the birthing themselves, on that magical night of visions: it was something they could never speak of; but ultimately, something that was unspeakable, unreal, that had to be seen to be believed: the truth, that others call myth.

* * * *

Review

The assimilation of **Demeter** (Latin **Ceres**) into the Olympian family was accomplished by severing her into two personae. As Demeter, she is the mother (or **meter**): **Deo** may be her original, and hence pre-Greek name, with her epithet of maternity added; it was interpreted as meaning the 'woman who meets you,' a name with decidedly sinister implications of Death; but others in antiquity attempted to interpret her name as 'Earth-mother' or 'Barley-mother' or 'Mother of the People.' All may be pure speculation, but it is clear that she was the Mother Goddess. She became a sister of Zeus, and an Olympian, but her daughter, the **Kore**, was denied Olympian status and was wedded to **Hades** (Latin **Pluto**) as **Persephone** (Latin **Proserpina**), a pacified version of her former chthonic identity as a **Perse**; and incorporated into the Olympian family as an in-law, visiting from the netherworld.

In Metaneira's House at Eleusis, Demeter disguises herself as a wet nurse witch and gives another name for herself as **Doso**, apparently the 'Giver.' In this role, she is impersonating **Hekate** (Latin **Hecate**), who represents the transcendent trinity of the Goddess, uniting maiden, mother, and witch. This transcendence also involves the conceiving of a son or **Koros**: Demeter herself never has a son (presumably, the son of so powerful a Mother might endanger Zeus); instead, that son is Persephone's, or ultimately Hekate's nurseling. He has many names, and represents the final pacification of Death, and its incorporation into the Olympian era: he is **Eubouleus** (the personification of the conspiracy that led to Persephone's abduction, as the 'Good Plan'); and **Plouton** (the 'Wealth' who visits as a friendly revenant); and **Triptolemos** (the 'Triple Warrior,' who was ostensibly Metaneira and Keleus's son, but ultimately the son of the 'Belly-person,' **Iambe** (**Baubo**) and **Raros**; just as the Goddess's ancient consort was often triple and serpentine, Triptolemos, although anthropomorphized as the ideal Koros, maintains the serpent identity: the cart for his Mission is propelled by serpents). Metaneira's other son **Demophoon** was a 'hero.'

For Discussion and Further Study

1. The *Homeric Hymn to Demeter* is the fullest telling of the myth of Persephone's abduction. Trace the interrelationships of the roles of **kore**, **meter**, and **pharmakis-trophos**. What events of the story does the teller either not know or suppress?

The heroine of *Alice in Wonderland* has an experience similar to Persephone's abduction. Compile a list of similarities between the two. The author Lewis Carroll was a pseudonym for the mathematician Charles Dodgson, who wrote the tale to entertain Alice Liddell, who was the daughter of a famous Greek scholar. Do you think he was thinking of Persephone or the Eleusinian Journey when he composed the story?

The theme of Death and the Maiden has been treated often in literature and art. Compile a list of examples.

2. Aristophanes parodied the Eleusinian Journey in his *Frogs* comedy. What metaphors are involved in his description of this Journey?

3. Consider what you have learned about the paradigms of heroes and heroines: what do you think the Eleusinian initiation meant (personally and psychologically) to the different classes and sexes of people who experienced it?

Maps and Genealogical Charts

✶

List of Illustrations

A Note on Geography

Do not expect the map of the world of Classical Myth to correspond exactly to what we might find in an atlas today; the topography from the Greco-centric point of view was more fluid than modern cartographers allow.

Ancillary Readings

Homer	*Odyssey* books 8-12
Homeric Hymns	*Demeter, Apollo, Hermes, Aphrodite*
Aeschylus	*Prometheus*
	Seven Against Thebes
	Oresteia (Agamemnon, Choephoroe, Eumenides)
	Suppliants
Sophocles	*Oedipus*
	Antigone
	Oedipus Coloneus
	Ajax
	Philoctetes
	Electra
	Women of Trachis (Trachiniae)
Euripides	*Bacchae*
	Ion
	Heracles
	Hecuba
	Hippolytus
	Medea
	Electra
	Iphigenia at Aulis
	Iphigenia Amongst the Taurians
	Helen
	Orestes
	Phoenician Women
	Andromache
Aristophanes	*Birds*
	Frogs
Apollonius of Rhodes	*Argonautica*
Apuleius	*Metamorphoses* (Amor and Psyche)
Vergil	*Aeneid* books 2&6
Ovid	*Metamorphoses*

Suggestions for Further Reading

Reference Works

Primary Sources:

W. H. Roscher, *Ausführliches Lexikon der griechischen und römischen Mythologie* (Hildesheim: Olms 1965, orig. 1884–1937)

General Surveys:

Michael Grant, *Myths of the Greeks and Romans* (New American Library-Dutton 1962)

Robert Graves, *Myths of the Greeks and Romans* (Penguin 1955, condensed version 1981)

Carl Kerenyi, *The Heroes of the Greeks* (Thames & Hudson 1952)

————, *The Gods of the Greeks* (Thames & Hudson 1959)

Larousse Encyclopedia of Mythology (Prometheus 1960)

Mark Morford & Robert Lenardon, *Classical Mythology* (Longman 1971)

John Pinsent, *Greek Mythology* (Peter Bendrick, orig. 1969)

Meyer Reinhold, *Past and Present: the Continuity of Classical Myths* (Hakkert 1972)

H. J. Rose, *A Handbook of Greek Mythology: Including its Extension to Rome* (Dutton-Penguin 1953)

Dictionaries:

Michael Grant & John Hazel, *Who's Who: Classical Mythology* (Oxford 1993)

Pierre Grimal (ed.), *The Concise Dictionary of Classical Mythology* (Penguin, orig. 1985)

J. E. Zimmerman, *Dictionary of Classical Mythology* (Bantam 1971)

Symbolism:

Robert E. Bell, *Dictionary of Classical Mythology: Symbols, Attributes, and Associations* (ABC-Clio 1982)

* * * *

Topical Subjects

Methodology:

Lowell Edmonds (ed.), *Approaches to Greek Mythology* (Johns Hopkins 1990)

Women's Studies:

Eva Cantarella, *Pandora's Daughters: the Role and Status of Women in Greek and Roman Antiquity* (Johns Hopkins 1987)

Christine Downing, *Goddess: Mythical Images of the Feminine* (Crossroads 1990)

Marija Gimbutas, *The Goddesses and Gods of Old Europe* (Berkeley 1982)

Esther M. Harding, *Woman's Mysteries: Ancient and Modern* (Bantam, orig. 1971)

Mary R. Lefkowitz, *Women in Greek Myth* (Johns Hopkins 1986)

Sarah B. Pomeroy, *Goddesses, Whores, Wives, and Slaves: Women in Classical Antiquity* (Schocken 1975)

Psychology:

Jean Shinoda Bolen, *The Goddesses in Everywoman* (Harper & Row 1985)

———, *The Gods in Everyman* (Harper & Row 1989)

Richard Caldwell, *The Origin of the Gods: a Psychoanalytic Study of the Greek Theogonic Myth* (Oxford 1989)

Joseph Campbell, *The Hero with a Thousand Faces* (Princeton, orig. 1949)

Paul Diel, *Symbolism in Greek Mythology: Human Desire and its Transformations* (Shambala, orig.1966)

James Hillman (ed.), *Facing the Gods* (Spring 1980)

John Weir Perry, *Lord of the Four Quarters: Myth of the Royal Father* (Collier, orig. 1966)

Otto Rank, *The Myth of the Birth of the Hero* (Random House, orig. 1914)

———, *The Double* (New American Library, orig. 1914)

Philip Slater, *The Glory of Hera* (Beacon 1968)

Carl Jung (et al.), *Man and his Symbols* (Dell 1964)

———, *Psyche and Symbol* (Doubleday 1958)

Emma Jung, *Animus and Anima* (Spring, orig. 1957)

Erich Neumann, *The Great Mother: an Analysis of the Archetype* (Princeton 1963)

Anthropology:

Walter Burkert, *Structure and History in Greek Mythology and Ritual* (Berkeley 1983)

Georges Dumezil, *Archaic Roman Religion* (Chicago, orig. 1966)

Mircea Eliade, *Cosmos and History: the Myth of the Eternal Return* (Harper & Row, orig. 1949)

G. S. Kirk, *Myth: its Meaning and Functions in Ancient and Other Cultures* (Berkeley 1970)

Edmund Leach, *Genesis as Myth and Other Essays* (Grossman 1970)

Lord Raglan, *The Hero: a Study in Tradition, Myth, and Drama* (Random House, orig. 1936)

Paul Ricoeur, *The Symbolism of Evil* (Beacon, orig. 1967)

Stith Thompson, *The Folktale* (Holt, Rinehart & Winston, orig. 1946)

Claude Lévi-Strauss, *Structural Anthropology* (Doubleday, orig. 1958)

Richard B. Onians, *The Origins of European Thought About the Body, the Mind, the Soul, the World, Time, and Fate* (Arno, orig. 1951)

Arnold Van Gennep, *The Rites of Passage* (Chicago, orig. 1908)

Jean Pierre Vernant (F. Zeitlin, ed.) *Mortals and Immortals* (Princeton 1991)

Ethnobotany and Religion:

Marcel Detienne, *The Gardens of Adonis: Spices in Greek Mythology* (Harvester, orig. 1972)

Richard Evans Schultes and Albert Hofmann, *Plants of the Gods: their Sacred, Healing, and Hallucinogenic Powers* (Healing Arts, 1992)

R. Gordon Wasson (et al.), *Persephone's Quest: Entheogens and the Origins of Religion* (Yale 1986)

Black Studies:

Martin Bernal, *Black Athena: the Afroasiatic Roots of Classical Civilization* (Rutgers 1987)

Frank Snowden, *Blacks in Antiquity: Ethiopians in the Greco-Roman Experience* (Harvard 1970)

on Mycenae:

George E. Mylonas, *Mycenae and the Mycenaean Age* (Princeton 1966)

———, *Mycenae, Rich In Gold* (Ekdotike Athenon 1983)

on Knossos (as Necropolis):

Hans-Georg Wunderlich, *The Secret of Crete* (MacMillan, orig. 1975)

on the Olympians:

Carl Kerenyi, *Zeus and Hera: Archetypal Image of Father, Husband, and Wife* (Princeton, 1975)

Walter Otto, *The Homeric Gods* (Thames & Hudson, orig. 1954)

Joan V. O'Brien, *The Transformations of Hera: a Study of Ritual, Hero, and the Goddess in the Iliad* (U Press of America 1993)

Walter F. Otto, *The Homeric Gods: the Spiritual Significance of Greek Religion* (Beacon, orig. 1954)

on Prometheus (and Sacrifice):

Walter Burkert, *Homo Necans: the Anthropology of Ancient Greek Sacrificial Ritual and Myth* (Berkeley 1979)

Marcel Detienne, *Dionysus Slain* (Johns Hopkins, orig. 1977)

Carl Kerenyi, *Prometheus: Archetypal Image of Human Existence* (Princeton 1963)

on Aphrodite:

Ginette Paris, *Pagan Meditations: the Worlds of Aphrodite, Artemis, and Hestia* (Spring, orig. 1946)

Geoffrey Grigson, *The Goddess of Love: the Birth, Death, and Return of Aphrodite* (Stein & Day 1976)

Paul Friedrich, *The Meaning of Aphrodite* (Chicago 1978)

on Athena:

Carl Kerenyi, *Athena: Virgin and Mother* (Spring 1978)

on Dionysus:

Carl Kerenyi, *Dionysus: Archetypal Image of the Indestructible Life* (Princeton 1976)

Walter F. Otto, *Dionysus: Myth and Cult* (Indiana, orig. 1933)

on Apollo:

Daniel E. Gershenson, *Apollo, the Wolf God* (Institute for the Study of Man 1991)

Carl Kerenyi, *Apollo: The Wind, the Spirit and the God* (Spring 1983)

———, *Asklepios: Archetypal Image of the Physician's Existence* (Princeton 1959)

on Artemis:

Carl Kerenyi, *Goddesses of the Sun and Moon* (Spring 1979)

on Hermes:

Norman O. Brown, *Hermes, the Thief: the Evolution of a Myth* (Random House, orig. 1947)

Carl Kerenyi, *Hermes: Guide of Souls* (Spring 1976)

Paul Radin (et al.) *The Trickster: a Study in American Indian Mythology* (with essays on the archetype and Classical myth by Jung and Kerenyi) (Schocken, orig. 1956)

on Delphi:

Petros G. Themelis, *Delphi: Museum Guide* (Ekdotike Athenon 1981)

on Herakles:

Georges Dumezil, *Destiny of the Warrior* (Chicago 1971)

G. Karl Galinsky, *The Herakles Theme: the Adaptations of the Hero in Literature from Homer to the Twentieth Century* (Blackwell 1972)

on Olympia:

L. Drees, *Olympia: Gods, Artists, and Athletes* (Pall Mall 1968)

on Theseus:

Anne G. Ward (ed.), *The Quest for Theseus* (Praeger 1970)

on Iason:

Jack Lindsay, *The Clashing Rocks: a Study of Early Greek Religion and the Culture and Origins of Drama* (Chapman & Hall 1965)

on Achilleus and Odysseus:

Gregory Nagy, *The Best of the Achaeans*, (Johns Hopkins 1979)

on Eleusis:

Carl Jung and C. Kerenyi, *Essays on a Science of Mythology: the Myth of the Divine Child and the Mysteries of Eleusis* (Princeton, orig. 1949)

Carl Kerenyi, *Eleusis: Archetypal Image of Mother and Daughter* (Schocken 1977)

R. Gordon Wasson, Albert Hofmann, and Carl Ruck, *The Road to Eleusis: Unveiling the Secret of the Mysteries* (Harcourt Brace Jovanovich 1978)

Continuity of the Classical Tradition:

Philip Mayerson, *Classical Mythology in Literature, Music, and Art* (Wiley 1979)

Dora and Erwin Panofsky, *Pandora's Box* (Princeton 1962)

Jean Seznec, *The Survival of the Pagan Gods: the Mythological Tradition and its Place in Renaissance Humanism and Art* (Harper & Row, orig. 1940)

W. B. Stanford, *The Ulysses Theme* (U Of Michigan, orig. 1963)

Index